"As with any new craft, *practice makes perfect*. Anyone who is willing to make a few mistakes and learn from them has the potential to be a great shoemaker."

AMANDA OVERS

Second edition 2021
First published by Make House Publishing 2019
hello@makehousepublishing.com
www.makehousepublishing.com

Edited & produced by
Amanda Overs at I Can Make Shoes

Art direction & book design by
Jessica Lau at Tiny Beast

Photography by
David Wilman

Post-production by
Begoña Toledo

Copyright © Make House Publishing 2021
Copyright photography © David Wilman 2019

All rights reserved. No parts of this publication may be
reproduced, stored in a retrieval system or transmitted,
in any form or by any means without prior permission
from the publishers. Amanda Overs asserts her moral
right to be identified as the author of this work.

ISBN - 978-1-9993653-1-8

A BEGINNER'S GUIDE TO
HOME SHOEMAKING

BY AMANDA OVERS

Founder of *I Can Make Shoes*

PREFACE
BY AMANDA OVERS

I fell into shoemaking in my early 20's after being a totally shoe-obsessed teenage girl. I had always thought I wanted to have my own shoe brand but once I started actually making shoes it became clear to me that I was more of a maker than a designer - my passion for design came much later.

After undertaking a traditional footwear course in my home town of Sydney, Australia I moved to London only to discover that without access to the machinery I didn't have the means to make shoes independently. Wanting to make my own shoes from home seemed like an impossible task and there really weren't any resources available at the time, so I decided to figure out a new way using modern methods to bring the craft into peoples homes.

The idea was to teach people how to make shoes from home without heavy machinery, making it a DIY craft that could be done alongside the likes of dressmaking or crochet, and thats when the *I Can Make Shoes* technique was born.

Fast forward 10 years and my shoemaking school, *I Can Make Shoes*, has taught thousands of students from all over the world! It's also paved the way for emerging and established shoe schools globally to teach a new and easily accessible method of shoemaking.

The past 10 years have seen *I Can Make Shoes* spark a movement in DIY shoemakers and open up a completely new sub-industry for 'at home' shoemaking.

With this supportive and encouraging approach, we're able to provide a place where students can express themselves creatively, inspire creativity in others and all the while creating beautiful shoes.

I've made so many amazing friends along the way and have had the pleasure of watching past team members and students go on to start shoe brands of their own.

This project is close to my heart and a huge personal milestone for me so I hope you enjoy it.

WHAT'S INSIDE
CONTENTS

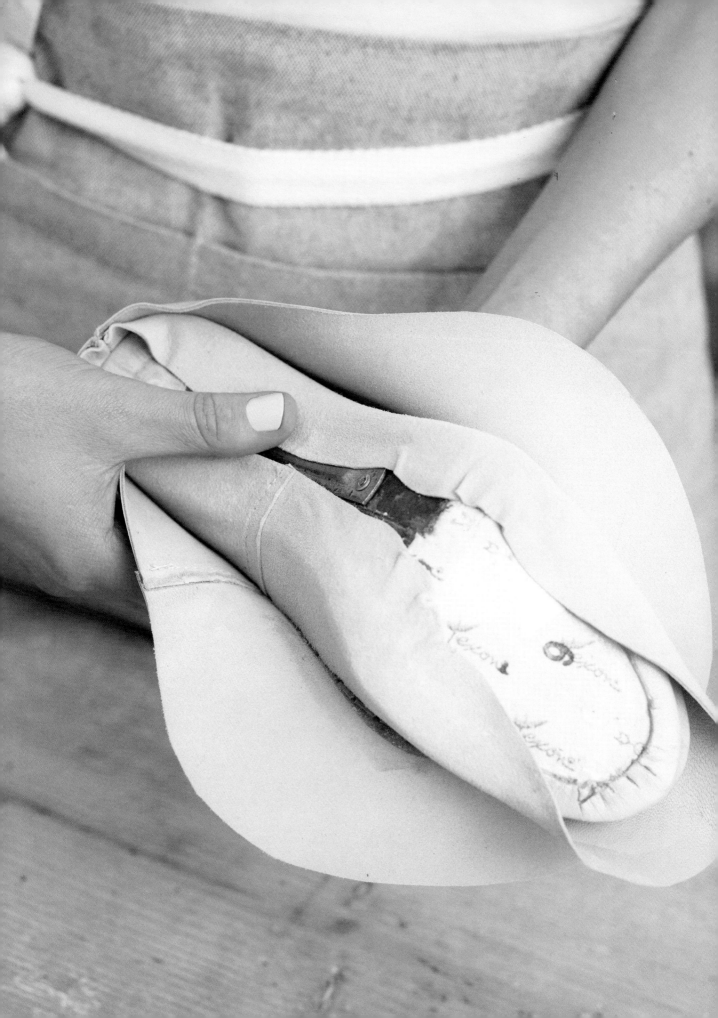

INTRODUCTION
I CAN MAKE SHOES

The *I Can Make Shoes* method which is taught throughout this book, is designed to simplify the shoemaking process to make it as easy as possible without the use of any heavy machinery.

This book was written as a launchpad for aspiring shoemakers, it's purpose is to outline the absolute basics required to get you started making your own shoes from home. Even though the book was designed with beginners in mind, it'll also come in super handy for those with a little experience.

The content covers the basic principles of shoemaking in the easiest and most achievable way possible. By making shoemaking easy to learn, it's my belief that it will encourage people to further develop their skills and move onto learning more advanced shoemaking techniques in the future. This first step is important to securing a new generation of shoemakers - you know what they say - *you've got to start somewhere.*

Here at *I Can Make Shoes* we aim to spread the love of the craft far and wide, and to us that means including people who are willing to make some mistakes along the way and build up their skills naturally at their own pace. With this in mind we have stripped it all back, explaining as much as possible whilst still keeping it as simple as possible.

I hope that this book will spark a love for the craft and inspire you to take your shoemaking up a notch, refine your skills, experiment with different materials, and maybe even have a go with some machinery. Shoemaking is a skill that you can continue to develop over a lifetime - practice makes perfect.

WHAT YOU'LL NEED
THE KEY COMPONENTS

Before we start making shoes, it's important to know the key components, what they do and why we need them. I've also included a glossary at the end for all the shoe terms mentioned throughout this book.

THE LAST

Lasts are the shoemaker's equivalent of a dressmaker's mannequin and are 100% essential to the shoemaking process. They are the blocks in which you stretch over the uppers to mould them into the shape of a shoe. With this in mind, before you start making your shoes you'll need to get some lasts that are the desired size, heel height and shape.

A question I get asked all the time is, "Can I just use my foot instead of a last?", which is a totally fair question, but the answer is no. You want your lasts to be the shape of shoes, not feet. Once you become a shoemaking addict you will naturally start to acquire a collection of different shoemaker's lasts. You can buy your lasts through the *I Can Make Shoes* online supply shop.

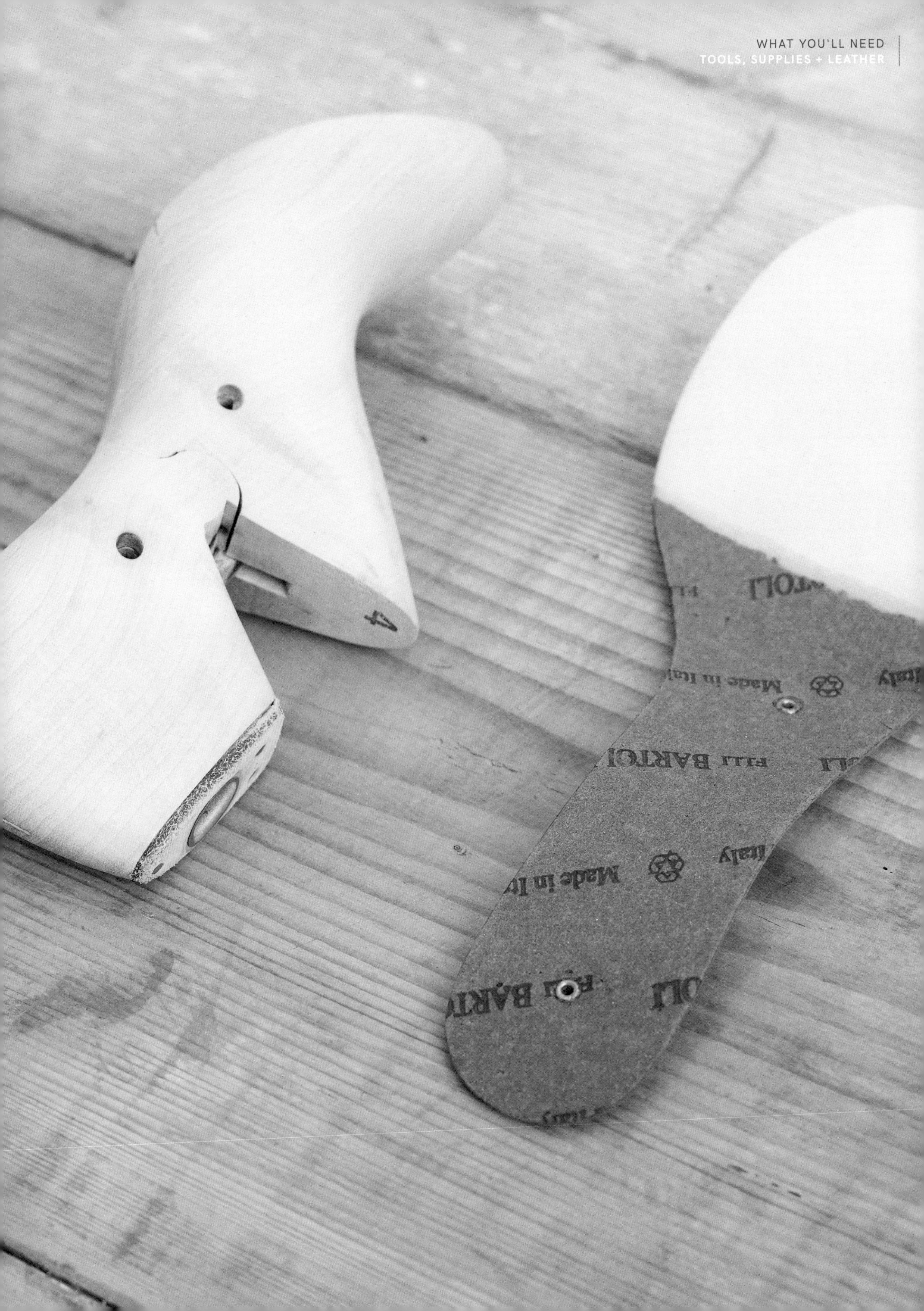

INSOLES

The insoles are the backbone of the shoes and are what hold it all together. For heeled shoes you need to use insoles with a steel shank. This is to hold the body weight and so that the shoes don't collapse in the arch area. For flat shoes you can also use a shank but I find this to be too stiff and prefer to have more flexible insoles, I recommend Texon® board 2mm thick.

UPPERS

The uppers determine the style of the shoes. We love working with leather but you can also use fabrics with interfacing or vegan leather alternatives. I recommend something with a good stretch to it that is no thicker than 2mm.

We stock all of these parts on the
I Can Make Shoes online supply shop,
making it easier for you to get started!

STIFFENERS

Shoe stiffeners are totally optional but if you want a good quality shoe that holds its shape, I highly recommend you use them. I use thermoplastic toe puff and counter stiffeners at the toe and heel area of the shoes to give them their structure. They are super easy to use and very forgiving for beginners. The stiffeners live inside the shoes and are not visible.

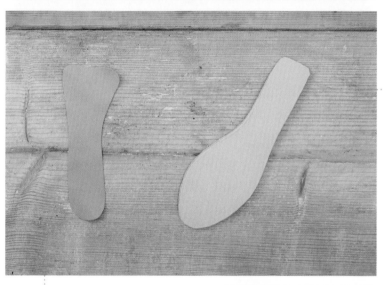

SOLES

The sole needs to be durable as it's the layer that is exposed to the ground. I recommend a thick cowhide leather. I like to use a 3mm veg tan leather as it's durable enough for a sole and malleable enough to cut by hand.

INSOLE SOCKS

Whilst insole socks are not essential for flat shoes, they are the finishing touch and can be padded with memory foam for extra comfort.

HEELS

The heels are usually made from a dense plastic or wood. If you are making heels out of wood, they need to be a chunky style as the wood will not be strong enough to support a stiletto style. Plastic stilettos will have a metal rod inside for extra strength.

GENERAL SUPPLIES
THE ESSENTIALS

In addition to the main shoemaking components, I've put together a list of general supplies that you'll need to get started.

Small Things
- Paper
- Masking tape
- Pencil & eraser
- Ruler
- Scissors
- Silver gel pen
- Craft knife
- Glue pot & spatula
- Craft foam
- Rubber crepe
- Clear book contact
- Cork filler (optional)

Sewing Machine

I use Janome Professional HD9 machines in my workshop, but any household machine suitable for denim should be fine. I recommend using a denim needle and a nylon or polyester thread as these are stronger than cotton threads and less likely to break.

Glue

Both of the glues that I use are vegan and from the German brand Renia. I use the non-toxic for 90% of the shoemaking process and the extra strong stuff for attaching the soles. The non-toxic glue is called Aquilim 315 and the extra strong stuff is called Colle de Cologne.

Both glues are contact adhesives so it must be applied to both of the surfaces you want to stick together. You'll need to let the glue dry before you stick - if it is still wet you won't achieve a bond. If you can't access these specific glues you can use any contact adhesive. Try contacting your local shoe repairer and asking them what they use and where they get it.

SHOEMAKING TOOLS
HANDY EXTRAS

Here is a list of shoemaking tools which will come in handy. Don't worry if you don't have all of these, there are plenty of household alternatives you can use instead.

Clicking Knife
This is a lovely cutting knife used for cutting leather and usually has a curved blade. You can use a craft knife or box cutter if you can't get one of these.

Safety Beveller
The safety beveller is used to skive or shave down excess bulky leather. At ICMS HQ we call this the 'potato peeler' because you use it just like that. Like the clicking knife, you can use a craft knife or box cutter in its place but the safety beveller is much easier to use.

Folding Hammer
This is one of my all time favourite shoemaking tools, it's used to flatten out a folded edge and is especially useful when it comes to folding around curves. I also use the folding hammer to smooth out my thermolastic stiffeners. A normal hammer works fine too though.

Awl
This little tool comes in handy for piercing through patterns onto leather and for many other miscellaneous tasks.

Leather Hole Punch
This is going to be essential if you are making shoes with lace holes or brogue details. Ideally you'd get one with a range of hole sizes.

Cutting Mat
Essential if you don't want to cut marks into your table top!

Dividers
Mostly used in patternmaking for ensuring that you have even spacing. You could also just use a ruler for this but it takes a little longer.

Drill, Screwdriver & Flat Topped Screws
Essential if you are planning on making shoes with high or mid heels.

Heat Gun
Let's be honest you can do this with your hair dryer. The down side is it'll take ages to heat up so if you can get your hands on a heat gun that would be ideal.

CHOOSING YOUR LEATHER
OUR RECOMMENDATIONS

You can use our method of shoemaking with any materials. We recommend leather as this is what we have used throughout this book, however you are welcome to use vegan alternatives.

Cow and Calf Skins

Calf skin is a great place to start for footwear in general, it is smaller and more lightweight than cowhide. Cowhides come in a huge variety of weights and finishes, it's usually cheaper than calf and is the most common type of leather used for footwear.

As a beginner I would recommend you think about finding a leather with stretch and a thickness of about 1.5-2mm.

Exotic Skins

Exotics such as ostrich, crocodile or alligator, eel, lizard or snake usually have zero-stretch making them very difficult for beginners to work with.

Kid Skin

Kid leather is made from goat and is super soft and light. I often find I need to back it with an interfacing if it's too thin.

Pig Skin

We like to use pig split skins for linings, as it's a breathable skin and super easy for beginners to work with. However you can use anything for your linings. Goat skins are also lovely and soft.

Veg Tanned Cowhide

There are lots of different sole leather options available; for beginners, we recommend you use veg tanned cowhides, approximately 3mm thick. Once you've built up your confidence you'll want to move onto a stiffer sole bend, it's pretty tough to cut by hand though.

Fabric

If you are using a thin fabric for your uppers, I would recommend you use an iron on interfacing with a stretch to give it some more strength. When you are using a material with a bias stretch you'll want to place your patterns so that the grain line is running from heel to toe. You don't need to worry so much with leather as it doesn't always have a clear stretch direction.

Vegan

There are lots of exciting new vegan materials coming onto the market so I recommend you try out any you can get your hands on. We like to use microfibre for vegan linings.

HOW TO DESIGN SHOES
TIPS + TEMPLATES

My biggest challenge with design has always been proportions and perspectives. I could never get my designs to look quite right, so once I started working with templates, I never looked back - they're my secret weapon.

I've put together some basic design templates to help you get started. Lightly trace them onto paper and let your imagination take over.

In a nutshell, these templates are just outlines of lasts (shoemaking blocks) with guidelines on them to help with proportions and perspectives. I've made the lines super faint so you can draw over them easily.

01 **HIGH HEEL**

02 **STILETTO HEEL**

03 **MID HEIGHT HEEL**

04 **FLAT SHOE**

HIGH HEEL
DESIGN TEMPLATE

HEEL SHAPE

If you want to design a different heel shape, just trace the upper section and get creative by drawing in your own heel.

STILETTO HEEL
DESIGN TEMPLATE

NOT QUITE RIGHT?

If your design looks a bit weird try holding it up to a mirror. This will show it to you from a whole new perspective and may highlight the areas that need a bit of work.

MID HEIGHT HEEL
DESIGN TEMPLATE

....

MAKE IT YOURS

Once you are really happy with a design you can add extra detailing to it. Try drawing on the stitching so you know where it should go and how many rows it should have.

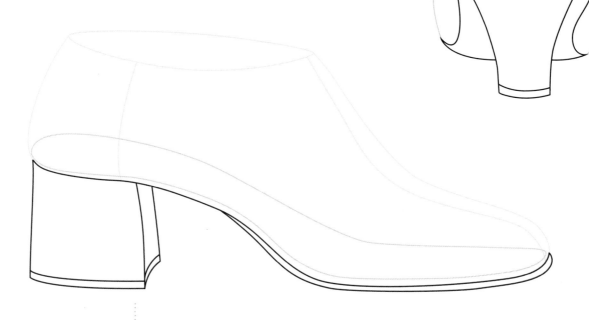

HEEL VARIATION

Notice the heel variation here which can completely transform the look of your design.

FLAT SHOE
DESIGN TEMPLATE

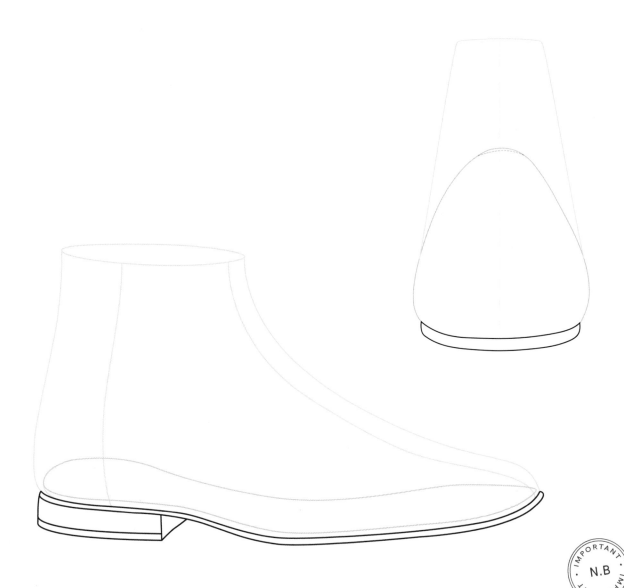

FORM AND FUNCTION

Always consider how your foot would go in and out of the shoe. Does it need a fastening? E.g. a buckle, zip or elastic. If so, think about where you would like it to go and draw it in.

N.B · IMPORTANT · IMPORTANT ·

PATTERNMAKING
BEGINNER'S INTRODUCTION

....

Let's be honest, footwear patternmaking can be very in-depth and intimidating, in fact, I could fill up a whole book just on this topic. For this book, I've put together a quick and easy way to make a footwear pattern which is a great introduction for beginners. In this example, we will be creating a pattern for a high heeled court shoe but you can apply the same principles to any last and create your own unique design.

If you are feeling more confident and want to get technical, there are plenty of resources out there to help you get stuck in. We recommend checking out some of the *I Can Make Shoes* YouTube videos or joining us in London for some private patternmaking tuition.

Start by choosing the lasts you want to make the shoes on and cover one of them with masking tape.

Try to overlap the pieces of tape to get a thick and flat layer covering the last. Try to avoid wrinkles and flatten them out with the side of your pencil, don't overthink this step.

Put a guideline down the front centre and back centre of the last. Next, we'll add in our back height point, this should be about a finger's width from the top of the last.

These lines are just to be used as a guide, so they don't need to be perfect. If you want to get more technical with the correct back height measurement, here is a formula to use: measure the length of the bottom of the last and then divide it by 5. Add 5mm to this measurement for ladies' shoes or 7mm for mens' shoes.

REMOVE THE EXCESS

Make sure you remove the excess tape from the bottom 'feather edge' of the last.

Designing your shoe onto the last can be as simple or as complicated as you like. For beginners we are going to keep this first style easy with a classic court shoe.

Think about where your toplines sit on the last and imagine how it would look on a foot. Make sure the front isn't too low or the sides too high. I'm not going to give you any technical measurements here because there is no right or wrong, this stage is all about looks.

Now time to get creative and draw your shoe design onto the last. This process is also called 3D designing.

Once you are happy with the design, you'll need to think about how you are going to lay it flat.

We usually use seams (joins) to do this, in this example we will do a side seam on the inside where it will be the most hidden and a dart back seam. To create the dart seam, mark 3/4 of the way up the centre back towards the back height point but making sure it's not cut all the way to the back height point.

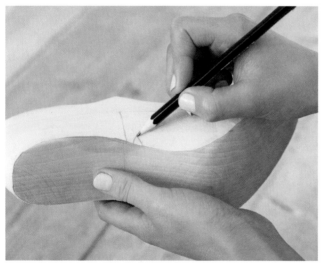

Add a little notch on the inside piece(s) of your pattern.

Since you are only making one pattern, you will need to flip it to get left and right feet. The little notch will help you remember to flip the pattern, so you don't accidentally make uppers for two left feet.

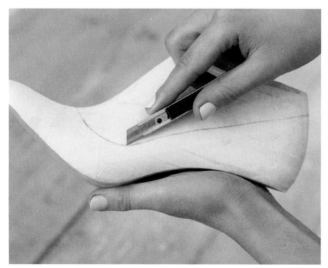

Cut the designs off the last with a craft knife.

Don't be afraid to cut right into the last, they are designed to take it. We want a nice clean line here. You'll also need to cut your side and back seams at this stage.

KEEP IT FLAT

*Make sure the tape is as
flat as possible before you
cut any slits into it.*

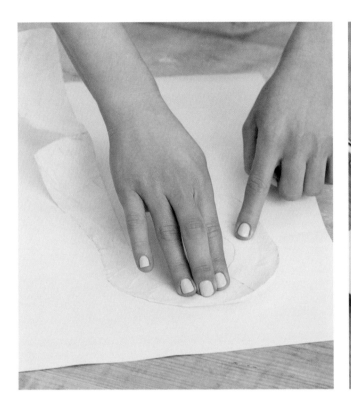

Lay your pieces flat on paper. When flattening your
tape onto paper, always stick down your toplines
first to conserve the shape of your design.

Once it's as flat as possible on the paper, you can use scissors to cut
little slits into any curved areas which won't lay flat on their own, this
is usually in the toe and heel areas. When all the tape has been laid
down flat on the paper you are ready to add in your pattern allowances.

*I use wallpaper backing
instead of pattern paper, it's
stronger and much cheaper!*

FOLDING OR TRIMMING ALLOWANCE

5mm on all toplines. This will become the folding allowance on your uppers and the trimming allowance on your linings. Some shoe designs have what we call a 'raw edge' in which case the toplines would not be folded. This means you can trace out your lining first and then remove the 5mm allowance from your pattern before you trace out your uppers.

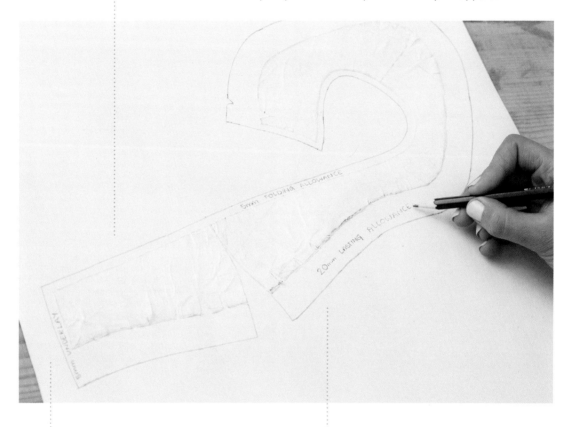

SEAM OR UNDERLAY ALLOWANCE

5-10mm on all joins. Sometimes it's a seam, sometimes it's an underlay, depending on the style of the shoe. For an underlay seam you only need this allowance on one side of the join .

LASTING ALLOWANCE

20mm on the bottom 'feather edge'. This allowance is so we can wrap the upper over the last and secure it underneath. This is arguably the most important allowance on any footwear pattern.

*To keep it simple there are **three main allowances** you need to know about, these will be more or less the same on all shoe patterns.*

THE DART BACK SEAM

*We won't be adding in any allowance here. We want
to shrink the pattern slightly so that when we pull it
over the last we can stretch it in place for a tight fit.*

Once you've added in your allowances,
you can cut out your final pattern.

Why add allowances? You will need to add allowances
so that we can lay the pattern flat onto the material to
cut out and then piece it back together for the perfect fit.

ONE PATTERN

*To ensure both shoes turn out the same
we only make one pattern for both shoes.
Just flip the pattern to get left and right feet.*

HOW TO MAKE
HIGH HEELED COURT SHOES

I always say if you can master a court shoe, you can make anything. In my opinion this is the best place to start for a beginner shoemaker, you've got a closed toe and heel meaning you'll need to insert stiffeners, you've got a heel to drill in and a reasonably easy upper to make so it's a good balance.

To get the best out of these instructions I recommend you read through the whole section first before you start. Here's what we are going to cover in this section.

01 **PATTERN**

02 **UPPERS**

03 **INSOLES**

04 **LASTING THE LININGS**

05 **STIFFENERS**

06 **LASTING THE UPPERS**

07 **SOLES**

08 **INSOLE SOCKS**

09 **STYLE VARIATIONS**

PATTERN
HIGH HEELED COURT SHOES

I used a high heel court shoe in the example for the *Beginner's Introduction to Patternmaking* on page 27 so you can simply follow that process to get started. In this section we will also look at how you can adapt that pattern to make variations of the same style.

PEEP TOE

The toe area has been cut away (on the last) and there is now a folding allowance added to the peep-toe topline.

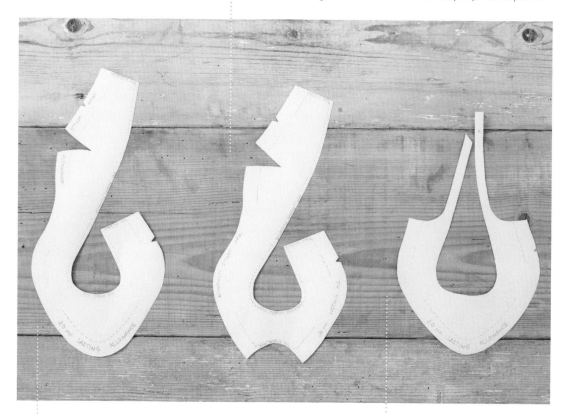

COURT SHOE

A court shoe or 'pump' is a great place to start as the classic construction covers most shoemaking techniques.

SLINGBACK

The heel section has been cut away (on the last) and the strap has been elongated for a buckle. There is no folding allowance on this topline, we call this style a 'raw edge'.

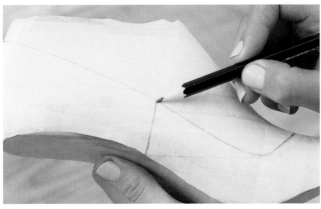

ADJUST YOUR ALLOWANCES

Your allowances will vary depending on the design of your shoe. Will you have a raw edge? Are you adding in straps? Do you have overlapping pieces?

Most of these patterns have side seams but you may want to experiment with a full back seam if your design will allow it.

UPPERS
HIGH HEELED COURT SHOES

In this section you will learn how to make the uppers of your shoes including preparing the pieces, attaching the linings and stitching it all together.
An industry term used for cutting is 'clicking' and stitching is called 'closing'.

Take your patterns and trace them onto the **underside** of your upper leather and lining leather.

I like to trace my patterns with a silver gel pen as it shows up nicely on most colours and is easy to clean off. Remember to flip your patterns for left and right feet. Then cut out your pieces as neatly as possible.

LEFT AND RIGHT

When tracing your patterns onto the leather you must flip your pattern over to get a left and right.

Lay your two upper pieces face down.

Draw on your 5mm folding allowance with a silver pen. If you aren't sure where this is check your pattern.

You'll need to put some small snips around the curves to help you when folding.

These snips should not go right up to the line, just about halfway.

GLUE BOTH SIDES

*For this section we will use the non-toxic glue, **Renia Aquilim 315.** This is a contact adhesive so it must be applied to both surfaces you want to stick together. You'll need to let the glue dry for about a minute before you stick, if it is still wet you won't achieve a bond.*

Put a thin brush stroke of glue across both sides of the line so you can fold.

Fold the topline of the uppers. When the two folds meet in corners, squeeze them together and snip off the excess.

REDUCE THE BULK

At this point if the leather is too thick you can skive down the fold with a safety beveller.

Piece together the sides.

Glue the folded edge over the unfolded edge,
with about a 5mm underlay and stitch in place.

AVOID THE STRETCH

*Most professional shoemakers will use
a topline tape (a strong non-stretch nylon tape)
along the topline before they fold. This is a step
that you can leave out if you are a beginner.*

IMPORTANT · N.B · IMPORTANT

FOR THE PERFECT FIT
*Follow the curve created by
the V shape to have a nice neat
curve at the back of the shoe.*

Once you've stitched the side seams in place you
can turn the upper inside out and fold it in half
so that you can stitch closed the back seam.

If you have a reasonably stretchy leather you can stitch up to 5mm away
from the edge. If your leather has very little stretch, go a little closer to
the edge. Repeat this step for your linings.

*Make sure that you stitch the lining **inside out**, so you close all the seams inside the shoes.*

N.B
· IMPORTANT ·

REDUCE THE BULK

You can use a safety beveller or a craft knife to skive away any excess bulk in the leather.

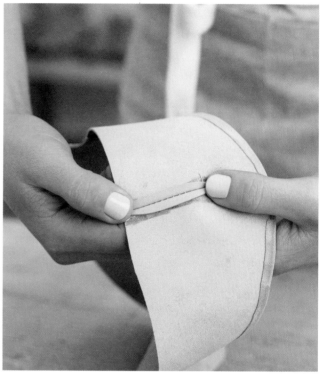

Use glue on both sides of the stitching to flatten out the seams.

Make sure the seams are completly flat and there are no air bubbles.

Next we'll piece the upper and lining together at the topline.

Flip your uppers inside out and glue along the topline. Flip your linings inside out and put a strip about 5mm down from the topline.

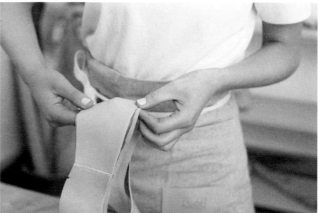

THIRD TIME LUCKY

*Don't get disheartened
if it doesn't fall into place
perfectly the first time
around. It can take a couple
of tries to get it to fit.*

Turn the upper the right way up and place it over
the inside out lining. Match up the back and side
seams and stick the toplines together.

Place the upper in the sewing machine and carefully stitch around the
topline as close to the edge as possible.

There will be an extra 5mm of lining around the topline.

We will cut this off later but we need to keep it at the back area for now. You can cut the excess lining from the front of the shoe at this stage.

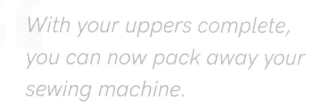

With your uppers complete, you can now pack away your sewing machine.

INSOLES
HIGH HEELED COURT SHOES

When making shoes with a high or mid heel you need to use an insole with a metal shank. This shank acts as the backbone of the shoe and supports the arch of the foot. The insoles we are using come with the shank already attached, we'll show you in this section how to trim them down to size and cover them, ready for lasting.

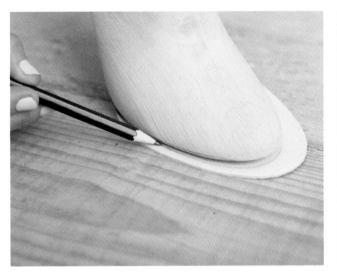

First things first, do your insoles fit the bottom of your lasts?

If not you'll need to trim them down to size or add extra Texon® board to the fronts to make them bigger. The perfect fitting insoles are crucial to the overall finish of the shoes.

THE RIGHT CUT

You may also need to trim a little off the back with a craft knife and if the pitch is off you may need to use a table vice to bend the shank a little until they fit perfectly.

Once you have your insoles fitting the bottom of the last perfectly, you can cover them with your lining leather so they are ready to use.

Trace around your insoles with a 15mm extra allowance onto the underside of your lining leather then cut them out.

Apply a thin, even amount of Aquilim glue to the whole top surface of the insole and to the **underside** of your lining leather.

Wait for the glue to become tacky, then stick the insole face down onto the glued surface and smooth it out with your finger tips.

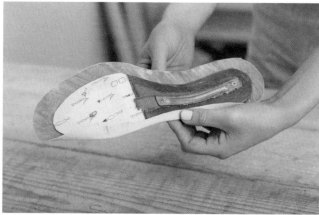

KEEP IT TIDY

To prevent a bumpy edge keep the pleats small around the curve, this should happen naturally as a result of pulling the leather away from the edge.

Turn the insole over and apply a thin, even amount of glue around the edge of the insole.

When the glue is tacky, fold the excess material over and stick it down. Use your thumb around the curves to create small pleats in the leather.

Trim or skive down any excess pleats. You want this surface to be as flat as possible!

LASTING THE LININGS
HIGH HEELED COURT SHOES

In this section we will be lasting the linings onto the insole boards. You may be asking yourself, what does this even mean? Let me explain; the process of stretching your uppers over the lasts is called 'lasting'. In two steps, we last (stretch) the lining layer and glue it in place onto the bottom of the insole, then later down the line we will do the same for the upper layer.

Tape the insoles to the bottom of the lasts using a small amount of masking tape at the front and back of the heels.

Here's where we are going to use that excess lining we left at the back of the uppers. Attach the uppers to the lasts by taping the excess lining we left on the backs.

KEEP IT CLEAN

When taping the backs of the uppers to the last, put the masking tape on the excess lining around the topline so you don't get sticky residue marks on your finished shoes.

Once attached to the lasts, check the back heights
match by lining up the tops of the lasts.

Check the back heights are positioned to match the measurement you
took on page 28.

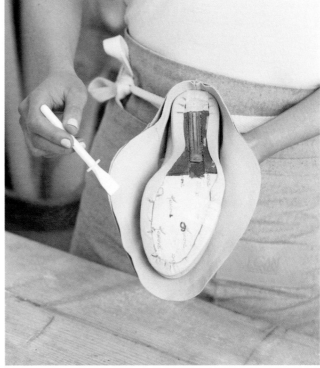

Coat the bottom of your insoles in Aquilim glue
right up to the edge.

Then glue a strip of glue around the inside edge of the lining,
about 10mm wide.

ATTENTION

*You MUST stay close to the edge
of the lining when applying glue here.*
*If you glue too deep into the lining this will
end up visible on the inside of the shoe,
not to mention very sticky on the foot!*

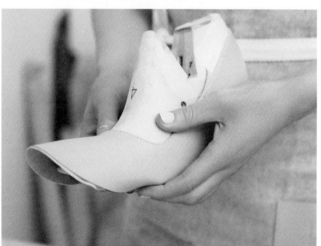

Stretch the upper forward and outward at the sides to create the desired shape.

Stick the lining onto the insole board to hold it in place. Make sure that from the top you have tight side lines of the shoes. Work your way around the insole sticking down the lining, make sure it is pulled tightly around the last.

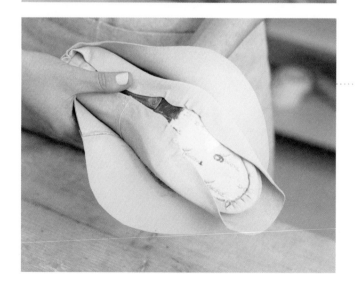

DON'T COMPROMISE THE SHAPE

Although you want it to be tight you must make sure that you are not pulling so tight that you distort the shape of the shoe from the top. Keep looking at the shoes from the top to check that you are happy with their shape.

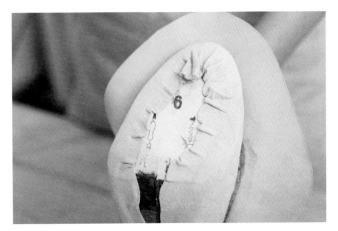

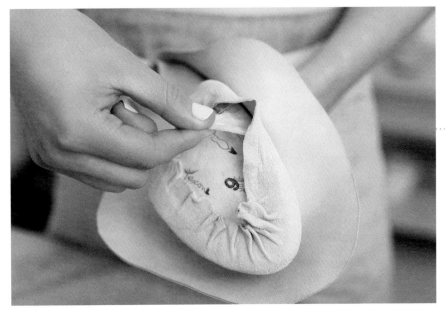

REMOVE THE TAPE

It's important to remove the tape otherwise you won't be able to get the shoe off the last.

You will need to create pleats around the toe and heel area, like you did with the insoles.

Remember, these pleats need to be as far away from the edge as possible. Pull up the lining to remove the masking tape, then re-glue in place.

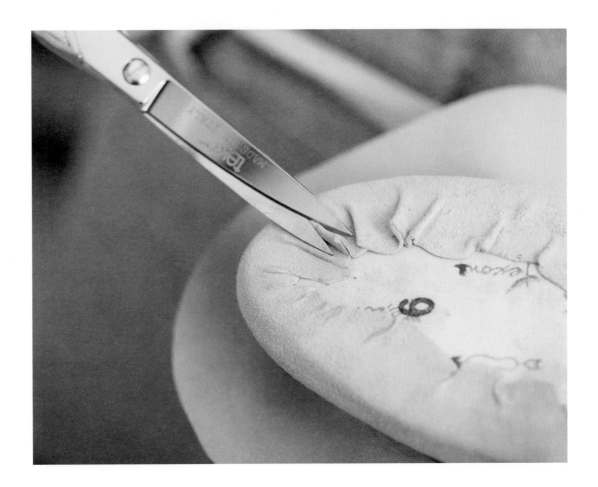

Before you trim away the excess, make sure that you match up the two shoes and are happy that they are symmetrical.

Then cut away all of the excess pleats so that the surface is as flat as possible.

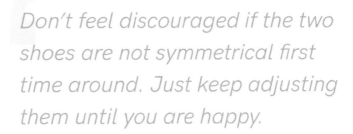

Don't feel discouraged if the two shoes are not symmetrical first time around. Just keep adjusting them until you are happy.

STIFFENERS
HIGH HEELED COURT SHOES

In this section we will be inserting the stiffeners over the top of the linings. This is a really important step as it is what will give your shoes their strength and shape once you remove them from the lasts. There are two stiffeners in this section: the 'toe puff' which goes in the toe area and the 'counters' which go in the heel area.

First we'll start with the toe puff which needs to wrap around the lining and be sealed at the bottom of the last.

Pull the upper right up to the stitching to reveal as much of the lining as possible. To insert the toe puff you'll need to heat it slightly on the shiny side with a heat gun to make it malleable.

PROTECT YOUR SURFACE

The heat gun may burn your surface so be sure to put something down under your toe puff like a heatproof mat.

Place the toe puff over the lining on the front of the shoes, shiny side down, stretch it over the last and seal it down under the shoe.

You'll need to keep using the heat gun to reheat it and mold it to take the shape of the last. You should end up with pleats under the toe area. Trim off the excess.

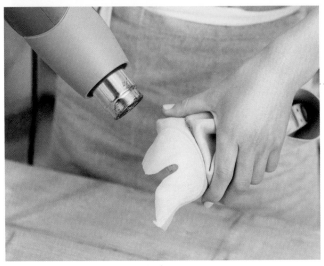

HOW HIGH?

The toe puff doesn't need to go all the way up to the stitching. Try to make sure it's not going over the widest part of the last, this is usually the joint of the foot.

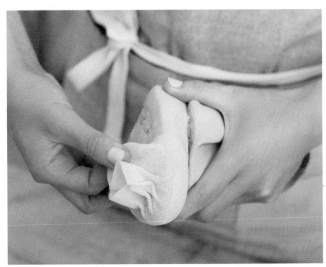

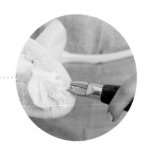

Next we will move onto the counter stiffener.

Lift your upper right up to the stitching, exposing as much of the lining as possible. This is important as the counter must be placed as close to the topline as possible.

CORRECT COUNTER

Traditionally shoemakers like to put the long edge of the counter on the inside of the foot and the short edge on the outside of the foot. I like to swap this, especially when making high heels, as I find that the shorter edge cups your heel nicer when in the high heel position and that the long edge helps keep the shape of the shoe when using thinner leathers.

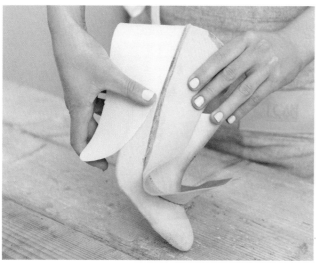

To insert the counter you must heat it slightly with the heat gun to make it malleable.

Once it's malleable place the counter so that the top of it is right up to the stitching, this will help you avoid a baggy topline. Use your hands to cup it onto the last and put a pleat into the back so that it fits snug.

SKIVED EDGE
Topline (also goes against the lining)

SHORT EDGE
Inside of the shoe

LONG EDGE
Outside of the shoe

NOTCH
Line up at the back seam

*If you're using the **I Can Make Shoes** products you should have a left and right counter. It can be tricky to remember which is which, so here's how to tell.*

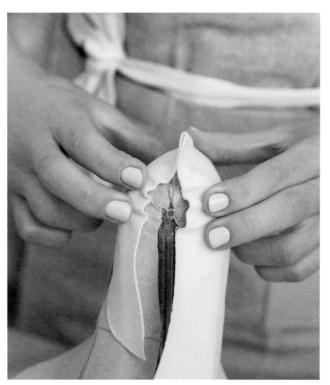
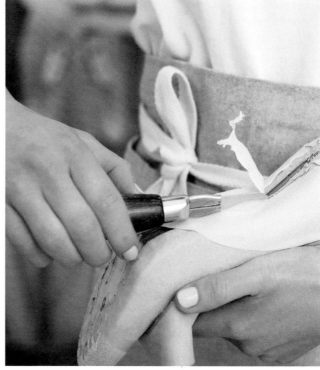

Quickly fold the excess into pleats while the counter is still malleable.

If it becomes too stiff just reheat it. Then you can trim away these excess pleats. Usually you will end up with one big pleat at the back which should be trimmed off once in place.

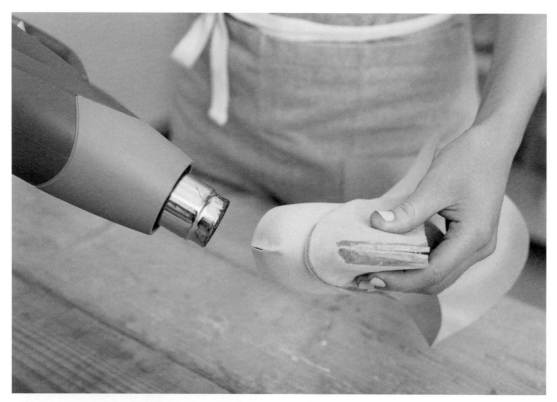

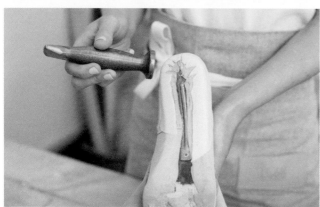

SMOOTH IT OUT

Make sure you have smoothed the stiffener neatly so that it doesn't show through your upper. If it's not going smooth, reheat it and just do it bit by bit.

Reheat the stiffener and use a flat hammer to smooth out the counter onto the lining so that it sits flush to the last.

I like to use a folding hammer for this step.

LASTING THE UPPERS
HIGH HEELED COURT SHOES

In this section we will be lasting the upper layer. This process is more or less the same process as we did for the lining but this time we go over the top of the stiffeners so that they are sealed between the two layers. You should be getting a pretty good idea of how your finished shoes are going to look at this stage.

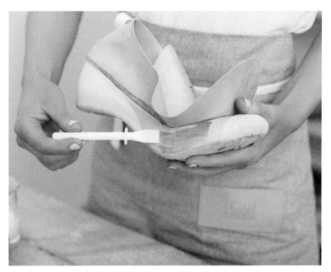 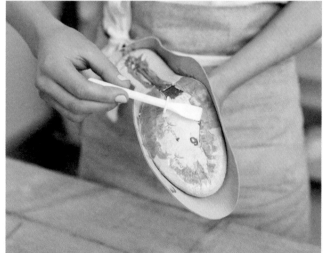

For extra strength, add some Aquillim glue to the uppers and linings in between the stiffeners and stick down the uppers.

Coat the base of the shoe with glue and the inside edge of the upper leather.

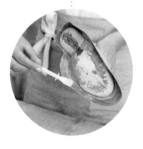

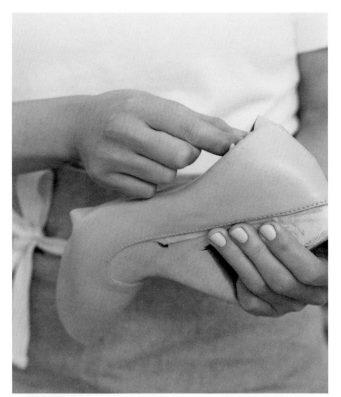

Stretch the upper over the last to mimic the shape created by the lining.

Work your way around the last sticking down the upper, make sure it is pulled tightly around the last.

KEEP IT FLAT

Make sure you keep the pleats as far away from the edge as possible.

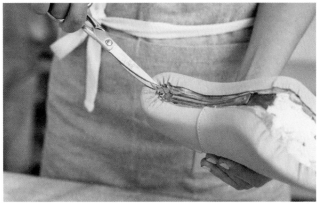

Once your uppers are firmly stuck down, trim away all of the excess pleats.

Make sure you pay special attention around the toe and heel area so it's as flat as possible.

DON'T OVERDO IT

The purpose of the cork filler is to make the bottom surface as flat as possible, so make sure you don't use too much.

Use a cork filler to fill the gap.

I like to use a cork filler to create a nice flat surface for your soles to go on. Cork filler isn't always easy to find so you can also use patches of leather or foam to fill the gap.

SOLES
HIGH HEELED COURT SHOES

In this section we will be creating a pair of soles and attaching them to the base of the shoes. Making a sole pattern is quite easy to do but it's really important that you get it 100% perfect before you cut it out of the leather. So re-doing the pattern multiple times to get it right is encouraged.

First step is to take some clear book contact and place it on the bottom of your shoe.

Using a pen or marker, trace around the feather (bottom) edge of the shoe.

DON'T LEAVE A MARK

To avoid any marks make sure the contact doesn't wrap up the sides of your shoe as it may take the finish off the surface of your upper leather.

N.B

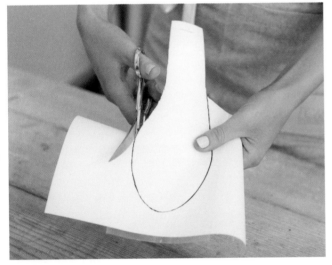

Lay it flat on paper and place your heel at the back of the sole pattern to mark where it comes to.

You'll want the sole to sit under the heel so draw in a 10mm underlay and cut away the excess. Double check your pattern before you cut the real soles. Once you are happy with your pattern you can cut it out in veg tan leather 3mm thick. Remember to flip the pattern to get a left and right.

SKIVE IT DOWN

I like to use a safety beveller to skive a little of the weight out from the underside of the end of the sole, this will help the heel sit more flat.

Line up the sole to the bottom of the shoes.

Using a silver pen, carefully trace around the sole onto the feather edge of the shoe.

GET A STRONG GRIP

*You'll want to use a stronger glue for attaching the soles, we use **Renia Colle de Cologne**. Be sure to allow 10-15 minutes for the glue to feel almost dry to touch before you stick. If it still feels tacky, you won't achieve a strong bond.*

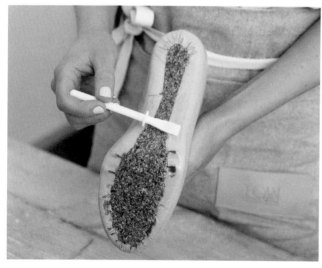

Coat the underside of the sole in glue.

Then coat the base of the shoe in glue right up to your silver pen line. It's really important that the glue goes right up to the line. Any gaps without glue means the sole will not stick there.

FOR AN EXTRA STRONG BOND

If you have your heat gun handy, heat up the glue on the sole and the base of the shoe before sticking for an extra strong bond.

Start with the toe and lightly touch the sole in place within your silver pen lines.

Then make sure the sides are sitting within the silver pen lines and gently touch it in place. Once you are happy with the position give the whole sole a strong squeeze around all of the edges and in the middle.

HEELS
HIGH HEELED COURT SHOES

....

This section is really fun for two big reasons - your shoes are almost finished and you get to use some power tools! During this section I will show you how to cover your heels and how to attach them to your shoes.

Place the heel on the underside of the leather and roll it from side to side.

Use the silver pen to mark out about 5mm extra on the top and bottom and enough for the leather to join up in the middle (with a little extra) then cut out.

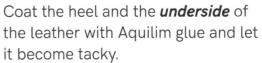

Coat the heel and the *underside* of the leather with Aquilim glue and let it become tacky.

Once it's ready to stick, start by placing the heel in the centre of the leather and smooth the leather around the heel without any air bubbles.

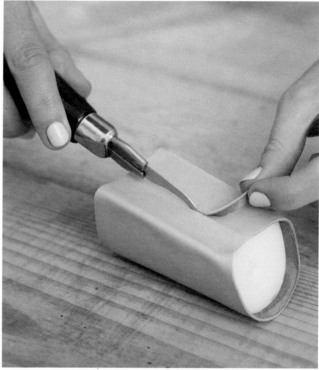

Find the middle of the inside of the heel where you want the leather to join.

Fold one side of the excess leather over the other. Take a sharp knife and cut through both layers of the leather to make a perfect join.

THE LEAF

For a curved heel or 'louis' heel, you may need to make a separate piece. We call this the 'leaf'.

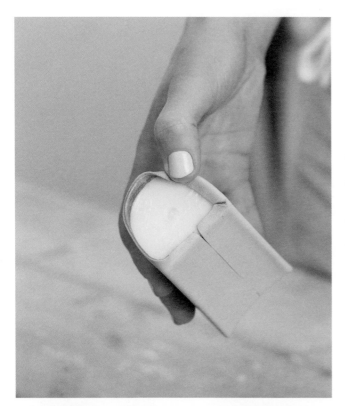

Apply some glue to the top and bottom of the heel and fold the excess over.

Trim away any pleats.

Hammer in your heel tips.

With a firm swing, hammer the tip all the way into the heel. Make sure you don't have any excess leather stuck in the holes for the heel tip to go in.

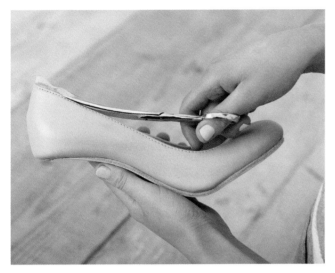

You can now remove the shoes from the lasts, yay!

Carefully cut away the excess lining from the back of the shoes.

Hold the heel in the desired position at the back of the shoe.

Drill two holes through the insole board to lightly mark the positioning onto the heels.

MIND THE SHANK

There is a metal shank down the centre of the insole so you must drill a hole on each side of this shank.

IMPORTANT · N.B · IMPORTANT

Once you've made a mark on the heels you can separate them from the shoes.

Drill the holes into the heel a little deeper.

Use a screwdriver to screw in two flat-topped, Philips head screws through the insole and into the heel.

Make sure these are tight and the heel is secure. We use 3/4 inch screws in our workshop but you can use any long enough to screw into the heel.

KEEP THE SHAPE

If this process distorts the back section of your shoe, reheat the upper in this area with a heat gun and stick it back on the last for 10 minutes, this will reshape it.

IMPORTANT · N.B · IMPORTANT

INSOLE SOCKS
HIGH HEELED COURT SHOES

Insole socks or 'insocks' are the final touch and can be pretty much any shape. Their purpose is to cover up the screws and to add some padding to the inside of the shoes. Sometimes you'll see just a teardrop shape and sometimes you'll see the insock mimic the entire shape of the insole. There's no right or wrong here just create a nice shape that works for you.

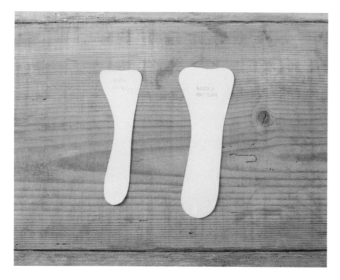

Cut out your foam to be about 5mm smaller than your insole sock all the way around.

Most of the time shoemakers will add some foam under the insock to add extra comfort. We use a 1.5mm thick memory foam but kids craft foam works great too.

MAKE IT YOUR OWN

You may want to use pinking shears or even a fake stitch on your insole sock to get a special finish.

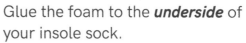

Glue the foam to the *underside* of your insole sock.

Apply Aquilim glue to both pieces. When the glue becomes tacky, press firmly together in position.

Using your pattern, mark the placement of your insole sock on the inside of the shoe.

I like to use a silver gel pen for this step so that I can see clearly where the glue should go.

Apply Aquillim glue to the underside of the insole sock (including the foam) and the inside of the shoes.

Once the glue is tacky, start by placing the heel area. Let the rest of the insole sock lay flat inside the shoe.

MAKE IT STICK

Press firmly in place using your thumbs. You've now finished your court shoes!

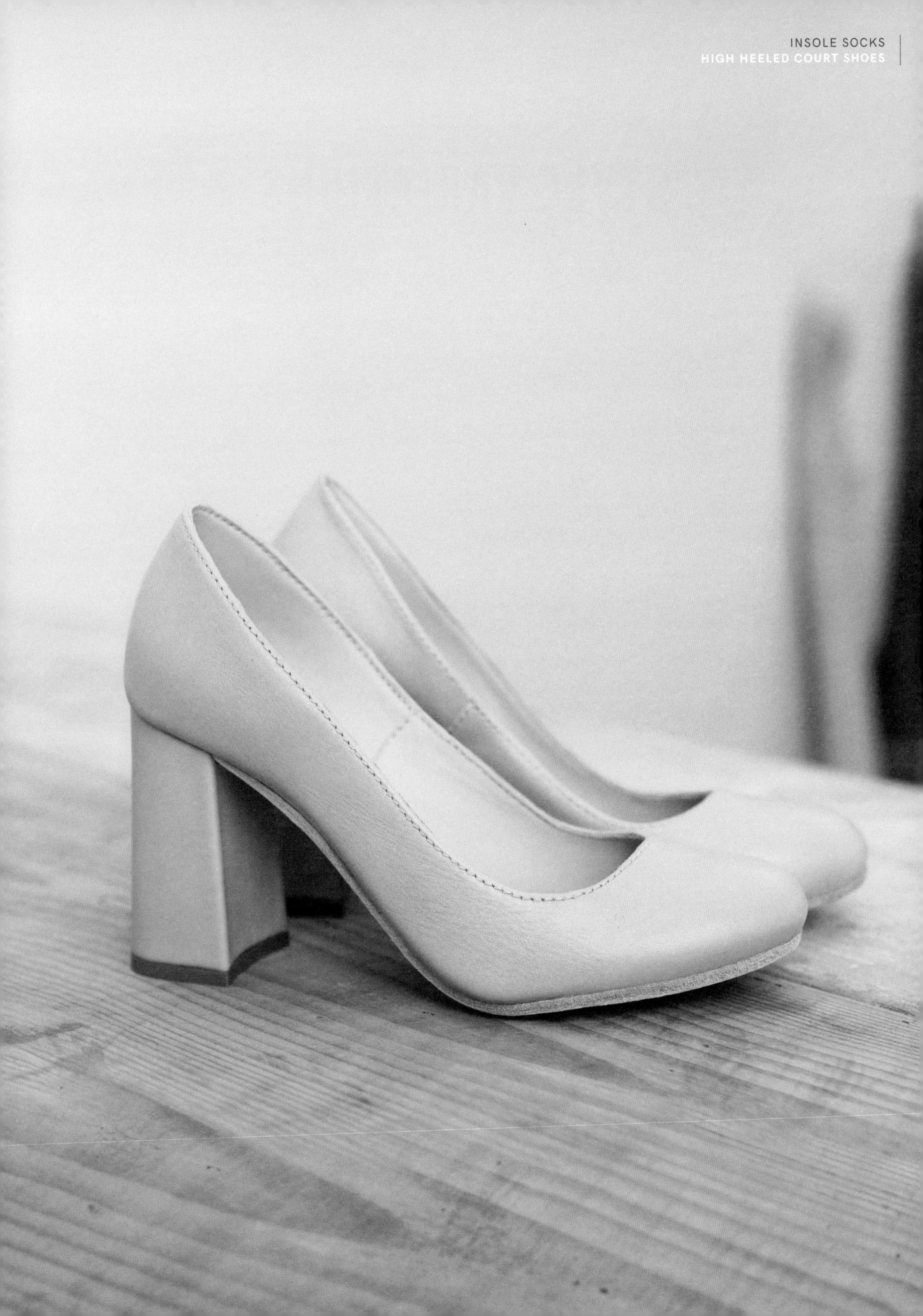

STYLE VARIATIONS
HIGH HEELED COURT SHOES

When making shoes the steps will more or less stay the same after you've made your uppers. Here are some examples of different styles you can make using the same techniques.

Peep toe shoe.

If you want to make a peep-toe shoe, the process would be exactly the same but without the toe puff. Here's an example of a finished shoe and how the upper would look. I've also added a loop at the back to insert an ankle strap.

Sling back shoe.

Same goes for a sling back but instead you'd leave out the counter stiffener. You may also need to add in a buckle or some elastic. Here's an example of a finished shoe and how the upper would look.

HEEL STYLE

Notice how different the style of shoe can be just by changing the heel.

HOW TO MAKE
FLAT SHOES

In this part of the book we are going to show you how to follow very similar steps to create completely different looking shoes - derby shoes and ballet flats to be specific.

All of these instructions are exactly the same for both mens and womens shoes but if you're making mens shoes, you'll need mens lasts.

01 **PATTERN**

02 **UPPERS**

03 **INSOLES**

04 **LASTING THE LININGS**

05 **STIFFENERS**

06 **LASTING THE UPPERS**

07 **SOLES**

08 **STYLE VARIATION**

PATTERN
DERBY SHOES

....

We used a high heel court shoe in the example for the *Beginner's Introduction to Patternmaking* on page 27 and for flat shoes it's pretty much the same process of drawing the design onto the last and cutting off your pieces. In this example we are doing a derby shoe which has two pieces; a front section and a back section.
You'll also need a **last bottom pattern** to create the insoles, shown here.

THE VAMP

The front section of the shoe including the tongue. We use the same pattern for the upper and the lining.

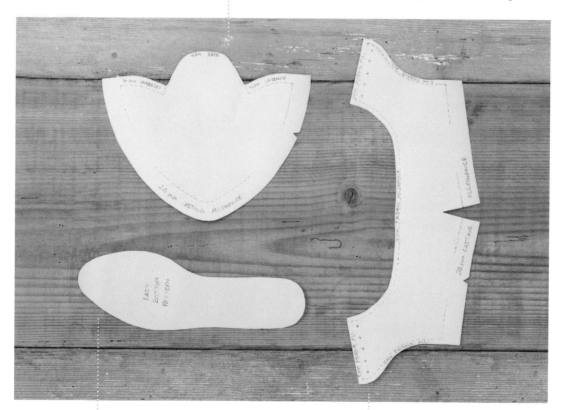

LAST BOTTOM PATTERN

The pattern used to make the insoles for flat shoes. The pattern should sit directly on the feather edge of the last.

THE QUARTER

This back piece is usually in a few separate parts called 'the quarters', but we are simplifying things by making it one whole piece with a dart seam in the back.

TWO PART PATTERN

With this derby pattern we want to make sure that the back piece sits over the top of the vamp. So you will need to make sure you have a 10mm underlay allowance on the vamp pattern.

To make your last bottom pattern, tape vertically down the bottom of the last from heel to toe then layer more tape horizontally to cover the rest of the last.

Make sure the tape is flat and doesn't wrap over the edges. Then using a pencil trace around the bottom (feather) edge of the lasts.

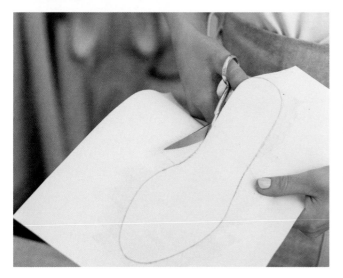

Carefully peel the tape off the last and lay flat on paper.

Following your pencil line, cut out the the bottom pattern and check that it fits perfectly.

UPPERS
DERBY SHOES

In this section I'm going to show you how to make the uppers for a classic derby style shoe (for ballet flats go straight to page 120). Once the uppers are stitched or 'closed' the assembly process is pretty much the same for all shoes.

Take your patterns and trace them onto the **underside** of your upper leather and lining leather.

Remember to flip your patterns for left and right feet. Then cut out your pieces as neatly as possible.

LEFT AND RIGHT

When working with multiple pattern pieces remember to cut out the small notches so you can tell your lefts from rights.

Lay your back piece face down.

Using a silver pen draw in your 5mm folding allowance on the topline.

GLUE BOTH SIDES

*For this section we will use the non-toxic glue, **Renia Aquilim 315.** This is a contact adhesive so it must be applied to both surfaces you want to stick together. You'll need to let the glue dry for about a minute before you stick, if it is still wet you won't achieve a bond.*

Apply a thin, even amount of glue on both sides of this line and allow it to become tacky.

Fold the topline of the uppers. When the two folds meet in corners, squeeze them together and snip off the excess.

AVOID EXTRA STRETCHING

Topline tape can be inserted at this stage to help with overall strength but this can be left out if you are a beginner.

At this point you can skive away any excess leather to reduce the bulk. I also like to put some seam tape where the laces will go to help avoid stretching.

Lay all of your vamp pieces face
down including the linings.

Glue the undersides of the tongue parts and stick
them together.

MAKE IT YOUR OWN

*You can leave the tongues raw
cut and un-stitched, but feel
free to stitch around them if
you like the look.*

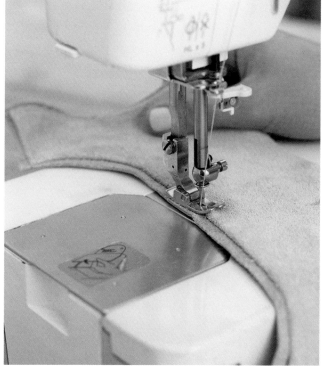

To put together the upper and lining of the back sections, flip both pieces face down.

On the lining, apply a strip of glue around 5mm down from the topline. It should go just past the laces area (up to where my finger is).

On the upper, apply Aquillim glue along the topline in the same area. **Make sure the sides are not glued together.** We need to keep them separate for now so we can insert the front section a bit later on, flick forward to page 95 to see how.

Place this piece in the sewing machine and carefully stitch the topline nice and close to the edge.

EXTRA LINING

There will be an extra 5mm of lining around the topline, we will cut this off later but we need to keep it for now.

FOR THE PERFECT FIT

Follow the curve created by the V shape to
have a nice neat curve at the back of the shoe.

Turn the upper inside out and fold it in half to line
up the back seam. Stitch it closed approximately
5mm away from the edge.

Repeat these steps for your lining, making sure that you stitch the lining
inside out so you close all the seams inside the shoes. Open and flatten
all the seams with a little glue, then use a safety beveller to skive away
any excess leather.

At this stage you can cut away the excess lining from the edges where your laces will go.

It is very important that you leave a little bit of excess right at the back, we will cut this off later.

Now for the tricky part, I recommend you read this whole section before you cut anything.

Start by flipping the stitched back piece upside down. On the **lining only,** cut a slit from the top of the side seam approximately 15mm horizontally towards the back dart seam.

Apply glue to the side underlay on the front
piece and the ***underside*** of the side overlay
on the back piece.

Sandwich the front section in between the upper and the
lining of the back section and glue the sides together.

Stitch the first side in place making sure you only stitch through the upper layers *not the linings*.

When you get to the top make sure you secure it with a backstitch.

Once you have the first side in place, fold the front section in half.

Glue the second side in place by sandwiching the front section between the upper and the lining of the back section. Then stitch the second side in place. Remember to only stitch through the upper layers not the lining.

CHECK BEFORE YOU STITCH

Make sure look at the upper from the front before you stitch the second side in place. This is just in case you need to shift things around a bit.

SECURE IN PLACE

*Gluing the pieces together first will help
hold everything in place while you stitch.*

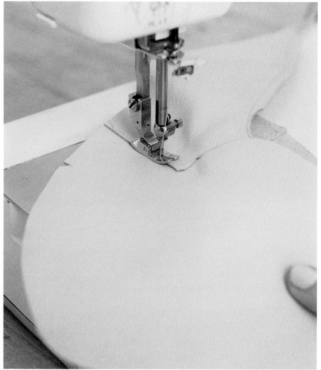

Once you are happy with the positioning you can glue the linings in place.

With everything glued in place correctly you can now stitch the lining
pieces closed. Be careful not to stitch the upper and lining side
seams together.

N.B
IMPORTANT · IMPORTANT ·

*If you stitch through all the
layers you will not be able to get
the stiffeners in properly so it's
important to keep them separate.*

Using an awl, mark the placement of the lace holes along the lace edge.

You may want to go over the prick marks with a silver pen so they are easier to see when you are punching the holes.

Using a leather hole punch, select the size of the holes you want to use and carefully punch the holes over the marks you made.

Try to make sure they are all the same distance away from the edge.

ADD EXTRA DETAILS

You can insert eyelets at this stage if you want them.

" *Thread in your laces and your uppers are complete!*

INSOLES
DERBY SHOES

Flat shoe insoles differ from high heel insoles because they don't need the metal shank. This is why we need a last bottom pattern so we can make the insoles ourselves. The process to cover the insoles is the same but with the additional layer of foam so you can use the technique from page 48.

INSOLE BOARD

For flat shoes we need movement in the insoles so I like to use Texon® board 2mm thick.

LEATHER OF CHOICE

The material you want to cover your insoles with.

LAST BOTTOM PATTERN

Your last bottom pattern ready from page 86.

MEMORY FOAM

For extra padding I like to insert a full layer of 1.5mm memory foam before covering the insoles.

Using your last bottom pattern, trace and cut out
your insoles on 2mm thick Texon® (insole) board.

Remember to flip your pattern to get left and right feet. Glue the foam
to the insole board and then cover the insoles using the same technique
outlined on page 48.

*Since these shoes are flat and you
won't be drilling in heels, you can add
in some foam padding at this stage.*

LASTING THE LININGS
DERBY SHOES

In this section we will be lasting the linings onto the insole boards. This process is exactly the same as the technique shown for the high heeled court shoes on page 52, feel free to flick back to refresh your memory.

N.B · IMPORTANT · IMPORTANT

ATTENTION

Make sure that the laces are fastened at the correct tension so that the uppers fit the lasts snuggly when lasting.

*Don't forget the golden rules of
lasting the lining from the high
heeled court shoes - match your
back heights, glue close to the
edge, always trim the pleats, and
remember to remove the tape!*

STIFFENERS
DERBY SHOES

In this section we will be inserting the stiffeners over the top of the linings. This process is exactly the same as what we've shown for the high heeled court shoes on page 58. We'll be using the exact same two stiffeners in this section, the 'toe puff' which goes in the toe area and the 'counters' which go in the heel area.

PROTECT YOUR SURFACE
Use a cutting mat or heat proof mat to make sure you don't burn your table.

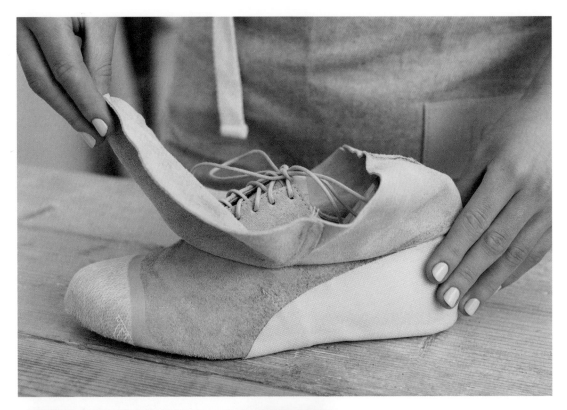

The shape of the last is different from a high heel so you'll find that you have less excess to trim at the end.

LASTING THE UPPERS
DERBY SHOES

In this section we will be lasting the upper layer of the derby shoes. This process is exactly the same as we did for the high heel example on page 64. Remember to make sure you keep all of your pleats as far away from the edge as possible on this layer.

N.B IMPORTANT · IMPORTANT

ATTENTION

Adding extra glue to the lining between the two stiffeners is especially important for flat shoes as you get a lot of movement in this area when walking.

Add in your cork filler to create a flat surface for your sole to go on. Remember you can use patches of leather if you don't have access to cork filler.

SOLES
DERBY SHOES

In this section we will be making the soles for the derby shoes. Soles for flat shoes will differ from the soles that we put onto high or mid height ladies' heels. The main difference is that we won't be drilling any heels in so we need to build up a stacked heel tip to give the shoes a decent amount of lift from the ground.

For this example we will be attaching a randing to the edge of the shoes.

What is randing? Randing is also sometimes called a 'mock welt' and is a stitched binding that runs around the junction of the upper and the sole.

GET A STRONG GRIP

*You'll want to use a stronger glue for attaching the soles, we use **Renia Colle de Cologne**. Be sure to allow 10-15 minutes for the glue to feel almost dry to touch before you stick. If it still feels tacky, you won't achieve a strong bond.*

Apply a thin, even amount of glue on the inside of the rand and the feather edge of the shoe.

Start on the inside of the shoe and stick the randing as tight to the feather edge as possible. Cut the end of the randing to join perfectly with the start point.

RANDING IS OPTIONAL

*Randing is available for sale on the **I Can Make Shoes** online supply shop. It's purely aesthetic though so you can skip and move straight onto the next step if you wish.*

To create the sole pattern, place
the shoe flat on a piece of paper.

Neatly trace around the feather edge of the shoe
making sure you don't angle the pencil too far in
or out.

On the pattern, draw a line in the
area where you want to have your
heel tip.

Repeat this step so you have two copies. Cut out
one with the whole sole pattern and cut out the
other with just the heel tip.

BEFORE YOU CUT

*Always double check your
pattern for any changes
before you cut the real soles.*

STRONGER SOLES

Most professional shoemakers will use a thick sole bend leather for their sole. However this can be really hard for beginners to cut so I recommend starting out with layering two pieces of 3mm veg tanned leather.

Once you are happy with the pattern cut them out of 3mm thick veg tanned leather.

You can use rubber or a dense EVA foam for a vegan alternative. Remember to flip the pattern for left and right feet. Then cut out 2-3 heel tips per shoe, depending on how much height your lasts will allow for.

Before we start stacking the soles, we need to rough up the smooth side of the leather.

Using the clicking knife (or any craft knife), lightly slice in a hash pattern. We only need to do this on one of the layers.

Roughing up the leather will help the glue to grip and bond the layers together for a stronger sole.

GET A STRONG GRIP

*You'll want to use a stronger glue for attaching the soles, we use **Renia Colle de Cologne**. Be sure to allow 10-15 minutes for the glue to feel almost dry to touch before you stick. If it still feels tacky, you won't achieve a strong bond.*

Glue the roughed up side of one layer and the *underside* of the other layer.

Give around 10-15 minutes of drying time and then carefully stick them together.

FOR AN EXTRA STRONG BOND

Remember you can heat this glue with your heat gun for an extra strong grip.

To give extra lift off the ground we are going to build up a heel tip using another two layers of soling leather.

Apply glue over the roughed surface and to the **underside** of the first heel tip.

Allow to dry then stick the heel tip to the sole. Repeat with the next heel tip(s), leaving the last one un-roughed.

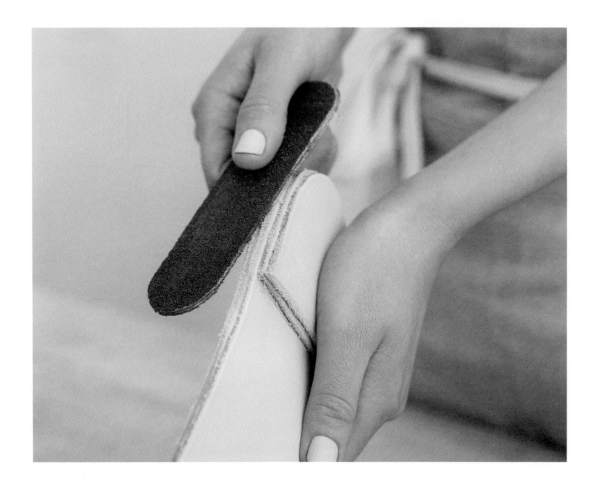

Once you've stacked all of the layers, you can start smoothing the edges of your sole unit.

I like to use a sandpaper board or a small handheld dremel.

If you don't have a handheld dremel, you can use ordinary sandpaper which does the job just as well!

BEFORE YOU GLUE

If you don't have randing, line up the sole to the bottom of the shoes and carefully trace around the feather edge with a silver pen.

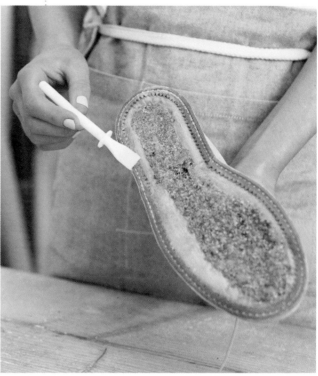

To attach the sole to the shoe, coat the underside of the sole unit in strong glue.

Then coat the base of the shoe in glue right up to your silver pen line or the edge of the randing.

STICK TO THE EDGE

It's really important that the glue goes right up to the edge of the soles and the shoe. Any gaps without glue means the sole will not stick there.

N.B
IMPORTANT · IMPORTANT

Starting with the heel, lightly touch it in place in line with your randing or silver pen line.

Then make sure the sides are sitting in the correct position and gently touch it in place. Once you are happy with the position give the whole sole a strong squeeze around all of the edges and in the middle.

Sand down the sole so it sits flush with the randing.

If you don't have randing be careful not to sand the side of your upper by mistake.

FIND YOUR FINISH

Once you've had a bit more experience you can experiment with different ways of finishing your soles for a more professional finish. Try adding an edge dye or buffing them with beeswax.

You can now remove your shoes from the last,
start by pulling out the heel and then wiggle
the front area off the last.

Carefully cut away the excess lining from the back of the shoes.
You have just made your own derby shoes, try them on for size!

*You'll need to fully
undo the laces so you
can easily remove your
shoes from the last.*

STYLE VARIATION
BALLET FLATS

The main difference between the flat pump pattern and the high heel is that we won't put a side seam in the flat. This is because we don't have the overlap problem in the pattern caused by the curve in the high last.

ADDING THE NOTCH

When tracing your patterns, don't forget to notch to the inside of your pattern.

RANDING IS OPTIONAL

*Randing is available for sale on the **I Can Make Shoes** online supply shop. It's purely aesthetic though so you can skip it if you wish.*

Ballet flat.

If you want to make a flat ballet pump the process of making the upper would be pretty much the same as the high heel court shoe and the process of lasting them would be the same as the derby shoe.

HOW TO MAKE
SUPER SIMPLE SANDALS

I love making sandals, they are so quick and easy, it's the most instant gratification you can get in the world of shoemaking. In this final shoemaking chapter I will show you how to make a really simple style and you'll see how you can apply this method to almost any style you choose in the future.

01 **FREESTYLE STRAPS**

02 **STYLE VARIATIONS**

FREESTYLE
SUPER SIMPLE SANDALS

Sandals don't need to be super complicated, here I will show you how to use your own foot as the last. If you are making them for someone else or to sell, you can use these same techniques on a sandal last.

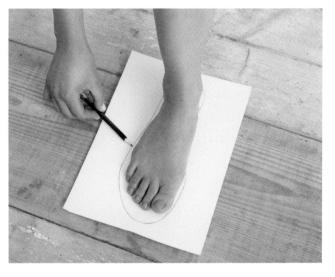 

To make the insole and sole patterns trace around your foot and add some extra width until you are happy with the overall shape.

You can then use this pattern to cut two left and two right out of 3mm thick veg tanned leather. These pieces will become your insoles and soles.

INSOLES

I've added an extra insole layer for this pair to give them a chunkier look. You can also add extra layers of leather to build up the heel tips.

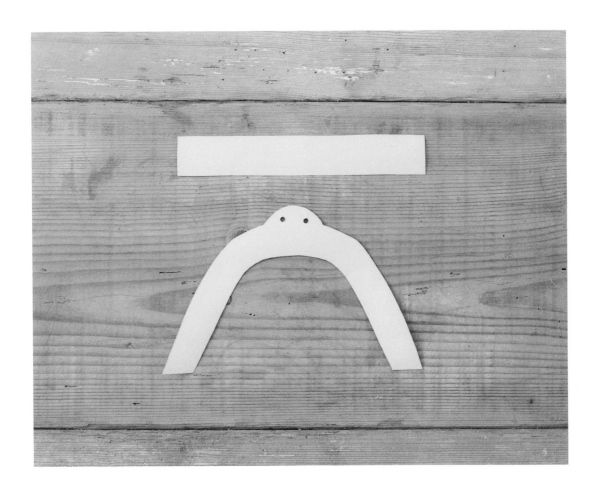

Here's what I mean when I say I freestyle my strap patterns. I literally cut out pieces of paper in shapes and put them over my foot to see how they look.

If the strap seems a little thin, I make a thicker one. If the curve isn't in the right place, I correct it until I've got it perfect.

I make my sandals in the most untechnical way, I do them without lasts and I totally freestyle it on the strap patterns.

Once you've got your strap patterns finalised, you can then cut the straps out of leather.

I like to use a veg tanned cow leather approximately 1-2mm thick. This way the straps can be left raw cut and won't need to be lined or stitched.

VEG TANNED LEATHER

This type of leather is great for sandals because it softens up over time, is thick enough to not require lining, and will eventually mould to the shape of your foot.

You can insert eyelets at this stage if you want them.

Make sure you use the correct size hole for your eyelets of choice.

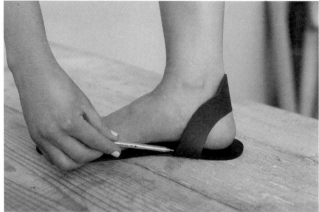

KEEP YOUR DISTANCE

Don't mark too close to the edge as you want to make sure the straps are secure under the foot.

Rest your foot on the insole and then overlay the straps in the desired position.

Mark the positioning of the straps on the insole approximately 5mm from the edge.

Cut an angled slit in the leather insole. This slit should be about 5-10mm away from the edge and should angle towards the centre of the insole.

Place your straps through the slits.

Put your foot or last into the sandal and tighten the straps to the desired fit.

Using a silver pen, draw boxes on the **underside** of the insoles where the straps will sit.

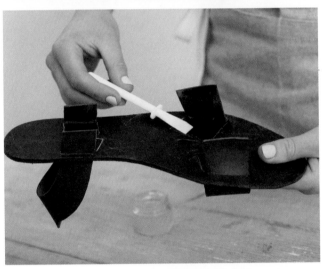

GET A STRONG GRIP

*You'll want to use a stronger glue for attaching the straps, we use **Renia Colle de Cologne**. Be sure to allow 10-15 minutes for the glue to feel almost dry to touch before you stick. If it still feels tacky, you won't achieve a strong bond.*

Glue the straps down in position under the insole.

Using a safety beveller, skive away any excess bulk from the bottom of the insoles.

Apply the strong glue to your insoles and soles right up to the edge.

Don't forget to rough up the sole and give it a blast with the heat gun to help the glue grip. Flick back to page 112 for a reminder on how to do this.

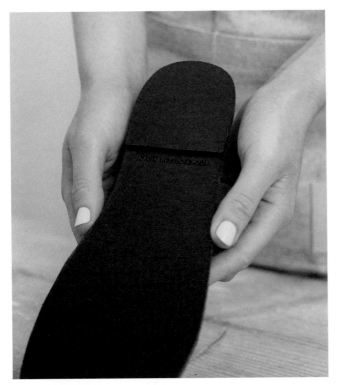

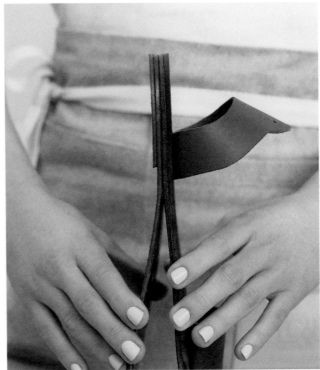

Once the glue has had some dry time, stick the heel area first and work your way up the sides to the toe area.

Give the edges a good squeeze the whole way around.

LAYER UP

I have added an extra insole layer here. You can also add a few extra heel tips here if you want that extra lift.

131

NEATEN THE SOLES

I like to add an edge dye coating to the soles after they have been smoothed down to create a neat finish.

Sand down the edges and add your finishing touches for your own super simple sandals!

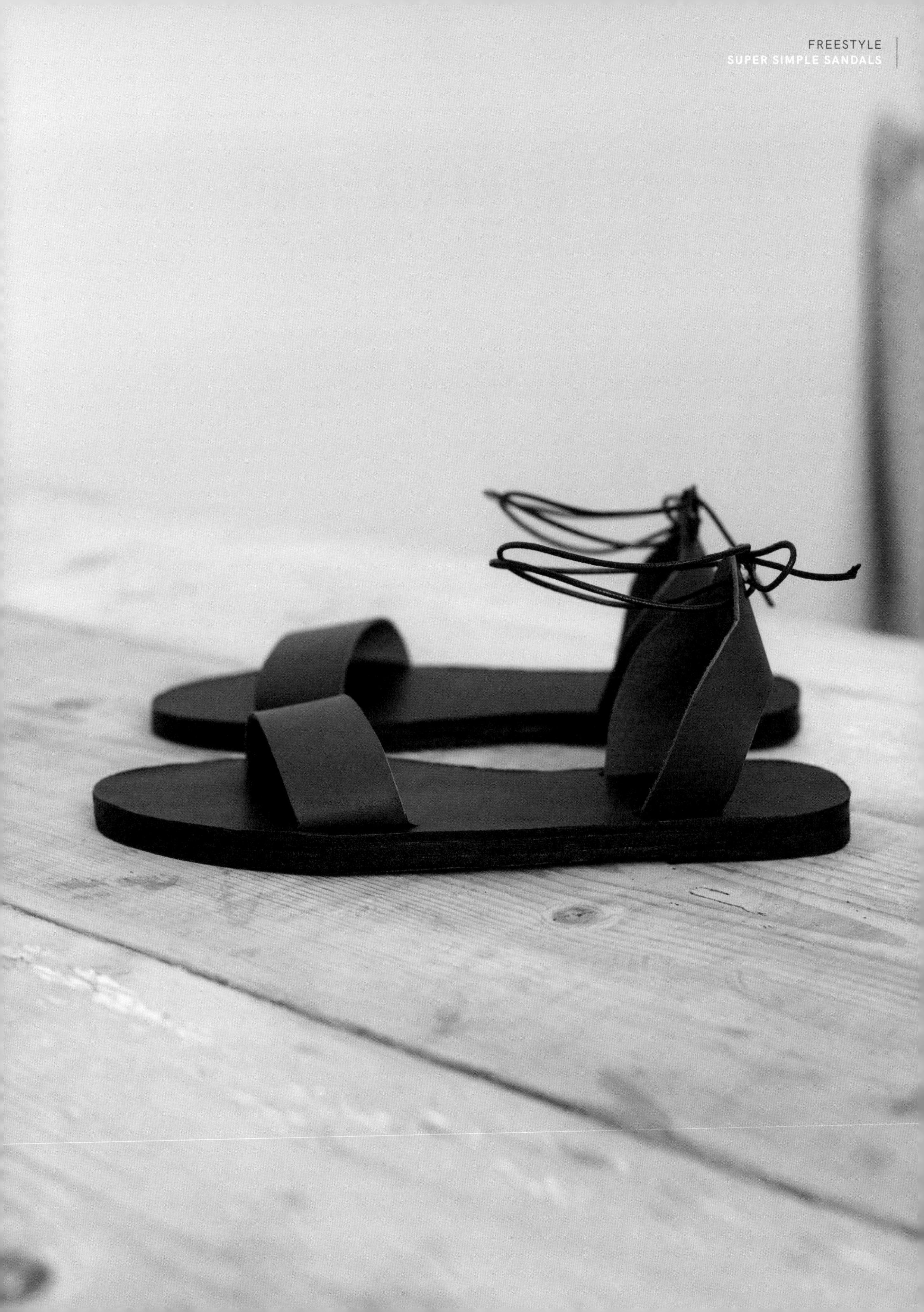

STYLE VARIATION
SUPER SIMPLE SANDALS

Here's an example of the exact same sandal except with a wider strap at the front. It's a subtle change but can give the sandal a totally different feel. You could try doing a cross over with two straps at the front or maybe just a small strap that goes over the big toe.

THE PERFECT FIT

When working with a wider front strap, try curving the edges so that the piece fits snugly over the foot.

Try experimenting with different strap and sole combinations.

On this style I have made a much thicker front strap for a more supportive fit, and have only added one layer of soling.

This back shape is one of my favourites, I often use this back and mix up the front straps.

EXTRA HINTS + TIPS

I've put together a list of tips to help fast track your shoemaking skills. You can also subscribe to our *I Can Make Shoes* YouTube channel for regular videos and tutorials.

LEATHERS

Using a leather with print
Trace out your pattern on the right side so you can see where to position the print on the shoe.

Find the nicest part
Leather is an organic material so some areas of the skin might be different. There may be some imperfections like holes or stretch marks so avoid them if you can.

Test the flexibility
When buying leather always stretch it in several directions to test the flexibility of the skin. Your material needs to be molded over the last so make sure you can fold it easily but it's still strong. In other words not too thin, not too thick.

Covering the insoles
Choose a soft leather (pig skin, lamb skin, kid skin) in order to pull all the pleats as far away from the feather edge as possible.

Don't wipe glue spillages
Just like wax, wait for the glue to set on the leather and gently erase it using a piece of crepe rubber.

DESIGNING

Hold your drawing in front of a mirror
Having a fresher point of view on what you are sketching will help you spot and correct any problem areas.

Think about the opening and fastenings
Always consider how your foot would go in and out of the shoe. Does it need a fastening? E.g. a buckle, zip or elastic. If so, where and how?

MARKING THE PATTERN

Mark a notch
Notches on the inside pieces of patterns will help you remember to flip your patterns and how to put together all your pieces once they are cut out.

Using a stiffer material
You might want to add some extra millimeters onto your lasting allowance if your leather is really stiff. When you have less stretch you'll need the extra leather to grip onto while you last the uppers.

Cross your lace holes
Draw a cross instead of a circle for lace hole positions on your pattern. The middle of the cross is more precise than a circle drawn by hand.

CUTTING OUT THE PATTERN

Conserve the shape
When flattening your pattern onto paper always stick down your toplines first to conserve the shape of your design.

Flatten the pattern
You may need to cut some small snips in the curved areas of the tape so it will lay flat. The higher the heel, the more volume you will have to flatten onto the paper.

THE UPPERS

Flip the pattern
When tracing out your patterns on the leather remember to always flip your pattern in order to get a left and a right shoe.

Adding snips to the topline
When folding toplines, one scissor snip in the folding allowance will give you a squared angle. Several tiny snips in the folding allowance will allow you to shape a smooth convex curve.

Always double check and test
Make sure you've got the right tension on your sewing machine by doing a test on a scrap of leather first.

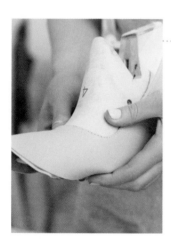

LASTING

Matching the pair
When lasting your second shoe, double check the back heights and the shape of the top lines all match.

Remove the masking tape
Make sure to remove the masking tape from the insole before you finish gluing the lining closed.

*Have more questions? Why not join our **Facebook Community?** You'll find lots of creative solutions from us and from your peers on how to fix home shoemaking issues.*

@icanmakeshoes.community

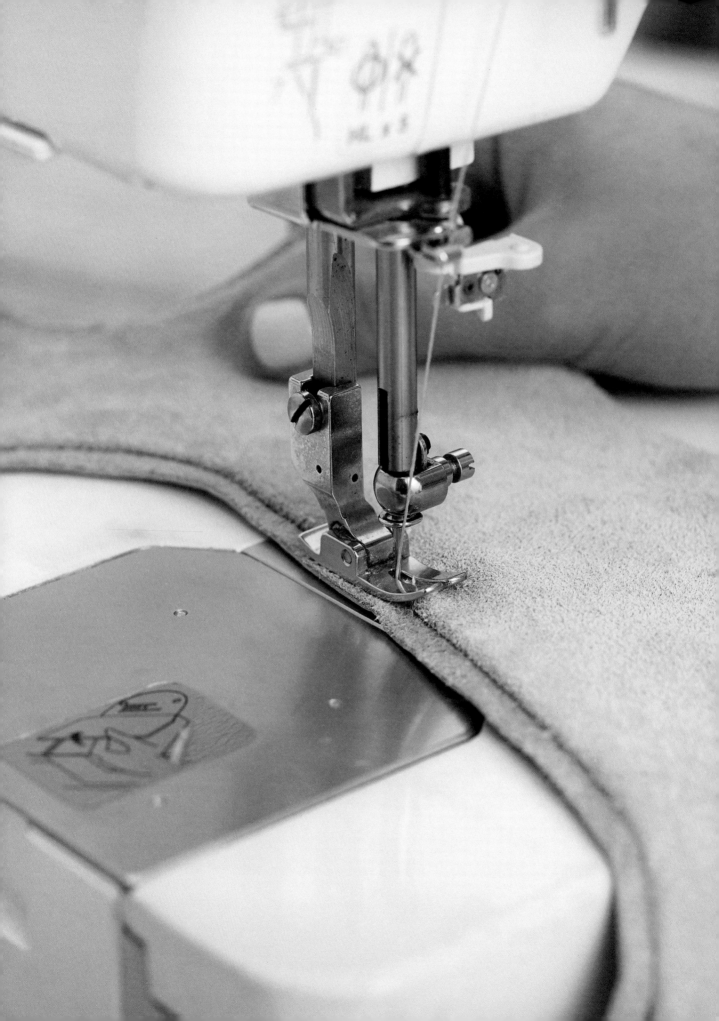

FAQS

Here are some of the questions I get
asked most regularly by my students.

Which sewing machine should I use?
We use flat bed Janome Professional HD9
machines, they are amazing and perfect for
beginners! We use them with denim needles
and nylon thread. Any domestic machine
that can handle denim should be fine for
home shoemaking.

Where can I get all the supplies?
You can get most of the supplies from the *I Can
Make Shoes* online supply shop. For everything
else we've got a detailed suppliers list on our
website - www.icanmakeshoes.com/suppliers-list

Can I buy leather online?
You can get most types of leather online however
I always recommend buying it in person if you can.
It's important to feel the stretch and thickness of
the leather and also check it for marks.

Can I use fabric instead?
Yes for sure, just use an iron on interfacing if it's
too thin. When you are using a material with a bias
stretch you'll want to place your patterns so that
the grain line is running from heel to toe.

Is the glue vegan?
The glues we use here at *I Can Make Shoes* are
vegan. We use a German brand called Renia.

**How can I make adjustments to the lasts for
a wider fit?**
A couple of ways - you can glue layers of veg tan
leather to the sides of the last and then skive down
the edges into the desired shape. Or you can use
a product called Milliput® to create adjustments to
the shape. Milliput® will need to be left overnight
to set and then be sanded down the next day.
Check out our YouTube channel for videos on how
to do this.

How to make shoes smaller?
If your shoes are too big and you want to shrink
them down a bit, you can start by putting a padded
insock inside. You can also get heel grips which
work great. Another top tip if you have a closed
back shoe, you can heat it up with a heat gun or
hair dryer and pinch the back (this is where the
counter stiffener is) to make it a little tighter.

How to make shoes bigger?
If your shoes are too small and you want to stretch
them out, you can start by taking your heat gun
or hair dryer and heating the shoes all over. Just
do one shoe at a time and with your hands stretch
out the shoes from the inside. This will loosen
up the leather and also stretch the thermoplastic
stiffeners that are inside the shoes.

SHOPPING LIST

Finding all the things you need can often be the hardest part. Here's a checklist to make the shoemaking experience a little easier for you.

I CAN MAKE SHOES SUPPLY SHOP

We pride ourselves in making shoemaking as easy and accessible as possible which is exactly why we decided to open our online supply shop. You can get all the essentials in one place and don't have to worry about minimum order quantities.

We sell all the essentials and the supplies which are hardest to find. For everything else we have a detailed suppliers list on our website which we update regularly.

www.icanmakeshoes.com/shop
www.icanmakeshoes.com/suppliers-list

Available online
- Lasts
- Insoles with shank
- Texon® insole board
- Thermoplastic stiffeners
- Sneaker soles
- Sandal soles
- Randing
- Heels
- Lining materials
- Memory foam

SPECIALIST SHOPS

Glue
We use Renia Colle De Collogne (Extra Strong) and Renia Aquilim 315 (Non-Toxic) throughout the book. You can buy it online from Algeos.com.

Cork Filler
We also buy this online from Algeos or you can try making your own by mixing ground cork with some glue.

Leather (Uppers & Linings)
Our favourite suppliers in London are GH Leathers and JT Batchelor but you can search for your local leather supplier.

Soles
If buying in sheets, you can get veg tanned leather from JT Batchelor or find your local leather supplier. Alternatively you can get sheets of rubber soling from Algeos.com.

Leather Hole Punch
A little bit more specialist but you can find on Amazon or eBay.

Awl
A common sewing tool you can easily find on Amazon or eBay.

LOCAL SHOPS

Heat Gun
You can find in your local hardware store, Amazon or eBay.

Drill
You can find in your local hardware store.

Screws & Screwdriver
You can find in your local hardware store.

Flat Top Hammer
You can find in your local hardware store.

Sewing Machine
You'll want to do some research online before you buy a sewing machine. Once you've decided on the one you want, do a search in your local area to see if you can buy it in person. We use Janome Professional HD9 machines in our workshop.

Craft Supplies
Pen, pencil, eraser, paper, masking tape, ruler or measuring tape, scissors, craft knife, silver gel pen, cutting mat. You can find all of these things in your local craft store.

GLOSSARY

Throughout this glossary I have referred to all of the terms as individual things but as we know shoes come in pairs so bear in mind that all of the components do too.

Awl
A small pointed tool used for marking holes in leather.

Back Height
The height of the back of the shoe in the achilles area.

Back Seam
The seam at the back of the shoe.

Ballet Flat
A style of flat shoe where there is a simple closed upper which encloses the foot. Often there is a small bow which sits on top of the vamp.

Closing
This is the industry term used for stitching the uppers together.

Clicking
This is the industry term used for cutting out the pieces for the upper and lining.

Clicking Knife
A traditional shoemaker's knife used for cutting the uppers and linings. I also use the clicking knife for lots of other processes involved with shoemaking.

Counter
A type of stiffener (see *Stiffener*) which is inserted within the upper, cupping the heel area to give shape and structure to the shoes.

Court Shoe *or* **Pump**
A style of heeled footwear where there is a simple closed upper which encloses the front and back of the foot.

Cutting Mat
A flexible type of mat that can be used for a range of arts and crafts endeavours.

Dart Back Seam
A type of stitched seam that will create a nice curved shape around the heel area of the upper.

Derby
A style of footwear where the laced up panel of the shoe is sewn on top of the vamp.

Dividers
A measuring compass with a screw used for patternmaking.

Feather Edge
The ridge running around the bottom edge of the lasts but also the bottom edge of the shoe.

Folding Allowance
An addition of usually 5mm to the toplines of the pattern where you will need extra leather to fold the topline over for a neat edge.

Folding Hammer
A small handheld hammer with a flat head on one side to flatten out seams and folded edges.

Handheld Drill
A power tool primarily used for making round holes, in the case of shoes it will be used to attach the heels.

Heat Gun
A power tool that blows hot air. You can use your hair dryer instead but it'll take much longer to heat up.

Heel
When describing the heel as a shoe component this is the block or stilt which holds up the height of the shoe. Heels come in all shapes and sizes and have a huge influence over the style of the shoe.

Heel tip *or* **Top Piece**
Fits onto the bottom of the heel and protects the heel from wear.

Hole Punch Tool
A tool used to cut out uniform holes in materials. It normally has a range of hole sizes to choose from on its turning head.

Insole
The insole is the heart of the shoe and sits beneath the foot. During the lasting process the lasting allowance of the upper is wrapped around the last and attached to the bottom of the insole holding the shoe together.

Insole Sock
Also known as 'insock', an additional piece of material, often with padding which is added to the shoe at the very end of the making process. They serve to cover up the insole board, screws/staples that attach the heels and they add comfort to the shoes.

Last
A shoe-shaped block that the shoe is built around. They come in left and right pairs and are normally made of plastic or wood. Lasts will determine the heel height, shape and size of the shoes.

Lasting
The process of stretching your uppers over the lasts to form them into shape.

Lasting Allowance
An addition of usually 20mm to the feather edge of the pattern where you will need extra leather to wrap around the bottom of the last.

Last Bottom Pattern
The pattern which fits the bottom of the last, it is normally used to trace out the insoles.

Leaf *or* **Tail**
The piece of material which covers the underside of the heel.

Lining
The lining is the part of the upper which sits inside the shoe and is in contact with the foot.

Notch
A small cut out 'V' shape which is marked on the lasting allowance on the inside edge of footwear patterns and pieces. It is generally a universal symbol used in footwear that determines whether it is the right foot or left foot. In footwear factories there can be several different notch symbols on the lasting allowance which also determine which size the upper is.

Nylon Tape
A type of self-adhesive tape which is made from nylon and has little-to-no stretch in it. It is used to reinforce seams or within straps to prevent them stretching out.

Oxford
A style of footwear where the laced up panel of the shoe is sewn underneath the vamp.

Patternmaking
In footwear, 'patternmaking' is the process by which patterns/templates are made according to the style and size of the shoe to be constructed.

Pattern Allowances
These are certain margins which are added onto the footwear patterns which factor in the material that is lost during the stiching and lasting processes, i.e. within seams.

Peep Toe
A style of footwear where there is an open toe and usually a closed back.

Quarters
The quarters are the side parts of a lace up shoe's upper.

Randing
This is a decorative addition which can be added around the feather edge of the shoe before the sole is attached. Randing mimics the traditional shoemaking technique called 'welting' and is often called a mock welt.

Raw Edge
This is when you leave the edges of the leather unfolded. Having a raw edge is quite common with leather as it doesn't fray.

Rubber Crepe
A pebbled latex sheeting which is commonly used as a raw material for cleaning excess glue of shoes. It is sometimes used to make soles for shoes.

Safety Beveller
A handheld knife which is used to skive away excess material. We call it the 'potato peeler' because it works in a similar way.

Screwdriver
A tool used for screwing and unscrewing (inserting and removing) screws. Also in this case used to attach the heels.

Seam
A seam is a join where two pieces of material are joined together.

Seam Allowance
An addition of usually 5mm on both sides of the pattern where there is a join that you wish to stitch together.

Seam Tape
Flexible adhesive tapes for reinforcing and reducing stretch (see *Nylon Tape*).

Shank
A reinforced strip of steel which sits inside the shoe between the insole and outsole. The shank gives support to the arch of the shoe and the foot and is therefore a vital part of high heeled shoes. In most footwear the shank is embedded within the insole.

Silver Pen
Traditionally used to mark out the patterns onto the leather. Silver ink tends to show up on most colours which is why it is used. It's the shoemaker's equivalent to dressmaker's chalk.

Skive
The process by which excess material is shaved down, normally from a seam, underlay or folded edge. Skiving can be done with hand tools or by machine. A '*skived edge*' is an edge of material that has been skived down.

Sling Back
A style of footwear where there is a strap which wraps around the back of the heel to hold the shoe on the foot.

Sole or Outsole
The layer in direct contact with the ground. They come in all different materials and are made to fit the last/shoe. Outsoles are normally made of a durable material to slow down the wear of the shoe and protect the upper. We use leather soles throughout this book.

Sole Bend
The part of the cow used for soles is called the 'bend' and it comes from the back of the cow.

Sole Unit
A sole which has been glued and stacked with multiple layers and has become one solid unit.

Stacked Heel Tip
Layers of soling material (usually leather) stacked to create a small heel lift for a flat shoe.

Stiffener
Traditionally made of leather or thermoplastics, stiffeners are inserted within the upper to give shape and structure to the shoes. Depending on the style of shoe, two types of stiffeners can be inserted - the 'counter' which cups the back of the heel and the 'toe puff' which cups the toe area.

Table Vice
A small and portable device which can be quickly clamped to any work surface and is used to hold an object secure so work can be performed on it.

Texon® Board
Texon board is a strong semi-flexible material made of cellulosic paper and used for insoles. Texon is the brand name of the material and whilst there are alternatives on the market they are generally still referred to as 'Texon' board.

Thermoplastic
A plastic material that becomes malleable when heated. Thermoplastic is often used for stiffeners within footwear (see *Stiffener*).

Toe Puff
A type of stiffener (see *Stiffener*) which is inserted within the upper around the toe area to give shape and structure to the shoes.

Topline
Any design line that is visible or sits on top of another panel on the upper.

Underlay
An underlay is a join where one panel of the upper sits below the other.

Underlay Allowance
An addition of usually 5-10mm to the side of the pattern which is the underlay of a join that you're stitching together. The top side of this underlay will be considered a topline.

Upper
The part of the shoe that covers the foot and essentially the part of the shoe that you see. In the simplest cases, such as sandals this may be nothing more than a few straps. Closed footwear can have more complex uppers with seams and separate panels.

Vamp
The front part of the shoe starting behind the toe, extending around the eyelets and tongue, towards the back part of the shoe.

I CAN MAKE SHOES

What is *I Can Make Shoes?* We're a female run independent shoemaking school based in London.

I Can Make Shoes is a private shoemaking school based in London, England. The school was founded in 2010 by Amanda Overs out of a desire to make her own shoes from home.

Fast forward to today and the school has organically grown into an internationally-renowned educational platform, servicing thousands of students from all over the world.

Amanda studied traditional footwear in Sydney, Australia and combined her traditional training with modern materials and self-tested techniques to create the *I Can Make Shoes* method. The method, which is taught throughout this book, is designed to simplify the shoemaking process to make it as easy as possible, thus giving complete beginners the skills to make their own shoes without the use of any heavy machinery.

Bringing the art of shoemaking into the at-home craft space has completely transformed how people view shoemaking and has allowed beginners to turn their kitchen tables into their new shoemaking workshop - a concept never shared before in the footwear industry.

The driving force behind *I Can Make Shoes* is to inspire and empower people through the craft of footwear. *"We're a team of shoemakers who all believe that the fashion industry, in general, can leave people feeling excluded and too embarrassed to explore their creativity. By simplifying the shoemaking process we've been able to create a place where beginners can develop their ideas and grow as designers and makers. This technique has helped to broaden the reach of the craft which I believe will have a lasting positive effect on the British footwear industry."* - Amanda Overs.

I Can Make Shoes has been behind numerous brand launches, trained high street footwear designers and been recognised by major publications including The Financial Times.

I CAN MAKE SHOES

Join our community...

Website *www.icanmakeshoes.com*
Instagram *@icanmake_shoes*
Facebook *@icanmakeshoes*
Twitter *@icanmakeshoes*
YouTube *@icanmakeshoes*

The driving force behind
I Can Make Shoes *is to inspire*
and empower people through
the craft of footwear.

YOUR NOTES

There's a lot to remember when making shoes for the first time, use this space to write down some reminders and important notes in your own words.

SUPPLIERS

You may also want to use this space to write down local suppliers so you don't forget them for next time.

*Special thanks to all the individuals
who made this book possible.*

PEOPLE

I Can Make Shoes Team
The amazing team at *I Can Make Shoes* who helped
massively in the preparation and crafting of this book.
www.icanmakeshoes.com/meet-the-teachers

David Wilman
The hugely talented photographer whose eye for
detail helped us make these steps visually beautiful,
clear and easy to follow.
www.davidwilman.com

Jessica Lau
The incredibly patient and creative layout designer.
Without her we would have no book. She's been
through all these steps so many times she's a pro
shoemaker now!
www.thisistinybeast.com

LEATHER, SOLES + TOOLS

GH Leathers Ltd
26 Cambridge Heath Road
Bethnal Green
London E1 5QH
+44 (0)207 538 4500
www.leathermerchants.com

A. A. Crack
Unit 16, Pennard Close
Brackmills Industrial Estate
Northampton NN4 7BE
+44 (0)1604 874 422
www.aacrack.co.uk

JT Batchelor Ltd
9-10 Culford Mews
London N1 4DZ
+ 44 (0)207 254 2962

WILLIAM KENT
Architect, Designer, Painter, Gardener, 1685-1748

WILLIAM KENT
Architect, Designer, Painter, Gardener, 1685-1748

MICHAEL I WILSON

ROUTLEDGE & KEGAN PAUL

London, Boston, Melbourne and Henley

First published in 1984
by Routledge & Kegan Paul plc

14 Leicester Square, London WC2H 7PH, England

9 Park Street, Boston, Mass. 02108, USA

464 St Kilda Road, Melbourne,
Victoria 3004, Australia and

Broadway House, Newtown Road,
Henley-on-Thames, Oxon RG9 1EN, England

Set in 11/13pt Photina Roman
and printed in Great Britain
by BAS Printers Limited, Over Wallop, Hampshire.

Library of Congress Cataloging in Publication Data

Wilson, Michael I., 1930–
William Kent.
Bibliography: p.
Includes index.
1. Kent, William, 1685–1748.   2. Artists—Great
Britain—Biography.   I. Title.
N6797.K4W54 1984   709′.2′4 [B]   83-24729

British Library CIP data available

ISBN 0-7100-9983-5

CONTENTS

ILLUSTRATIONS

PREFACE

No comprehensive survey of William Kent's remarkable career has appeared since 1948, when the late Margaret Jourdain published her admirable pioneer study. As 1985 will mark the tercentenary of Kent's birth, it seemed therefore that the time was ripe for a fresh look at his achievements in the context of his period – hence this book. In it I have attempted to present a broad overall survey of Kent's work against the background of a narrative-style account of his life; this approach, it is hoped, will best convey to the reader the involved manner in which the two interacted upon each other, and will also reflect the impossibility of dividing up his varied activities into unrelated compartments – with the possible exception of landscape gardening, which consequently receives a chapter to itself. The book is therefore not a catalogue of Kent's work but rather an introduction to it, leaving the reader free to decide which of the several avenues of Kent's work he or she may wish to explore further, whether it be painting, architecture, design and decoration, or landscape.

For the most part I have rendered the spelling of original eighteenth-century MSS. material into its modern equivalent and have made other small editorial changes where these seemed to be justified.

In preparing this book I have received help in various ways from a number of people to whom I would now like to express my thanks, especially the Rev. W. A. Atkins; Canon J. L. Badger; C. G. C. Boydon Esq.; Professor P. Dixon; Miss Rebecca Ferguson; J. Fleming Esq.; D. F. Foxon Esq.; His Grace the Duke of Grafton; K. D. Holt, County Archivist for Humberside; C. P. C. Johnson and N. Colley of the Lincolnshire Archive Office; the Rev. J. A. A. Lodge; A. R. N. Ratcliff, Chief General Manager of the Eagle Star Insurance Co.; Miss K. Rorschach; Dr. J. W. Shiels of the Borthwick Institute of Historical Research, York; and the Rev. T. C. Willis.

Above all, thanks are due to Peter Day, Keeper of the Collections at Chatsworth, and to those of my friends and colleagues at the Victoria & Albert Museum who have so generously supported me with advice and practical help during the preparation of this work. A special debt of gratitude is owed to Miss A. G. Hatchman who typed the manuscript.

Permission to quote from both MSS. and published material has been received from the following and is gratefully acknowledged: K. R. Adam Esq.; C. Cottrell-Dormer Esq.; Croom Helm Ltd; His Grace the Duke of Devonshire and the Trustees of the Devonshire Settlement; Victor Gollancz Ltd.

Illustrations

The illustrations in this book are reproduced by kind permission of the following: The British Architectural Library, RIBA, London, 49, 69; The British Library, 71; The Chatsworth Settlement Trustees, 1, 3, 21, 53, 74, 76–9, 83, 84; Country Life Ltd, 25, 26, 29, 30, 36, 91–3; The Department of the Environment (Crown Copyright; reproduced with the permission of the Controller of HM Stationery Office), 5–9, 23, 24; A. F. Kersting, 27, 28, 94–6; E. de Mare, 70; The National Maritime Museum, 50, 51; The National Portrait Gallery, 46, 47, 64; The Royal Academy of Arts, 4; The Royal Commission on Historical Monuments (England), 72; The Victoria & Albert Museum, 2, 20, 35, 37, 41, 43–5, 57–61, 67, 68, 100; The Trustees of the Wallace Collection, 31, 33; special thanks are also due to Sally Chappell for 2, 10–20, 32, 34, 35, 38, 42, 48, 52, 54–63, 65–8, 73, 75, 80–2, 88, 90, 97–100; and to Krystyna Socholik for 85–7 and 89.

A Note on Dating

Until 1752 the English calendar year began on 25 March, the period 1 January to 24 March being reckoned not as the first months of the new year but as the last months of the old. This potentially confusing situation is normally simplified by the use of double dates, e.g. 1 January 1745/6. The transition from old year to new would be expressed as e.g. 24 March 1745/6 followed chronologically by 25 March 1746.

1 Portrait of Kent by Luti, Rome, 1718. The confident-looking sitter was then aged 33

CHAPTER ONE
A SECOND RAPHAEL

William Kent, one of the most remarkable English artists of his own or indeed any other generation, was born towards the end of 1685 at Bridlington in Yorkshire. The registers of St Mary's parish church there record the marriage, on 27 October 1684, of William Cant and Esther Shimming, and the baptism on 1 January 1685/6 of their son, also called William. The lax spelling standards of the time later enabled him to adopt the alternative spelling of Kent with perfect freedom, and in fact contemporary records for this area of Yorkshire show that both versions of the name were used with equal impartiality.[1]

Kent's place of birth is further confirmed by a newspaper report of 1713 (see p. 9) which states clearly that it was Bridlington, and this report was itself based on facts supplied to the newspaper by one of his patrons. Any remaining doubts about his parentage are removed by a reference in his will to his sister Esther, who was presumably named after her mother.

We have no idea what the elder William did for a living, although there has always been a suggestion that he was not well off, and the circumstances surrounding his son's attempt to start a career in London seem to bear this out. Similarly we know nothing of the younger William's childhood and formative years, except that he was one of those 'who in arts, in their early dawns of life show a natural genius in drawing, especially, which is the root and foundation of fruitful genius.' This comment is by Kent's contemporary, the engraver George Vertue, whose maddeningly terse manuscript notes about the art scene in eighteenth-century London are nevertheless invaluable.[2] It is in fact ultimately to Vertue that we owe our scanty knowledge of Kent's early life, the entire span of which is contained in the following brief paragraph:

> When young unexpectedly he demonstrated his youthful inclinations to drawing. Being apprentice of a coach painter and house painter – from him he came to London without leave or finishing his apprenticeship. His parents' or friends' circumstances not being in a condition to forward his practice and the expense of a profession, they had the good fortune to find

some gentlemen of that country [i.e. Yorkshire] to promote his studies,
raised a contribution, and recommended him to proper persons at London,
to direct him to Italy, where he went with Mr. J. Talman and Mr. W. Locke
aged about 20 (certainly 1710 by sea).

The interpretation of this account has usually followed that of Horace Walpole,
who edited Vertue's notes and used them as the basis of his own *Anecdotes
of Painting*, first published in 1762–71. Walpole's version of Kent's escapade
is as follows:

He was . . . put apprentice to a coach-painter; but, feeling the emotions of
genius, he left his master without leave, and repaired to London, where he
studied a little, and gave indications enough of abilities to excite a generous
patronage in some gentlemen of his own county, who raised a contribution
sufficient to send him to Rome, whither he accompanied Mr. Talman in
1710.[3]

This picture of the talented youth absconding without hesitation, breaking
his indentures, and setting off immediately for London to seek his fortune, has
the romantic appeal of all such success stories from Dick Whittington onwards.
Moreover our knowledge of Kent's character enables us to picture him taking
these momentous steps with gaiety, enthusiasm and boundless self-confidence.

However, a closer reading of Vertue's admittedly meagre account raises
doubts as to the accuracy of Walpole's version. Had Kent not first gone back
to Bridlington, it seems most unlikely that his relatives could have done much
on his behalf once the two hundred-odd miles between Bridlington and London
separated him from them, especially at a time when communications were
bad, to say the least – for even in good weather the journey to the capital
by means of cumbersome, springless stage-coach could take four days. And
one is bound to question how a young aspiring artist from the north, without
any connections at all, could hope to attract to himself sufficient attention
unaided, even in a London very much smaller than it is today.

A more reasonable solution (which can also be read into Vertue's account)
therefore suggests that Kent, after leaving the anonymous coach-painter, first
returned home, determined to search out a more satisfying career. As his
employer's business is said to have been in Hull, some twenty-five miles away,
Kent could feel safe from immediate repercussions. Confronted with this *fait
accompli* his family, probably already under the sway of that good-humoured
personal charm to which many of his contemporaries, as well as his own letters,
were later to bear witness, brought him to the notice of local influential worthies who, it was hoped, might be able to do something for the wayward young
man. His impulsive behaviour on this occasion is highlighted by another of
Vertue's disclosures; Kent, it seems, was 15 years old when apprenticed and
20 when he finally left his master, so he cannot have had much more time
to serve. To walk out at this point in his career surely points either to a

monumental row with his employer or else to unbearable frustration, boredom and impatience with what he no doubt by now considered a menial and degrading occupation utterly unworthy of his talents.

It is difficult not to believe that Kent was already known in Bridlington (and perhaps farther afield) before this, as something of a local prodigy; his abilities as an artist can hardly have gone unnoticed in a relatively small and predominantly sea-going and rural community where such gifts are not common. But no doubt it was quite another matter to convince prospective patrons – shrewd Yorkshiremen all – that his was a talent worth backing financially. The fact that patrons were evidently forthcoming probably owed as much to Kent's persuasive tongue as it did to his artistic promise; it is significant that the chief impression conveyed by his letters is one of cheerful loquacity, of a kind calculated to browbeat the most hard-headed of backers into grudging acquiescence. (Here it is worth noting that although his family may have been poor Kent was certainly not ill-educated. Clearly he was articulate, and although his letters lack style they are no worse in this respect than those of many of the landed gentry who became his patrons; this also applies to his spelling, although he does have a distressing tendency to miss out letters from words and words from sentences – perhaps due to haste. His handwriting is almost always entirely legible.)

It seems logical therefore to discard the original image of the ex-apprentice arriving in London unknown and unheralded, in favour of the more prosaic but also more probable scenario in which he arrives bearing letters of introduction from burgesses and others at home to fellow Yorkshiremen in London – men who have 'made good' in the City, who have the right contacts and can introduce him to others who will know what to do with this strong-willed but promising young artist, of whom great things are expected back home in Bridlington.

In fact, there was only one thing to be done. William Kent must be sent to Italy, where he could develop his talent for painting at the very fountain-head of art itself and receive instruction from the best Italian masters. It should be stressed that this decision was not instantaneous; according to Vertue, Kent spent a whole year in London before going to Italy and thus had ample time to acquire those friends and patrons whose support was vital to his progress. Once the Italian venture was settled, however, the necessary money was found, and in July 1709 Kent set off. His goal was Rome, where he finally arrived early in 1710.

Even if Kent had not himself wanted to settle in Rome, his patrons' wishes had to be respected, and these would almost certainly have placed Rome first on his itinerary. Central to the Renaissance and its aftermath was a consuming interest in the ancient Classical civilizations, especially that of the Romans (the contribution of the Greeks not being fully appreciated until the later eighteenth century). The Classical world, it was felt, held the secrets of order, balance and harmony in political and social life and in the arts; Rome had been the centre of that world, the source of all its power, wealth and artifacts. Those who lived in European countries other than Italy wanted to acquire art objects from the Classical past, as well as paintings and drawings by Renaissance and later artists. The first great English collector of antiquities was Thomas Howard, Earl of Arundel, in the early years of the seventeenth century; to him, it was quaintly said, 'this angle of the world oweth its first sight of Greek and Roman statues', but many others followed his example, either in person or by proxy. Indeed, during the eighteenth century the English passion for collecting got somewhat out of hand and was by no means restricted to the fine arts. Charles Burney, the eighteenth-century music historian, records that in their enthusiasm for the music of Corelli, 'the English were said to have stripped Italy, not only of many of its best pictures and statues, but of all its valuable violins.'[4]

It is therefore a reasonable assumption that William Kent's original patrons despatched him specifically to Rome with instructions to buy up on their behalf suitable examples both of paintings and of antique statuary. No doubt their enthusiasm was fired by reading such recent books as Joseph Addison's *Remarks on Several Parts of Italy &c* (1705), in which was to be found the following passage, full of exciting promise: 'No part of the antiquities of Rome pleas'd me so much as the ancient statues, of which there is still an incredible variety. The workmanship is often the most exquisite of anything in its kind.'[5] It would be Kent's task to secure part of that 'incredible variety' and to ship it back home, in return for the financial support he was receiving.

Kent's various patrons can be divided up into three groups. The original consortium that first despatched him to Italy is composed for the most part of shadowy, anonymous figures. However, there exists a letter from Kent addressed to 'Mr. Saml. Gale at Mr. Tewkes in the Old Change near Cheapside, London,' dated 17 April 1712, in which Kent briefly sketches out his life in Rome. Samuel Gale (1682–1754), though not much older than Kent, was just the sort of man to have interested himself in the fortunes of the young painter. Godson of Samuel Pepys, and son of Thomas Gale, Dean of York, Gale was a Customs official by profession and a dedicated archaeologist and antiquarian who from 1717 to 1740 was Treasurer of the newly re-formed Society of Antiquaries. His non-Yorkshire origins (he was a Londoner) and comparative youth at the time of Kent's departure for Italy do not necessarily preclude him from having been one of the latter's patrons, and he would certainly have been very keen to obtain Classical antiques.

Kent concludes this letter in his usual breathless style as follows: 'I am very well and please to give my service to Mr. Popplewell and all good friends; we are in hopes of seeing Mr. Oddy. . . .' The Rev. Popplewell and Mr Simon Oddy have not been further traced and there is no record of Mr Oddy's arrival in Rome. However, Kent also mentions 'our good friend Mr Talman' and 'our friend Mr Lock', both of whom had accompanied him from London to Rome. Daniel Lock (to whom Vertue strangely gives the initial W.) seems to have been an amateur connoisseur whom Kent describes to Gale as living 'by books and prints'. John Talman (1677–1726) is better known; he was the son of the distinguished architect William Talman and, like Samuel Gale, became a celebrated antiquary and scholar. This was to be his second visit to Italy; he had been there during a previous Continental trip lasting from 1698 until 1702. In the Bodleian Library is preserved a small vellum-bound volume containing copies by Talman of the letters which he wrote to his father and others during the first part of his second visit, and these give us some fascinating glimpses of the progress of himself and his companions.[6]

Even before leaving England Talman described to his father (12 May 1709) an incident which shows not only that he himself already had a reputation as a connoisseur, but also that Kent too had made some useful connections:

> The other day Mr. Kent the painter who goes with me [to Italy] was carried to my Lord Sutherland, who enquired of him how he went to Rome and with whom; he making answer, with me, 'What! (says my Lord), Talman is going to Rome again to bring home a design for Whitehall.'

The reference to Whitehall is an indication of the interest then being taken in the possibility of building a new palace and government complex to replace the old, burnt-out palace. Later this scheme was to concentrate on the provision of a new Parliament House, in which Kent himself was to be involved (see pp. 167–71).

At the time of their leaving Talman seems to have had no clear idea of what he was going to do in Italy, but in fact he was to spend several years there, making – with the aid of assistants – highly competent drawings and sketches of antiquities, as he later explained in a letter of 31 May 1710:

> I must beg leave to tell you that now my employment is to cause abundance of fine drawings to be made in several parts of Italy relating to architecture, which I have coloured as the originals to give a lively idea of Italian gusto in their beautiful manner of ornamenting the insides of buildings.

He eventually returned to England in 1715, where in 1717/18 he was elected Director of the Society of Antiquaries, with Gale as Treasurer.

But all this was in the future. For the present his energies and those of his companions were directed towards their voyage. They set sail in the *Swallow* in July 1709; on the 22nd of the month they were at Deal 'waiting for a wind', and were still waiting at Spithead on 5 August. After this things improved; Gibraltar was reached on 22 September, and landfall finally achieved at Leghorn on 15 October. On 18 November they reached Florence and remained there until the following April. The British consul at Florence was Dr Henry Newton, who in 1712 returned to England to become Master of the Foundation of St Katherine-by-the-Tower; he commissioned the newly arrived Kent to paint a picture for him, thus probably becoming the eager artist's first patron in Italy, and seems to have been generally kind and helpful towards the three young men.

From Florence Talman wrote gloomily to his father complaining of lack of news from home as well as lack of money. 'My companions have had letters above 3 weeks ago. . . . Just now, to mortify me more, Mr. Kent received another letter from England – it's very hard I shou'd be forgot that have writt so often' (18 February 1709/10). 'Mr. Kent has received 4 letters and Mr Lock 4, 1 of which is a bill with money' (4 March). However, all was well when they reached Rome at the beginning of April, for money awaited Talman there. For Kent, things were probably less simple; he needed the support of patrons, and it seems – from a letter which Talman wrote to Dr Newton on 5 July 1710 – that the original ones back in England were either replaced by or supplemented with new ones quickly found in Rome: 'For the keeping of poor Mr. Kent abroad at study for some years our English gentlemen have been so publick spirited (which humour I pray God encrease for the honour of England) as to give him generous assistance; his bashful temper and inexperience in writing has been the cause of his not troubling you with a letter of thanks for all your favours. . . .'

Two of these new patrons are in fact mentioned by Kent in his letter to Samuel Gale, in the concluding passage:

> Sir, I'll beg leave you'll please to take care of this picture and drawings for Sir Wm. Wentworth; not knowing where to send them, I took the liberty to trouble you until Sir Wm. sends for them. . . . I send them by one Mr. Massingberd, a Lincolnshire gent. I hope Sir you'll please to do me this favour, for Sir Wm. is my very good patron, and I shall think myself very much oblig'd to you, so please to excuse these from your humble servant Wm. Kent.

Sir William Wentworth (mistakenly called 'Sir John' by Vertue), of Bretton Park near Wakefield, was a young baronet who from 1709 until 1712 was completing his education by making the Grand Tour of Europe. We do not know the circumstances of his first meeting with Kent – though Yorkshire connections were again perhaps involved – but he was sufficiently impressed by the latter's talents to make him (according to Vertue) an annual allowance of £40 for a period of seven years. At the same time, however, it is obvious from Kent's letter that Sir William, like his other patrons, expected him to carry out commissions in return for his subsistence. His *rapprochement* with Sir William was rapid, for the baronet arrived in Rome at the beginning of April 1710 and left again on his travels on 22 August that same year. For the best part of a year he stayed in Geneva, spent a few months at Utrecht, and was back in England some time during the spring of 1712; towards the end of May Bretton Park welcomed its lord and master home again. Samuel Gale, it seems, probably did not have the responsibility of looking after Sir William's property for long.

It is clear that during this early period Talman helped Kent out with money, though he himself was often short of funds owing to the non-arrival of drafts from England. In a letter to Daniel Lock from Naples on 20 December 1710 he writes: 'I wou'd beg you to assist Mr. Kent with money for a week, when I will pay interest if required.' Little is known of Lock, who comes only briefly alive in a letter which Kent wrote from Rome on 13 August 1712: 'Mastr. Lock is out of favour [i.e. out of sorts] this hot weather which makes him very uneasy, and indeed [it] is hotter than ever I felt it.'[7] Nevertheless Lock, Talman and Kent formed an evidently cheerful and compatible triumvirate during the early months in Rome; as Talman explained to his father on 9 May 1710, 'I do not live with my companions, we are all in separate lodgings, but [we] agree very well and every Thursday we spend in seeing some fine palaces, as last Thursday we saw [the] Borghese Palace. . . .'

Talman's attitude towards Kent seems to have been avuncular, almost paternal, although he was Kent's senior by less than a decade. There is evidence of this in a letter written to Kent on 8 November 1710 from Naples, while Talman was paying a short visit to that city:

> Dear Billy: I hope you don't take it ill that I have not writt, which hasn't proceeded from forgetfulness of my friend, but from the abundance of curiosities I note down every night. I hope you study hard; by Xmas I hope to be in Rome. The situation of this city is not to be imagined; I find the churches rich to excess, but tell Mr. Lock here are no Momo's, Pasqualino's or Paolucci's. . . . I live very cheap and enjoy serene weather – pray you or Mr. Lock write often and you'll much oblige your true friend – John Talman.

There is no record of anybody else ever having addressed the mature Kent as 'Billy'. In Talman's letter of 20 December to Lock we find the rather touching injunction, 'Keep my Bill safe', indicating a genuine affection which had its first test when Kent failed to reply to the letter addressed to him at Naples. Talman was perhaps the first but by no means the last of Kent's friends to discover that he was a bad correspondent, as we shall see. The letter was followed up by another, couched in understandably injured tones and dated 6 December:

> I wrote to you Nov. 8 but have had no answer. I am sorry you forget your friend; if you had so much to write at nights as I have you and Mr. Lock might be excused. I hope you study very hard. Immediately after Xmas you'll see your humble servant and true friend – J. Talman.

So far as we know the friendship endured, at least for a time; after all, both Talman and Lock are mentioned in Kent's 1712 letter to Gale. But it is reason-

[7]

able to suppose that as each pursued his chosen path their ways gradually diverged. A clue to a possible cooling of relations is contained in Talman's exhortation to Kent to 'study very hard'. Obviously he took a keen interest in Kent's progress – perhaps too keen, for in 1714 the harassed student complains in a letter that Talman is 'continually preaching to me that I may be a great painter'.[8]

Others, however, had the same idea. Of all Kent's earlier patrons, it is Burrell Massingberd, the 'Lincolnshire gent' of Ormsby in that county, who is to us the most interesting, because a considerable part of the correspondence that arose between Kent and himself after his return home in 1712 has survived.[9] Most likely they met in Rome. Massingberd not only supported Kent financially but was also the medium through which a friend, Sir John Chester of Chicheley Hall in Buckinghamshire, decided to do the same; these two, together with Sir William Wentworth, formed the second main group of patrons whose assistance enabled Kent to continue his career. In a momentous letter (undated) Massingberd informs Kent that he is sending him 'in money and goods', twenty guineas plus another £20 from Sir John Chester, whose contributions had been quite unsolicited, as the letter makes clear; 'Speaking of my intentions to send you some money in order for your support at Rome, and mentioning the hopes we had of your becoming a great painter if you continue the same diligence I left you inclind'd to, he said the design [i.e. intention] was so good that as he is a great lover of the arts he would readily, without being asked, contribute towards it.'

Massingberd explains that he is to arrange with Kent what Sir John is to receive in return for his generosity. Both these patrons made full use of Kent's talents, for not only was he required to act as agent in acquiring genuine artifacts for their collections (to say nothing of mundane domestic items such as soap and treacle), but they also expected him to use his own artistic skill in making copies of original paintings for them. Already in the letter announcing their joint financial support to Massingberd says that Sir John would like 'a copy of Guido's *Aurora*', and continues, 'and what you send him besides is left to yourself.' His own wants were comparatively simple – or so he probably thought. 'For me, I desire you will send also a copy of the *Aurora* and one of Guercini's *Vesper* with the sleeping woman over the chimney in the Villa Ludovizia . . . and anything else of your own which you think fit, and if you send me more than what you can well afford, you will be sure of more money the next year to make it up.'

At first, however, Kent caused his patron to have serious misgivings. Letters remained unanswered and the expected goods – paintings, statuary and prints – failed to arrive. Massingberd's shipping agents at Leghorn reported that 'Mr. Kent acknowledges receipt of your letter but doth not mention a word of returning you any answer not forwarding your things to us. . . . Mr. Kent doth not mention a word of sending you anything to our address' (2 and 20

October 1713). Their letters are a continuous catalogue of failure in getting Kent to reply to them or even to track him down. The injured patron replied that 'I think Mr. Kent very negligent that he neither writes to me nor sends any things for your house to be forward[ed] to England as I have for some time expected of him' (30 October 1713). When goods did eventually arrive there was more heart-searching. Writing to Kent on 9 December 1713 Massingberd complains that some of the recently arrived books have pages and plates missing. 'I also miss the Naples soap, the six Florentine medals, the 2 dictionaries which I left with you, but hope to hear of them shortly with the marbles and many more fine knick-knacks to put me into humor, for I can't but complain you have very much neglected me though Sir W. Wentworth says you are long [?] enough to him, his pictures came all safe but my case was very much damaged.' Insult was thus firmly added to injury.

In response to this Kent at last began to excuse himself. 'You may assure yourself that my not writing is not out of disrespect or not being mindful of your generosity and Sir John's, but the truth is I had as leave make a drawing as write a letter. I shall remember what you desire to have me copy. I have begun one thing, the *St. Michael* of Guido Reni, and shall do the rest in time, but my master will have me do pictures of invention.' This appears to be a polite hint that his teacher (perhaps Benedetto Luti) disapproves of his spending too much time making copies for patrons and would prefer him to exercise his own imagination rather more freely. In fact he had already done so publicly, to some purpose.

In its issue for 5 August 1713 the newspaper *British Mercury* carried the following report: 'Mr. W. Kent, born at Bridlington in Yorkshire, is said this year to have gained the annual prize given by the Pope in the Capitol for painting.' Kent had already communicated the news to Massingberd in a letter of 3 June 1713: 'Now Sir thinking you'll be glad to hear of any improvement, about two months ago the Pope gave the subjects to be drawn for the young painters; I made a drawing of my invention, about 200 figures, and have won now the prize, the ceremony being at the famous Capitol, and the cardinals give the medals to painters, sculptors and architects. Cardinal Dado [Bado?] gave me mine and bid me study.' In his reply of 4 August 1713 Massingberd signifies his approval, though qualifying it with some regrets over the non-appearance of expected items. 'I congratulate you on the Pope's medal which I think is the second you have won and I hope you will get it every year you draw for it. The French newspaper said it was a German that won it, but I showed my letter to Mr. Gale and he got it altered in [the] English news and added the place of your birth.' (This makes it clear that it is to Samuel Gale we owe full and final confirmation of Kent's Bridlington origins.)

The medal was of silver, bearing on one side a portrait of the reigning Pope Clement XI (Giovanni Francesco Albani), and on the other an effigy of St Luke, patron saint of artists. It was Kent's prize in an annual competition organized by the Accademia di S. Luca in Rome and was included in the sale of his effects after his death; however, though certainly gratifying, his success was not quite so outstanding as he allowed his friends at home in England to believe.

The competition was a three-tier event. In each of the three fields of painting, sculpture and architecture there were three classes, and in each class three prizes were offered (though not all were invariably awarded). The prizes were handed out at an annual ceremony on the Capitol which included much rhetoric and a performance of a specially composed musical work.[10] In the list of prizewinners for 1713 'Guglielmo Kent Inglese' is placed second in the second of the painting classes, for which the set subject was *A Miracle of S. Andrea Avellino*; first prize went to Franz Georg Hermann from Kempten in Swabia, a pupil of Pellegrini. Another first (in Class I) went to Cosmas Damian Asam of Bavaria, later to become one of the most celebrated artists of the German Late Baroque and, as a painter, streets ahead of Kent both in technique and in imagination. In stating that 'it was a German that won it', Massingberd's French newspaper was therefore not so far from the truth. But neither the newspaper nor Massingberd appreciated the complexities of the competition, and it seems likely that Kent was not anxious for people at home in England to learn all the details.

Confirmation that a mistakenly rosy view of his achievement flourished unchecked at home is given by the antiquarian Ralph Thoresby. In 1715 Thoresby published an account of the items in his own private collection, and amongst these was a drawing by Kent (given to Thoresby by Samuel Gale), who is described as 'an ingenious artist now at Rome, where he won the prize of drawing this year, from all the students in that science, for which his Holiness presented him with two silver medals of his own bust, with St. Luke on the reverse.'[11] Having thus doubled Kent's original prize at a single stroke, Thoresby then makes the following statement: 'He was also the first of the English nation who was admitted into the great Duke of Tuscany's Academy of artists, which is an honour to his native county of York.' So it would have been, if it could be proved. To date, however, no evidence has appeared that Kent was ever received into the Florentine Academy. Nor, for that matter, is there any for Massingberd's hint that the Papal medal was not the first of such awards that Kent had received. All one can say is that Kent was probably not too concerned to correct inaccurate reports about himself and his artistic prowess, provided these were favourable.

'Good dear Kent, study hard that you may answer the character I have of you, and if you stay 7 or 8 years longer and we should live till then I hope to have a staircase for you to paint a la Italiano the first thing you do, and I believe if Sir John Chester is alive he will have another.' Thus wrote Massingberd earnestly in his letter of congratulation. Elated by the news of the Papal medal, he clearly believed that in William Kent he had backed a winner. Fortunately he could not know that much of his protégé's future success was to be in quite other directions than painting and that he himself was to have no part in it. For the moment, therefore, it is pertinent to examine the background and probable development of Kent's painting studies.

By the time Kent arrived in Italy the arts both there and throughout Europe generally, following the stimulating era of the Renaissance, had been additionally enriched by the Baroque phase, now drawing gradually to a close. Skilfully used by the Church as a propaganda weapon in its war against the new Protestant religions, Baroque art played shamelessly upon the emotions of the spectator; the word 'theatrical', though so often used to describe it, can nevertheless hardly be bettered. Amongst the chief technical ingredients of the Baroque style were illusionism and tricks of perspective, effects of light and shade (*chiaroscuro*), colour, an all-pervading sense of movement, and the fusion of painting, sculpture and architecture which at the highest level of inspiration could produce a supreme masterpiece such as Bernini's *Ecstasy of St Teresa* in the Cornaro Chapel of Santa Maria della Vittoria, Rome. Here, above and around the altar, a *coup de théâtre* confronts the astonished visitor who sees a marble yet uncannily lifelike figure of the saint swooning in ecstasy as a smiling marble angel prepares to plant a shining gold arrow in her heart; painted angels float on stucco clouds above, and three-dimensional sculptured portraits of members of the Cornaro family look on from theatre-like boxes at the sides of the sanctuary.

In the field of pure painting the brutal realism of Caravaggio is often cited as typifying the Italian Baroque style, but in fact it is only one aspect. Equally if not more important is the work of Annibale Carracci, with – to a lesser extent – his cousin Ludovico and the school of painters that followed their lead. Carracci combined a new sense of freedom with profound respect for the principles of design, harmonious composition and facility of ornament found in the work of the great masters of the High Renaissance, especially Raphael. These principles formed the basis of the training given at the celebrated Academy founded in 1585 in their native Bologna by Annibale Carracci and his cousins, Ludovico and Agostino. Annibale, however, spent the latter part of his career in Rome, where his most famed achievement was the interior decorations of the Farnese Palace, a fine re-creation in contemporary terms of the spirit of Raphael.

Thanks to their Protestant background and northern temperament, many English artists and *cognoscenti* found the full-blown emotionalism of the more extreme manifestations of Italian Baroque too much to stomach. Even the Venetian school in the magnificently colourful tradition of Veronese was regarded askance by some. The work of the Venetian painter Sebastiano Ricci (1659–1734), his nephew Marco Ricci (1676–1730) and Sebastiano's pupil Pellegrini (1675–1741) was known and to some extent appreciated in England, where all three artists were actually resident, on and off, between 1708 and 1719. Yet John Talman, writing to Dr Newton from Rome in 1711, is scathing in his comments on Sebastiano: 'I hear two very pitiful painters are setting out for England to paint the cupola of St. Paul, the one Signor Rizzi [sic] from Venice, the other Sigr. Franceschini, a Bolognese. . . . Rizzi of Venice everyone knows to be no more than a scene painter.' Nevertheless scene painting, rightly or wrongly, is what much of Baroque painting is about. (In fact, the cupola was eventually painted by James Thornhill.)

It was the Romano-Bolognese school of the Carracci which, to the English mind, had best succeeded in transmitting the values of the Renaissance whilst avoiding the worse excesses of the Baroque, and this too may have been a powerful reason behind the selection of Rome as Kent's main base in Italy. The last great exponent of the Bolognese style, Carlo Maratta (b. 1625), was still living and teaching in Rome, although a very old man; he was President of the Accademia di S. Luca at the time of Kent's award, but died in that same year (1713) aged 88. His best-known pupil at the time was Giuseppe Chiari (1654–1727), from whom Kent seems to have received some instruction. However, though evidently an admirer of both these painters, Kent apparently selected as his principal teacher another artist influenced by Maratta, Benedetto Luti (1666–1724).[12] A Florentine with a good sense of design and colour, Luti had a lively style which to some extent was untypical of the Romano-Bolognese academic tradition, but this does not seem to have troubled Kent, whose critical faculties were in any case probably not well developed at that time.

The illusionism of the Baroque found its most universal expression in the painting in fresco of ceilings and staircase walls with *trompe l'œil* scenes – saints in glory, Classical gods assembled on Olympus, architectural vistas and so on. Luti himself had painted one such ceiling, on the apotheosis of Pope Martin V, in the Palazzo Colonna in Rome. The technical formulae for this type of decoration had in fact been established in the pre-Baroque era by Antonio Correggio (notably in the cupola of Parma Cathedral dome, 1526–30), but it was the Baroque artists who pushed optical tricks such as foreshortening to their ultimate limits, often with dazzling effect (the descriptive Italian term for such extremes is *di sotto in sù* – from below upwards). Examples of this sort of thing already existed in England before Kent left for Italy, mainly in the work of Antonio Verrio and Louis Laguerre at places like Windsor Castle, Hampton Court, Chatsworth and Burghley House. However, Kent is unlikely to have seen much if any of this, and even if he had he could hardly have been prepared for the wealth of *trompe l'œil* masterpieces which he encountered in Italy. Their effect was no less considerable on connoisseurs like Massingberd, whose ambition to have Kent paint him a staircase 'a la Italiano' was entirely predictable.

Massingberd's faith in Kent's abilities and promise were unshakeable, even touching. In a letter dated 8 July 1714 he announces further gifts of £20 each from himself and Sir John Chester, adding that he had intended to send more but 'my money in town grows short.' He also urges Kent on to fresh efforts, lapsing into Latin for special emphasis: 'I have nothing to add but to beg you'll study and not think of coming over *donec Raphael Secundus eris* [until you have become a second Raphael]. Don't stint yourself in study and ambition and another 7 years may produce wonders, and your advancement shall always be the desire and endeavour of . . . etc.'

He need not have worried. For the time being Kent showed no signs at all of wanting to return to England – he was enjoying himself far too much in Italy and especially in Rome which was, as he told his patron, 'the best place to make a painter'. The Eternal City at this period was in fact a place of strong contrasts between abject poverty and great luxury. The streets were poorly paved and very dirty, elegant houses were jostled by ill-built, ugly looking dwellings, and many of the magnificent remains of ancient Imperial splendour were half-buried in a weed-covered mass of medieval rubble whilst others had been converted into unsuitable housing for the poor. The often bizarre juxtapositions of ancient and modern buildings in eighteenth-century Rome have been faithfully and atmospherically recorded by those two great topographical masters of the period, Giovanni Battista Piranesi and Giovanni Paolo Panini. But living costs were low (Kent wrote to Gale that one could easily survive on £50 a year) and there was usually something of interest going on, much of it in connection with religious observances. 'There is always a great concourse of foreigners of all nations drawn hither by curiosity, devotion, and the conclaves', wrote one visitor, and Kent himself remarks to Samuel Gale that 'shortly we shall have a new set of saints made which is the occasion of a great many strangers coming.' A number of these arrivals were from England, and they could look forward to a warm welcome from their fellow-countrymen living in Rome; the English formed a high proportion of the tourist or semi-permanent population and had their own coffee-houses, clubs and taverns, as well as their own private social groups meeting in each others' houses and lodgings. Thomas Lord Raby recommended his kinsman Sir William Wentworth 'to lodge at one Charles Brown's, a Scotchman, who has the best lodgings in Rome, and is a very honest man and ready to assist his lodgers, tho' I believe he is a little dear, however 'tis agreeable to have the help of one that knows the town as well and is one's countryman and honest, which is a rare thing amongst the Italians' (letter dated 25 February 1710). 'Here are a great many English', noted Sir William in his reply (17 April), so many indeed that all Mr Brown's lodgings were taken; however, the visitors' excited expectation of witnessing the selection of a new Pope and all the attendant ceremonies had been dashed, since 'the Pope is recovered of his illness which most people thought he would have gone off with. . . .'[13] At the same time (26 April), John Talman was advising Dr Newton that 'Rome appears a new city, and the Pope notwithstanding his indisposition has perform'd most of the functions of the week [Holy Week], at which were present more English gentlemen than were to be seen in the Holy Year.' 'At present we have about eight or ten gentlemen', writes Kent to Gale in a description of his own immedi-

2 Drawing inscribed 'Wm Kent a view at Tivoli', dating from Kent's Italian period. The incongruous Egyptian element was not without influence on him in later years

ate circle, and it is easy to imagine him as the central figure in it, for he seems always to be have been popular. His letters to Massingberd likewise regularly contain lists of the visiting gentry, as well as tantalizing glimpses of the current festivities: 'At present for the sake of one of the new saints has been for this week past every night fireworks and serenades and much Bacchanal work' (13 August 1712). On a quieter note, the members of Kent's own immediate circle seem to have been in the habit of meeting regularly for the purpose of admiring their own acquisitions of prints, drawings, bronzes and suchlike, for in the letter to Samuel Gale Kent writes: 'I can assure you we remember our friends every Thursday night, being the curiosity day.'

In spite of all these distractions he did, however, make serious efforts to learn the art of fresco painting, perhaps urged on by the example of Luti: 'I have lately been learning to paint in fresco, for my master is a-painting a ceiling of a church' (letter to Massingberd, 16 April 1715). Between June and October 1714 he made an extensive tour of north Italy (see pp. 25–7), keeping a journal in which he not only noted down the various places visited and works of art seen but also other details, including some interesting notes on the technique of fresco. Early in 1717 Massingberd hopefully sent over the measurements for a 'ceiling piece', and Kent dutifully expressed his pleasure at the commission, adding: 'If Sir John Chester will please to send a measure I shall do one for him before I leave Rome.' In the same letter (15 February 1717) he makes an interesting reference to the subject matter for Massingberd's ceiling: 'Mr. Talman was here this morning and would have me done this ceiling after the grotesk manner, but I think it will not be well unless the whole was so. I believe you may remember this sort of painting as what the Ancients used, but I am resolved to do a thought of my own.'

The 'grotesk manner' to which Kent refers was later succinctly described by Robert Adam as meaning 'that beautiful light style of ornament used by the ancient Romans in the decoration of their palaces, baths and villas'.[14] The word in this context comes from the Italian *grottesche* (grottoes); it was originally used at the time of the Renaissance as a reference to the excavated buildings of ancient Rome, and was then applied to the style of decoration found within them. The rediscovered style was freely interpreted by the Renaissance artists – for example, Raphael and his school in the famous arcaded gallery in the Vatican known as the Logge.

Grotesque-style decoration consists basically of all sorts of fantastic human and animal figures, scrolls, garlands and ornament of all kinds, painted in a flat, two-dimensional linear manner, and all too often giving the impression of being a somewhat barren exercise in mere space-filling. Examples of it existed in England before Kent's time – notably in Inigo Jones's Queen's House at Greenwich – and Kent himself was to employ it more than once after his return home (see pp. 50, 157). But for the moment he felt it to be inappropriate and preferred to let his imagination take over. By way of practice ('both to force my invention and to have practice to paint in fresco', as he himself wrote) he undertook to paint the ceiling of S. Giuliano dei Fiamminghi (the church of the Flemish community in Rome), in the Via del Sudario, with a scene showing the glorification of the saint; the agreement is dated 12 July 1717. At the back of the journal in which he recorded his north Italian trip he also describes the actual painting of this work, calling it 'the first proof of my painting in fresco':

> After having placed my cartoon and left nails where I might put the pieces up again after it was cut, when the mason had put on the plaster as much as I thought, I trac'd the outline of my drawing upon it and so began to paint – but I found the *arriciatura* [plaster foundation] being very dry, was forc'd to paint very fast until such time as the ceiling was wet for five or six days, and then was no more put to the inconvenience to paint a piece at a time.

This fascinating if involved account is supplemented by remarks on the making up of the various colours used in fresco, all of it being additional to some three pages found elsewhere in the journal and describing (in a mixture of English and Italian) the general principles and technique of fresco painting.

The journal account is dated 15 September 1717 and Kent speaks as though he had already completed the work by that date. In fact, however, the church records show that work continued until 9 December, when the scaffolding was finally dismantled. Kent was assisted throughout by the plasterer, a certain Maestro Domenico, and for his work received a small token payment of fifteen gold *scudi*. The painting still exists, and shows the apotheosis of St Julian surrounded by admiring angels. Although the technique is hesitant and the colours over-bold, it is not without charm, and moreover remains the only example in Rome of a Baroque ceiling by an English artist. Kent was pleased with it – so pleased that he contemplated doing another; it had, he told Massingberd, 'succeeded very well – the next Spring if I have time I shall paint the next in chiaroscuro' (18 January 1717/18).

Meanwhile he continued to work on the project for Massingberd. 'Your ceiling piece is almost done', he wrote on 15 June 1717. 'I have made two figures that represent Music and Poetry; here is your friend Mr. Hewet that comes to see how it goes on and will inform you how your poor painter does when he comes home.' There was a slight hitch when a letter from Ormsby revealed that the original measurements were misleading and that consquently the painting was too big. Kent had already expressed his doubts on 3 April 1717: 'This measure of your ceiling piece seems to be very long. . . . I hope there's no mistake.' Now his hope was that he would be able 'to adjust without doing another'. Apparently he succeeded, for eventually the 'ceiling piece' was finished and despatched to England early in 1718. 'I should be glad to hear if you have received your ceiling piece and if it fits the place, and beg you'll

3 *The Return of the Prodigal Son.* A competent easel painting by Kent in the manner of
Sebastiano Ricci, in which the architectural background is at least important as the figures.
Probably painted in Italy

excuse the faults, being the first. ... Now am still at work upon Sir John's
ceiling piece which I do upon two large cloths for the convenience of bringing'
(15 March 1718).

The ceiling decorations for Massingberd and Chester were not of course true
fresco, since they could not be painted *in situ* and had to be done on canvas,
and in fact the majority of Kent's mural decorations in England were also to
be painted on canvas. The Massingberd ceiling has not survived, but Sir John's
may still be seen at his country seat Chicheley Hall. The subject is the esoteric
one of *Mercury Watching Herse and her Sisters Before the Temple of Minerva*,
and in composition it has been compared to Veronese's *Esther Before Ahasuerus*
which Kent may well have seen in the church of S. Sebastiano when he visited
Venice in 1714. In a letter to Massingberd (who seems always to have acted
as a go-between for Sir John) of 18 February 1717/18 Kent not only proposes
the subject for the painting but also discusses its siting above the staircase
according to the measurements he had been given, and his readiness to 'divide
the rest of the cove where there are no windows and paint basso relievos'.
On 15 March he followed this up with further suggestions, a sketch of the
staircase and a letter from an architect friend, Giacomo Mariari.

This man, who is otherwise unrecorded, was evidently already well known
to Massingberd, for in 1712 the latter had sent Kent a consignment of black
and red crayons and pencils, with instructions to divide them up with 'Sig. Ja-
como from me, with my service to him, and let him know if he were in England
I daresay he would find encouragement, for ... there are fifty new churches
to be built in London upon the publick charge and I don't hear that any models
are yet fixed upon.' (Massingberd refers here to the Act of 1711.) Mariari is
probably also the subject of a passage in a letter from Talman to a Mr Wallop,
despatched from Rome on 25 April 1711, in which there is a reference to 'a
humble servant of yours, Giacomo, who made drawings for your house', and
who wished to enquire why he had not been paid for his work. He may well
have been a member of Talman's team of architectural draughtsmen. In his
latter to Massingberd Mariari proposed further alterations to the staircase and
offered to supervise them himself; however, nothing came of this and indeed
the 'ceiling piece' was never installed over the staircase.[15] For by the autumn
of 1719 Sir John had decided to demolish Chicheley Hall as it stood and to
get a competent Warwickshire master-builder, Francis Smith, to rebuild it.
When this was done, Kent's painting was installed not over the staircase, but
in the entrance hall.

Kent did not neglect easel painting. In 1714 he found himself inspired by
an incident from Homer's *Iliad* – the occasion 'when Agamemnon sent to
Achilles for Briseis, a subject that has never before been done and I hope will
do very well', as he told Massingberd (24 November). The following year it
was Homer again ('Venus a-conducting Helina to Paris') plus a painting of
the Holy Family; all – as he was careful to point out to Massingberd – were

pictures 'of my own invention', continuing defensively, 'it's true they take a great deal of time, but it is more to my study than copying twenty.' Moreover the *Holy Family* was intended 'for my next shew of pictures here', indicating that from time to time he was in the habit of holding exhibitions of his own work, probably mainly for the benefit of English friends and visitors. His greatest success in this field seems to have been a commission from Cardinal Ottoboni, on the subject of Cyrus, King of Persia, instructing the Jews to build the temple at Jerusalem. 'It consists of a great many figures; if I succeed the honour may be something but the profit no great matter' (19 June 1716). The painting was publicly exhibited and excited much comment. 'When it was exposed there was great enquiry what school it was of and who was the author, which gave a great satisfaction to my friends here' (8 October 1715). It does not seem to have occurred to either Kent or his friends to interpret the general mystification about the stylistic interpretation of his painting as anything other than a compliment. A letter of 15 November 1718 mentions two life-size works on themes of Classical mythology intended for the Duke of Queensberry and Lord Lempster respectively (both visiting Rome), but it is not entirely clear whether these were also of his 'own invention' or merely copies. He certainly continued to supply copies, and refers to them from time to time in his letters, mentioning amongst others a figure by Maratta, a landscape by [Gaspard] Poussin and the group of musicians from Veronese's *Feast at Cana* for Massingberd, and Domenichino's *Diana and her Nymphs* and Correggio's *Leda* for Sir John. After his death his studio still contained a number of other copies that he had made, most if not all probably dating from his Italian period; they included another version of Reni's *Aurora*, *The Death of Germanicus* after Pietro da Cortona, a *Holy Family* after Maratta, a portrait of a boy after Rubens, and a *Virgin and Child with St John* after Giovanni Lanfranco (a pupil of Agostino Carracci). Of Kent's own easel work also probably dating from the same period there remained two different versions of *Venus and Aeneas*, a figure of Mercury, a group of *Mercury, Venus and a Cupid*, and *The Discovery of Cassandra*, as well as four untitled canvases described simply as 'histories'.

Even while he was still at work on the ceiling project for Massingberd, and a full two years before he actually returned to England, pressure of work and the effort of keeping his patrons happy seems at last to have begun to tell on him. 'I am hard at work now and will study hard to despatch some things that will be agreeable to my generous friends when I come home. I can assure you I am quite weary with living this poor melancholy life, but I hope I shall be reviv'd when I see all my friends in England' (15 June 1717). There were other reasons too for his depression, as we shall see (p. 32).

Throughout all these years he was under constant pressure also to keep up the flow of purchases made for his patrons and to send over all manner of things to England. By no means all were works of art. At the lighter end of the scale, for instance, Massingberd asks him to buy three fans, confessing archly, 'To tell you the truth it is for a lady I am going to commit matrimony with', the other two being for her mother and sister. Italian fans were highly prized, it seems, and not only by women; John Talman sent several home as presents to male recipients including his father. Rome was famous for its perfumes (and, surprisingly, its greyhounds), Naples for silks and soaps, Venice for glass and crystal, Milan for swords and other metalwork; to have an agent on the spot who could obtain such delectable luxuries as these was too good an opportunity to miss, as Kent and other temporary expatriates like him soon discovered.

In the more serious field of antiquities, the purchase of paintings and statues, in itself an onerous task, was further complicated by the need to ensure that such fragile items were packed sufficiently well to withstand the long and arduous journey to England. Writing to Kent on 5 July 1714 Massingberd makes a heartfelt plea: 'When you put up any more pictures for me [I] beg you will put oil paper next the painting, for the last were so scratched . . . as lessened the value very much.' To his shipping agent Samuel Winder he was even more severe; complaining about the damage done to his purchases unloaded from the ship *Scipio Galley*, he alleges that 'they were very much damaged, the marbles all misplaced and put into the wrong boxes and some of them broke with the Naples soap among them which run out and spoiled all the papers. . . . the *Aurora* was roll'd up with straw and strips [?] and dirt which it will never recover and one of the *Galateas* had a cut with a knife or scissors no less than 5 inches into the painting' (15 October 1715). It was safer to entrust goods to willing Tourists returning home: 'I hope you will not let any English gentlemen come over that you can be so free with, without sending something,' wrote Massingberd to Kent (14 May 1713), and in another letter points out that it is unwise to entrust Scotsmen with errands, since 'if any mistakes should happen they live a little too far off' (4 August 1713).

There could even be awkward brushes with the law; Kent tells of what he modestly calls 'an imbroglio' in which he and another patron, young Thomas Coke (later to play a prominent part in his life), got into trouble with the authorities for trying to send a Classical sculpture of Diana out of the country. Although Coke had paid for the statue, he had inadvertently broken a Papal law concerning the export of art works, and for a time things looked very ugly, with Coke being threatened with imprisonment and Kent, as his abettor, with banishment from Rome. Everything was eventually put right, no doubt with the aid of massive but inevitable bribes, although Kent goes into no detail, merely remarking laconically that 'at last all was adjusted and he has got the statue.' It eventually came to rest at Coke's country seat in Norfolk, Holkham Hall, and is still there.

There can be no doubt that despite Massingberd's respect for Kent's talents he often found his protégé exasperating to deal with, notably in his failure to answer letters, carry out commissions satisfactorily, or display any kind of business acumen. For a time – though he later tried to make amends for this – Kent seems to have treated Massingberd's financial support and the necessity to keep a tally of his commissions with an artist's typical disdain for such mundane matters, evoking such *cris de coeur* from his patron as 'When I take so much pains to be particular to you I must desire you'll be a little more so to me' (1712?), and 'I desire also you will give your mind a little to accounts though [not] so much as to spoil your hand by that stiff science but to let me know how matters stand between us' (4 August 1713).

On the other hand Kent's patience with his patron must often have been quite sorely tried. Sir John Chester seems to have been agreeably complaisant, if we may judge from a letter from that gentleman to Massingberd dated 30 October 1715: 'I shall be very ready to give all the encouragement I can to Mr. Kent, whose performance pleases me extremely and makes me wish for that [which] he hath lately done for me' (probably the copy of Correggio's *Leda*). On the occasion of the Pope's medal he had been pleased to say that he was 'glad to hear that Mr. Kent came off with so much honour' (23 August 1713). Massingberd, however, was made of different stuff. A reading of his letters leaves one with the abiding impression that here was one of life's dedicated moaners, ever ready to temper pleasure with some kind of small, carping criticism. Like attracts like, and it is therefore no surprise to find that the fans procured for Massingberd's fiancée did not suit. 'My humble service to your lady; I am sorry the fans were not to her mind, but indeed here is nobody that does [them] well, otherwise I would send another', wrote the unabashed Kent.

More serious, however, was Massingberd's attitude to money. Doubtless it was right and proper that he who paid the piper should call the tune, but Kent clearly found it irksome to be constantly badgered about finances: 'I am glad to hear the boxes came safe but what I mentioned about the prices what they cost me you need not wonder, for I can assure you [they] cost me more' (8 June 1718). At one point he seems to have sensed that Massingberd suspected him of living beyond his means, for he replies with a spirited defence of his activities and points out that his patrons are likely to benefit from them as well: 'The money you are pleased to send me, it's true I spend it, but have got a fine collection of prints and drawings, which makes some of our poor spirited gent[lemen] that are here say I must be rich to buy such things, but if I live to come home they will be a pleasure to you to see, and what you like shall be at your service.'

It may have been one of the 'poor spirited' gentry who in 1716 nudged Sir William Wentworth into suggesting that it was time for Kent to come home; Kent himself certainly believed that someone was telling tales, remarking resignedly, 'I imagine some envious person has put it in his head that I have been [here] long enough.' On the other hand, Sir William's contribution towards Kent's maintenance had initially been for seven years; that time was up, and we can perhaps forgive the young baronet for feeling that he was now entitled to see some return for his money in the shape of a real, Italian-trained artist painting away energetically 'a la Italiano' at Bretton Park.[16]

But it was not to Bretton Park that Kent was eventually to return, nor even to Burrell Massingberd's Ormsby. Greater prospects were in store for him and new fields of creative activity awaited him, of some of which he can at this time have had only the faintest inkling, of others none at all.

CHAPTER TWO
TRAVELS IN ITALY

That famous phrase, the Grand Tour, probably makes its first appearance in a book of 1670, *The Voyage of Italy*, by Richard Lassels. Although the tradition of the Tour is at least a century older, by the time Lassels wrote his book it was recognized as the ideal method of rounding off the education enjoyed by young gentlemen of fortune, and of filling in that awkward interval between their finishing formal schooling and coming of age. 'Travelling preserves my young nobleman from surfeiting of his parents, and weans him from the dangerous fondness of his mother', writes Lassels;[1] amongst other benefits it takes the youth 'more than four notches lower, in his self-conceit and pride', teaches him languages, and causes him to appreciate his own country better and to study how he can best serve it. And the chief goal of the journey, continues Lassels, must be Italy, where the young traveller may 'season his mind with the gravity and wise maxims of that nation, which hath civilized the whole world, and taught Man manhood.' Here two or three years should be spent 'in learning the language, viewing the several courts, studying their maxims, imitating their gentle conversation, and following the sweet exercises of music, painting, architecture and mathematics'. After three more years passed in France, the traveller 'will be ready to come home . . . a man most complete both in body and mind, and fit to fill the place of his calling.'

Provided he stayed the course, that is – for the Tour was fraught with dangers, and some of those who undertook it never returned. Amongst the perils – the intensity of which varied at different times and in different places – could be listed robbers and bandits of all kinds, common thieves, local wars with their inevitable contingents of disgruntled weapon-happy soldiery roaming the countryside, pirates at sea, weather conditions, even wild animals such as bears or wolves. Prior to the mid-seventeenth century, Protestants travelling in Roman Catholic countries, especially Italy, stood in considerable personal danger from the Inquisition unless they kept very quiet about their beliefs. Above all, there was the ever-present threat and all too frequent reality of sickness in a hundred different forms. Lord Raby, writing to Sir William Wentworth on 17 December 1709, delivered a solemn warning: 'Pray take care of your health, for Italy is a dangerous country and had like to have made an end of me.'

Fortunately the young Tourist did not have to face these multifarious dangers alone, for he was invariably accompanied by servants (their number proportionate to his rank) and by a tutor, also originally called a governor, while an overseer or trusted family servant took general charge of the practical and financial arrangements. This was certainly the case with Thomas Coke, the 15-year-old heir to Holkham in Norfolk, who set off on the Tour on 21 August 1712. His chief mentor (chosen by his guardians) was Dr Thomas Hobart, a Fellow of Christ's, Cambridge, and a qualified medical practitioner whose professional training was likely to stand the party in good stead before the journey was over. Hobart's lieutenant was an Italian, Domenico Ferrari, who later became librarian at Holkham, while the mundane financial and everyday details of the Tour were administered by a household steward named Edward Jarrett. It is thanks to Jarrett's meticulous keeping of his accounts that we owe much of our knowledge of the Coke party's progress and activities on this Tour. The principal volume is entitled 'An Acct. of the Moneys . . . Recd. of Mr. Hobart upon Acct. of . . . Thomas Coke Esq . . . for cloaths, necessaries, extraordinarys, travelling expenses and other paymts, from August the 21: 1712'.[2]

The cavalcade from Holkham spent some considerable time in France and its members did not arrive at their first significant Italian stop, Turin, until November 1713. Here, rather surprisingly, Ferrari left them and returned to England, though he was later to accompany Thomas Coke's younger brother Ned on a similar Tour as tutor. From Turin, however, they made good speed via Genoa, Pisa, Florence, Venice, Ravenna and Spoleto to Rome, reaching the Eternal City on 7 February 1714. The account books show that the precocious Thomas immediately set about buying paintings, drawings and prints, as well as a set of 'instruments to learn architecture'. 'I am become since my stay in Rome a perfect virtuoso, and a great lover of pictures', he wrote with boyish enthusiasm to his grandfather, Sir John Newton, on 24 May 1714.[3] To the seventeenth and eighteenth centuries a virtuoso implied a connoisseur, a collector of antiquities, a student of the fine arts – often, a subtle combination of all three. 'I would have him then to be not only a virtuous man but a virtuoso too', wrote Lassels when describing the qualities of the ideal tutor. The term dilettante originally had similar connotations, though it later came to imply a generally lighter and more trifling approach to weighty matters than that of the virtuoso. There was certainly nothing trifling about Thomas Coke: on the other hand the account books indicate that he was as ready to be diverted as any young adolescent of his age. A succession of dancing, fencing and mathematics tutors engaged *en route* probably reflects his governor's concern for his education rather than his own interests. But a liking for music is especially notable in the form of visits to the opera and the frequent purchase or hire of musical instruments, especially the flute. On 30 April 1716 Thomas Coke bought no less than three harpsichords at once, for the sum of 29 *louis d'or*. Other interests, healthy though probably innocent, are reflected in an entry for 13 May 1713: 'My master gave to a pretty woman: 5s.'

It is therefore not surprising that this high-spirited yet fundamentally serious-minded youth should have taken a liking to a fellow Englishman of similar disposition and only a dozen years older than himself – William Kent, to whom he was probably introduced in March or April 1714. Kent's first reference to him is in a letter to Massingberd of 16 May: 'Here is one Mr. Coke a-buying a collection and has bespoke of six of the best painters a picture, and one I am to do as big as the life.' This was indeed a promising start, and more was to follow; payment for a drawing or similar item probably explains an entry in Jarrett's book made on 1 June: 'Paid to Mr. Kent: 60 pauls' (a paul or *paolo* then being the equivalent of 10 pence sterling). This is the first of many entries concerning Kent, and the extent of his influence with Coke may be measured by the fact that, although Jarrett itemizes most of the payments in the account book in some detail, those to Kent are more often than not simply noted as 'Paid to Mr. Kent by my master's orders', without any further elucidation.

We do not know exactly where Coke met Kent, but the studio of Benedetto Luti or that of Giuseppe Chiari would seem to have been as likely a place as any; what more natural than that the young gentleman, visiting those artists in the course of his perambulations round the establishments of celebrated painters in Rome, should be introduced to his fellow countryman who was studying painting there. Kent soon proved his usefulness in other spheres; an architectural tutor engaged by Coke and named 'Signor Giacomo' can surely be none other than Giacomo Mariari, his introduction effected by Kent.

It is clear that Coke found the budding artist to be a congenial companion, for on 6 June 1714 – indeed, almost as soon as they had met – he took Kent off with him on a tour of some of Italy's northern cities before himself preparing to spend the winter as a student at the Turin Academy. Kent, writing to Massingberd on 24 November 1714 after returning to Rome, says that Coke had mentioned the project to Giuseppe Chiari, asking whether 'he thought it would be an advantage to me', and that Chiari had enthusiastically advised him to take up the offer. Probably he required but little encouragement. So together he and Coke visited Siena, Florence, Bologna, Ravenna, Venice and Padua, our knowledge of this trip being considerably enlarged by a journal in which Kent recorded some of his impressions of the sights, chiefly paintings.[4] He listed the various paintings seen, and on the blank pages made rapid sketches of those pictures which particularly impressed him. Not all were on public view, and obviously his being in the company of a rich young English Tourist gave Kent the *entrée* to private collections which he would not otherwise have seen. At the same time Jarrett's account book shows that money opened doors of a good many semi-private establishments; for example, entrance both to the Villa Borghese and to the Palazzo Farnese cost the visitors 3 pauls, to the Palazzo Barberini 9 pauls.

Architecture, however, also figures in the notes, though to a lesser extent. In fact, it is interesting to speculate that it may have been Thomas Coke's undoubted enthusiasm for architecture which first prompted Kent to take rather more than a passing interest in that branch of the arts, notwithstanding his friendship since 1712 with Giacomo Mariari. With Coke to guide him he entered fully into the spirit of the tour, and although his comments on architecture are brief compared with those on painting, they are not without interest. Of Siena, their first stop on the journey, he records that 'the most remarkable thing here is the cathedral, a Gothick style fane', but also notes that it contains traces of the 'Roman gusto' (i.e. Classical taste); as usual his wording is obscure, but he appears to be referring to the relief busts of Popes set in roundels which occupy the spandrels of the arches. Similar busts in the Clock Court at Hampton Court are amongst the earliest indications of Renaissance taste in England. On the other hand, at the villa built by Giuliano da Sangallo for Lorenzo de'Medici at Poggio a Caiano it seems to have been the spectacular garden grotto which most took his fancy (see p. 202). But for us today it is the following passage concerning Venice which has the greatest relevance:

> We arrived July 22; the next day went to see the noble place [Piazza] of
> St. Mark and in the afternoon to St. Giorgio Maggiore – the architecture of
> Palladio, the ceiling in the library divided into several divisions with
> painting. . . .

Here his attention was apparently caught less by Palladio's great church than by the library in the adjoining convent, a magnificent apartment constructed between 1641 and 1643 to the designs of Baldassare Longhena. Much of its interest is due to the unusual ceiling which consists basically of a flat-centred vault with segmental excisions down both sides to allow for the lunettes from which the room gets its light. Down the centre of the ceiling is a series of paintings with wide spaces between each one. As usual Kent describes these paintings (by Girolamo Coli and Francesco Gherardi) at some length, but in the end it was the ceiling design itself which stayed longest in his memory, for years later he was to reproduce it in the library at Holkham Hall.

In view of Kent's awakening interest in architecture at this time, it is significant that near the end of the volume in which he wrote up the journal of his tour there are several pages of notes written in Italian; these are concerned with perspective and architectural theory and are illustrated with sketches and diagrams. The section is headed by the titles of two books from which it would seem the notes are taken; these are *Paradossi per Praticare la Prospettiva senza Saperla*, by Giulio Troili, called Paradosso (Bologna, 1672; Kent's was the later edition of 1683), and *Lo Ignanno degl'Occhi, Prospettiva Pratica*, by Pietro Accolti

[26]

(Florence, 1625). Although at the time Kent's chief use for these notes was probably to help him get the correct perspective in fresco painting, they no doubt came in useful again later on when he had to face the practicalities of building.

If Kent's architectural interests had been aroused by his young friend (patron somehow seems to be too formal a word to use at this stage in their relationship), they certainly did not die when, at Padua, the time came for the travellers to part, Coke to continue his journey by stages to Turin, Kent to return to Rome. At Padua, for example, he especially noticed 'the church of St. Giustina, the architecture of a great gusto being of the Ionic order' – a notably succinct summary of this great, severe Renaissance cathedral, built between 1530 and 1560. At Vicenza, 'Here is a famous Amphitheatre of Palladio and several other palaces – the plan of the theatre of this form [here he makes a sketch] ornamented with statues and basso relievos with fifty marble pillars.' At Mantua he visited the astonishing Palazzo del Tè, although here once again it was the painting that excited him, above all the famous and frightening *Sala dei Giganti* which he was moved to call 'the finest of all Giulio Romano's works'. It is also significant that, as he told Massingberd, 'At Parma I stayed almost two months to copy some things for my study from the famous cupola of Correggio's.'

His expenses had been subsidized by Coke as far as Parma, after which he may have been forced to economize somewhat, in view of his long stay there; on 7 September he notes in the journal: 'Write this at the Peacock in Parma upon my bed, not having more room.' He also carefully jots down the cost of his transport from Parma to Modena, and writes to Massingberd that he was glad to find money awaiting him at Rome, 'for by travelling I had ruined all my clothes and had nothing to buy more, which money you sent me has set me up again.'

All in all, we may conclude that he returned to his painting studies with his imagination enriched and his artistic horizons unexpectedly enlarged. It was about this time also that the most momentous event in his life took place – his first encounter with Richard Boyle, third Earl of Burlington.

This young nobleman, destined to lead a revolution in English taste, had succeeded to his title in 1704 at the age of 10, with estates in Ireland, Londesborough in Yorkshire, Chiswick in Middlesex, and London's Piccadilly. Little is known of his early life; he was brought up by his widowed mother and was described in 1713 by a contemporary as 'a good natured pretty gentleman, but in Whig hands'. On 17 May 1714 he too, like Thomas Coke before him (though at the rather later age of 20), set off on the Grand Tour, travelling through the Netherlands and Germany to Italy, with Rome as the inevitable goal. The anonymous account book of the journey (at Chatsworth) records the names of five gentlemen who accompanied him. One of these could have been his governor (at 20 years old he was almost too old to have a tutor), though it is not clear which. Another was the painter Charles Jervas, who after his return from Italy succeeded in building up what many considered to be an inflated reputation, although his links with Burlington House remained strong. A Tourist rich enough to afford the luxury often included in his entourage a drawing master whose task it was not only to give tuition but also to record such objects, buildings or topographical views as took his patron's fancy *en route*, and this may have been Jervas's original function. On the other hand a second artist also travelled with the Burlington party, although his name does not appear in the account book for the outward journey; this was Louis (anglicized to Lewis) Goupy, who in Vertue's words 'was thought proper to be engaged by the young Earl of Burlington to go with him [on] the tour of Italy and to Rome, as his singular favourite and painter.'[5] Unfortunately the high hopes which Goupy – who is best known today as a painter of fans – doubtless had of this promising appointment were destined to be dashed (see p. 59).

There is little in the record of this, the first of the two visits that Burlington was to make to Italy, to suggest that his behaviour and interests at this time were any different from those of the more serious-minded yet still zestful young Tourists such as Thomas Coke. Payments for mundane, even frivolous items appear throughout the journey; they include wine, coffee, chocolate, packs of cards, ribbons, a carnival costume, and quilts, baskets and milk for the pet dogs, as well as such necessities as '3 fanns to keep off flyes'. Burlington's love of music (probably inherited from his mother), is attested by visits to the opera, the hire of harpsichords in Rome, Florence and Venice, and the acquisition in Paris on the way home of two harpsichords and a bass viol. One of his more expensive purchases whilst in Rome was that of a diamond ring costing 1,350 crowns. Yet, like Coke, Burlington also applied himself conscientiously to artistic matters, notably in the purchase of pictures, and it is in this connection that he is assumed to have first met William Kent.

His arrival in Rome was not unheralded, for Massingberd has already fore-warned Kent in typical fashion. Anxious to get his hands on a statue of Meleager in the Palazzo del Pigneto, Massingberd says that he is ready to give £200 for it if Kent can arrange the purchase quickly, 'for my Lord Burlington is coming full of money and it is a hundred to one but he will have it. . . . When Lord Burlington comes you will I hope have his encouragement because he loves pictures mightily, and if I had not been so unfortunate as to be out of town all the time from his first resolutions to travel to the time of his setting out I had been introduced to him and would have recommended you and also begg'd his assistance to bring me over a box of pictures' (5 July 1714). It was perhaps fortunate that he could not foresee just how unnecessary his introduction would have been for Kent's future advancement.

Meanwhile Burlington had no sooner arrived in Rome (30 September 1714) than he became ill, perhaps of a fever, and remained so until Christmas, being attended for part of the time by the Papal physician. During all this time – from 3 October until 27 December – he never left his lodgings. Nevertheless he was able to purchase a painting by or after Annibale Carracci on 17 November and another, by Viviani, on 7 December. The interesting suggestion has been made that the paintings were bought through Kent, who may have called unprompted to offer his services as artistic adviser to this latest important arrival on the Anglo-Roman scene.[6] Certainly he would have had no inhibitions about doing so, and it may well have been his refreshing lack of servility plus an engagingly unaffected self-confidence that helped to endear him to so many people. Vertue remarks on Kent's 'civil and obliging behaviour', but there is no reason to suppose that he specifically shared James Boswell's expressed 'admiration for persons of high birth', or that there was anything of the toady about him. Had there been, he would certainly never have gained the friendship of either Coke or Burlington. In the case of the latter, the connection with Yorkshire also doubtless worked once again in Kent's favour. This connection was closer than is perhaps generally recognized, for in 1651 Burlington first appears as an alternative spelling of Bridlington, whence the first Earl (created 1664) took his title.

Alternatively, Kent may originally have been asked by Thomas Coke to call on Burlington, to present his respects in an ambassadorial capacity. Although Coke and Burlington never met in Italy, and it is doubtful whether they had ever done so previously in England, each would have known something of the other's movements through gossipy letters from home, in an age when the circle of society and its doings was very much smaller than it is today. But whatever the original impulse behind Kent's first meetings with Burlington (and Vertue specifically states that they first met in Rome), his young Lordship's subsequent purchases of paintings certainly suggest that he may well have been guided by Kent in making them, for they included a Pietro da Cortona, a Domenichino, another Viviani, and two Marattas.

It is important to retain a sense of proportion about Kent's position in the English community at Rome, and not to suppose that he held some sort of pre-eminent position there, despite his long sojourn. There were other English artists, some reputable, some less so, all of them ready to act as advisers and guides, as the following passage written by Lord Raby (who does not even mention Kent) in a letter to Sir William Wentworth shows: 'Pray make my compliments to Mr. Dumvil . . . and desire him to tell you how you may find Mr. French the English painter at Rome. . . . I must advise you that if you would buy any pictures there, rather to take the advice of French than of any other, for there is one Edwards an English painter who is very officious to his countrymen but is wonderfully sharp and loves to get as much from them as he can' (25 February 1710). It is also of interest that at no point during their correspondence does Sir William mention Kent either, even though the letters cover the brief period during which he became Kent's 'very good patron'.

On 5 February 1715 Burlington left Rome on the first stage of his journey home (he reached England on 30 April), and Kent returned to his painting studies and his commissions on behalf of Burrell Massingberd, Sir John Chester and Sir William Wentworth. Had any of them but known, Kent had already established a good relationship with the man who was to be his chief patron for the remainder of his life. For the present, however, life for Kent continued much as before. No doubt from time to time he received written or verbal news of Thomas Coke, who by May 1715 had left Turin and embarked on a kind of mini-Tour through Switzerland, Germany and France, intending afterwards (as he wrote in a letter to his grandfather) to 'pass one more winter in Italy, to confirm myself in the language and the virtuosoship of that country'.[7] Coke's acquisitions on this tour were mainly books, which had evidently now become a passion that was to remain with him for the rest of his life; the books bought during 1715 became the nucleus of the future great library of Holkham, in the care of the erstwhile tutor Ferrari.

On Christmas Day 1715 Coke and his party left Marseilles for Sicily, arriving at Palermo on 16 January 1716. By May they had reached Naples, where there was a cheerful reunion with Kent; the fact that his travelling expenses to Naples and his accommodation bills there were paid for him suggests that he went there by invitation rather than on his own initiative. He at once reassumed his role as artistic adviser, effecting an introduction between Coke and the painter Francesco Solimena, from whom Coke then commissioned two pictures. At the time this artist clearly exerted considerable influence on Kent, who wrote telling Massingberd that 'Solimeno [sic], a modern painter, has put better ideas into my head in respect to colouring' (9 June 1716). The account book also records payment for 'pictures and drawings that he [Kent] bought for my master at several times'.

In June Kent returned with Coke to Rome. Here the latter plunged once again into picture-buying, and (advised no doubt by Kent throughout) commissioned works from a number of artists whose work is perhaps rated somewhat lower today than by their contemporaries; they included Luti, Garzi, Conca and Procaccini. There were, however, two new but interlinked developments which held considerable significance for the future. First, Thomas Coke began to buy classical statuary, beginning with a bust of the Emperor Lucius Verus which had come to light during dredging operations in the port of Nettuno, and an unidentified bas-relief which cost him 60 crowns. In 1717 his purchases of pictures, statues and books during the four months he spent there before leaving finally for home amounted to almost 4,000 crowns. The embarrassing 'imbroglio' over the statue of Diana which was to take place in 1717 arose out of this deliberate policy of acquiring statuary.

Second, Giacomo Mariari was re-engaged during August and September 1716, receiving payments for his tuition and for supplying drawing paper, and an additional present 'for going about the town with my master and learning of him architecture'. There can be little doubt that the ever-growing size of his collection of pictures, statues and books, coupled with a keen practical interest in architecture, had already sown the seed in Thomas Coke's mind of a fine new Classical-style mansion at Holkham which should provide a fitting setting for these treasures.

In September he whirled Kent off again with him to revisit several cities in northern Italy including Florence, Parma, Piacenza and Modena. At the last-named there could well have been disaster, for Kent fell ill. Of all the hazards which faced Tourists and other expatriates in Europe, sickness was perhaps the most feared. It was possible to take sensible precautions against wild animals, brigands, common thieves and other hazards, and the chances of survival were fairly good. Against disease there was little or no defence; God's will, whatever it was, would most certainly be done. The letters of Massingberd and of Kent himself are regularly punctuated by such realistic phrases as 'if we should live till then' and 'if I live to come home'. At least this stoical attitude ensured that Tourists did not allow themselves to be intimidated by the possibility of illness, any more than by the risks of robbery or even murder. It is this attitude which Kent himself reflects in his 1712 letter to Samuel Gale, when he writes: 'About a month ago we lost Sir John Read, a patron of arts, which died of the small-pox, which was lamented by us all, but as it happened we had a clergyman, which was some satisfaction to us; they had sent his body for England.' (Evidently, in the very heart of Roman Catholicism, an Anglican parson was providentially available in the hour of need. Kent was no Papist; some years later – 15 February 1717 – he firmly reassures Massingberd as follows: 'I imagine by a word in your letter you are afraid I should change my religion, but there's no fear of that', even though he has been spending a lot of time with Cardinal Ottoboni and is about to paint the ceiling of S. Giuliano dei Fiamminghi.) Smallpox was of course the scourge above all others; even John Evelyn in an earlier age had not escaped it, contracting it at Geneva and narrowly cheating death. Luckily Kent's illness at Modena was of a less serious nature, and thanks to the attentions of a Dr Pammazini (paid for by Coke) he soon recovered. However, his recovery may not have been entirely complete, for in a letter to Massingberd written on 15 February 1716/ 17 after returning to Rome he says that he has come back sooner than intended, owing to his having caught cold whilst making a copy of Correggio's cupola painting in the cathedral at Parma, which had been the next stop on the itinerary after Modena. (Thus for the second time in two years this important and powerful work exercised its spell upon him, although its actual effect on his own painting is not easily discerned.) It is instructive that neither in this letter nor in the one immediately preceding it (8 October 1716), which is written from Florence, does Kent actually tell Massingberd that he is travelling again with Coke. Obviously he feared a lecture on time-wasting, and perhaps even more the possible loss of his valuable subsidy. After the bout of sickness, whatever it was, he seems (so far as we know) to have enjoyed good health almost to the end of his life.

Returning to Rome once again with Kent in January 1717, Thomas Coke indulged in a final orgy of acquisition before at last setting off for England in the spring, the faithful Dr Hobart still in attendance. During the final period in Rome he also had further sessions of architectural tuition with Mariari. He did not land until a year later (18 May 1718), having been deflected *en route* by many interesting places and events, including an abortive attempt to take part in the siege of Belgrade (neatly defeated by Dr Hobart acting in collusion with Coke's guardians and the Austrian authorities). Undoubtedly Kent must keenly have regretted the final departure of his enthusiastic young patron (for so he had become), and he may well have found it hard to settle down again to his studies and commissions after the excitements of the past months. There is perhaps more than a hint of disgruntled dissatisfaction and boredom in his uncharacterisitic comment to Massingberd, 'I can assure you I am quite weary with living this poor melancholy life, but I hope I shall be reviv'd when I see all my friends in England.' It is significant that this letter is dated 15 June 1717, only a few weeks after Thomas Coke had left Rome for good, and perhaps amongs his 'friends in England' Kent, unknown to Massingberd, was silently numbering Coke and already looking forward to their future reunion. It is probable also that his own half-formed intentions to return eventually to England took positive shape from this time onwards.

Escape, however, was not quite so easy. For one thing he felt the need to be fully equipped as a painter before returning home. On 8 June 1718 he tells Massingberd that whilst hoping to return no later than next year he is 'resolved to have a trial here of the difficult and different parts of painting and not run the hazard to begin when I come home. I long to see England, but the desire I have to do something makes me delay the more.' The following 15 November he writes: 'I am still in my resolution to get out next Spring, and my Lord Lempster has agreed with a very good sculptor to come along with me. . . . I hope to have him do ornaments in stucco after the Italian gusto.' At this stage it was clearly Kent's intention to set up at home in some way as a purveyor of Italian art, with help from patrons; Lord Lempster, for example, had already entered into a contract with the unnamed sculptor 'to give him so much a year'. Kent continues his letter on the same theme: 'I am making all preparations and continually a-drawing ornaments and architecture and getting things that I think will be necessary for use in England, but I am afraid by what I hear that our [English] gusto is still in the little Dutch way – fine burnish'd paint that all the figures look like glass bottles and not like Nature.' (This, incidentally, must be one of the most succinct yet devastating assessments of second-rate Dutch painting ever penned.) Evidence that Kent was still in direct or indirect contact with Thomas Coke is supplied in the very next sentence of the letter – a sentence whose light sarcasm at the expense of contemporary English taste pierces the fog of Kent's contorted style like a beacon: 'Mr. Coke had a fine picture of Domenichino and another of Carlo Marrat[a] and a very large one of Giuseppe Chiari, but we hear the English critic[s] do not like 'em, which gives me small encouragement to venture where they are so great judges in painting and architecture, but however I hope the encouragement of my friends will make me despise these Gothick gusto.' His irony is the more understandable when one recalls that almost certainly he himself guided Coke in the purchase of the offending pictures. The word 'Gothick' (invariably at this time spelt with a final k) is here used in a pejorative sense, as it had been for the past hundred or so years; it had yet to be invested with that kind of amused tolerance which later was to spring from Kent's own dabblings in a pseudo-medieval idiom, much less with the cheerful respectability that Horace Walpole was to bestow upon it through his creation of Strawberry Hill in the 1740s. When Alexander Pope described Kent to Lord Burlington as 'a wild Goth ... from a country which has ever been held no part of Christendom', he was deliberately if humorously evoking a picture of an uncouth savage (and incidentally including Burlington in the fun with a provokingly sly reference to Yorkshire).[8]

About one month later Kent writes again to Massingberd in the same vein: 'Now I'm a-making all preparations [so that] I can come to England next Spring, and will content myself to see France alone, and not go into Flanders. I lay what little money I have on prints and stucco figures [such] as heads and feet etc., which will be of great use to me when I cannot see the antiques. I now am make [sic] a study of ornament that will be proper to adorn about my paintings if [I] can introduce the Italian gusto into England.' By 'the Italian gusto' Kent here seemingly refers to mural and ceiling painting, while the 'ornament' he was studying was probably the kind of grotesque-style decoration which – disposed in panels – he later used as a surround to the painted centrepiece of more than one ceiling (e.g. in the Red Velvet Room and Gallery at Chiswick House).

His next sentence in this letter is a *cri de coeur*: 'I hope you will be so kind as to send me some assistance to come home.' He has already referred to 'what little money I have' two sentences earlier, and is clearly determined that Massingberd shall be left in no doubt about his financial situation. For despite his encounters with Coke and Burlington no other source of hard cash had yet replaced the faithful support of Massingberd, Chester and perhaps, to a lesser extent, Wentworth. Their patronage remained essential to him for some months longer. Then, at last, in late autumn 1719, came the time for Kent to leave Italy and return home, and even the journey itself provided a foretaste of things to come, for he travelled from Paris to London in the company of Lord Burlington, himself on the way back from Italy.

Burlington had been in Italy since the summer of the same year. But this second visit was not the somewhat desultory Tour that the first had been;

it was much shorter, and moreover was made with a specific purpose in mind – namely, to acquire as much first-hand information as possible about the Renaissance architect Andrea Palladio and his buildings, most of which were in and around his native Vicenza. Behind this mission, which was evidently infused with a sense of zeal and urgency, lay a conversion every bit as important and far-reaching to the cause of English art and architecture as that of St Paul to the Christian faith, though not perhaps quite so sudden.

Part of this conversion may well have been due to the influential writings and philosophy of the third Earl of Shaftesbury (1671–1713), who in a series of works published between 1709 and 1712 sought to establish new criteria of taste and aesthetic judgment. He equated taste with morality and the standards of daily life with those expressed in the arts, especially painting and architecture. 'Thus are the arts and virtues mutually friends; and thus the science of virtuosos and that of virtue itself become, in a manner, one and the same.'[9] But the gentleman of taste, the virtuoso, should beware of taking his learning too far: 'I am persuaded that to be a virtuoso (so far as befits a gentleman) is a higher step towards the becoming a man of virtue and good sense than the being what in this age we call a scholar.'[10] Obvious enthusiasms of any kind were to be strictly avoided, and a façade of dignified reserve presented at all times to the world.

This was heady enough stuff to a young nobleman already more than usually interested in the arts. But the probable impact of Shaftesbury's philosophy upon the receptive mind of Burlington was undoubtedly sharpened by the publication in 1715 (the very year of Burlington's first return from Italy) of two works in three folio volumes whose importance to English architectural history can hardly be overstated.

The first was volume I of the famous three-volume series *Vitruvius Britannicus* by the Scottish-born architect Colen Campbell (1676–1729). *Vitruvius Britannicus* is a collection of engravings of seventeenth- and early eighteenth-century British buildings, mainly country houses, by architects of the period including Wren and Vanbrugh (both of whom were still living) and Campbell himself. The series was in fact a propaganda exercise to promote the cause of Classically inspired architecture based ultimately on the theory and practice of the Romans. Even the title proclaims this, for Vitruvius was a Roman military engineer of the first century AD whose manuscript work on architecture was rediscovered amidst great excitement in about 1486 and republished at Rome; it subsequently formed the basis of much Italian Renaissance architectural theory. The 'British Vitruvius' of Campbell's title in fact refers to Inigo Jones, the first and up to that time almost the only man in Britain to have understood and put into practice the principles of Italian Classical architecture in buildings such as the Whitehall Banqueting House (1619–22) and the Queen's House at Greenwich (1616–35).

Even more significant, however, was Campbell's reference in his preface to 'the great Palladio, who has exceeded all that were gone before him and surpassed his contemporaries, whose ingenious labours will eclipse many and rival most of the Ancients.' Andrea Palladio (1508–80) was certainly one of the most important Italian Renaissance architects to absorb and re-interpret the Classical Vitruvian style. However, it is doubtful whether his work would have been so well known or his influence so widespread outside Italy had he not published in 1570 his own contribution to architectural study, *I Quattro Libri dell'Architettura*. Inigo Jones himself owned a copy of this which he freely annotated during a visit to Italy in 1613–14. But it was not until 1715 that the first complete English edition was published in two volumes in London, edited by an immigrant Italian architect from Venice, Giacomo Leoni. Here then was the second of the two works whose publication was to make 1715 such a memorable year, especially for Lord Burlington.

For the scales now fell dramatically from his Lordship's eyes. Shaftesbury had already declared that 'One who aspires to the character of a man of breeding and politeness is careful to form his judgement of arts and sciences upon right models of perfection.'[11] Burlington had all the necessary aspirations; the Vitruvian-Palladian architectural ideal would now provide him with the 'model of perfection', with Campbell to demonstrate its application in an English context. Having reached some such stage in his thinking, it must have galled Burlington extremely to recognize that instead of largely frittering away his time in Italy he could have employed it to greater purpose and in more serious and rewarding pursuits. However, having only recently returned to England there could be no question of his going back to Italy, at least for the present. Instead, he nailed his colours to the mast by inviting Colen Campbell to undertake the remodelling of his seventeenth-century London home, Burlington House in Piccadilly (at that time little more than a country road).

This did not happen immediately, for curiously enough in 1716 Burlington first asked James Gibbs, an architect schooled in the already unfashionable Baroque tradition, to undertake the work; this suggests that Gibbs was engaged before his Lordship's conversion was complete – even, perhaps, by correspondence while Burlington was still away in Europe. At all events, Gibbs was replaced by Campbell in 1717, and the rebuilding then began in earnest in strict accordance with the tenets of Palladio. Indeed the façade was closely based on one of Palladio's own buildings, the Palazzo Iseppo da Porto at Vicenza.

Burlington's contacts with Campbell at this time must undoubtedly have served to attract him ever more strongly to the Classical cause, and to make finally clear to him that his own primary artistic interest was in the field of architecture – notwithstanding his generous patronage of the other arts, notably music. About this time he appears to have designed and built (doubtless in close consultation with Campbell) the single-storey Summer Parlour adjacent to his Jacobean family mansion at Chiswick. We have no information as to the precise moment at which Burlington felt himself called to assume the leadership of what soon became known as the Palladian movement. The time was nevertheless especially ripe for such a movement. With the death of Queen Anne and the accession of George I in 1714 the Whigs swept the Tories from power in a political *bouleversement* that affected the entire social structure of the country, and the widespread submission by the landed gentry to the disciplines of Classical architecture was one of the most obvious and striking signs of the change. The Palladian style, indeed, was the outward and visible expression of Whig philosophy, which looked to Classical sources for authority, precedent and inspiration.

By 1719 Burlington had made up his mind. Though he had undoubtedly gained much from his association with Campbell during the past four years, he was learning at second hand – almost, it could be said, at third, for Campbell himself had never been to Italy. The time had now come for a return visit to that country, with the set purpose of studying the work of Palladio; then, and only then, would he, the third Earl of Burlington, be a virtuoso in Shaftesbury's sense of the word, fit and ready to lead his fellow countrymen into the bright dawn of a new Classical age. Leaving Campbell in charge of operations at Burlington House, he sped back to Italy.

In the autumn of 1719 William Kent set off from Rome in the opposite direction. He travelled as far as Genoa with his old patron Sir William Wentworth, who was once again in Italy, but at Genoa exchanged the old for the new, for there he was reunited with Burlington. 'I met him at Genova', he wrote excitedly to Massingberd on 15 November, 'and he would make me promise to stay for him here; he was agoing towards Vicenza and Venice to get architects to draw all the fine buildings of Palladio, and return back here which I expect every day.' This letter was written from Paris, where Kent confessed he was having some difficulty through 'being alone, and not speaking the language well . . . but I hope in a little time to see my good friends in England; that will be a great satisfaction for all my troubles.' His luggage had been sent on in advance: 'I sent directed to you all my things, 1st a long box with pictures in it for you and Sir John Chester and some sketches I have done for myself, and a square box with my prints in it and some little pictures (some for you), two boxes of wax boys and heads, legs and arms' (i.e. painters' props).

It has been suggested that Kent met Burlington at Genoa by prearrangement. The evidence seems to point to the contrary. In his letter to Massingberd Kent states that he would have set off sooner but was delayed 'by waiting longer for Sir Will. Wentworth than I expected'; this does not suggest any kind of time-table. Having met Burlington at Genoa, 'His Lordship lik'd my designs so well, both painting and architecture, that he would make me promise at least to begin to paint for him the first when I come over, which if he comes soon may be with his Lordship.' As yet there is nothing very definite here; Kent gives the impression that he is kicking his heels in Paris, waiting about at his Lordship's behest, but is not going to wait for ever.

On the other hand this may all have been a subtle but deliberate ploy, to put Massingberd off the scent and to conceal the fact that his protégé had already been snatched away from him by a richer and more powerful patron, whether by fortuitous accident in Genoa or by design plotted through previous correspondence. (Certainly Vertue states that Kent was 'directed' to join Burlington's retinue at Paris.)

Whatever the truth of the matter, it is clear from Kent's letter that he and Burlington had already re-established the rapport which had subsisted between them in 1714–15. Even more importantly, Kent was becoming an enthusiastic convert to the Palladian creed. 'Since I have left Rome and Florence [I] cannot bear to see anything, except two fine palaces of Vitruvio in Genova that my Ld. carry'd me to see, which he has order'd to be drawn.' In the same letter this sentence is then followed by one of the most remarkable of all Kent's written comments: 'I hope by his Lordship's encouragement and other gentlemen who may have a better gusto, than that dam'd gusto that's been for this sixty years past'.

Literacy was never Kent's strong point; the stronger his feelings, the more contorted his style. The meaning here, however, is clear. He intends to play his full part in bringing about that fundamental change in taste at home now perceived to be so essential. The evident fervour of his conviction is a striking tribute to Burlington's powers of persuasion, for in this respect Kent was no mere opportunist and, as his subsequent career was to prove, never wavered in his devotion to the Palladian cause. Eventually he came to think of himself and Burlington as prophets, sharing the misunderstanding and contempt which is all too often the prophet's lot – 'As for what you and I do, it may be esteem'd a hundred years hence, but at present does not look like it, by what I see doing in the arcades of Convent Garding', he once wrote to Burlington (16 November 1732), moved to resigned despair by some ill-conceived alterations being carried out to Inigo Jones's famous piazza.[12] The social presumption of this implicit claim to be considered on an equal footing with Burlington obviously did not even occur to him. It merely reflects the genuine friendship and esteem which each had for the other almost – it seems – from their first meeting, which continued throughout their lives, and which was certainly one of the oddest yet most fruitful associations in the history of human relationships. Genuine affection, uninhibited by class distinction and uncomplicated by any suggestion of homosexuality – which our permissive age too readily assumes – glows through the opening sentence of this same letter (the main purpose of which was to recommend a new servant to Burlington), despite Kent's usual trouble in expressing himself clearly: 'My Lord: The person I mention to you for a servant in your house, is such a one, that I don't know but by people loving and living with them may in time think the same way, as I flatter myself I do with you.' (Even Burlington himself sometimes had trouble in unravelling Kent's contorted syntax. In two separate letters to his wife written in October 1728 the Earl makes the following wry comments: 'I have yours of the 9th by this post, and another from the Signor, more allegorical than ever. . . . I have had a letter from the Signor, if possible more in the clouds than ever. . . .')

Meanwhile the future, which a year ago had seemed so nebulous, was suddenly beginning to take shape. Less than a month later Massingberd received another letter, this time from London. After a ten-year absence William Kent was once again back in England. Significantly, the letter came from Burlington House. 'After a dismal journey from Paris . . . [I] got safe here with my Ld. Burlington and am lodg'd in his house, and he will have me begin to paint for him the first thing that I do, which is the fine room in his new building. I have already made the design, which he seems to be much pleased with.'

CHAPTER THREE

SWIFT SUCCESS

It is not surprising that Kent, having been away for so long from his native country, at first obviously felt somewhat lost and bewildered; this appears in his next letter to Massingberd, 19 January 1719/20. 'You may imagine I am not a little disturbed at the hurry of this country; for being quite a stranger to the extravagant taste of the English virtuosi in painting, sculpture and arch[itecture] that I don't know where I am when I am once out of the gates of Ld. Burlington's house, where I think you may see a true Palladian front.' Bemused alike by the pace of London life and the state of English artistic taste, only the gleaming new façade of Burlington House served as a visible reminder of what he had left behind and as a promise of better things to come (though he must also surely have rejoiced at his first sight of Inigo Jones's Banqueting House). The winter climate was an additional reason for taking a jaundiced view of life in England. 'I hope it will not be so long before I have the happiness to see you, though the season is a little troublesome and the change of air from that of Italy that since I came I have had a great cold but hope it will be nothing' (10 December 1719). A few weeks later: 'I am still at work here [Burlington House], the days being so short and cold to an Italian constitution that I keep [to] my little room, only twice a week I go to the Operas where I am highly entertain'd, and then think myself out of this Gothick country' (30 January 1719/20). Burlington House was to be his principal haven for the rest of his life.

The 'true Palladian front' of the mansion was, as we have already noted, based on a genuine Palladian model and indeed can still be traced, despite the additions of 1866. Sadly, however, the nineteenth century also destroyed the imposing gateway, modelled by Campbell on the York House watergate which was at that time wrongly attributed to Jones, and also the superb semi-circular Classical colonnade that enclosed the forecourt. (This is held by some experts to have been the work of James Gibbs but by others that of Burlington himself. Following demolition of the gateway in 1868 the colonnade was removed to Battersea Park where it lay unerected for many years. It is last mentioned in a newspaper account of 1892,[1] after which it disappears from record and from view.) London had not seen such spectacular new domestic architecture since the building of the Banqueting House a century earlier. The average passer-by, however, was not privileged to enter the house and view the fine new apartments, richly decorated in the Classical manner that was soon to become the interior style of so many town and country houses throughout Britain.

An important part of the decorations consisted of painted ceilings, and although both Pellegrini and Sebastiano Ricci had already been employed at Burlington House not all the ceilings had been completed; their completion was to be Kent's first task in England. His letter to Massingberd of 10 December 1719 had already indicated that he was to paint Burlington's new 'fine room'; by 19 January 'I have made a sketch in colours for the Great Room in the front, and all the rest of the ornaments that are to be *al Italiano*.' The theme of the Great Room or Saloon ceiling is a *Banquet of the Gods*; Kent followed it up with an *Assembly of the Gods* for what is now the Secretary's Room, and, significantly, an *Apotheosis of Inigo Jones* (Plate 4) for a third room (this painting, a roundel, is now over the main staircase). All three paintings are executed in oils on canvas, and all have survived. Kent finished them in 1720, probably by early summer.

Unless viewed from a considerable distance *trompe l'œil* ceiling and mural decoration is seldom entirely successful, however gifted the artist; indeed, some would say that it can never be successful. The architect Roger Pratt (who died in 1685, the year of Kent's birth) wrote: 'But as for those [figures] which are ascending, or sitting as it were there, they cannot but be represented to us with much shortening and distortion, and so have something of harsh and monstrous in them, though performed by the most experienced masters in that curious art of perspective, as will most evidently appear to all men upon the least observation.'[2] It follows therefore that the effects of mediocre artists in this genre can be disastrous. Kent's work at Burlington House is perhaps not quite so poor as is sometimes claimed, but it certainly shows that his powers were inadequate to cope with the task he had set himself, despite his long apprenticeship in Italy.[3] The most conspicuous failing both here and elsewhere is his extremely shaky grasp of the basic principles of human anatomy – all too often the limbs of his figures look as though they are formed from plasticine. It must also be said that notwithstanding the comparative success of the ceiling at S. Giovanni dei Fiamminghi his treatment of perspective remained hesitant. The modern visitor to Burlington House has only to step from the Saloon into the adjoining Council Room, comparing Kent's rather dark and dreary *Banquet of the Gods* with the far more colourful and technically assured *Cupid before Jupiter* by Sebastiano Ricci, in order to appreciate the contrast. (The space now occupied by the Council Room was originally filled by the staircase, which was moved to its present position in 1816.) Echoes of Veronese, whom Kent

4 *Apotheosis of Inigo Jones*. Architecture personified, enthroned between a portrait of Jones and
a drawing or engraving of the south front of Campbell's Burlington House; indeterminate
Classical buildings in the background. Painted 1720 for one of the rooms in Burlington
House and now over the main staircase there

clearly admired (at the time of his death his studio contained two copies of
ceiling paintings by the great Venetian master), are faintly discernible, and
the *Apotheosis of Inigo Jones* is a tolerable essay. But all in all these ceilings
must have been a sad disappointment to Lord Burlington.

Yet nothing in Burlington's subsequent behaviour gave the slightest hint
that he was in any way dissatisfied with Kent's performance – quite the reverse,
in fact. Already by June 1720 Kent was working for two powerful noblemen
to whom he must almost certainly have been recommended by Burlington – the
Duke of Chandos and Viscount Castlemain. For Chandos he is said to have
painted three ceilings in the Duke's magnificent new palace at Canons, Mid-

dlesex, completing them by 1725, although only one – on the theme of Leda and the Swan – is mentioned in the inventory of the house. Canons was a huge Italianate palazzo designed by James Gibbs in a Baroque rather than a purely Classical style; it was built out of the fortune amassed by the Duke in his capacity as Army Paymaster, and no expense was spared to make it as sumptuous as possible both inside and out (for example, it was at Canons that the newly fashionable wood, mahogany, was first used as panelling on any large scale in Britain). Predictably, expenses outran resources; the Duke's heirs were forced to demolish the house, and with it went Kent's ceilings.[4]

The same fate befell his work for Lord Castlemain. The Viscount's mansion, Wanstead in Essex, was Colen Campbell's first large-scale essay in the Palladian style, and indeed the first full physical statement of the Palladian creed. Built between 1715 and 1720, it expressed in its regular planning, in its Classical ornaments and in such details as the enormous, temple-like portico (which was to become an almost essential feature of subsequent eighteenth-century country house architecture) the full realization of the theories set out by Campbell himself in *Vitruvius Britannicus*. In the circumstances Kent's commission *circa* 1721 to decorate the Great Hall ceiling – which he did with a painting showing the Times of Day – was almost inevitable. Possibly he rose to the challenge more successfully than at Burlington House, but this we cannot know, since in 1824 – with distressing but sadly all-too-familiar disregard for an architectural monument of seminal importance – Wanstead was demolished. Some indication of the esteem in which Kent was already held in the earlier part of his career may be seen in the fact that Lord Castlemain not only commissioned a full-length portrait of him by William Aikman, as Vertue noted in 1725, but set it up over the fireplace in the Great Hall, a conspicuous position in which it was seen and noted by the diarist Mrs Lybbe Powys during her 1781 tour in East Anglia.[5]

The evidence of Burlington's partiality towards Kent, which is implicit in the commissions at Burlington House, Canons and Wanstead, nevertheless pales into insignificance when placed beside The Affair of the Kensington Palace Rooms (as Sir Arthur Conan Doyle might have called it). In 1718 the aged Christopher Wren was most unfairly and unceremoniously swept by the tide of fashion from his office as royal architect or Surveyor, and was replaced by William Benson, an incompetent poseur with more pretensions to literature than to architecture – which was not saying much. Benson only lasted a year in office, but he and his successor Sir Thomas Hewett (who, although equally incompetent, at least had the sense to leave actual designing to professional deputies) provided for George I a new suite of state rooms at Kensington Palace. The question of decorating these in a suitable manner now arose. Confident in his position and secure in the knowledge that he was England's greatest mural artist, Sir James Thornhill (1675–1734), the Sergeant Painter or official royal artist, duly submitted designs for decorating the first of the new apartments, known as the Cupola Room. These were shown to the King, who approved one of them; he also later approved a painted model of the room. Thornhill was asked to name his price, and quoted £800. He then sat back and waited for the commission to fall into his lap.

Thus no great imagination is required to visualize Thornhill's rage and fury when, early in March 1722, he learned that the commission had instead been given to William Kent. In Vertue's telling phrase 'a mighty mortification fell on Sir James Thornhill',[6] and indeed this was a blow from which the unfortunate artist never recovered professionally. Kent, on the other hand, set to work with such a will that already by May 1722 he had completed more than half the decorations. The main feature was octagonal coffering painted on the coved ceiling in blue and gold against a background of simulated marble, the centrepiece consisting of a great painted Garter star. The scheme was later completed on the walls with painted trophies, pilasters of wood painted to look like fluted stone, a relief carved by Rysbrack, and a series of gilded antique statues of Roman gods in marble niches ('a terrible glaring show', complained Vertue). Coffering was much used by the Romans as a decorative device, and Kent must have seen many surviving examples of it in Italy. Geometrically shaped panels (the coffers), more usually recessed into plaster than painted, are arranged in regular patterns, and the panels themselves decrease in size towards the top of the ceiling or dome, giving an optical illusion of height. This is notably successful at Kensington, where the actual ceiling is only slightly concave; painted shadows aid the deception. Trophies – great clustered groups of impedimenta, usually Roman arms, armour and other military accoutrements – were another reminder of Classical times; Kent's trophies are painted in an illusory, three-dimensional manner, as at Kensington, though other artists of his own and the following generation (such as Robert Adam) preferred their trophies in high relief of wood, stone or plaster.

Some years later Kent was to repeat, to some extent, the successful formula used in the Cupola Room. In 1734 Vertue recorded that 'Mr. Kent finished a small staircase with ornaments [and] basso relievos at Hampton Court.'[7] This was the Queen's Staircase, still extant, with a flat ceiling again painted – to a high standard – with coffering and central Garter motif, and with panels in *grisaille* (grey monochrome) of nautical and other emblems on the walls, the main panel at ground level showing Neptune crowning Britannia.

This is the point at which to ask exactly how it was that the relatively unknown and untried Kent succeeded in snatching a plum job from under the nose of the established and justly celebrated court painter Thornhill. Money certainly played a part. In Vertue's account, the Vice-Chamberlain (also confusingly called Thomas Coke), having received Thornhill's quotation of £800, 'without more ado takes Mr. Kent to Kensington and asked him what he would have for the same painting to be done; after having considered he answered 300 pounds, which was agreed to and he set to work.'[8] On the other hand, there exists a written proposition from Kent in which he quotes £300 if using Prussian Blue in the colouring or £350 if Ultramarine should be thought more appropriate, and it was this last which was actually chosen. (The proposition, dated 28 February 1721, is written in French, the court language used to assist the King, who knew no English.) Economy was much in the air at the time; money for the Kensington Palace state apartments was pared down to the minimum, so it is perhaps not so surprising to find that their decoration was also made the subject of close financial scrutiny.

Part of the answer may also lie in the personality and conduct of Thornhill himself. According to Vertue, his knighthood and his appointment as Sergeant Painter (both 1720) were acquired 'by great favour of the quality and interest of the Surveyors and Officers of the King's Works', presumably meaning Benson and/or Hewett. However, instead of resting on his laurels Thornhill then behaved very foolishly. He spread it abroad that the men to whom he owed his position were incompetent, 'declared himself opposite to all their interests, and by drawing and designing, and demonstrating their ignorances in the art of building, he would set himself up against them for the place of Surveyor or Architect, and in short for all in all.'[9] According to another account, he 'dabbled in architecture, and stirred up much envy in that profession by announcing a design of taking it up, as he had before by thinking of applying himself to painting of portraits.'[10] In fact it seems all too plain that, to some extent at least, he was his own worst enemy. In this situation almost any competitor for an official commission was assured of a hearing, and Kent must have seemed the embodiment of Nemesis to the ungrateful Thornhill's former supporters. 'Therefore they have play'd him this trick', remarks Vertue grimly.

His mortification must have been completed by the knowledge that in substance if not in form the idea of coffering on the Cupola Room ceiling had originally been his, and that almost certainly Kent knew this and made use of it. A drawing by Thornhill now in the Victoria & Albert Museum is inscribed by him 'For the cieling [sic] of the Great Room at Kensington': in this, Kent's angular Classical coffering is replaced by lozenge-shaped, leaf-like forms and his Garter Star by an exuberant chrysanthemum head, but there is no mistaking the general overall pattern set by Thornhill and no escaping the conclusion that Kent followed a path already partly mapped out for him. He even used Thornhill's chrysanthemum, together with other formal floral motifs, as a centrepiece of the ceiling coffers.

Vertue adds a postscript to the episode, according to which Thornhill, in a last despairing effort to wrest the commission from Kent, wrote to the Vice-Chamberlain expressing his willingness to do the work 'for what any other would do it – but was rejected.' His bid had failed, but less for the two reasons we have so far examined than for the third, more significant than either of them. Again Vertue sums it up succinctly: 'Besides, the Lord Burlington forwarded Mr. Kent's interest as much as lay'd in his power at Court, and strenuously opposed Sir James.' Brought up from childhood as a good Whig, Burlington was still only 20 when in 1714, on the death of Queen Anne, he was swept into the orbit of the newly established Whig court. Despite his youth, honours were heaped embarrassingly thickly upon his head; he immediately became a Privy Councillor, and in 1715 was appointed Lord Treasurer of Ireland, Vice-Admiral of the County of York, and Lord Lieutenant of both the East and West Ridings. Later, in 1730, he received the Garter and in 1731 became Captain of the Gentlemen Pensioners.

Apart from the Lieutenantship of the Ridings, these posts were virtual sinecures. Taken together, however, they ensured that he had the ear of anybody who mattered at court, and undoubtedly this made his promotion of Kent's interests a far easier matter than it might otherwise have been. He was further helped by the fact that Sir Thomas Hewett, the Surveyor, had already met Kent in Rome in 1717, had visited his studio there and had watched him painting Burrell Massingberd's 'ceiling piece' (see p. 16).

From a purely artistic standpoint, mere partisanship on behalf of Kent cannot entirely explain the implacable opposition to Thornhill evinced by the Burlington faction at court. The Sergeant Painter was after all the finest mural artist that England had ever produced. It requires a great effort of the imagination to visualize the Painted Hall at Greenwich Hospital as Wren left it, ready for decoration – a huge, bare, oblong apartment with a flat, white and totally blank ceiling some 5,500 ft in area, the only ornament in the whole vast room being the moulded capitals of the pilasters in the piers. How much greater was the imagination which Thornhill needed, and found, to fill this great expanse and later the Upper Hall beyond it with a carefully orchestrated riot of architectural detail, naval trophies, ships, shells, fruit, flowers and people – all executed in paint with a technical mastery and an overall command and purpose unrivalled in England and not often surpassed abroad. Greenwich was and is Thornhill's finest work; he left, however, many others of high quality and similar genre ranging in size and scope from the cupola of St Paul's cathedral to the staircase at Hanbury Hall, Worcestershire, as well as a considerable corpus of designs for theatrical scenery and stage settings.

None of this availed him in 1722; indeed, his former career was in part his downfall. In the first place, his public commissions, as at Greenwich and St Paul's, fatally linked him with the discredited Tory party in general and with Wren in particular. It was unthinkable that an artist of the old regime should be allowed to execute important public works for the new government and party, especially when the same artist had not hesitated to bite the hand that had fed him. In the second place, the style in which he painted was outmoded and was furthermore also inevitably associated with the Tories. The typical Baroque ceiling draws the eye upward, past a multitude of subsidiary figures, until it rests upon a central personage, whether saint, Classical god or secular ruler; the theme almost invariably presents an apotheosis of this

[45]

central figure. In England the technique had been used to reinforce the claims to divinely approved supremacy of every monarch from James I to Anne. It was calculated to compel the instant attention of the onlooker or visitor and to force home a blatant political message by means of sheer visual saturation. Neither the message nor the means by which it was conveyed were acceptable to the new Whig administration, groping its way towards a constitutional monarchy as we understand the term today.

In any case, complete overall coverage of walls and ceilings with illusionistic painting was a florid Baroque manifestation no longer in tune with the Classical theories of Burlington's circle. Painting there might indeed be, but an actual painted scene – it was felt – should be restricted to the central area of the ceiling, while any other painting in the same room should be purely decorative, taking the form of architectural devices, imitation sculpture and so on. It is no coincidence that Kent's central ceiling paintings at Burlington House and at Kensington retreat once again into the confines of heavy plaster frames which inhibit the full effects of illusionism. It was no longer the business of mural painting to indoctrinate or distract, but rather to emphasize the general richness and decorative harmony of the whole. In 1732 the Earl of Oxford significantly noted that he had found the dining room of the Angel Inn at Bury St Edmunds 'much decorated (as Mr. Kent's phrase is, and those that follow him)' by the landlord's artist nephew.[11] To the Palladians, mural art was primarily decoration, and not an end in itself.

Perhaps we have here a clue to Burlington's early faith in Kent's powers as an artist. In Knapton's well-known portrait of Burlington at Chatsworth there is a lurking obstinacy in the mouth which suggests that, once having made his mind up about something, the Earl did not easily change it. If he had secretly found Kent's Burlington House paintings disappointing, he was not going to admit it, nor alter his opinion of Kent's abilities. What therefore must his pleasure have been to discover, through the designs for the Kensington Palace rooms, that as a purely decorative artist Kent showed signs of even greater promise, especially in the careful control and organization of ornament. This fact was later to be of crucial importance in the decoration of Chiswick Villa.

Despite the apparently irresistible momentum generated by the Burlington faction on Kent's behalf, some officials still harboured lingering doubts about his suitability for the work. These doubts were expressed in the form of a three-man commission appointed by the Office of Works in May 1722 to report on Kent's progress with the painting of the Cupola Room (Plate 5). The members of the commission were themselves artists; Jan Van der Vaart and Alexander Nesbitt specialized in landscapes, whilst Jacob Rambour was himself an ornamental painter. They were somewhat taken aback to find the ceiling already 'better than half done', after only about two months' work, and proceeded to make the following unfavourable comments:

5 Kensington Palace: the Cupola Room, 1722, with Rysbrack's *Roman Marriage* relief over the fireplace. The coffering and most of the architectural decoration are painted

> 'Tis our opinion, that the perspective is not just; that the principal of the work, which consists in ornaments and architecture, is not done as such a place requires. Mr. Nesbitt adds that the boys, masks, mouldings etc., far from being well, he has seen very few worse for such a place; and Mr. Rambour affirms that the said work, far from being done in the best manner . . . is not so much as tolerably well perform'd.[12]

They then suggested that Prussian Blue had actually been used although Ultramarine had been chosen, thus implying that Kent was cheating the authorities out of their money.

Much if not all of this can be attributed to sheer professional jealousy, especially in the case of Rambour. Kent was well prepared for it. He was no stranger to criticism; at the time of his winning the Papal medal reports had reached him from Paris (so he told Massingberd) that the painters there 'are jealous . . . and say it's a trifle to get the medals, but I had the honour that a cardinal told the Pope a Protestant had drawn a miracle better than a Roman Catholic – not that I make myself the more, but let them come and draw, to see how easy [it is] to get from twelve or thirteen that drew in the Capital' (26 January

1713/14). Now he had hardly set foot in England before he was roundly pro-
claiming defiance: 'Engagements I have for more work makes all these poor-
spirited English daubers rail, and make parties against me, but I hope to overcome them all' (letter to Massingberd, 30 January 1720). The backing of a
powerful patron was undoubtedly a significant factor in this attitude. Certainly
no action seems to have been taken on the commission's report, and an attempt
by the authorities in August 1722 to solicit the joint opinion of two celebrated
painters, Michael Dahl and Charles Jervas, likewise came to nothing. Dahl
nervously declined to serve, and Jervas had diplomatically left town. The Office
of Works then gave up all efforts to control Kent, and paid him £350 on completion of the ceiling, which is executed in oils on plaster. He next painted the
wooden walls with architectural ornament in tones of olive grey, gold and
brown, using in part a *sgraffito* technique in which a top layer of paint or plaster
is scratched away to reveal a second layer beneath. This time the Office of
Works was tardy with payment and Kent was forced to lodge an official com-
plaint; it had the desired effect and in June 1725 he was paid £324 2. 7d.
for the walls, which he had probably completed some considerable time
previously, government departments being what they are.

In fact long before 1725 Kent had moved beyond the original commission
to decorate the Cupola Room to a progressive scheme of work involving all
the other main rooms in the new sequence. His timetable for this may be set
out as follows, together with the payments he received:

1722–3	The King's Drawing Room (£500)
1723	The Privy Chamber (£300) and the King's Bedchamber (£150)[13]
1724	The Presence Chamber (date found on ceiling plaster) and Council Chamber (£300 each)
1725–7	The King's Gallery (£700), Great and Little Closets (£150 each) and Staircase (£500)

Not all of Kent's decoration in these rooms has survived, but we still have
the King's Drawing Room, Presence Chamber, King's Gallery, Staircase and
Privy Chamber. Together with the Cupola Room, they add up to a unique
survey of Kent's different decorative styles.

The ceilings of the King's Drawing Room (Plate 6) and Privy Chamber are
traditional in that in each a central oval painting on canvas showing a typical
mythological scene is linked to the walls of the room by coving decorated with
simulated architectural and sculptural ornament; the subjects respectively are
Jupiter and Semele and *Mars and Minerva* (Mars wearing the Order of the Garter
and representing George II, Minerva standing in for Queen Caroline – Baroque
conventions died hard, even with Kent). But the paintings are deeply recessed,
and their heavy plaster settings serve to reduce them still further to the level
of huge cameos, decorative rather than illusory, and totally divorced from their
surroundings rather than merging into them.

6 Kensington Palace: ceiling of the King's Drawing Room. *Jupiter and Semele*, 1722/3

The Presence Chamber is very different (Plate 7). 'The ceiling in imitation of the antient Roman subterranean ornaments', states Vertue, and adds disparagingly, 'poor stuff'.[14] In fact this is Kent's first use in England of the so-called 'grotesque' style which some seven years previously had been urged upon him by John Talman as a suitable theme for Massingberd's 'ceiling piece'. As we have already seen, there was nothing originally subterranean about the style, and Vertue's misapprehension merely stems from a common failure to understand its origins; it was not until 1738, with the first discoveries at Herculaneum, that these origins became clearer to a wider audience. Meanwhile Kent's decorations in the Presence Chamber were the first to have been seen since Inigo Jones had made use of the grotesque style on the coving of the Queen's Bedroom in the Queen's House at Greenwich, and despite Vertue's opinion they certainly do not deserve to be dismissed as poor. On the contrary, they are lively, colourful (blue, red, green and gold on a white ground) and perfectly fitted for their purpose, which was solely that of cheerful decoration. No wonder they caused distress to those brought up in the Baroque tradition who had hitherto preferred to ignore the grotesques of Jones (which were probably not painted by Jones himself but by another artist such as John de Critz). Determined to introduce a much-needed breath of fresh air into the whole business of mural art, Kent introduced the style into two other rooms at Kensington from which it has since been erased, the King's Bedroom and the Council Chamber; chronologically, in fact, the King's Bedroom was actually the first of the three to be so decorated. Kent received £150 for it, and £300 each for the Presence and Council Chambers.

For the ceiling of the King's Gallery Kent chose a different solution. Here he set up in line down the centre a series of seven paintings on canvas on the theme of Ulysses, six octagonal in shape, the central one oval, flanked by other painted roundels and oblongs. The canvases are linked by a series of ornamental motifs derived from Classical architectural and sculptural decoration, and executed in white and grey on a gold-flecked ground suggestive of mosaic. Although these motifs have an affinity with the grotesque style, they are of a more robust character actually identified at the time by the somewhat misleading overall title of 'mosaic', and were altogether less revolutionary in concept. This kind of work (which is also found in the King's Drawing Room and Privy Chamber) could safely be left to others, and in fact a section of the mosaic ornament in the King's Gallery is signed and dated 1726 on the back of the canvas by an otherwise unrecorded artist named Franciscus De Valentia.[15] Kent meanwhile got on with painting the main and subsidiary canvases in his studio. The Ulysses pictures are not outstanding, but again it must be emphasized, in fairness to Kent, that as items in an overall scheme of decoration they perform their function admirably. As a further sign of Kent's moving away from the old Baroque tradition, they are painted as *quadri riportati* – that is, as normal pictures without foreshortening. In veering towards this kind of

7 Kensington Palace: ceiling of the Presence Chamber, 1724. Kent's first essay in the 'grotesque' style, as startling today as when it was originally painted

approach Kent was clearly influenced by the work of Guido Reni, whose *Aurora* ceiling fresco in the Casino Rospiglioso at Rome he had copied for both Massingberd and Sir John Chester, and which he mentions in an interesting passage concerning the former's 'ceiling piece' which had just been despatched to England. 'I must advise you', he warns his patron, 'if any wise critics should think fit to speak, that the painters here, when the place is little, don't paint the figures entirely so much shorten'd as in high places, but rather choose Guido's way as in the *Aurora* &c. and then to paint the figures not so dark lest it should look heavy.'

This attitude makes his treatment of the King's Staircase at first sight all the more surprising. Most of the decoration, through four levels, is in *grisaille* and consists mainly of 'mosaic', trophies, and imitation sculpture in fake

8 Kensington Palace: detail of the decorations on the King's Staircase, 1725–7. The painted archway, through which can be glimpsed some grotesque-style ornament, shelters a pageboy, some ladies of the Court, and two Yeomen of the Guard

niches. However, on the upper part of the north and east walls, and intended to be viewed from below, Kent presents us (in paint) with a series of four balustraded arcades, in which are grouped a motley crowd of characters, all of them life-size portraits of people attached to the court of George I, and some still identifiable. These include a valet named Ulric in Polish national dress, two Turkish servants originally captured in Hungary who became influential *eminences grises* at court, and Peter the Wild Boy. (Found loping about on all fours in a forest near Hamelin, Peter never learned to speak properly and eventually became a social embarrassment; he died in 1785 in seclusion at Berkhamsted.[16]) Other remarkable figures in this gallery include some Yeomen of the Guard, a tall Scotsman, a Quaker, an assortment of court ladies and even some children.

It is said that George I himself made this selection from those who daily surrounded him, and it is of course possible that Kent's reversion here to an apparently archaic formula was to some extent dictated by royal preference. Whatever the reason, one's initial reaction to the King's Staircase is that it is in the tradition of Baroque illusionism in general and of painted staircases in particular, of which the grandest example in this country is that other King's Staircase at Hampton Court painted by Antonio Verrio and completed by him in 1702. The basic idea of placing figures within a simulated architectural setting, though used by the Romans, was first successfully exploited in post-Classical times by Andrea Mantegna in the *Camera degli Sposi* (Room of the Betrothed) at the ducal palace in Mantua (1474: Mantegna's figures also were contemporary portraits, in his case members of the ruling Gonzaga family). Though scale and emphasis changed over the centuries, the formula thereafter remained the same. Kent completes it at Kensington with another well-tried device, a painted ceiling 'window' from which more onlookers peer down on to the staircase below; one of these, florid-faced and somehow quizzical, is himself, another a lady friend, two others possibly his pupils, and the rest friends and musicians (Plate 9). Through no fault of his, the ceiling is too low and the illusionistic effect therefore lost. (The same miscalculation also mars the mausoleum ceiling of his patron, the great Duke of Chandos, at Little Stanmore church in Middlesex, where a little porthole of blue sky is so obviously painted as to make the visitor smile. This ceiling, however, is not by Kent but by Gaetano Brunetti, although at one time the Duke suggested that Kent's ceiling painting – on canvas – in the principal bedroom at Chandos House, St James's Square, should be re-sited in the mausoleum, or 'Monument Room' as it was called.[17])

Yet we should be careful not to dismiss the Kensington staircase merely as a competent exercise in an outworn genre. Competent it certainly is; indeed, it is one of Kent's most successful attempts at decorative art (Horace Walpole grudgingly called it 'the least defective work of his pencil'). As to genre, it is equally certainly based on ancient precedent of which Kent had undoubtedly

9 Kensington Palace: detail of the ceiling above the King's Staircase (before restoration), showing a self-portrait of Kent (second from right) with friends. The lady has sometimes been identified as his mistress, Elizabeth Butler

seen many examples whilst in Italy. One of the more likely sources for his inspiration may have been the *Sala Regia* in the Quirinale Palace at Rome; here, early in the seventeenth century, Agostino Tassi – with the assistance of Giovanni Lanfranco and Carlo Saraceni – painted an architectural setting of arcades and balconies containing groups of half-length figures including several turbaned Turks, together with a few Chinese and Africans. But the architecture is much fussier than Kent's and most of the figures far more agitated than his. The important point to remember is that this particular version of the formula was not well known in England. The figures in the mural compositions of Verrio, Laguerre and Thornhill were not normally confined behind balustrades or galleries (except for a few examples such as in the Saloon at Blenheim Palace, where Laguerre's painted half-length spectators – which also include a self-portrait of the artist – peer disconcertingly over a simulated parapet at living occupants of the room). Moreover full Baroque illusionism, as we have seen, demanded overall treatment of walls and ceiling, such as Verrio gave to the Heaven Room at Burghley House; this was the sort of thing that had caused Lord Shaftesbury to write in disparagement of 'those wilder sorts of painting . . . in fresco upon the walls, the ceilings, the staircases, the cupolo's and other remarkable places either of churches or palaces'.[18] Kent's staircase at Kensington, on the other hand, is controlled and restrained; only a small proportion of the available space contains figures (which, it should be said, are probably the best he ever painted), and far from spilling out all over the walls these are kept firmly in bounds by the constraints of the painted architecture. By complaining that 'all these paintings are so far short of the like works done here in England before by Verrio, Cook, Streeter, Laguerre, Thornhill, Ricci, Pellegrini &c.',[19] Vertue reveals, first, his total misunderstanding of Kent's decorative style and, second, his failure to recognize that it was drawn directly from original Italian sources and was not based at second hand on a collection of grandiose but tired and outworn clichés. No doubt he also failed to notice that the background ceiling seen through the painted arches of the Kensington staircase is decorated in that same Roman grotesque style which he so despised (Plate 8).

In 1727, on the accession of George II, Kent gained a valuable ally in the new Queen, Caroline of Ansbach, who whilst outwardly enduring constant snubs and even insults from her overbearing husband was nevertheless a force to be reckoned with, for despite appearances 'her will was the sole spring on which every movement of the Court turned.'[20] In politics she was discreetly but decisively active; Sir Walter Scott, in the course of a succinct literary portrait of her, remarks that 'it was a maxim of Queen Caroline, to bear herself towards her political friends with such caution, as if there was a possibility of their one day being her enemies, and towards political opponents with the same degree of circumspection, as if they might again become friendly to her measures' (*The Heart of Midlothian*, chapter XXXVII). Although George II on his own admission took no interest in the visual arts, the Queen – a lively, intelligent and cultured woman – probably took an active part in formulating the final decorative touches to the Kensington Palace rooms. Certainly (despite an imperfect command of English) she took pleasure in the company of the Whig intelligentsia at court, who provided a congenial collective escape valve from the intense boredom of life with the King. Indeed, when the Princess Royal heard that George II's mistress Lady Suffolk had retired from court, she remarked feelingly that she wished he would take a fancy to someone else, 'that Mamma might be a little relieved from the *ennui* of seeing him for ever in her room.'[21]. The close links between the Burlington faction and the Queen were further strengthened by the appointment of Burlington's wife as a Lady-in-Waiting. Against such a background it is not surprising to learn that on finishing his work at Kensington Kent obtained (24 January 1727/8) one of the first of the several official posts to which he was to be appointed over the years, that of 'History Painter and Keeper or Preserver of the Paintings of the Royal Palaces for life', at an annual salary of £100. A 'history painter' of the period concerned himself with the representation of incidents in ancient history, Classical mythology and the scriptures and it should be said that this was (in Vertue's words) 'a new constituted place purposely for him', not a traditional office. Nevertheless, in this capacity his first major task (1729) was to take down Rubens's ceiling paintings in the Banqueting House for cleaning and re-lining – perhaps none too soon, for they were officially described as being 'in danger of wholly perishing'. The work took some time but was not without its rewards. On the back fly-leaf of the notebook in which he had written up the account of his north Italian tour of 1714 he now proudly made a brief entry as follows:

> The 12th day of January 1733/4 the King and Queen came to the Banqueting House at Whitehall, and came upon the scaffold forty foot high to see the paintings of Rubens that I had restor'd – his Majesty was pleas'd to tell me I had done them exceeding well – the Queen told me I not only deserv'd thanks from the King but to [sic] all lovers of painting.

This was praise indeed, coming from a monarch whose expressed dislike of 'boets and bainters' is well known, but although modern conservationists might not agree with his Majesty in this instance, Kent's work did at least help to preserve the ceiling for posterity.

During 1729–31 he also carried out important restorative work to Verrio's mural paintings at Windsor Castle, including the two main staircases and no less than fifteen ceilings, for a total payment of £1,200. Later years were to see the restoration of painting in the Chapel (1736), repainting of the decoration on the window side of St George's Hall (1746), and the repainting of the decoration on the cupola of the Guard Chamber, which had been obliterated during structural repairs (1747). At Hampton Court, on the other hand, his work seems to have been mainly original, and during 1732–5 he decorated the Queen's Staircase and the Guard Chamber (see p. 43).

The Keepership, however, was not Kent's first official appointment, for already in 1726 he had been granted the somewhat surprising post of Master Carpenter to the Office of Works. Despite its prosaic title this was one of the four key positions essential to the full political control of the Office of Works and its architectural activities; the posts of Surveyor, Deputy Surveyor and Master Mason were already held by Palladian nominees, and so Kent's appointment usefully completed the take-over. The duties of his post in no way interfered with his painting at Kensington or with private commissions, of which the most important at the time was the decoration of Houghton in Norfolk.

Houghton was brand new, begun in 1722 for Sir Robert Walpole (1676–

1745), George I's able First Minister. Although as a landowner Walpole conformed more nearly to the traditional Tory image of a hard-drinking, hard-hunting squire, as a politician his new house was bound to express his Whig beliefs and so he chose Colen Campbell as his architect. Campbell had already dedicated one of his designs in *Vitruvius Britannicus* to Walpole (vol. II, 1717); this, however, was not used, and instead Campbell produced one of the most interesting and influential houses of the entire Palladian movement, the plan or variations of it being repeated many times subsequently. A feature of the plan was the inclusion of four square towers, one at each corner of the house, and though these were later (*circa* 1729) capped by Gibbs with uncharacteristic domes, Campbell's designs (also published in *Vitruvius*) show that he himself had envisaged crowning them with roof pavilions, as used by Inigo Jones at Wilton House. In fact it is Jones and not Palladio whose influence is most clearly sensed at Houghton, where amongst other Jonesian touches the 40-ft cubic entrance hall is a deliberate echo of the hall at the Queen's House, Greenwich.

It might be thought that Kent, placed as he was in or about 1725, was the natural choice as chief decorator at Houghton. However, Horace Walpole asserts that his father Sir Robert was 'persuaded' to employ Kent, which suggests some discreet pressure from the Burlington group. Horace goes further and states that because Kent's colouring was so bad – 'more raw and undetermined than that of the most errant journeyman to the profession' – Sir Robert deliberately restricted him to *grisaille*.[22] It is true that the decorations at Houghton are mainly in the mosaic manner with much simulated sculptural and foliated ornament on gold backgrounds, and that the staircase is in the monochrome architectural style used on the greater part of the Kensington staircase, which dates from the same period. There is nevertheless quite a lot of restrained colour at Houghton, such as the green, pink and white of the scroll-work in the ceiling of the White Drawing Room, to say nothing of a painting on the Saloon ceiling of Phaeton driving the chariot of Apollo. In addition to these two ceilings and the staircase walls, Kent also decorated the ceilings of the Marble Parlour (Dining Room) and the State Bedroom, the latter with a *grisaille* painting of Aurora. Although in this last instance Horace Walpole was perhaps correct in stating that restraints were placed on Kent in the matter of colouring, he seems like so many others to have missed the essential fact that Kent's mosaics and grotesques were part of a whole new decorative canon, not a second-best alternative forced upon an artist unskilled in the older Baroque manner.

Kent's work at Houghton was probably antedated by the commission to decorate the entrance hall at Ditchley Park, Oxfordshire, for in 1726 he was paid £250 for painting the ceiling there. His employer was the Earl of Lichfield, for whom James Gibbs had recently rebuilt Ditchley in a plain but imposing manner. For the ceiling Kent provided a competent *Assembly of the Gods* contained within a heavy oval gilt frame; in addition he provided for the walls two large canvases depicting scenes from the *Aeneid*. Almost certainly he designed the opulent frames for the latter, each with a heavily moulded egg-and-dart border surmounted by a bay leaf swag, in the centre of which is a bracket supporting a bust of a literary *alumnus*. The motif of bust, bracket and swag is repeated as a sequence in the hall, not merely over the two paintings; this, plus the general sense of unity, the Jonesian quality of the doorcases and chimney-piece and their close resemblance to corresponding ones at Houghton, makes it very probable that Kent was the originator of the entire decorative scheme. If so, he gained experience which was very soon to be of great value to him at Houghton.

A further most interesting parallel occurs at Ditchley; this concerns the figures modelled on the pediments of three of the principal doorways in the hall. The figures represent Poetry, Music, Geography, Astronomy, Geometry and Sculpture, and both in appearance and attributes they very closely resemble similar figures over the doorways of the central hall at Mereworth Castle, the imitation of Palladio's Villa Rotonda at Vicenza which Campbell had built in 1723 near Tonbridge in Kent. This similarity can hardly be a coincidence, but should rather be taken as evidence of the impact of Mereworth and its interiors on Kent – something which seems all too often to have been ignored.

Meanwhile the dispute with Sir James Thornhill continued unabated. Whilst Kent was working at Kensington, *circa* 1727, Thornhill discovered that the new decorations demanded the painting and gilding of panelling and cornices. This was a new departure; formerly panelling had been stained, grained and varnished, so that, for example, plain deal could be made to look like walnut or even marble – a typical Baroque trick. It had not normally been painted, and gilding was only used on occasion to pick out some of the architectural features. Wholesale painting and gilding was now to be carried out at Kensington by an underling of Kent's named Howard. What irritated Thornhill was not so much the scheme itself as the fact that gilding in the various royal palaces was supposedly the monopoly (and no doubt a profitable one) of the Sergeant Painter. 'I cannot help thinking it is a great encroachment on the office, as well as on my patent', he wrote to the Office of Works in injured tones. This time he seems to have succeeded, for the order to Howard was cancelled. Yet in other respects ill fortune continued to dog his footsteps. There exists a manuscript of about 1730 in which Thornhill petitions George II for money owing to him, and which contains the following affecting if ungrammatical paragraph:

As he succeeded Sigr. Verrio as History Painter to his late Majesty, by warrant under his Grace the Duke of Newcastle, and a fresh warrant to serve his present Majesty by his present Majesty's particular order; entitled to the same advantages as his predecessor had, which was 200L per an.: being the same as the King's Face Painter enjoys etc. Yet instead of ever receiving one shilling, has been disgrac'd and supplanted in his royal Majesty's favour and business by the overbearing power of the late Vice Chamberlain Coke and the present Earl of Burlin–n, by obtaining signs manual for others, to the great detriment of your Petitioner, not only in painting for the King, but in all other business both public and private.[23]

The identity of the 'others' is plain. If it is true that Thornhill really had been promised the post of History Painter, then he had yet another legitimate grievance against Kent. As usual, however, the opposition was too strong for him, so that in the early 1730s we find Vertue declaring that Thornhill 'has been long unemployed even in his own way of history painting' (though here Vertue continues to cite Thornhill's aspirations to architecture as the chief reason for his downfall).[24]

There were others at this time, of considerably less standing than Thornhill, who also believed that they had genuine grievances against Burlington and Kent. Vertue tells us that Lewis Goupy, who had travelled in Italy with Burlington on the latter's first tour, eventually returned home (after a probable second visit to Italy), 'expecting to be caressed and much valued, having also a genius to paint histories as well as portraiture'. Instead he found 'Mr. Kent . . . who so far engrossed his Lordship's favours – by merit or cunning – which dislodged Mr. Goupy.'[25] The disappointed artist ended his days in 1747 as a drawing master. Another painter, Henry Trench, apparently knew Kent in Rome and met Burlington there; he too had been a prizewinner at the Accademia di S. Luca, had studied with Chiari, and in comparison with Kent was 'looked upon to be the better painter of the two by much'.[26] Yet he made no headway when he visited England in 1722–3 except for a single small commission executed for Sir Thomas Hewett and now lost. Dispirited, he returned to Italy, was back in England again in 1725 and died the following year. The clue to this non-career perhaps lies in Vertue's revelation that Trench, keenly feeling that Burlington was misguided in preferring Kent to Trench himself, at some time 'took an occasion to write an expostulatory letter to this nobleman setting forth the difference of merit on his side more than Kent's – but this had no other effect but only, as sometimes Lord Burlington would read it to Kent, by way of mortification – and mirth.'[27] We need not assume that Kent and Burlington went out of their way to spoil Trench's chances. They simply refused to take him seriously – which was another method of achieving the same result. Another possible explanation for Trench's failure to make his mark is that he was naturally lazy. Writing to Massingberd on 8 June 1718 Kent says that he and Giacomo Mariari are keen 'to hear how Mr. Trench succeeds in his paintings, for he has not done one picture here.'[28]

Ridicule, however, is a two-edged sword, and both Burlington and Kent experienced its sharpness, especially at the hands of William Hogarth (1697–1764). Soon after Kent returned to England, he joined an artists' Academy set up in 1720 by the painters John Vanderbank and Louis Chéron in St

[59]

Martin's Lane. Another early entrant to this school was Hogarth, recently embarked on a career as an engraver in his own right having failed to complete a seven-year apprenticeship to a silver-engraver.[29] Almost certainly he met Kent at the Academy, but though we have no record of their acquaintanceship it is unlikely to have been cordial, for Hogarth's notorious mistrust of foreign art and artists extended also to those who allowed themselves to become unduly influenced by such things. His attitude towards Kent and Burlington became abundantly clear in February 1723/4 when he published his satirical engraving *Masquerades and Operas* (also sometimes known as *The Taste of the Town*). This was primarily an attack on debased standards and foreign influences in the theatre, especially the craze for Italian opera, of which Burlington was a powerful patron. However, in the background Hogarth introduces a view of the main gateway of Burlington House; on the apex of its pediment (inscribed 'Academy of Arts') stands a figure labelled 'KNT', posing like a Roman emperor though with palette and brush in hand, while two reclining figures named respectively 'MIel ANGELO' and 'RAPHAEL URB[ino]' gaze up at it adoringly. Before the gate stand three gentlemen, one of whom is very probably intended to represent Burlington himself. Hogarth thus clearly indicated his contempt for those who, he felt, had been responsible for introducing false values into the nation's artistic life. A similar though later print entitled *Taste, or Burlington Gate* (1731) is better known, but cannot be positively said to be by Hogarth, though often ascribed to him. Doubts about its authorship cannot have done much to console either Kent or Burlington, who here saw themselves lampooned even more tellingly and unmistakably, together with the Duke of Chandos and Alexander Pope, both of whom were closely associated with the Burlington group.

Commentators on Hogarth and his attitude towards Kent and Burlington often make the point that he was Thornhill's son-in-law and infer (sometimes even state) that he took up the cudgels in a spirit of filial partisanship. Certainly he was ever ready to campaign against injustice in all its forms, and equally certainly he greatly admired and respected Thornhill. However, *Masquerades and Operas* appeared five years before the famous elopement and marriage with Thornhill's daughter Jane on 23 March 1729, while, as we have already noted, *Taste, or Burlington Gate* is perhaps not by Hogarth at all. Furthermore it was not until 1724 that Hogarth actually joined Thornhill's own Academy and so probably first came into close and regular contact with his future father-in-law. *Masquerades and Operas* must therefore be seen as stemming purely from Hogarth's own views and opinions, uninfluenced by consideration for Thornhill.

In 1725 Hogarth made an even more direct attack on Kent, in the form of a print satirizing an altarpiece which Kent had painted for the church of St Clement Danes. The painting showed a celestial choir and instrumentalists and was a disaster, for two main reasons. In the first place, it seems quite simply to have been a bad picture, revealing only too well just those deficiencies in Kent's technique which were not so baldly exposed in his decorative painting. In the second place, some of the musical angels were thought to bear an unacceptable likeness to the Princess Sobieski, wife of James the Old Pretender, and her children. On these grounds the painting was taken down and bundled away into the vestry during 1725. On 5 October Hogarth added insult to injury by publishing his print. This is basically a copy of the painting itself, though Hogarth probably exaggerates Kent's faulty figure drawing. The satire however – as so often with Hogarth – lies not so much in the picture as in the long caption beneath it; this states that the painting has been removed 'to prevent disputes and laying of wagers among the parishioners about the artist's meaning in it' and then goes on to identify different areas of the composition such as 'E/An angel tuning an harp; F/The inside of his leg but whether right or left is yet undiscover'd; G/A hand playing on a lute; H/The other leg judiciously omitted to make room for the harp.' Kent never forgot this, as Hogarth was later to discover to his cost. Ironically it is mainly through the medium of Hogarth's print that we today know what the painting looked like, since it was destroyed during the Second World War. There is an unflattering tradition that for some years it used to be brought out periodically, not for liturgical use but to adorn the music room of the Crown and Anchor, a public house in the Strand.[30]

In 1724 Kent was engaged to paint another altarpiece, this time for St George's church, Hanover Square. Although both paintings seem to have been produced at about the same time, it would seem probable that the St George's one came first, for had the church authorities in Hanover Square heard about the furore raging at St Clement Danes they might well have withdrawn the commission. As it was, the altarpiece was finished, apparently gave no cause for offence or dissatisfaction, and is still *in situ* in the church. The subject is the Last Supper and in its general design the painting bears some resemblance to Poussin's treatment of the same subject in a canvas originally in the royal chapel at St Germain-en-Laye and now in the Louvre. Kent probably knew it from an engraving which was made in 1673. Considerable re-touching has somewhat obscured the merits and/or defects of his own picture, which is in any case now overshadowed by a magnificent seventeenth-century east window of Flemish stained glass put in during the nineteenth century. Nevertheless it can confidently be said to be the best of Kent's tiny output of religious paintings (the 'small *Madonna*', *St Peter* and *Christ Bearing His Cross* which remained in his studio after his death are lost), and amongst the best of his non-mural paintings as a whole. For a long time Kent's authorship was forgotten and the picture ascribed to Thornhill – a situation which would have pleased neither artist.

Even this altarpiece figured in the running battle between Kent and Thornhill. In 1728 Thornhill instituted legal proceedings against a patron, Benjamin

Styles of Moor Park in Hertfordshire, on the grounds that he had not been paid the £3,500 owing to him for decorating the house. According to Vertue, 'Mr. Styles refus'd to pay, alleging . . . that Sir James had not done his part with care nor finished his works as he was capable to do. . . . A strong party at Court being all of the Office of Works, Mr. Kent's friends and interest, no doubt endeavoured to foment this difference and slur the reputation of Sir James, tho' it was the true opinion of the several artists, judges [i.e. expert witnesses including the painters Dahl and Richardson] in this case, that Sir James had excelled in this work, particularly as he designed it to rival all his competitors.'[31] The case was settled out of court just before it was due to begin; however, as part of the agreement Thornhill insisted that for each of eight paintings of the Heroic Virtues he should receive the same price 'as Mr. Kent had for that altarpiece at St George's Church, Hanover Square. . . . Sir James is resolved to take no less.' No records exist of the transaction between Kent and the authorities of St George's, but it is relevant that Hogarth's caption to the parody on the St Clement Danes altarpiece asserts that the parish paid £60 for it.

There now briefly reappears upon the scene the half-forgotten and faintly pathetic figure of Kent's erstwhile patron Burrell Massingberd. In the summer of 1724 he wrote from Lincolnshire to suggest that Kent should paint an altarpiece on the subject of the Last Supper for the church at Boston. Kent replied with some enthusiasm on 23 July 1724: 'I am oblig'd to you for recommending me to paint that altar piece you speak of, it's a subject I like and I am engaged to paint the same subject for the new church in George Street near Hanover Square.' He went on to state that the dimensions he had been given would necessitate a picture 10 ft high by 14 ft long, and that his price would be £300, plus another £100 for 'the architect part in wainscot and gilding'. A month later he wrote again, reducing his price to £250, and enclosing a design for the frame. He was not to know that on the very next day (21 August) a certain John Browne of Boston – perhaps a churchwarden – was to write to Massingberd with some depressing news. 'The subscribers met last Tuesday, at the Vestry, to consult about the enterprise. I show[ed] them your letter. They all thought Mr. Kent's proposal too much money, and like true Englishmen if they don't strike while the iron is hot grow very cool upon the matter. So [I] verily believe there will be nothing more done in it.' He was quite right – nothing was, and the church remained without its altarpiece.

Perhaps this episode finally convinced Massingberd that Kent no longer needed him. There is no cause to doubt the sincerity of Kent's original intentions, as expressed for instance in a letter of 16 August 1718: 'I hope to keep my resolution for next Spring without fail and then if it please God to see my most oblig'd friends, and shall accept of your kind offer to come to you before I go to make myself known in London.' Fate, however, had other plans for him, as he explained on 3 June 1720: 'I was in hopes to see you before this, but I have had the good fortune to be introduced into good business which I know you'll [be] amongst the rest of my good friends to be glad to hear.' He is, he tells his patron, at present engaged 'upon the greatest works in England [for] Lord Burlington, Lord Duke Chandos and Lord Castlemain; until I have fixed these work[s] a little I am afraid [I] shall not be at liberty to come into the North, but wish to see you and if you should make a step to Sir John's I would not fail to meet you.'[32] He was still making excuses in 1724, for the first of the two letters about the Boston altarpiece begins: 'Dear Sir; I thought to have call'd on you in my way with Ld.Burlington to Launsburry [Londesborough] but I found so much difficulty in getting to you and I being a bad horseman that at this opportunity it will be impossible.'

This apparent reluctance on the part of Kent to put himself out for Massingberd, despite all the protestations of gratitude with which – after his initial shortcomings – he had liberally larded his letters from Rome, must have been bitter medicine for his patron, forced to look on whilst others richer and more powerful than he helped his protégé towards fame and fortune. It will not have escaped Massingberd's notice that although Kent was willing to journey to Buckinghamshire and even as far afield as his native Yorkshire he was evidently not willing to make that extra effort which would have taken him into Lincolnshire. No doubt they met in London on one or more occasions, but that would not have been the same.

It is easy to charge Kent with ingratitude, but again it must be stressed that we need not doubt his good intentions; he was young, there would be plenty of time to go up to Lincolnshire, and meanwhile a sensible artist with a career to make took good care to please powerful patrons who could make or break that career. When, a few years later in 1729, Massingberd died at a comparatively early age (predeceased by Sir John Chester in 1726), it is to be hoped that Kent felt genuine sorrow at the passing of one whose material aid and enthusiastic support and encouragement had been of such vital importance to him during the long years in Italy.

CHAPTER FOUR
THE SIGNOR AND HIS FRIENDS

Once comfortably installed at Burlington House after his return from Italy, it cannot have taken William Kent long to appreciate just how wide and varied was the circle of Lord Burlington's friends, a circle to which he himself was now fully admitted. Some of its members had at one time or another been guests like himself under Burlington's roof and enjoyed the Earl's hospitality as well as his patronage. Foremost amongst them was George Frederick Handel (1685–1759), who had been made welcome at Burlington House almost since the time of his first arrival in England in 1710 as an already celebrated young composer in the service of the Elector of Hanover (he was then 25). Handel returned to Hanover in the summer of 1711, but by autumn 1712 he was back again in London, where life was so congenial and the prospects for employment so good that he simply did not bother to leave. 10 January 1713 saw the production of his opera *Teseo*, which had been astutely dedicated to the 18-year-old Lord Burlington, and it was not long before Handel became not merely an honoured and frequent visitor to Burlington House but was actually given rooms there which he used more or less permanently until 1718. A potentially awkward situation arose in 1714 when, following the death of Queen Anne, Handel's deserted and aggrieved employer the Elector of Hanover ascended the English throne as George I; the patronage of Burlington was perhaps additionally valuable in helping to smooth the errant composer's return to royal favour, though this was not achieved until the following year.

It is sometimes suggested that Handel and Kent were both living at Burlington House at the same time. This is not so. Although Handel doubtless continued to pay frequent visits there, he had moved his main base to Canons in 1717, taking up an offer from James Brydges, Earl of Caernarvon and subsequently Duke of Chandos, to become his director of music. At Canons Handel wrote most of his instrumental *concerti grossi*, the Chandos Anthems, and the first of his English oratorios, later known as *Esther*. But when Kent arrived on the scene he will have found that much of London's musical gossip revolved round the newly formed Royal Academy of Music and its preparations to launch a new season of Italian opera. This body was not a training school for young musicians, as is its modern namesake, but a profit-making company which aimed to promote financially successful musical ventures, primarily in the field of opera (public orchestral concerts in the modern sense being at that time virtually unknown). Its chief patron was the King, and Burlington was prominent amongst the directors, who between them raised a fund of £50,000. A powerful stimulus was doubtless the South Sea Bubble mania then raging.

When Kent arrived back in England Handel had not long returned from a talent-spotting expedition to Germany, where at the Electoral court of Dresden he had succeeded in signing up for the Royal Academy several celebrated singers including the soprano Margherita Durastanti and the *castrato* Francesco Bernardi Senesino. A letter from Handel written – in French – to Lord Burlington from Dresden on 15 July 1719, announcing his success in securing the singers, is still preserved at Chatsworth. With stars of this calibre in its musical firmament the Royal Academy could not but prosper, and the whirlwind speed of Lord Burlington's second visit to Italy in 1719, whence he returned with Kent in tow, is at least partly attributable to his anxiety not to be away from home for too long while such momentous events were in train.

At this point we encounter a slight mystery. Writing to Massingberd on 30 January 1719/20 Kent (it will be recalled) says that he finds it too cold to go out, except that 'twice a week I go to the Operas where I am highly entertain'd', which could be taken as a compliment to Handel and the Academy. The snag is that no operas were performed in London between the summer of 1717 and 2 April 1720, when *Numitor* by the Venetian composer Giovanni Porta was the Academy's first presentation (to be superseded after five performances by Handel's brand-new opera *Radamisto*). Whatever Kent saw, therefore, it cannot have been opera. During the winter of 1719/20 only two theatres were open in London, those of Drury Lane and Lincoln's Inn Fields, and these two between them presented a varied diet of plays ranging from mutilated Shakespeare (*The Taming of the Shrew; or Sawney the Scot*: Lincoln's Inn, 21 December) to the still-living Vanbrugh's *The Relapse* (Drury Lane: 3 December, 29 January) interspersed with more ephemeral pieces. A curious feature of almost all these performances was the interpolation of song and dance acts, foreshadowing the later music hall or vaudeville, while on one occasion during December a rare vocal and instrumental concert replaced the drama at Lincoln's Inn. It can only have been these tenuous links which prompted Kent to use the misleading term 'Operas' when what he really meant was plays.

At first sight it might seem that in any case he was not particularly musical. Years later, in January 1738/9, he attended a performance of Handel's latest oratorio *Saul*, and wrote of it to Burlington in the following terms: 'The oratorios go on well, I was there with a handsome widow, fat, which has given much diversion to the looker-on and we was in the box you used to have. There is a pretty concerto in the oratorio; there is some stops in the harpsichord that are little bells – I though it had been some squirrels in a cage.'[1] These chatty comments, however amusing, tell us nothing whatever about the musical and/or emotive qualities of what is generally acknowledged to be one of Handel's finest works. The adjective 'pretty' seems misapplied to what was probably an organ concerto performed by Handel himself, according to his normal practice, as an interlude during the oratorio, while Kent's reference to the 'little bells' apparently betrays that kind of ear which is easily titillated by sudden and unexpected splashes of orchestral colour though remaining less receptive to actual musical content.[2]

In fact, however, it seems clear that Kent's usual flippant style concealed a genuine love of music. His early interest in opera is signalled in a letter to Massingberd of 26 January 1713/14 in which he announces that in Rome 'the operas are begun', and it surfaces again in a letter to Lord Burlington of 16 November 1732 at Chatsworth: 'My Lord [Bruce] for his good Lady has taken the box next to yours in the Opera; the new woman [Celeste Gismondi] I like extremely, though it's not the fashion to like her nor the present opera.'

In a later letter to Massingberd (18 January 1717/18) Kent makes an individual if typically confused comparison between French and Italian music and painting which deserves quotation: 'I am inform'd that in England we are inclined a little to the French gusto in painting but can assure you I never design to follow it – for if they understood painting as well as they do music and consider the difference between the French music and the Italian, I can assure them there is just the same in painting; as the French music is most ungrateful to the ears, so is their painting to the eyes.'

An interest in the organ and its music is perhaps discernible in a brief note, made during the 1714 tour with Thomas Coke, that in the cathedral of Santa Giustina at Padua 'the organ is counted famous for a variety of stops.' However, he does not mention that on this occasion the party were treated to an organ recital, apparently arranged for their benefit, for the account book shows that payments were made both to the organist and to 'the man that blew the bellows'. Later on Kent himself was actually to design an organ case (see p. 116).

While the full extent of Kent's musical knowledge must remain problematical, it is certain that Handel knew a good deal about painting; he collected pictures, and eventually owned two Rembrandts. In 1724 or earlier he left the shelter of Canons and set up his own establishment at 57 Lower Brook Street (now 25 Brook Street), where he lived for the rest of his life. Nearby in newly built Hanover Square a conveniently handy parish church, St George's, was in building (architect John James) and was completed early in 1725; Handel became a regular worshipper there. It is therefore tempting to wonder what he, with his connoisseur's eye, made of Kent's *Last Supper* altarpiece.

The waning popularity of Italian opera received its most severe blow on 29 January 1728, for this date saw the first performance of John Gay's clever parody *The Beggar's Opera*, in which native English was used instead of the Italian language, lofty sentiments and improbable plots were replaced by a low-life romp involving robbery and double-dealing, gods and goddesses gave place to criminals and whores, and tuneful traditional airs were substituted for more high-flown music. Although the Royal Academy of Music was wound up in June 1728, Handel struggled on for another thirteen years, through a variety of financial crises and in the face of ever-growing public indifference to opera. But eventually he abandoned this form of his art altogether and concentrated mainly on oratorio, to which he had been giving increasing attention for some time.

Seemingly Handel bore no ill-will towards John Gay (1685–1732), despite the damage to his reputation done – no doubt innocently enough – by the poet, who was also originally a member of the Burlington circle. Before Handel went to Canons he and Gay had been in amicable residence together at Burlington House – the old house, that is, before Colen Campbell remodelled it – as Gay records in the first edition of his *Trivia* (*circa* 1715):

> Yet Burlington's fair palace still remains;
> Beauty within, without proportion reigns. . . .
> There Hendel[3] strikes the strings, the melting strain
> Transports the soul and thrills through every vein;
> There oft I enter (but with cleaner shoes)
> For Burlington's belov'd by ev'ry Muse.

When Kent first came to Burlington House Handel, as we have seen, was no longer actually living there. Gay, however, certainly was, though intermittently. Improvident, easily offended and quick to lose heart, he was something of a trial to the several generous patrons who supported him throughout his career and of whom Burlington was amongst the earliest. Alexander Pope described him as 'quite a natural man, wholly without art or design, and spoke just what he thought, and as he thought it.'[4] In this respect at least his character must have been similar to that of Kent (they also shared an interest in food). The poem 'A Journey to Exeter' is a descriptive travelogue written in 1715; this was a holiday trip funded by Burlington, to whom Gay rightly dedicated the poem and whom he addressed in the opening lines: 'While you, my Lord, bid stately piles ascend . . . I journey far.' Sometimes the Burlingtons took Gay with them on their own travels; thus we find Pope writing to Gay (13 July 1723) that he has been told 'that both Lady Burlington and yourself were immediately to return from Tunbridge, and that my Lord was gone to bring you back.'[5]

As it happened, it was probably through his name being linked with that

10 Frontispiece to Gay's *Poems*, 1720. The circular Classical temple (here rendered oval by Kent's imperfect technique) probably derives from the ancient Temple of the Sibyl at Tivoli

of Gay that William Kent first became known to a wider public. In 1720 Tonson and Lintot published in two volumes the first collected edition of Gay's works, Burlington subscribing to fifty copies. The engraved frontispiece was by Kent, making his bow as a book illustrator. He had learned the skills of etching and engraving whilst in Italy, though such examples of his printmaking as have survived from those years eschew imagination and are copies of paintings by artists such as Maratta. A few manuscript notes on the technique of etching are to be found towards the back of the journal which he kept whilst touring north Italy in 1714. Theory seems here to have shortly preceded practice, for in a letter of 7 January 1714/15 (possibly to Samuel Gale) John Talman announces, 'I send you . . . the first fruits of Mr. Kent's etching, the distich I got for him from a prelate, so you see we are at work.' (A distich is a two-line verse: it often serves as the caption to a print and is engraved with it.) The frontispiece to Gay's *Poems on Several Occasions* (Plate 10) is unremarkable but seems at least to be of Kent's own invention, representing an Arcadian scene complete with a Classical temple (see p. 203), shepherd and shepherdess, and cherubs. His inspiration here was the first poem in the collection, 'Rural Sports', written in imitation of Virgil. Two other engravings which accompany the poems, though not signed, are undoubtedly his work. One, an illustration to 'The Shepherd's Week', depicts contemporary country girls and lads disporting themselves in an atmosphere of innocent bucolic enjoyment, and again reflects the general tone of the poem. The other engraving prefaces Gay's 'Dione: A Pastoral Tragedy' and is an unremarkable composition of *putti*, Classical fragments including an altar, and naturalism in the shape of a tree and a vague mountainous background. Despite Kent's practical experience in the medium (admittedly not extensive, it would seem), his technique in these engravings is hesitant and unsure, and it is noteworthy that after the *Poems* he never again signed a print 'W.Kent inv.et fecit', preferring to leave the actual engraving to others.

However, what really must have made the town sit up and take notice of Kent was not these rather feeble engravings but the extraordinary outburst of extravagant praise with which Gay greeted him in volume II of the *Poems* (in Epistle IV, dedicated to 'The Right Honourable Paul Methuen, Esq.'). Gay's theme is that true worth is not appreciated in its native surroundings. For this he had of course the highest Scriptural authority ('A prophet is not without honour . . .'), but to choose William Kent as his example could be said to be unfortunate.

> Why didst thou, Kent, forego thy native land,
> To emulate in picture Raphael's hand?
> Think'st thou for this to raise thy name at home?
> Go back, adorn the palaces of Rome;
> There on the walls let thy just labours shine,

And Raphael live again in thy design.
Yet stay a while; call all thy genius forth,
For Burlington unbiased knows thy worth;
His judgement in thy master-strokes can trace
Titian's strong fire and Guido's softer grace;
But oh, consider, ere thy works appear,
Canst thou unhurt the tongue of envy hear?
Censure will blame, her breath was ever spent
To blast the laurels of the eminent.

In giving this wildly inflated view of Kent's artistic powers Gay was obviously relaying the views of others, for during the few months that elapsed between Kent's arrival and the publication of the poems Gay himself can have had little time to form a balanced view of the painter's abilities – even supposing he was competent to do so. The flattering reference to Burlington, as being the only connoisseur with enough acumen to detect Kent's genius, nevertheless also suggests that there were others who felt less certain of it; furthermore the entire passage was a needless provocation to those already disposed to regard Kent as an upstart and a charlatan, by no means eminent and certainly not laurel-crowned. It played directly into the hands of such critics and must surely have given rise to much satirical laughter at the expense of both Kent and Burlington. One can imagine Thornhill and Hogarth later savouring its ironies together as their vendetta against Kent intensified.

In 1724 Kent is said to have designed some scenery for one of Gay's dramatic works, *The Captives*, performed at Drury Lane in January of that year.[6] More permanent were the illustrations to Gay's *Fables* (volume I). On 22 November 1726 Gay wrote to his friend Brigadier-General James Dormer a letter containing what he called some 'little trifling news of the town' and included the following: 'I am about to publish a collection of Fables entirely of my own invention to be dedicated to Prince William, they consist of fifty, and I am oblig'd to Mr. Kent and Wootton for the design of the plates.'[7] John Wootton's illustrations to the *Fables* are concerned on the whole with animal subjects (in which, together with landscapes, he specialized), whilst those of Kent deal mostly with the human aspect. This is perhaps unfortunate, for there can be no denying that Kent's figure drawing on occasion arouses in the viewer a sense of unease; attitudes look stiff, proportions wrong. It is tempting but misguided to take into charitable account the mental adjustment required of an artist used to working on a large scale and in distorted perspectives who is suddenly compelled to produce drawings of ordinary size and content. More relevant is Gay's comment, in the same letter to Dormer, that 'the work is . . . delay'd only upon account of the gravers, who are neither very good or expeditious.'

Nevertheless Kent's illustrations are really rather charming, and we may readily agree with Horace Walpole's opinion that 'such of the drawings as he designed for Gay's *Fables* have some truth and nature.'[8] In 'The Mother, the Nurse and the Fairy' (no. III), the original drawing for which is in the British Museum, Kent evokes a scene of almost cosy domesticity, in which the stern Palladian setting is considerably softened by the solicitous attitudes of the two women bending over the infant in its cradle (Plate 11). From personal experience Kent knew all about 'The Painter who Pleased Nobody and Everybody' (no. XVIII), and has perhaps put something of himself and his studio into the accompanying illustration (Plate 13). Now and then there are examples of useful observations (a country barn in 'Pythagoras and the Countryman', no. XXXVI – original also in the British Museum – the interior of a theatre in 'The Two Monkeys', no. XL), and his lively imagination seized gleefully upon such subjects as enabled him to indulge his emergent taste for the bizarre and the unexpected ('The Elephant and the Bookseller', no. X, 'The Universal Apparition', no. XXXI). One of the most interesting illustrations is the one which accompanies the fable of 'The Butterfly and the Snail' (no. XXIV). Kent's picture shows a formal garden with trees, a pleached alleyway, a fountain, and a couple of urns with a gardener leaning against one of them, whilst in the background is a two-storeyed building surmounted by a domed lantern and very closely resembling the Casina in the grounds of Lord Burlington's house at Chiswick (Plate 14). The Casina – also called the Bagnio – was a sort of outdoor banqueting house, and though now long vanished it appears as Plate 26 in volume III (1725) of *Vitruvius Britannicus*, where it is described by Campbell as 'The first essay of his Lordship's happy invention, anno 1717'. It was thus considerably more important architecturally than its function as a garden folly would otherwise have warranted, and Kent's inclusion of it in this little illustration was probably both a measure of its impact upon his artistic consciousness and a delicate compliment to his patron. As a building the Casina was not particularly original, revealing clearly the combined influence of Inigo Jones and Colen Campbell, but it doubtless enjoyed the prestige accorded to all 'firsts' and indeed appears again in the background of a portrait of Burlington painted about 1720 and attributed to Jonathan Richardson (National Portrait Gallery, Plate 46).

In the poem 'A Journey to Exeter' Gay had sketched a word-picture of Burlington enjoying an idyllic rural seclusion at Chiswick, 'Where Pope unloads the boughs within his reach/The purple vine, blue plumb, and blushing peach.' These two lines have a certain poignancy, for, as his friends well knew, the branches of most ordinary trees were beyond rather than within the reach of Alexander Pope (1688–1744), who had been noticeably deformed by sickness at the age of 12 and whose health since then had seldom been better than poor. But Pope's physical frailty was compensated for by agility of mind, poetic genius, and a depth of Classical learning that made him an indispensable theorist to the Palladian group. He and his parents had been taken under Burlington's wing in 1716, when they moved from Binfield near

11–14 Four illustrations to Gay's *Fables*, 1727:

11 'The Mother, the Nurse and the Fairy', no. III.

12 'The Elephant and the Bookseller', no. X.

[72]

13 'The Painter who Pleased Nobody and Everybody', no. XVIII.

14 'The Butterfly and the Snail', no. XXIV. The building is Burlington's Casina at Chiswick

Windsor to Chiswick, and, although very proud, Pope was not above accepting financial help from Burlington which in 1719 enabled him to purchase the lease of a Twickenham house ever afterwards known as 'Pope's Villa'. Thus Pope never actually lived at Burlington House; he was, however, a frequent visitor and struck up lasting friendships with Gay, with Handel (whose sagging reputation he later helped to restore with a six-line panegyric in the fourth volume of his *Dunciad*, 1728) and, of course, with Kent.

When Kent appeared on the scene Pope had already published *The Rape of the Lock* (1712) and most of his translation of Homer's *Iliad* (1715–20), described unkindly by his contemporary Richard Bentley as 'a pretty poem, but not Homer'. Although the quality of his work may originally have attracted the patronage of Burlington, a rapport was quickly established between them which was sustained until Pope's death in 1744. On Burlington's arrival at Dover in 1715 after his first Grand Tour, a number of gifts which he had brought back for Pope were confiscated by the Customs and only released after the payment of a bribe. Pope was an indefatigable correspondent, and a constant stream of notes and letters flowed from Twickenham to Chiswick, Burlington House or Londesborough on all subjects ranging from politics to the gift to Burlington of a puppy born to Pope's Great Dane, Bounce ('Be pleas'd to let the bearer know if you would have the puppy, in which case I will bring it with me and be its foster-father' – undated letter at Chatsworth). Pope's tone throughout is one of genuine respect and affection for Burlington. 'Pray make my sincere compliments to Lord Burlington, whom I have long known to have more mind to be a good and honourable man than almost any one of his rank', he writes to Gay (13 July 1723).[9] Burlington himself was not a good correspondent ('Remember this is the third letter I have write', notes Kent reprovingly to his patron on one occasion); he seems to have disliked letter-writing and his letters usually contain some excuse for not having written sooner or for brevity. But the tone in them towards Pope is warm, and undoubtedly reflects Burlington's very high regard for him. 'From one that I love and value as I do you, even rebukes are pleasant', writes the Earl (6 February 1738/9) in response to yet another gentle plaint from Pope that his letters remain unanswered, and concludes: 'I long to see you, and am with the most sincere affection, my dear Pope, ever yours Burlington.'[10] Words such as these surely go deeper than the empty platitudes of the age. Any distancing between poet and patrician was due not to differences in their social status but to the wider range of Burlington's responsibilities, both private and public. No doubt Pope understood this, though there are occasional hints in his letters that he sometimes felt just a little neglected – 'My Lord: It's so long since I've had the honour and pleasure of seeing you, tho' I have twice or thrice seen your flying horses and chariots pass by my door, that I've some cause to fear you have quite forgot a man who (I faithfully assure your Lordship) can never forget to be yours. ... I am much disappointed to miss you so often, as yesterday, and again this afternoon. No man is more your Lordship's faithful servant' (two undated letters).[11]

It was greatly to Burlington's credit that he numbered amongst his closest friends not only fellow Whigs but (after 1714) Tory sympathizers, including the politically tainted Henry St John, first Viscount Bolingbroke, who having been one of Queen Anne's most powerful ministers had been abruptly tumbled from office on her death. Moreover Gay favoured the Tories, and so did Pope; the latter also had the additional disadvantage of being a professed Roman Catholic at a time when the faith was inevitably linked in the public mind with Jacobitism.

William Kent, having lived with Catholicism for nine years without adopting it, was probably less frightened of it than the majority of his countrymen. At all events he seems to have found Pope the most congenial of all Burlington's friends, and the admiration seems also to have been mutual. Invited to supply illustrations for Pope's edition of Homer's *Odyssey* (1725/6), Kent produced some of his most accomplished and interesting work in this field, mostly in the form of head- and tail-pieces, (Plates 15–19), the final one being a cameo-like portrait of Pope himself, in profile on a medallion supported by two typically Kentian *putti*. The engraver was Peter Fourdrinier who had arrived in this country from Amsterdam in 1720.

15, 16 Two head-pieces from Pope's edition of the *Odyssey*, 1725/6

17–19 Three tail-pieces from the *Odyssey*:

17 Vol. I, bk iv. Triton with sea-monster

18 Vol. II, bk vii. Fountain with mermaids and dolphins

19 Vol. V, bk xxiii, Trophy of armour and weapons

'Mr. Kent could tell you how often I talk'd of you, and wished for you';
Pope's aim here is to confirm his devotion to Burlington, to whom he is writing
(19 December 1798), but the words also suggest the frequency of his meetings
with Kent, which he himself confirms in another letter to the Earl: 'I go
frequently to him [Kent], not only thro' the affection I bear him, and the respect
I pay to his genius, but in good earnest to learn what I can, and as often as
I can, of yourself and my Lady' (28 November ?1736). Such meetings were
not necessarily decorous. A typically rambling, effervescent letter from Kent
to Burlington (27 January 1738/9) paints an unexpected but libellous picture
of the poet in his cups: 'Pope is very busy, last night came to me about eight
a-clock in liquor and would have more wine, which I gave him; you may
tell Mr. Bethel he's very sorry, so am I he's not well, but he lays it all [on]
his not taking a cup of red.'[12] On 28 November following Kent writes again

[77]

to his patron: 'My service to Mr. Bethel and tell him his friend Pope is the greatest glutton I know, he . . . dined with Mr. Murray and Lady Betty and was very drunk last Sunday night.'[13] These references to Pope's drunkenness were part of a standing joke amongst the group, for the delicate and sickly Pope was necessarily the most abstemious of men: Kent invented the episodes because he knew they would amuse Lord Burlington. (They did: the first letter – which also includes the reference to Handel's *Saul* – is endorsed firmly on the back, in Burlington's own hand, 'Mr. Kent's to be kept.') Pope's self-discipline in the matter of drinking was seemingly also imposed upon his guests, for it is said that he would place a single pint of liquor before two people, drink a couple of small glasses himself, and then retire saying politely, 'Gentlemen, I leave you to your wine.'

On the other hand we need not doubt that whenever and wherever Kent foregathered with his cronies, conviviality was the order of the day, to a greater or lesser degree. He himself, it seems, was no mean toper, and is described by Pope in a letter to Lady Burlington (September 1738) as being 'very umbrageous in his drink'.[14] We have Kent's own intriguing account of a supper party which he gave for a select company that included Pope and Lord Oxford. 'Not one drop of wine being left in the cellar when my Ld. went, I bought of Mr. Wright some excellent claret and Scotch sack and Cyprus Esquisito; I have had but one feast in my room since you went, but I can assure you, was drank fourteen bottles of wine in one setting and neither I nor company was sick or sorry for the next day', wrote the genial host to Lady Burlington (14 December 1738), and continued, 'but as all my feast[s] are generally talk[ed] of, it's diverted the gent[lemen] and other wits *abasto cose.*'[15] Obviously a Kentian dinner party was something of an occasion, as well as being an English manifestation of the kind of 'Bacchanal work' that Kent himself had reported from Rome in 1712.

Food as well as drink clearly played an important part in Kent's life. 'The doe you sent was extremely good, the more you send the better', he tells Burlington (27 January 1738/9), and one can almost see him patting his stomach with satisfaction as he writes.[16] 'I thank you for the salmon. Will you eat of it the day you come? And a mutton steak in the manner of that great master, Signior Kent?' (Pope to Burlington, undated).[17] Thanks to such good living a natural tendency to put on weight had resulted, by the time he reached middle age, in an undeniably stout figure. A portrait of Kent painted at Rome *circa* 1718 by Benedetto Luti (Plate 1) shows that the young man in his early thirties already had a pronounced double chin. By the time Bartholomew Dandridge produced his better-known portrait almost twenty years later, the double chin, heavy jowl and plump cheeks foreshadowed in Luti's painting had arrived with a vengeance (Plate 47).

Yet fat people are often said to be more contented and good-humoured than thin ones, and this was certainly true of Kent. His brand of bluff humour was

20 This canine suppliant sketched by Kent may have been a member of the animal-loving
Burlington household

not necessarily always appreciated by those who found themselves on the
receiving end of it, like the unfortunate lady in the following anecdote recoun-
ted by Horace Walpole; 'My Lady Townshend made me laugh t'other night
about your old acquaintance Miss Edwin. . . . My Lady says, she was forced
to have an issue made on one side of her head, for her eyes, and that Kent
advised her to have another on t'other side for symmetry.'[18] (But it is refreshing
to find that here Kent was also able to poke fun at one of the most sacred
canons of Palladianism.) His 'civil and obliging behaviour' (see p. 81) no
doubt enabled him to be on good terms with most people, but he seems also
to have inspired real affection, as well as being valued for the amusing garrulity
of which his letters can give us only a faint echo. 'The greatest news I have
to tell you is that the Signior is in perfect tranquility, enjoying his own being,
and is become a happy but plumper copy of General Dormer', writes Pope to
Burlington (27 November 1736), and refers in the next sentence to Kent's
'sweetness of manners'.[19] Fatness is also often equated with laziness, but
although Kent obviously enjoyed his creature comforts we need not in his case
take too seriously such phrases as 'that lazy mortal the Signor' (Burlington
to Pope, 6 February 1738/9); this was all part of the fun, and in fact Kent
must have worked with some dedication throughout most of his career. On

the other hand Vertue attributes his final illness partly to 'his high feeding and [mode of] life and much inaction', which suggests that at least in his last years he succumbed to temptations which he had formerly resisted, though perhaps not always successfully.

When or from whom he first acquired his nickname 'the Signor' (or 'Signior', as most of his friends – though not Burlington – spelt it) is unknown, but it stuck, and became a feature of the gentle fun and raillery which was constantly poked at him, and of which he was evidently a complaisant and good-natured butt (though giving as good as he got).[20] The choice of title was perhaps due less to his long sojourn in Italy *per se* than to a conjectural tendency to lard his conversation with anecdotes beginning 'When I was in Italy . . .' and to the habit of lapsing suddenly in his letters (and therefore probably in his speech) into Italian. 'My Lady Dorothy tells me I am to have a doe [sent down from Yorkshire]. If it should come, I shall make a *Fiesta di mangiare tutte in un giorno*' (letter to Lady Burlington, 14 December 1738; Kent seems to have been especially fond of venison).[21] A report to Burlington on the progress of work at Chiswick produced the following: 'Polly *con grand lavori di spalli* has done the stucco pavement and has *datto una sempli-ci-vernice* to some of the pictures; I desired he would let the rest alone' (10 November 1738).[22]

Chiswick is again the subject of the following passage in a letter of 27 January 1738/9: 'My Lord Lovell [the erstwhile Thomas Coke] desires his service to you, and this day goes to Chiswick with Marchese Sacchette; my Ld. told him Mich. Angelo was an Ignorante in archetr.; *come nostro Michll. Angelo – nove non ci niente che value.*'[23] On another occasion Kent introduces a more personal note; 'My Lord: I received yours, am sorry to hear you had so bad a cold, *io spero che la purgazione* has carried all off before this time.'[24] Nevertheless not all his Italianism was on this generally mundane level, for at some point he compiled a *Breve Compendio delle Metamorfosi di Ovido*, perhaps as an aid to learning the language. This manuscript summary of the famous *Metamorphoses* is not especially 'breve', consisting of 210 octavo pages, and it also poses a problem in that it does not seem to be in Kent's own handwriting; the script is noticeably neater and indeed finer than his. Nevertheless the title-page unequivocally proclaims it to be 'da Gulielmo Kent'. There is no date, although the watermark indicates that the paper is of Italian make, pre-1705.[25]

Kent was scarcely ensconced at Burlington House before Burlington announced his impending marriage, the news of which Kent then passed on in a letter to Burrell Massingberd (30 January 1720): 'Lord Burlington is going to be married to Lady Dorothy Savile, so I hope the *vertu*[26] will grow stronger in our house and architecture will flourish more.' Of some significance is (i) the reference to 'our house' indicating that he is already quite at home and feels himself one of the Burlington household, despite having been a regular part of it for less than two months; (ii) the reference to architecture at a time when his primary interest is generally supposed to have been in painting; (iii) his expectation that the arrival of Lady Dorothy will increase rather than decrease the artistic and intellectual activities of the circle surrounding her husband-to-be. In this last Kent was not disappointed, for the new Countess seems to have taken to the circle of Kent, Pope, Gay and the rest like the proverbial duck to water.

Lady Burlington, daughter of the second Marquess of Halifax, was a talented young woman who enjoyed and patronized the theatre whilst also sharing her husband's love of music, especially opera. Her own creative abilities lay in the field of drawing in general and in that of portraiture in particular. Vertue recounts a visit which he paid in the early 1740s to either Chiswick or Burlington House (it is unclear which), where he 'had the opportunity of seeing a room adorned with crayon paintings [of] heads [in] great numbers hung all round the room done by Lady Burlington, who has painted in that way with great success and with much application, and to be sure is a most fine and excellent genius.'[27] Her surviving works (such as two portraits of her daughters, now at Chatsworth), though pleasant enough, hardly bear out such extravagant praise, much less Vertue's subsequent comment that 'these works may well be esteemed an honour to the art and a glory to this nation . . . worthy of the regard of such a noble lady.' Far more appealing to the modern eye are the racy caricatures of opera singers, family friends and others for which she was also celebrated and which reveal a quick eye for instant characterization (Plate 21). Vertue, however, also makes the point that Lady Burlington's tutor in 'the art of drawing and painting in crayons' was Kent himself, and no doubt the lessons provided a good opportunity for teacher and pupil to get to know each other better.

There is no evidence that Lady Burlington benefited greatly from Kent's tuition, but on a personal level she would certainly have endorsed Vertue's judgment of him as 'an ingenious man, and of civil and obliging behaviour'. To her, as to the rest of the circle, he quickly became 'the Signior' or sometimes 'Kentino', and they corresponded regularly, he relaying such snippets of gossip as he knew would interest her when she was out of town – for example, an account of a royal Drawing Room or levée which he attended in October 1738; the King, he told her, was in black and wore a hat 'with a white feather and gold lace, the Princesses very fine. . . . Several ladies that had fine necks, I was told they call'd them Cupid's Kettledrums. . . .' On her own appointment as a Lady-in-Waiting to the new Queen in 1714 she helped her husband to promote Kent's cause at court, dropping his name at suitable moments and relaying back interesting snippets of court gossip: 'pray let the Signior know that his Majesty was yesterday full of commendations of the two pictures' (letter to Burlington, 1731).[28] In return Kent executed various household commissions for her. 'I hope the Signior has remembered about my tables and glasses', she writes from Bath in 1735, perhaps referring to new furnishings that he was to obtain or even to design for her. In lighter vein, she was ready to join

21 Kent in an idle moment, sketched (perhaps by Lady Burlington) in pencil and brown crayon

in any kind of communal jape that had Kent as its target. There exists at Chatsworth a petition addressed to Lord Burlington, couched in long-winded and legalistic language, in which the signatories – their tongues lodged firmly in their cheeks – pray his Lordship to spare a tree (growing in the grounds at Chiswick) which Kent had ordered to be cut down, apparently because it interfered with his ideas for the garden. After a long preamble it continues:

> We, your Honour's humble Petitioners who have many years known, accustomed & frequented the said Tree, sitten, reposed or disported under the Shade thereof yea and seen the said William Kent, the Agent & Attorney of . . . Sathan, solace himself with Syllabubs, Damsels, and other Benefits of Nature, under the said Tree, Do, for ourselves & our prosperity . . . petition and pray that the said Tree may remain, subsist, continue & flourish in his place, during his or her natural life (not being absolutely certain of the Sex of the said Tree) to enjoy the Small Spot of Ground on which God and your Lordship's Ancestors of ever blessed memory have placed it.[29]

The principal signatories to this document were Lady Burlington and her daughters, together with the Duke of Grafton, his son Lord Euston, and Alexander Pope. The handwriting throughout is Pope's and in fact it was probably he who conceived the idea in the first place. We do not know whether Kent was overruled as a result of the petition, but if so he no doubt accepted defeat with cheerful good grace.

The petition dates from about 1741, but it was not the first occasion that Pope and Lady Burlington had savoured between them a similar joke at Kent's expense. On 29 October 1738 Pope had written to the Countess humorously proposing Kent for the well-endowed living of Eyam (Derbyshire), which was in her gift and which was expected to fall vacant in the near future. 'He is as learned, tho' not so courteous as Bishop W-x; as eloquent tho' not so courtly as G-t; as well-bred tho' not so bookish as H-re, and (to sum up all) has a good a taste as R-le, and as good a stomach as all the clergy put together. . . . I think your Ladyship begins to find the excellent person at whom I point (or rather to *smoke* him, for he is very hot, and very fat),

> Of size that may a pulpit fill,
> Tho' more inclining to sit still.

And . . . I presume to name him, and defy any objections, viz. Mr. William Kent.'[30]

Though Pope's intention here is to divert, there is perhaps an implied criticism of the established Church in his assertion that Kent's only possible motive in accepting the living would be 'to get into a soft pulpit, where is a soft cushion, to lay his soft head', bringing to mind some of Hogarth's satirical representations of contemporary clergy. In fact he pursued the theme again a year later in a letter to Lord Burlington, this time seriously proposing a candidate for another living, whilst expressing the hope that whoever was appointed to Eyam would be 'the best preacher in England', upright, honest and compassionate.'If such a man cannot be found, I wish I had it [the benefice] myself, or that Mr. Kent would take Orders, for we are e'en as good Christians as most parsons' (15 October 1739).[31] In the enjoyment of this badinage it is easy to forget that Pope was a Roman Catholic. As for Kent's religious beliefs, these are a matter for conjecture. It is probable, however, that whilst holding fundamental if fuzzy beliefs, he adopted towards the Church of England the secularist attitude typical of the period, and significant that in a letter to the Countess of Huntingdon he remarks *en passant*: 'I never will have a good opinion of over-religious people.'[32]

The relationship between Pope and Lady Burlington seems to have been founded on an admiration both mutual and sincere. She had first captivated him by her attentions to his aged and dying mother, and seems always to have been thoughtful of his needs, however simple. He admired her artistic gifts: 'My real services ... attend yourself and Lady B. – I hope she paints; I hope you build', he writes to the Earl,[33] and in 1732 he produced verses 'On the Countess of Burlington Cutting Paper' (i.e. making the decorative designs that preceded the era of the silhouette). Pope himself was to some extent a connoisseur of painting, and on being asked 'Which gives you the most pleasure, sir, poetry or painting?' replied: 'I really can't well say; both of them are extremely pleasing'.[34] In fact he had once aspired to become an artist, and as a young man had spent some eighteen months lodging with Charles Jervas and being instructed by him in the techniques of painting and drawing. His talent it seems was small, however, though not so small as he made out in a letter to Gay of 23 August 1713: 'I comfort myself with a Christian reflection that I have not broken the Commandment, for my pictures are not the likeness of anything in heaven above, or in earth below, or in the waters under the earth.'[35]

As man and wife the Burlingtons appear to have been generally content (Pope stated his belief that their joint welfare was 'nearer akin than with most married people'), and the letters which passed between them (each addresses the other as 'My dear Child') are full of genuinely solicitous enquiries about each other's happiness and health – which in her case was not especially good and caused her to make visits to Bath and Tunbridge Wells in order to take the waters. An attachment which she formed for the Duke of Grafton did not apparently disturb the basic relationship with her husband. As she grew older her temper grew shorter and her rages famous; according to Horace Walpole she cursed roundly and blasphemed, even on her deathbed in 1758. It is possible that she was responsible for the uncharacteristic misunderstandings and ill-will that seem to have clouded Kent's last months (see p. 244). The waspish Lord Hervey paints an unflattering picture of her in his 'Poetical Epistle to the Queen':

[Let] Dame Palladio, insolent and bold,
Like her own chairman, whistle, stamp and scold. . . .[36]

But he also refers to her 'mason-husband', and clearly had little time for either of them (nor they for him – his various scornful comments about Chiswick Villa had struck home). Nor should we take seriously the assessment made of her by her uncle Lord Winchilsea (who disliked most people anyway), when in 1736 he called her 'the wickedest [most] mischievous jade upon earth', accused her of 'lying and making mischief, abusing everybody, imposing upon her husband and exposing him only to show her own power', and recommended 'some correction and some wholesale severity such as sending a lady down into the country'.[37] By this he probably meant Londesborough, which the whole family including Lord Burlington himself seem to have found a place of extreme boredom. 'I am sure you don't expect any news from this place', wrote the Burlingtons' daughter Charlotte,[38] echoing many similar phrases to be found in her parents' letters to each other, although the Earl was a conscientious landlord and spent a good deal of time in Yorkshire when he would far rather have been at Chiswick.

The Burlingtons had three daughters, of whom two survived childhood. The elder, Dorothy (b. 1724), was perhaps her parents' favourite, and after her untimely death was to be described by her sorrowing mother as 'the comfort and joy of her parents, the delight of all who knew her angelic temper, and the admiration of all who saw her beauty'. Unhappily and unwisely, as it turned out, she was married on 9 October 1741 to the Duke of Grafton's heir, Lord Euston, whose subsequently notorious ill-treatment of her was widely held to have been a more immediate cause of death than the smallpox from which she officially died less than seven months after the wedding. She was not yet eighteen. Fate was somewhat kinder to the younger sister, Charlotte (b. 1731). Her father's pet name for her was The Monkey, but to most other people she was known as Cha. To both girls Kent was obviously one of the family, filling an avuncular role. In a letter to her father from Chiswick (12 December 1743) Cha relates that 'Mama has bought a mare . . . and I got upon her and rid three or four times round the yard and Mr. Kentino stood and laughed at me all the time.' Kent's interest in food was well known to the children, as the following two extracts, again from letters by Cha, will show: 'I did think of writing to Mr. Kent today but perhaps . . . somebody will ask him to dine with them, then maybe he will stay till 8 or 9 o'clock, and then if I did send him anything good to eat he would not care much for it at supper and then perhaps it wou'd not be so very fresh to eat tomorrow' (to her mother, 30 October 1742). 'Mr. Kent went away yesterday morning and took all the potted hare with him so I can't tell his opinion of it yet, but I dare to say he will like it wondrously' (to her father, 11 October 1743). Nevertheless Kent obviously kept a watchful eye on both children when their parents were away from

[85]

home: 'Mr. Kent has been to see us twice and he dined with us', wrote Dorothy to her mother from Chiswick on 25 November 1736, and when earlier that same month she herself had been taken ill with some sudden childish ailment Kent (as he reported in a letter to Lady Burlington) was quickly at her bedside, assessing the situation and the measures taken for her relief and recovery.

It may seem somewhat strange that on 23 October 1741, in the midst of the furore that followed Dorothy's tragic marriage, Cha attended an important ball given by Sir Thomas Robinson, with Kent as her chaperone: 'There were none but people of the finest fashion, except Mr. Kent, Mr. Cibber, Mr. Swiney, and the Parsons family. . . . Kent came as governess to Lady Charlotte Boyle . . .'[39] However, such an entertainment (to which she had no doubt been looking forward for some time) was just the thing to take the child's mind off unpleasant goings-on at home, and who better to escort her than the faithful family friend, her parents being in far too agitated a state to attend themselves.

In 1748 Cha married Lord Hartington, the Duke of Devonshire's son and heir, who as a contrast to the dissolute Lord Euston was kind and generous to his young wife, and was moreover greatly beloved by Burlington. 'No man alive can love you more than I do', wrote the latter to his future son-in-law (12 July 1745), perhaps regretting that he had no son of his own, devoted though he was to his daughters. It was through Cha, his sole surviving heir, that Burlington's lands and possessions eventually passed into the hands of the Devonshire family. Yet her life too, though happy, was cruelly short, for she died in 1754 aged only 23, but not before she had borne four children.

In the company of people such as these Kent socialized and passed his days. His humble origins in Bridlington must have seemed light-years away, although bequests to his sister and her children in his will are an indication that he maintained some sort of contact with his relatives. On the other hand the Burlington circle of which he had so effortlessly become part had many more fringe members than those described here. In addition to those who have already been mentioned such as General Dormer, Lord Bolingbroke and Charles Jervas (whose connection with the circle probably explains his reluctance to comment on Kent's work at Kensington Palace, when invited to do so by the Office of Works), there were Sir Clement Cotterell, the brothers Bryan and Ferdinando Fairfax (the latter always referred to by Kent as 'Nando'), Sir Mark Pleydell of Coleshill, Berkshire,[40] General John Campbell, and numerous others to whom there are only passing references in letters and elsewhere. Amongst them all Kent moved with an easy familiarity, totally unabashed by rank or position – 'by no means a respecter of persons, but using sharp speeches to the greatest', as Pope puts it – self-possessed and self-assured. Pope summarized it antithetically as 'his violence of temper and ungovernable spirit of dominion'.[41] His good humour was irresistible: 'Nurse Read is rejoiced that he is coming back, he is such a pure good humour'd man', wrote Lady Burlington to her Lord on one occasion. At the other end of the social scale he was 'the little rogue Kent' and 'the honest Signior' to Lord Bruce, Burlington's brother-in-law, and he gave away to posterity more about himself and his character than he realized when he concluded a letter to Burlington (27 January 1738/9) with the words: 'There are a hundred more wild things that cannot be write, so hope to see you soon. . . . Wm. Kent.'

One further aspect of Kent's private life remains to be examined here. 'I wonder when the time will come that I shall be in love', he writes jocularly to Lady Burlington (7 October 1738).[42] He never married, and somehow his whole life-style suggests that of the cheerful bachelor. Nevertheless men who have Kent's obvious zest and appetite for life are not often celibate, though for professional or other reasons they may – as he plainly did – wish to keep their public and private lives entirely separate. When he died Kent left most of his money to 'Elizabeth Butler, of the parish of Saint Paul Covent Garden' and her two children. Horace Walpole describes her, without actually naming her, as 'an actress with whom he [Kent] had long lived in particular friendship', and it has sometimes been suggested that it is she who accompanies Kent in the self-portrait painting on the staircase ceiling at Kensington Palace. There is no proof of this, and Vertue is perhaps nearer the mark when he simply says that Kent left the bulk of his money to 'a favourite mistress', implying that others had preceded her. Nevertheless there is no disputing the fact that a talented actress named Elizabeth Butler did exist contemporaneously with Kent; though not of the first rank she appeared continuously at Drury Lane in a variety of parts between 1726 and 1742, and towards the end of her career became a lessee of the same theatre. In 1740/1 she moved from Leicester Fields to a house in King Street, Covent Garden, and was seemingly a fairly wealthy woman by the standards of the time.[43] Having in mind Kent's close interest in the theatre it seems virtually certain that this successful actress was the same woman who filled for him the role of a wife, perhaps also of a mother to his children, and who supplied a background of intimate domesticity which even his best friends could not provide.

CHAPTER FIVE
DECORATIONS AND FURNITURE

There can be no doubt that originally Kent's friends and patrons, and presumably Kent himself, regarded him first and foremost as a painter. Yet it must soon have become apparent that his boundless energy and enthusiasms were not to be confined within the techniques and conventions of a single branch of art. The idea that his career can be divided up into neat chronological bundles, each representing a different phase of interest and development, is totally misconceived; indeed, amongst the most striking aspects of that career are the relative speed at which Kent adopted his various interests, the manner in which they developed concurrently instead of consecutively, and the entirely natural way in which one grew progressively out of another.

In the field of architecture, for instance, it is often assumed that Kent showed no interest in the subject until he was introduced to it by Burlington. Yet, as we have seen (pp. 26–7), it may well have been his trip to northern Italy in 1714 with Thomas Coke, coupled with his earlier friendship with Giacomo Mariari, which first opened his eyes to the architectural felicities of Palladio and others. Already in 1715 he tells Massingberd that he has been speaking to John Talman 'of your improvement, that you was become a convert to the Italian gusto in building' (12 October), and offers to help his patron design a summer house, an offer which is repeated on 9 June following: 'if you marked in your letter the form and the measures, then we could make a design agreeable to our climate.' Undoubtedly this design would have been Classical in idiom. When, therefore, in 1719 Burlington first began to communicate his new-found evangelistic zeal for the Palladian creed to Kent, he was not dealing with somebody entirely ignorant of Italian Classical architecture, and it is significant – as has also been noted (p. 80) – that in 1720 Kent expresses the hope that as a result of Burlington's marriage architecture, not painting, will 'flourish more'. It did, not as a result of the marriage, but as the practical outcome of Burlington's visits to Italy.[1]

The Earl's first ventures into architecture were the Casina and the Summer Parlour, both created at Chiswick in about 1717 under the tutelage of Colen

Campbell. Other products of the years prior to 1725 were a mansion, Totten-ham Park, Wiltshire (for Burlington's brother-in-law, Lord Bruce), and a dor-mitory for Westminster School, the design for which was published in 1721 and completion achieved in 1729. Both show the continuing influence of Campbell (who, however, fades inexplicably but completely from the picture during the early 1720s) and an early if hesitant awareness of Inigo Jones; Tottenham Park (since rebuilt) was on the square Wilton/Houghton ground-plan with corner towers, whilst the Westminster dormitory echoed the arcaded loggia of Covent Garden, though with a severity of purpose which aroused much comment at the time. (Tottenham, however, having been commissioned in 1720, antedates Houghton and therefore, while it may have been conceived in consultation with Campbell, is actually the earliest of its type.)

It was in 1725 that work began on what has since become Burlington's best-known building, the famous Chiswick Villa (Plate 22). He seems to have been considering the project ever since returning from Italy in 1719, but the final impetus came from a fire which partly destroyed the old Jacobean family mansion at Chiswick. There was never any intention in Burlington's mind of actually living in the Villa; it was to be a gallery for the suitable display of his considerable collection of paintings and sculpture (much of it amassed in Italy), while the basement beneath was to house his library.

The general exterior appearance of the Villa is of a relatively small, square building, with a central octagonal dome, an imposing portico and staircase on the entrance front, and a slightly less imposing staircase on the garden side. It had three obvious prototypes – Palladio's Villa Rotonda (1552–3) at Vicenza, the Villa Rocca Pisani (1576) at Lonigo by Scamozzi and Campbell's newly completed Mereworth Castle. Of these three buildings, Burlington had undoubtedly seen the first and third for himself, and knew the second from engravings in his possession. Yet Chiswick is much more than a mere amalgam of the other three; it demonstrates a boldness of touch and certainty of purpose that marks Burlington out as an able and inventive architect in his own right, not merely a clever imitator of others. To take a single example, the segmental lunettes which pierce the drum of the dome at Chiswick are not found at any of the other three villas and indeed were unknown in northern Europe at the time. Burlington, however, knew that Scamozzi had used them elsewhere, judged them suited to his present purpose, and so introduced them – sublimely indifferent to the cries of astonishment which greeted this innovation.

The interior planning is equally imaginative, in fact more so, since for the actual shapes of the rooms Burlington went right back, via Palladio's original drawings, to the plans of Roman baths. The rooms relate to each other and to the overall plan as a whole according to the Classical theory of 'harmonic proportions', giving balance and symmetry; nevertheless within these limi-tations Burlington succeeded in designing an apartment of striking originality. This was the Gallery on the garden side, composed of three distinct sections

22 A drawing by Kent of Chiswick Villa showing the entrance portico and part of the octagonal dome. The sculpture is Rysbrack's statue of Palladio, while the figures in the foreground may represent Lord Burlington with Kent himself. The impudent dog is a typical touch of graphic Kentian humour

– a rectangular, apsidal-ended section in the centre, with a circular section at one end and an octagonal one at the other. Even Palladio himself had but rarely used round or octagonal shapes, and English architects prior to Burlington had stuck firmly to squares and rectangles. The Chiswick Gallery is proportionally small (though it seems to the visitor larger than it actually is, due to clever illusionistic scaling-down of the doorways and decorative details), but its subsequent influence on the spatial planning of British architects far outweighed its size.

Another very influential innovation at Chiswick was the introduction into domestic architecture in this country of the coffered domes and half-domes associated with Roman baths and other public buildings. It is quite possible, however, that Burlington's interest in the joint architectural and decorative uses of this device was stimulated by Kent's use of painted coffering in the

Cupola Room at Kensington, completed at about the same time as work began at Chiswick. Kent's involvement at Chiswick was inevitable and to some extent predictable. The ceilings of the Red and Green Velvet Rooms and of the Gallery (central section) are each – in the accepted Classical manner – divided up into nine sections or panels by a grid-like pattern of heavy beams with decorative plaster mouldings. Kent ornamented the panels of the Red Velvet Room and Gallery with paintings in his mosaic manner, unspectacular yet well suited to their purpose. The colour schemes – pink, green and gold on white in the Gallery, light blue on yellow ochre in the Red Velvet Room – are fresh and attractive, and the centrepiece of the Red Velvet Room ceiling, on the subject of Mercury presiding over the Arts, is a bright and tolerably competent *trompe l'œil* that includes a simulated architectural background. (The centrepiece in the Gallery is a scaled-down version of a Veronese, attributed to Ricci.) The ceiling of the Summer Parlour is undoubtedly also the work of Kent, consisting mainly of grotesques in red, blue and pink on white, with two roundels of symbolic children and, in the main central roundel, four tiny oval landscapes framed in cartouches. The lightness of touch both here and in the Gallery is a salutary corrective to the belief that everything Kent did was necessarily heavy in effect. It could even be said that it was in these rooms, rather than at Kensington or Houghton, that he perfected his purely decorative technique in painting. Nevertheless, for his really important contributions to Chiswick we should look elsewhere.

Early in 1720 Lord Burlington had contacted Kent's former mentor John Talman with a view to purchasing Talman's collection (inherited from his recently deceased father William Talman) of drawings by Palladio, Inigo Jones and John Webb. The acquisitive Earl had already, whilst in Italy, scooped up a cache of Palladio's original drawings which he is reputed to have discovered in the stables of the Villa Maser, near Trevino. The transaction was made in stages, the last of which seems to have been reached in April 1721, and in view of his former association with Talman William Kent was doubtless the go-between throughout. In 1724 or thereabouts Burlington conceived the idea of publishing some of the designs and Kent was given the task of editing them. Perhaps Burlington thought it would be a good introduction for him to the serious business of architecture. Obsessed by his vision of Kent as a great pain-ter, he may not fully have appreciated the extent to which his protégé was already taken up by architectural matters or the confidence with which Kent, having visited the site of the new Chicheley Hall in 1720, wrote to Massingberd that 'I think the whole design will not be much amiss, though if things had not been gone so far I believ'd I should have given my opinion to have had some alterations.' The book, *The Designs of Inigo Jones*, finally appeared in two volumes in 1727, with a long list of subscribers whose names read like a roll-call of the contemporary nobility – there are no less than thirteen dukes. Lurk-ing shyly amongst them like drab weeds in a bed of gaily coloured blooms are the names of Burrell Massingberd and Sir William Wentworth, the former in particular no doubt glad to pay for the privilege of still being associated, however remotely, with his one-time dependant. Care must be taken not to confuse this book with a similar-sounding publication, *Designs of Inigo Jones and Others*, which was brought out by Isaac Ware shortly before 1733 and which also contains designs by Kent.

Kent's book, like that of Ware, has no descriptive text except for comments on the plates. In addition to the designs of Jones, many of which are for the proposed Whitehall Palace, the book also includes designs for Palladio's Venetian church of S. Giorgio Maggiore, several of Chiswick Villa and a number by Kent himself; amongst these are found the interior of the Cupola Room at Kensington Palace, a design 'for a Public Gallery with paintings and statues', and five plates of chimney-pieces. The latter are heavily indebted to Jones, who had evolved a weighty two-stage arrangement, the upper portion of which above the mantelshelf was frequently surmounted by a pediment and framed a painting (or, by Kent's day, a mirror); it was in fact known as a 'tabernacle frame'. Jones's door-frames were equally distinctive, being severely rectangular and again almost always surmounted by the triangular pediment or its broken variant, sometimes supported on scrolled volutes. Above all, chimney-pieces, door-frames, cornices, ceiling beams, window-frames – these presented surfaces on which an unending series of decorative Classical mouldings could be formed in wood, stone or plaster, in the ancient patterns such as egg-and-dart, bead-and-reel, Vitruvian wave or scroll, Greek key or meander, dentil, bayleaf garland and the ubiquitous acanthus.

All this Kent – as his designs for chimney-pieces show – lifted lock, stock and barrel from Jones, in the general sense if not in the particular. Certainly he overdid things on occasion: Horace Walpole rightly remarks that 'His chimney-pieces, though lighter than those of Inigo, whom he imitated, are frequently heavy; and his constant introduction of pediments and the members of architecture over doors, and within rooms, was disproportionate and cumbrous.'[2] But there seems little doubt that the chimney-pieces at Chiswick were designed by Kent as the first-fruits of his editing of Jones's drawings, and this probably also applies to the door-frames as well. Perhaps 'designed' is not quite the right word in this context, for in fact several of the Chiswick chimney-pieces are flagrant borrowings from Jones; nevertheless their very lack of originality points to their being amongst Kent's earliest efforts in the field of applied architecture.

If such over-dependence upon established models betrays the hand of a comparative novice, there is another feature at Chiswick which just as surely announces a bravura touch which can only be that of Kent. The ceiling of the Blue Velvet Room (Plate 24) is an extraordinarily elaborate affair, its main part seeming to rest on pairs of console brackets which project from the wall above the cornice; the superimposed ranks of gilded Classical mouldings

23 A corner of the Blue Velvet Room at Chiswick. Kent's portrait of Pope over the larger door is complemented by that of Inigo Jones, by William Dobson

24 Chiswick: ceiling of the Blue Velvet Room, unmistakably Kentian though probably based on a design by Cherubino Alberti. The central painting of Architecture with attendants is certainly Kent's. Cleverly silhouetted against a background of graduated gold dots, the figures stand out with three-dimensional clarity

enlivened with panels of grotesques gleam against an azure background, and in the centre of the ceiling is an allegorical painting of Architecture as a female figure surrounded by *putti* bearing drawing instruments, her head surmounted not by a crown but by a Corinthian capital. This last somewhat ludicrous conceit must surely be the work of Kent, but it is redeemed by the magnificence of the ceiling as a whole. Regrettably we cannot credit Kent with the overall design, for Burlington's purchases from Talman included one very similar design by Cherubino Alberti (d. 1615), a mural painter of Rome, and this was probably the starting-point for the Blue Velvet Room ceiling. What we can envisage, however, is that the extrovert Kent had the necessary vision and Italianate background to persuade a hesitant Burlington – perhaps against his better judgment – that this exuberant and defiantly Baroque ceiling would not look out of place amidst the more conventionally Classical felicities of Chiswick.

The extent of Kent's involvement in the creation of Chiswick must remain for the most part conjectural, but equally there is no reason to doubt that at Chiswick his powers as an architect-cum-interior decorator were first seriously tested. Chiswick became and remained Lord Burlington's favourite spot; as well as an architectural masterpiece the Villa was a popular place of pilgrimage to which the public were admitted by ticket, and he could afford to ignore the sarcastic comments of uncomprehending critics such as Lord Hervey who gave his unasked opinion that the Villa was 'too little to live in, and too large to hang to a watch'. Kent shared Burlington's affection for it – though not perhaps to quite the same extent – and over the years kept an eye on things there when Burlington was obliged to go to the north. 'I have not been at Chiswick for three weeks', he writes in 1739 to the Countess of Huntingdon, a phrase which suggests that for him so long a gap was unusual.[3] On 12 September 1738 he writes to Burlington at Londesborough of a visit which he has paid to Chiswick in the company of Joseph Pickford, a master mason often employed in Palladian circles: 'I got to Chiswick to do what we had to do: the gate [Inigo Jones's – see p. 165] will be quite finished in two or three days; the other door that was taken down in that place is put up again and when all this work is done he is to begin the cascade. The rest of the things are doing in the house as you ordered.'[4] A month later he writes again: 'My Lord: I hope you received my last in which I gave you the particulars of what was doing here and at Chiswick. I since have been at Chiswick and have order'd the pantry in the new house as they call it [i.e. the Villa] to be done in the same manner as the rest, that all the dirt may be out at once' (10 November 1738).[5] Everything now being neat and tidy, the question was – would the family be coming down for Christmas as usual? A further letter was despatched to Londesborough, containing a slight note of pathos from the faithful friend and retainer: 'I hope you'll keep ChristX at Chiswick; after so many years I have not miss'd that I shall be so fanciful as to think it will be the last I shall ever be there' (28 November 1738). Fanciful indeed – but sadly this failed to do the trick, for on the following 14 December he was forced to write to Lady Burlington in a vein of resignation: 'I must make myself as happy as I can, finding you don't think of keeping ChristX in the old place. . . . I should have been glad you had been here and shall be glad to see you return all in good health.'[6]

Chiswick without Burlington was like a ship without its captain. 'I lay there the other night', wrote Kent to his patron on 16 November 1732, 'but though I love it, was too melancholy for want of them I wish to see.'[7] The French topographical artist Jean Rigaud was employed (as Vertue tells us) 'to make drawings of this noble Lord's house and gardens, which he did in several parts making 8 views.'[8] Unfortunately Rigaud succeeded in annoying Burlington, to whom he 'gave great disgust', as Vertue puts it (he overcharged); the drawings, however, remain, and are our best evidence of the incongruous appearance presented by the beloved Villa in its close proximity to the seventeenth-century mansion, notwithstanding a somewhat tentative Classical frontage which seems to have been added to the latter soon after 1715 under the initial influence of Campbell and *Vitruvius Britannicus* (a drawing by Burlington of this façade exists at Chatsworth). A cohesive architectural scheme was attempted; for instance, in *circa* 1730–5 Burlington connected his youthful Summer Parlour to the Villa itself by means of a two-storey 'Link Building' in the style of the Villa though differentiated from it; the Jacobean house was also already connected to the complex by means of a two-storeyed gallery.[9] But no amount of integral planning could have concealed the disparate styles, a fact which makes it impossible today to regret the demolition of the older house which took place in 1788.

The interiors of Chiswick Villa are rich but subdued; it is as though an impatient Kent, conscious of his new powers, was held in check only by the restraining hand of Burlington. Where that hand was momentarily lifted (as in the Blue Velvet Room), the result was both striking and startling. Things were very different at Houghton. Lord Hervey was right, in that Chiswick is after all a miniature, though perfect in all its parts; it was never intended as a dwelling house and was not so used during Lord Burlington's lifetime. Houghton, on the other hand, is a sizeable Palladian mansion, and it was here that Kent first came into his own as an interior designer and decorator. (Indeed he 'designed all the ornaments throughout the house', according to Horace Walpole in *Aedes Walpolianae*.) His activities in this field seem to have followed on quite naturally from his painting of the staircase at Houghton and in fact probably not only progressed concurrently with it, but also coincided with the later phase of his work at Chiswick. The building of Chiswick (though not necessarily all the decoration) was completed in 1726; the decorations at Houghton are post-1726, since a prominent motif which recurs throughout them is the Garter, which Walpole did not receive until that year. Houghton was finished in 1735, though the main rooms were habitable long before then.

The basic planning of a Palladian mansion provided for a suite of intercon-nected ceremonial apartments on the first floor, or *piano nobile*, in imitation of Italian Classical practice. External access to these was usually by way of the typical imposing portico and stairs. The ground floor contained rooms of a more private character for the use of the family – dining rooms, breakfast rooms, 'book rooms' (as at Chiswick), service rooms, kitchens, even bedrooms. Almost invariably the ground floor was visually separated from the upper floors in that its exterior walls were 'rusticated', i.e. clad in large blocks of stone which could be either smoothly finished or given a rough, rock-like appearance; the ground floor area itself was often actually called 'the rustic'. Naturally, however, the state rooms received the most attention from architects and decorators, since they were individual status symbols within mansions which were themselves status symbols – and none more so than Houghton. Sir Robert Walpole was out to impress, to establish himself and his family in the public estimation as being foremost in his native county of Norfolk and amongst the first in the country at large. The new house had also to be in the Classical manner with which the new Whig aristocracy (of whom Walpole was the political leader) had identified itself under the artistic leadership of Burlington; hence the choice of Campbell as architect, and then of Kent as decorator. It is salutary at this point to remind ourselves again that the innova-tions of the Palladian school were not universally welcomed. In 1732 Edward Harley, second Earl of Oxford, whose leanings were unashamedly Tory, visited Houghton and poured scorn both on what he considered to be a piece of preten-tious nonsense, and on its originators: 'The measure of the hall, as well as the plan of the house, are exhibited in that ignorant rascal's book called *Vitruvius Britannicus*, the editor Colin Campbell. . . . The house as it is now is a composition of the greatest blockheads and most ignorant fellows in archi-tecture that are.'[10]

Lord Oxford's further considered judgment on Houghton was that 'it is neither magnificent nor beautiful, there is a very great expense without either judgement or taste.' Indeed he may well have found the sheer opulence of the interior decoration somewhat overwhelming, for there is no denying that at Houghton Kent allowed his enthusiasm for Classical ornament to run riot. The profusion of ornate gilt mouldings in all the state rooms, the heavy com-partmented ceilings, the chimney-pieces and door-frames (as well as Campbell's 40-ft galleried hall) all reveal the clear and continuing influence of Inigo Jones, but without his discretion and selectivity. It has also to be said that as regards Kent's interior schemes, and more particularly at Houghton, not enough atten-tion has been paid to the influence on him of Campbell's interiors at Mereworth; these are equally opulent and must surely have been known to Kent, though it does not seem that he had any part in them. However, a set of twelve chairs in the Long Gallery at Mereworth is specifically assigned to him, and several side tables in his manner are also to be found there.

Above all, he did at Houghton exactly what was required of him in providing

25 Houghton: the Saloon (west side). Kent at his most opulent, his furniture here gracing the setting for which it was designed

a rich, indeed sumptuous, setting for the large house parties which it was Walpole's custom to hold twice a year, when the other members of the government came down to Norfolk to hunt, discuss politics amongst themselves and the local gentry, and drink themselves under the table, for ten days in summer and a further twenty days in November; these informal gatherings were called Walpole's 'congresses'. Most, no doubt, came away suitably impressed by what they had seen – as was, of course, the intention. In a letter to Lord Carlisle dated 9 December 1731, Sir Thomas Robinson describes just such a house party there, at which there were between twenty and thirty guests, with 'as much cheerfulness and good nature as I ever saw where the company was so numerous'. The impression made upon him by Houghton, then almost finished, was the opposite of that received by Lord Oxford, and deserves quotation at some length: 'I believe it is the best house in the world for its size, capable of the greatest reception for company, and the most convenient state apartments, very noble, especially the hall and saloon. The finishing of the inside is, I think, a pattern for all great houses that may hereafter be built: the vast quantity of mahogany, all the doors, window-shutters, best staircase &c. being made entirely of that wood; the finest chimnies of statuary and other fine marbles; the ceilings in the modern taste by Italians, painted by Mr. Kent and finely gilt; the furniture of the richest tapestry, &c; the pictures hung on Genoa velvet and damask . . . in short, the whole expense of this place must be a prodigious sum, and, I think, all done in a fine taste.' Another visitor commented that throughout the whole house 'the fitting up, for instance doors, door-cases, windows and cornishes [sic] &c. &c. is as magnificent as you can conceive, and in as great a style as any single room in England.'[11]

However, one man's taste is another's poison. Palladian interiors, like Palladian architecture, were anathema to some, who considered them ostentatiously vulgar. In his series of paintings *Marriage à la Mode* (circa 1743) Hogarth managed to take another sideswipe at Palladianism in general and Kent in particular in the second picture of the series, *Shortly after Marriage*. Here the dissipated young nobleman and his cuckolding girl-wife are shown against the background of a typical Kentian interior, sometimes said to be the saloon at 5 Arlington Street, the house to which Walpole moved from Downing Street in 1742 after falling from office.

Inevitably the building of Houghton overstretched Walpole's resources. Before it was built he had once remarked to Sir John Hynde Cotton that 'to construct a great house was a high act of imprudence in any minister.' After its completion Sir John reminded him of this, at which Walpole confirmed what he had said, adding 'Your recollection is too late; I wish you had reminded me of it before I began building, it might then have been of service to me.'[12]

Some of Sir Thomas Robinson's points deserve further examination. The 'Italians' who worked on the ceilings included the celebrated immigrant stuccoist Giuseppe Artari who, often collaborating with his fellow-countryman the equally talented Giovanni Bagutti, had already worked for Vanbrugh, Gibbs and Campbell (for the latter, at Mereworth). The wall-coverings of Genoese velvet and damask (some of it still *in situ* today) echoed Kent's own Italian experiences. The great chimney-piece in the Marble Parlour or State Dining Room appropriately features a carved marble panel representing the worship of Bacchus; this is by John Michael Rysbrack (1694–1770), and is amongst the earliest examples of co-operation between Kent and the famous sculptor, immigrant son of a Dutch landscape painter (they had probably first met in connection with the Cupola Room at Kensington Palace, where in 1723 Rysbrack had completed a large bas-relief on the subject of a Roman marriage). Most remarkable of all, the lavish use of mahogany throughout the house showed that Walpole was not going to be outdone in splendour by even such a Maecenas as the Duke of Chandos; the doorway of the Saloon alone is said to have cost £1,000. The spectacular, almost over-night rise in the popularity of mahogany at this time was due to a combination of different factors, chief amongst them being a drying-up in the supply of European walnut (formerly the fashionable wood) coupled with the removal in 1733 of the duty on timber imported from British North America and the West Indies. This made it possible to import large quantities of mahogany from Jamaica, though this source was soon supplanted by the former Spanish South American colonies of Cuba, San Domingo and Puerto Rico. Mahogany had a compelling new colouring, a rich dark red; moreover it was stronger than walnut, far more resistant to wood-worm, and – since the trees were larger – could be cut into much bigger planks. This last quality was of course especially valuable in the construction of panelling.

At this point it should be stressed that neither at Houghton nor at any other site where he was employed was Kent on hand full-time to supervise the work being carried out in his name. Like the Adam brothers later in the century, with numerous commissions on their books simultaneously, Kent could only make periodic visits to his projects, relying for the rest of the time on foremen and supervisors. At Houghton the executant of both Campbell's and Kent's designs was Thomas Ripley (d. 1758), another Yorkshireman and Kent's predecessor in the office of Master Carpenter. He was not thought of highly by his contemporaries, who considered him to be unimaginative and incompetent; Pope made three known unflattering poetic references to him, and other attacks included the following devastating couplet:

> So Ripley, till his destined space is filled,
> Heaps bricks on bricks, and fancies 'tis to build.[13]

Vanbrugh was coarser. When in 1721 he learned that Ripley had succeeded Grinling Gibbons as Master Carpenter, 'such a laugh came upon me, I had like to beshit myself.'[14] Had he known that in 1726 Ripley would succeed

26 Raynham: the Hall, completed 1730. Although at one time this apartment was ascribed by some to Jones, we need not doubt Kent's authorship, which also extended to the benches, frames and angled side tables

him as Comptroller of the King's Works he might have laughed less immoderately.

Sir Thomas Robinson in a revealing passage points out that Kent's non-attendance on site coupled with his fondness for the bottle sometimes led his clients into greater expense than should have been necessary. 'The Signior, as he was call'd, often gave his orders when he was full of claret, and he did not perhaps see the works for several months after; he had indeed a pretty concise tho' arbitrary manner to set all right, for he would order without consulting his employers three or four hundred pounds' of work or more to be directly pull'd down, and then correct the plan and bring it to what it ought to have been at first.'[15]

During his period of work at Houghton Kent was also employed not far away at Raynham Hall, at the behest of Charles, second Viscount Townshend. Lord

Townshend was Walpole's brother-in-law as well as his neighbour, but political and personal rivalry between them was exacerbated by the building of Houghton. As Lord Hervey put it, 'Lord Townshend looked upon his own seat at Raynham as the metropolis of Norfolk, was proud of the superiority, and considered every stone that augmented the splendour of Houghton as a diminution of the grandeur of Raynham.'[16] So bitter were his feelings that he invariably left home whenever Walpole entertained at Houghton, referring acidly to the 'Bacchanalian orgies' which took place there.

None of this, however, prevented his employing Kent, who worked at Raynham between 1725 and 1732. Thus some of the decorations and other features probably antedate those at Houghton; on balance they certainly appear more restrained, even hesitant, suggesting that Kent was still feeling his way in this area of work. Lord Oxford, visiting Raynham on his 1732 tour of Norfolk, was predictably scathing: 'The rooms are fitted up by Mr. Kent, and consequently there is a great deal of gilding; very clumsy over-charged chimney-pieces to the great waste of fine marble.'[17] The principal painted features are the staircase, with simulated statuary and other sculptural ornament (Plate 27), as at Houghton, and the mosaic ceiling of the 'Belisarius Room' (taking its name from a painting by Salvator Rosa which formerly hung there) with a central medallion showing Fame admiring a bust of Pope. But Kent was also responsible for architectural alterations within the house, which dated in essentials from the seventeenth century. The planning of the entrance hall and staircase are assigned to him, and other structural alterations were also made, including one which especially irritated Lord Oxford: 'Kent has parted the dining room to make a sort of buffet, by [introducing] the Arch of Severus; surely a most preposterous thing to introduce a building in a room, which was designed to stand in the street.'[18] Preposterous or not, the result was not unsuccessful (Plate 28). Following a visit to Raynham in December 1731, Sir Thomas Robinson wrote that 'It has lately been . . . prettily ornamented in the inside by Mr. Kent.'[19] The insipid adverb entirely fails to do justice to the quality of Kent's work at this house.

James Adam, on a visit to Raynham in 1759, found on the other hand that 'The apartments have been fitted up by Mr. Kent but are by no means elegant or pleasant.'[20] This too shows a lack of sympathy with Palladian ideals – mere elegance and pleasantness were not amongst Kent's priorities. On a technical point it is interesting to note that the staircase decorations at Raynham are amongst the very few examples of Kent's painting to be applied directly to the plaster in oils; others are at Stowe (the hall ceiling) and at Kensington Palace. Most of his work in this field is on canvas, probably being painted in his studio and placed *in situ* when completed. An example of this occurred at Chicheley Hall, where a focal point of decoration was a large tabernacle frame in the east wall of the entrance hall; the problem of how best to fill this frame was put to Kent, as Sir John Chester explained in a letter to Mas-

27 Raynham: the Staircase. A smaller but more elegant version of the Houghton staircase,
with typical and effective *trompe l'œil* decoration here painted directly on to the plaster

28 Raynham: the State Dining Room. Kent's screen in imitation of a Roman triumphal arch annoyed his critics

singberd dated 29 February 1723/4: 'My son [-in-law] Toller was with Mr. Kent for his advice about the niche of the tabernacle in my hall, which I had thought of finishing with my own marble [i.e. a bust of himself], which at first Mr. Kent seem'd to approve but since inclines to a statue painted; if you should see him before you leave the town I desire you'll present my service to him and let him know . . . that if he determines for the latter I hope he will do me the favour to paint it and [I] shall leave the price to him.' In the end Kent chose to paint a *chiaroscuro* figure of Mercury (now removed), for which he was paid twelve guineas.

A feature of the same entrance hall is a screen of three arches resting on marble Corinthian columns, above which runs the landing gallery; this screen divides the entrance from the staircase hall behind. The suggestion has been made that this feature was designed by Kent, and some weight is given to this by the fact that payment to Henry Flitcroft for the drawing is recorded in the household accounts for 1722. As Lord Burlington's draughtsman (see p. 167) Flitcroft – at this time a young man only 25 years old, and as yet with no career of his own – would have been the obvious person to translate Kent's ideas on to paper. But the grammar of Classical architecture does not permit arches to rest directly on capitals, as in the Chicheley screen, and therefore any idea of Kent's authorship for this feature must surely be discarded; even at this early stage in his professional architectural work he would never have committed such a solecism. On the other hand there seems no good reason why the young Flitcroft should not have been given the opportunity to produce his first individual work here, which would explain the ungrammatical nature of the composition (though not why it escaped correction).

It is interesting to note that the tabernacle in the hall at Chicheley is repeated in essence (though on a slightly larger and more ornate scale) at Ditchley Park, where Kent and Flitcroft also worked together. Both tabernacles moreover are found on the left-hand wall as the visitor enters through the front door, and both face the fireplace across the hall. Precise dates are impossible to determine, but of the two schemes Ditchley was probably the second to be completed (Kent was paid for his ceiling in 1726). It seems certain that Kent, even if not the originator of the tabernacle idea at Chicheley Hall (and he probably was), brought it with him to Ditchley a few years later.

Much of Kent's interior decoration, however successful, is derivative. The same cannot justly be said of his furniture. In its opulence, richness and general effect it is often said to recall the Italian Baroque furniture (especially Venetian) which Kent will have seen during his years in Italy. There is some truth in this, although the discerning eye will note that Genoese influence is at least as much if not more important than Venetian. On the whole, though, Kent's furniture is unmistakably his own, and, together with numerous unattributed pieces immediately stemming from it, forms a unique contribution to the history of eighteenth-century English furniture. Furthermore, taken as a whole, it encourages speculation as to the direction in which Kent's talents might have taken him, had he not come under the influence of Burlington and the Palladian circle. He is sometimes thought of as a Baroque artist *manqué*. No more powerful evidence for this view could be found than his furniture designs.

It will be recalled that in 1724 negotiations took place between Kent and Burrell Massingberd about an altarpiece for Boston church (p. 62). The price was to include a design for 'the woodwork that's to be about the picture'. Frames for paintings and mirrors may well have been the first items of moveable furniture designed by Kent, although like his chimney-pieces other frames of his invention were a fixed part of general decorative schemes. This was no doubt at least partly true of a scheme at Kensington Palace which he produced at the express command of Queen Caroline in 1727. His fee of £50 covered the following:

> For drawing the sides of the Drawing Room, with all the pictures sketcht in proper colours, designing and drawing the mouldings and ornaments for all the picture frames, glasses etc.; for drawing the Gallery with all the pictures sketcht in proper colours, the frames drawn with ornaments, at large, and for the sconces and glasses.[21]

The point that the frames in the drawing should be seen to contain recognizable paintings is surely an important one. It is made again in *The Designs of Inigo Jones*, and indeed these and other contemporary designs show that some significance was attached to the placing of paintings in relation to the overall decorative scheme (see also note 11 to this chapter).

Kent may well have taken his first decisive steps in designing free-standing furniture at Houghton, where he provided two magnificent suites of seat furniture – chairs, armchairs and settees – in distinct yet related styles. He thus became the first English architect and decorator of note to provide furniture for settings which he had himself created, and totally in keeping with them. Because of this unified purpose Kent's furniture looks entirely misplaced in a different environment from that for which it was intended, unless the new setting is in a style very similar to the original.

According to Walpole, Kent 'gave designs for most of the furniture at Houghton, as he did for several other persons.' Moreover it was undoubtedly at Houghton that for the first time he 'attracted much notice by his skill in interior arrangements – he could plan bookcases, cabinets and chimney-pieces; hang curtains with a grace; introduce ornaments in wood or stone, and in short, do all, and more than all, that the upholsterer aspires to now.'[22] Yet evidence of Kent's involvement in providing the original designs for known pieces is comparatively rare and often circumstantial. The state bed at Houghton is certainly by him (Plate 29), and was executed in 1732 by the London firm of Turner, Hill and Pitter for the huge sum of £1,219 3s. 11d. – another example of Sir Robert Walpole's extravagance. (Lord Oxford, on his 1732 visit to Houghton, makes the following interesting comment: 'I took notice of Sir Robert's own bedchamber; the bed is shut up in a box, a case made of mahogany with glass, as if it was a cabin, the room small, my Lady's picture over the chimney.'[23] This cannot have been the state bed itself, but the fact that Sir Robert's bed was apparently housed inside a kind of glass case makes some museum display techniques seem more tolerable.) A design for a sumptuous table for Houghton appears as plate 41 in the collection entitled *Some Designs of Mr. Inigo Jones and Mr. William Kent*, published in 1744 by Kent's disciple John Vardy (d. 1765). The original drawing for this is in the Victoria & Albert Museum (Plate 35); what the engraved plate does not show are the two small caricatures of Italian clerics which the irrepressible

29 Houghton: the green state bed, 1732. Perhaps the most sumptuous single piece of furniture ever designed by Kent

Kent has sketched on the same page, presumably rapidly illustrating some anecdote of the moment.

Vardy's publication also shows a design for a small 'Table at Lord Burlington's at Chiswick', and an example of the same, identical in every detail though slightly different in its proportions, is also to be seen in the Victoria & Albert Museum. The most active period for the provision of furniture at Chiswick was probably the 1730s, though not all of it was necessarily designed by Kent. Representative bills (preserved at Chatsworth) include one from John Boson dated 11 September 1735 for the provision and carving of 'two rich glass frames, two mahogany tables, two stands with boys' heads', total £43, and a bill for upholstery of various kinds from the executors of Stephen Langley totalling £218 (11 April 1735).

The Chiswick furniture was later removed to Chatsworth, where we now find Kent's magnificent table from Wanstead, his scarcely less magnificent library writing tables and several other items. Another plate from Vardy (no. 42) shows one of a pair of settees made in 1731 by the cabinet-maker James Moore the younger for Sir John Dutton at Sherborne Lodge, Gloucestershire, and now at Temple Newsam. The family archives reveal that Kent was concerned in 1728 with the remodelling of the house, so it is reasonable to suppose that he furnished not only the original design for these settees but also supplied drawings for other items including four window stools *en suite* with the settees and six hall chairs, all of which are in his distinctive style.

Of the various cabinet-makers associated with Kent the most important were James Moore the elder and Benjamin Goodison, more especially because they were employed by Kent (in his capacity as Master Carpenter) on various royal works. Moore in particular supplied the furniture for the 'new apartment' at Kensington Palace; these pieces had been designed by Kent and consisted chiefly of side tables, some supported by sphinxes (see note 21). But even the finest cabinet-maker must have found that translating Kent's designs into actual pieces of furniture was often a daunting task.

For Kent's furniture is architectural in its conception and much of its decoration, and shows no understanding of the particular and peculiar qualities of wood. Indeed some of his ideas positively invite deterioration – splitting, warping and so on. Pieces made in the spirit but not to the letter of Kent's designs have often survived much better, and it is important to recognize that there are many more extant items of furniture which reflect Kent's general influence than there are pieces specifically attributable to him. This perhaps better than anything else bears out Horace Walpole's comment that 'Kent's style . . . predominated authoritatively during his life; and his oracle was so much consulted by all who affected taste that nothing was thought complete without his assistance';[24] Walpole then goes on to state specifically that furniture, including 'frames of pictures, glasses, tables, chairs &c.', was one of the subjects on which fashionable society regularly sought Kent's assistance. Hence the considerable corpus of 'Kentian' pieces to be found today.

There is of course no mistaking Kent's general style, which is exemplified mainly in the form of seat furniture, frames, tables and pedestals, all of it ceremonial in character. His chairs and settees, with or without arms, are the items which bear the closest imprint of his Italian experince, both in their defiantly Baroque appearance and such details as the use of Genoese cut velvet upholstery. At Houghton the original upholstery remains on each of the two sets of seat furniture, being crimson and rose for the Saloon (matching the same on the walls) and crimson and cream for the other set. Arms are scrolled over at the ends, legs are square-section with human or animal masks at the knees, and the wood is mahogany tastefully gilded in part or in whole. But it is the nature and scale of the ornaments which make Kent's furniture style so distinctive. The accepted Classical friezes – dentil, acanthus and so on – are still used when and where appropriate (mainly on tables and case furniture), but their restraint is offset by a huge variety of fluid ornamental forms ranging from interlinked chain-like motifs carved in relief to the three-dimensional carved swags of fruit and flowers, husks and foliage which Kent regularly suspends between the legs of his settees and tables. Many of these are sufficiently naturalistic as to suggest early Rococo overtones; in this con-nection, and in view of the fact that the original French Rococo style was based on natural rock and shell formations, it is interesting to observe that one of Kent's favourite decorative motifs, and a useful 'trade-mark' by which his per-sonal style may be identified, is the scallop shell. His most striking employment of this beautiful form (commonly also used, it should be said, by many Italian Baroque artists) is in the head of the state bed at Houghton; here the shell, which is in relief of green velvet with gold ornament, is in two parts – an inner and an outer – and occupies almost the entire height of the bed-end. It is completely successful, and we may agree wholeheartedly with that visitor to Houghton in 1738 who described the bed as 'very rich and very elegant, and not overdone'.

Kent has other individual trade-marks besides the scallop shell. One is a curious shallow patterning like fish-scales which he very frequently applies to the legs of seat furniture and tables. There is no convincing precedent for this in Italian Baroque furniture, although it is occasionally met with on French examples of the period (such as a pair of side tables now in the Courtauld Institute of Art, London). Kent could have got the idea from French engraved designs (the work of Nicholas Pineau being especially relevant here), or simply from the 'mosaic' style of ceiling decoration. Another of his idiosyncrasies is a scroll-like support resembling an architectural bracket on end and used very frequently for tables and settees; this is also often a favourite area for the fish-scale patterning. Scales and shells are often combined together in effective ornamentation, not necessarily confined to furniture; for example, on the ceil-ing of the Summer Parlour at Chiswick the four landscapes in the central

30 Armchair from the set of twelve designed (together with four stools and two settees) by Kent for the Saloon at Houghton. Gilt mahogany, upholstered in crimson and rose cut velvet

31 Armchair, Venetian, early eighteenth century. This illustrates the type of furniture the influence of which was to appear in Kent's own designs

roundel are each given a painted cartouche frame decorated with scaling and surmounted by a scallop shell.

Kent's tables are intended mainly to be decorative rather than functional. King of them all is the huge square table now in the State Dining Room at Chatsworth (though not a dining table) but originally at Wanstead; it rests on scroll supports, and two giant scallop shells form an important part of the decoration. (It should be said that there are some doubts about Kent's authorship of this piece.) In the same room are two gilt side tables which Kent supplied *circa* 1735 for Lord Burlington at Chiswick. Side tables, console tables and pier tables are the three varieties most usually associated with Kent, and all are intended to stand against a wall. (Console being the architectural term for a bracket, a console table properly has front supports only and is screwed to the wall at the back, although the term was also confusingly used for side tables in general including those with four legs. A pier table is placed against the wall between two windows, since architecturally speaking a pier is the

32 Tail-piece from the *Odyssey*. Further proof that the influence of Italian Baroque furniture was still fresh in Kent's mind after his return to England

33 Armchair identical to a pair designed by Kent for Chiswick and now at Chatsworth. Pinewood carved and gilt, upholstered in crimson and green cut velvet on a light ground

wall-space between two apertures.) On these three types of table Kent again used a rich vocabulary of ornament, usually carved from softwood and partly or wholly gilded. While Classical friezes such as dentil or meander are found beneath the table top, and sometimes also at its base, there is often – as in the seat furniture – much additional carved ornament of a naturalistic though controlled character in which familiar ingredients such as the scallop, acanthus, floral swags and human or satyr masks again play a large part. The origins of a vogue for a type of console table having a single support in the form of an eagle with outstretched wings may well lie with Kent; certainly it became a popular formula, as did also a variation having intertwined dolphins instead of the eagle. A pair of magnificent eagle console tables reliably attributed to Kent may be seen at Ditchley Park. Sometimes dolphins and eagle are combined in a single piece, as in two especially fine console tables at Mereworth also attributed to Kent. Following the practice of Italy (where Kent will have seen many imposing side tables and absorbed much of their general

34 Tail-piece from the *Odyssey*. A side table in Italian style, foreshadowing a number of similar designs that Kent was to produce for his patrons over the years

35 Design for a side table at Houghton. The clerics are evidently a light-hearted reference to Kent's Italian days, and do not appear in the engraved version (plate 41 in Vardy's *Some Designs of . . . William Kent*)

36 Side table in the Saloon at Houghton. One of Kent's most imposing essays in this *genre*, incorporating the Garter motif (a compliment to Walpole), as well as many of the usual ingredients of his style

style), all the tables have heavy tops of marble, or at least of that ancient imitation known as *scagliola*. According to the sale catalogue of his effects Kent himself, at the time of his death, owned no less than four examples of this kind of table; the description of three of them is 'An Italian marble table on a rich carved and painted frame', and the fourth is identical except that the frame is described as 'gilt' rather than painted.

In a different category are two fine library tables designed by Kent for Chiswick and now at Chatsworth. These are free-standing pieces in mahogany with gilt metal mounts, the top resting on pedestals whose outer ends (curved in one, angled in the other) are linked by an arch across the kneehole. The rich effect of both these tables indicates the new importance now given to libraries in house planning; from the seventeenth-century idea of the library as a private sanctum or 'book room', often little bigger than a closet, it had become (through the general spread of learning and Whig insistence on the importance of a Classical education) one of the larger public rooms in the house, in which various social activities could take place. It is true that Burlington's ground-floor book room at Chiswick Villa hardly fits into the latter category, but the private sanctum continued to co-exist with the larger library in many

37 Table formerly in Chiswick Villa and closely based on plate 40 in *Some Designs of . . . William Kent*

38 Settee and chairs: plate 42 in *Some Designs of . . . William Kent*. The bottom left-hand design gives two alternative suggestions for the chair back

39 Settee based on the design in plate 42 of *Some Designs of . . . William Kent*: made by James Moore in 1731 for Sir J. Dutton

houses, and there may well have been a library in the old Jacobean house at Chiswick for which Kent's table was intended.

In a class entirely by itself stands the organ case which appears as plate 47 in *Some Designs of . . . William Kent*. It is not known when or for whom this was designed (or indeed if it was ever made), but it is for a chamber or domestic instrument, not a church organ, and as such is the first known example of a vogue which was later taken up by several well-known eighteenth-century architects and cabinet-makers, including Thomas Chippendale, Thomas Johnson, John Linnell, Robert Adam and James Wyatt. The organ cases which they designed reflected the rising status of an instrument which owed much of its popularity to the success of Handel's organ concertos. Kent's case (which makes no visible provision for the organ console) is in the architectural manner of his wall-furniture, but moreover in view of his remark about the organ in Santa Giustina, Padua (see p. 66), it is significant that this design is entirely based on his recollections of Italian church organs. Basic to the Italian organ case as it evolved at the time of the Renaissance is a strongly architectural framework enclosing three or more round-headed arches in

40 Design for an organ case: plate 47 in *Some Designs of . . . William Kent*. Presumably intended for domestic rather than church use, but entirely Italian in conception

41 Mirror-frame attributed to Kent and perhaps designed for Frederick, Prince of Wales, at
Kew Palace or Carlton House

which the visible pipes are disposed; ornamental cross-bars are placed centrally across the front of each group of pipes. This distinctive treatment is peculiar to Italy and is not found elsewhere in Europe. Kent, however, repeats it in his design, and although his arrangement of the pipes is somewhat different and the carved ornament is from his personal vocabulary, the two carved angels clinging to the pediment have many close relatives in Italy (including two similarly situated at S. Giorgio Maggiore in Venice).

Kent is known to have designed a number of stands or pedestals, either in sets or in pairs; there are good representative examples from Chiswick at Chatsworth and others at Hampton Court. Usually of pinewood carved and/or gilt, they taper towards the bottom, frequently include the fish-scale patterning and the acanthus motif, and as frequently also feature a human head with or without torso; on the head rests a platform which usually simulates the capital of a column. On the platform were placed candelabra, sculptured Classical busts or bronzes (General Dormer being a noted collector of the latter), or perfume burners – these last being necessary adjuncts to socializing at a period when elegant clothes belied the all-too-often unwashed state of the bodies which they concealed. A telling instance of the need to sweeten the atmosphere is provided by a passage in a letter of 1728 from Lord Hervey to his friend Stephen Fox, in which his Lordship relates that on the previous evening: 'At Court . . . there was dice, dancing, crowding, sweating and stinking in abundance as usual.'[25]

There exist numerous pieces of furniture of the more ceremonial type outlined above, which bear all the hallmarks of Kent's style but which cannot

42 Tail-piece from the *Odyssey*. Here are all the ingredients of the familiar eagle console table associated with Kent, though assembled in reverse order

43 Eagle console table in Kent's manner. Pinewood carved and gilt, with green *verde antique* marble top

be directly attributed to him, such as the set of six typical settees of gilt wood in the Double Cube Room at Wilton dating from *circa* 1735. In several instances these pieces are so closely linked with schemes of architecture and interior decoration stemming directly from Kent as to make his ultimate authorship a virtual certainty. An outstanding example of this is the magnificent King's Chair at the Treasury, of softwood carved and gilt with claw-and-ball feet and lion masks at the knees, and with a large decorative cresting-piece in which two *putti* suspend a crown over a cartouche carved with the royal monogram GR; the arms rest on dolphin supports. The chair was made some time between 1729 and 42 – that is, well within Kent's lifetime. Yet in fact the element of doubt associated even with pieces such as these only serves to emphasize the extent to which his all-pervasive influence filtered through to those cabinet-makers who had the ability to assimilate and reproduce his style. Just as in the 1760s and 70s Thomas Chippendale, John Linnell and others were to rein-terpret the ideas of Robert Adam, so men such as Benjamin Goodison and Mat-thias Lock created 'Kent' furniture of quality, adding to it fresh characteristics

44 Settee in Kent's manner (especially the laughing satyrs carved on the arm-terminals). A piece typifying Kent's influence on a number of cabinet-makers

of their own. Lock in particular was not afraid to mix the pomposities of Kent with the frivolities of the true Rococo. This is to be seen not only in his original drawings and published pattern books of engravings (such as *A New Drawing Book of Ornaments, Shields, Compartments, Masks etc.,* 1740), but in actual examples of his work. Especially notable is a large mirror-frame, now in the Victoria & Albert Museum, which was carved by Lock in 1743. At first sight this appears to be impeccably Kentian, but closer examination reveals a considerable amount of naturalistic animal and plant life amongst the decoration, and at the very top of the frame in the centre, where Kent would have put a scallop shell or some such formal motif, Lock has carved the head of a hare. Although this is a detail which can be justified by the general theme of the decorations, which is that of the chase, it adds at the same time a touch of humour which one feels might well have appealed to the Signor himself.

Lock's mirror-frame is designed *en suite* with a large marble-topped console table standing beneath. This is a formal grouping very typical of Palladian furniture, yet curiously enough seldom used by Kent himself, except at

45 Kentian bookcase, conceived in the typically architectural manner reserved by the Palladians for such pieces

Houghton and Devonshire House. Certainly no examples are illustrated in the 1744 *Some Designs of . . . William Kent*. We should not ignore the value of this collection of plates in spreading the knowledge of Kent's furniture style amongst those who had not previously seen his work for themselves.

In 1739 we find Kent writing to the Countess of Huntingdon, 'The easy chairs will be done this week and shall be sent.'[26] Despite this he is not generally associated with furniture designed primarily for comfort and everyday usage. (One regrets the disappearance of the 'mighty pretty cradle, designed by Kent' in which according to Horace Walpole the Prince of Wales's fourth son, Henry Frederick, born on 26 October 1745, was first publicly displayed to an admiring Court; seemingly the cradle no longer survives in the Royal Collections.[27]) It should not be forgotten that in fact Kentian furniture, intended as it was for parade, for show and as a foil for the richly decorated rooms in which it was intended to be set, represents a mere fraction of the pieces produced during the period and is largely untypical of them. A floridly carved foursquare gilt chair by Kent has generally little in common with the flowing mahogany lines of a more ordinary chair of the period, except that the latter may be quite heavily carved on the knee, often with a lion or human mask – both favourites with Kent. His influence may also be detected in those chairs which have a heavy lion's-paw foot instead of the more usual and popular claw-and-ball foot of Oriental origin. The wider and more generalized impact of his style may be seen in various pieces of case furniture – bureaux, bookcases and the like – which demonstrate the same architectural approach to design and the same inclination to treat the new mahogany, for ornamental purposes, as though it were stone rather than wood. (The prodigal use of solid mahogany at this time soon had to be replaced by veneering, except for chair and table legs.) The closest affinity between Kent's furniture style and functional pieces is probably best demonstrated in a number of extant library tables and commodes (ornamental chests-of-drawers) which have arched supports and applied decorative terminals, each of which ends in a lion's foot and has at its top a lion's head with a gilt brass ring in its mouth.

Kent's own furniture is entirely individual and belongs emphatically to his period and to the settings for which it was designed. It was not intended for popular use, as that of Hepplewhite or Sheraton was to be. One might therefore be forgiven for supposing that it had no further influence beyond Kent's own lifetime. This would be a mistake. When in the 1760s Robert Adam was first called upon to provide furniture for his patrons, he turned for inspiration to the work of Kent, whom he had always respected. Thus it is that, although Adam evolved his own distinctive and highly influential style in furniture, his early pieces clearly show the Kentian influence in their general appearance, even if their decoration already contains elements of the familiar Adam grotesques. An armchair now in the Victoria & Albert Museum, one of a set of chairs designed by Adam for Sir Lawrence Dundas, is ornamented with typi-

46 Portrait of Lord Burlington attributed to Richardson and probably painted between 1717 and 1719, before the Earl's second visit to Italy. The Earl's coat and turban are a brilliant red. The Casina at Chiswick appears in the background

47 Portrait of Kent by Dandridge, *circa* 1730. He wears the casual turban which in the privacy of the home replaced the formal wig and kept shaven heads warm

cal sphinxes and Greek honeysuckle in relief, but its square outlines and
ceremonial appearance are pure Kent. Moreover there are sets of seat furniture
at Osterley House by both Adam and his rival Sir William Chambers which
in form (although not decoration) closely resemble a similar set at Rousham
House, where Kent worked for General Dormer. Chambers, on a tour of country
houses spread over the years 1745–8, took the trouble to sketch a chair by
Kent which he spotted on his visit to Tottenham Park; clearly he too believed
that it was possible to learn from the Palladian genius.[28]

Kent himself, it seems, was no more diffident about his powers as a furniture
designer than he was about any of his other abilities. In 1734 he wrote to
the Earl of Huntingdon mentioning that he had heard 'that my Lady Huntingdon writ something in relation to the furniture, in which, if I can be of any
service, I shall always be ready to give my advice.' This enviable self-confidence
cannot alter the fact that Kent's furniture succeeds magnificently in doing exactly
what its creator intended – enhancing and enriching its surroundings, and
bearing impressive witness to the wealth and social standing of those patrons
who had commissioned it.

CHAPTER SIX
ROYAL COMMISSIONS AND GOTHICK GUSTO

Any list of Kent's influential patrons must invariably be headed by the Crown, in the impersonal sense in which – for example – he had received the commission to decorate Kensington Palace. But at the same time he worked for members of the royal family on a more personal basis. Queen Caroline required him to provide further decorations for the Palace (see p. 105) and in 1736 work began on a new Library which he had designed for her, facing on to St James's Park. This was a free-standing, single-storey building of double cube dimensions (60 × 30 × 30 ft), coolly elegant within, its single chamber lined on three sides with arched recesses to contain the books; at the junctions of the arches brackets supported busts of past queens of England carved by Rysbrack. Kent's designs (preserved in the Soane Museum) show that his original intention had been to have projecting bookcases, as in Wren's Library at Trinity College, Cambridge, with the busts accommodated in niches at the ends of these. Projecting bookcases were indeed put in, but at a later date and on a far smaller scale than Kent had envisaged. The ceiling was coved, with a rich cornice, and at each end of the room was a typical marble chimney-piece; when the Library was demolished in 1825 – to provide a site for York House – the chimney-pieces survived in part and were transferred to the State Apartments at St James's Palace, where they still remain. Sadly the Queen did not live to enjoy the scholarly peace of her new Library. It was completed in October 1737; a month later she was taken ill whilst actually in the Library, and soon afterwards was dead.

In 1730 Kent had started work at Kew House, at the behest of Frederick, Prince of Wales. Kew House (which stood opposite the so-called 'Dutch House', still to be seen within the grounds of Kew Gardens) was described by John Evelyn in 1678 as 'an old timber house', and was probably of Tudor origin. Prince Frederick leased it from its owners the Capel family, and it is tempting to believe that he deliberately selected it because of its close proximity to Richmond Lodge, which, as he well knew, was a favourite retreat of his parents (especially his mother) with whom he was constantly at loggerheads and who

48 The Queen's Library, St James's, as furnished during the Regency period

would thus be suitably irritated.[1] His commission to Kent to make improvements at the house resulted in what seems to have been an almost complete rebuild, with interior redecoration to match. Since it was all demolished in 1802 our knowledge of the exterior and the plans is perforce based mainly on engravings in Sir William Chambers's publication of 1763 entitled *Plans, Elevations, Sections and Perspective Views of the Gardens and Buildings at Kew*. It has to be confessed that the appearance of the house as re-created by Kent was plain to the point of boredom, the main façade consisting of a central three-storey block flanked on each side by a shallow two-storey projection and a long, single-storey lateral wing. The almost total lack of any kind of exterior adornment imparted a barrack-like appearance to the whole. None the less Kew was important as being Kent's first venture into the field of actual architecture. This probably explains its stilted, mannered style, the first essay of a pupil who has all the necessary vocabulary but still lacks the confidence to employ it freely. It is faintly surprising that Burlington, to whom Kent must surely at one stage or another have submitted his designs for opinion, allowed his protégé to raise such an uninspiring building.

The interiors were a different matter. Unfortunately Chambers does not illustrate any of them in his book, but we can glean some idea about them from his comments in the text. On the ground floor were semi-private apartments including a room known as the Cabinet, a Gallery, and a suite of rooms for the use of the royal 'Bedchamber Women' (although probably not so designated until after the Prince's marriage in 1736 to the Princess Augusta of Saxe-Coburg). Kent is specifically credited with the ceilings and chimney-pieces in the Cabinet and Bedchamber Women's dining room, and with the ceiling of their drawing room. Details are not given, except in the case of the Gallery which is also credited to Kent and described as having a blue wainscot with gilt ornaments – an interesting colour scheme which instantly brings to mind the Blue Velvet Room at Chiswick. A grand staircase with a ceiling by Kent led up to the main rooms on the first floor, where several other ceilings by him were to be found, in particular that of the Grand Drawing Room 'designed and I believe painted by Mr. Kent with grotesque ornaments, in party colours and gold. The center compartment represents the story of Leda'.[2]

The fact that Kew House was also known as Kew Palace after Kent's reconstruction was probably due less to its size – it was not unduly large – than to its royal resident;[3] however, the cumulative impression conveyed by the interiors may also have had something to do with this, for they do seem to have been suitably palatial. Moreover, although Chambers provided no interior views, at least one does exist. This is found in a painting by Charles Phillips in the Royal Collection which shows Prince Frederick carousing with a band of hunting cronies in one of the rooms at Kew. The apartment is lofty, with columns and pilasters against the walls which are painted with imitation stone blocks and hunting trophies. Over the fireplace is a portrait of Frederick's sister the Princess Anne in hunting costume; this was by Mercier but unfortunately has since vanished. Walpole remarks on having seen it at Kew in 1761 'in the Long Blue Room',[4] presumably the lower Gallery, but this does not seem to be the room shown in the picture. Plate 34 in Vardy's *Some Designs of . . . William Kent* shows a chimney-piece decorated with hunting motifs and a similar hunting portrait (in this case a man, perhaps the Prince himself), but though described as being 'for the Prince of Wales' there is no positive evidence that it was designed for Kew.

Chambers also assigns to Kent the furniture in both the main and ground floor galleries, the Dressing Room, and the Grand Drawing Room in which 'the chimney-piece, the tables, glass frames, and all the furniture were designed by the same ingenious artist.'[5] The cabinet-maker concerned may well have been the younger James Moore, who is known to have worked for Prince

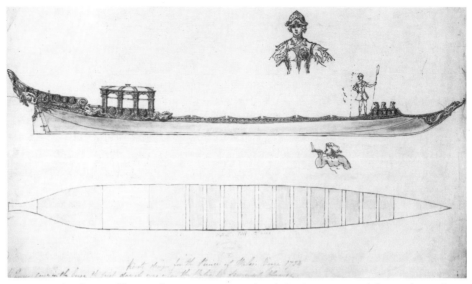

49 Design for the royal barge. The accompanying sketch for the watermen's livery shows that Kent's usual enthusiasm for a scaly effect was here especially appropriate

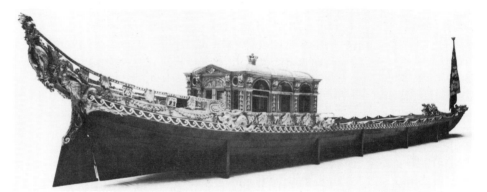

50, 51 Two views of the royal barge. The exuberantly carved stern, though a *tour-de-force* in its own right, is nevertheless in the British naval tradition of the seventeenth and eighteenth centuries

Frederick between 1732 and 1734. A possible survivor of the Prince's furniture (though not necessarily from Kew) which bears all the hallmarks of Kent's style is an oval mirror-frame now in the Victoria & Albert Museum (W86–1911). The focal decorative point of this piece is an elaborate crest which features the Prince of Wales ostrich feathers and coronet against a scallop shell background – a successful combination of motifs which Kent was to use to even greater purpose on the stern of the magnificent barge which he designed for his royal patron in 1731–2 (Plate 50).

In the days when London's streets were narrow, cobbled and ill-maintained, and before the building of the Embankment, much traffic – both official and

[130]

unofficial – went by water, i.e. the Thames. As a means of transport, therefore, the Prince of Wales's barge was not solely a luxury. It was long (63 ft), low, and built for speed, following the basic design of a wherry, and although we still have Kent's original drawings showing the plan of the hull and an elevation (Plate 49) it is highly unlikely that he could have produced them without professional consultation, most probably with John Hall, the Thames shipwright who eventually constructed the boat.[6] There are also drawings showing details of the carving on the stern and on one of the windows of the state cabin, and these were later reproduced by Vardy in *Some Designs of . . . William Kent.*

Apart from its beautiful lines the barge's chief glory is its carved decoration, which is on a scale so lavish that it can only be described as Baroque. The figure-head is a gilded dolphin; in the prow six sea-lions lean out like anthropomorphic passengers, whilst the stern sweeps back and upwards to terminate in the huge trophy in which the scallop shell and royal crest are supported by dolphins and mermaids. Acanthus leaves and scallop shells, all strongly carved in deep relief, decorate the exterior of the elegant state cabin (Plate 51). This is square in shape, with double doors at each end and open windows, and contains wall seats upholstered in green velvet, much gilding, and a painted ceiling whose chief motif is the royal arms. This last may have been the work of the gilder Paul Petit, who of all those artisans and craftsmen employed on the barge received the highest payment – almost £260. John Hall the shipwright received just under £140, while the carver James Richards, who had succeeded Grinling Gibbons as Master Carver to the Crown in 1721, received £150.

The original complement of the barge was intended to be twelve oarsmen, but the number was later increased to twenty-one, eleven to starboard and ten to port. There was also a barge-master, one John Hill. He and his crew were fitted out with magnificent if rather fanciful uniforms including blue hose, black velvet caps (a fur one for Hill), and large, round silver-gilt badges designed by the famous silversmith Paul de Lamerie. With his usual taste for marginalia Kent has sketched the head and torso of one of the oarsmen on the same sheet as his drawing of the barge. This was by no means his only venture into the field of costume design. In December 1731 Prince Frederick was host at a masquerade at which – dressed as a shepherd – he was flanked by eighteen huntsmen each specially costumed by Kent in a fantastic outfit which included green waistcoats, leopard skins, gloves and feathered caps.[7] Nor, in this connection, can we ignore Horace Walpole's famous anecdote about the 'two great ladies' who persuaded Kent to design gowns for their respective birthdays. 'The one he dressed in a petticoat decorated with columns of the five orders; the other like a bronze, in a copper-coloured satin, with ornaments of gold.'[8] However often it may be quoted this passage never ceases to fascinate costume historians and admirers of Kent alike, and to arouse in them feelings of regret that these two remarkable dresses were not preserved.

The gaily costumed crew of the royal barge were augmented on occasion by two musicians playing French horns, although their function was probably more to act as a two-tone klaxon than to supply soothing music; on that crowded highway the Thames this was a practical consideration. Music *per se*, when required, was supplied by a complete ensemble travelling in another barge, as in the case of the famous Water Music which Handel had written for George I in 1717. Indeed 'a Set of Musick' filled one of two other barges which accompanied Prince Frederick's new barge on its first official journey down the Thames, which took place on 8 July 1732. The Prince escorted his mother, brother and five sisters from the landing-stage at Chelsea Hospital to Somerset House (a Tudor Renaissance mansion, not yet rebuilt by Sir William Chambers) to view the progress of some picture restoration there. The party then returned by water to Chelsea, no doubt again to the strains of music – perhaps even those of the Water Music itself.

This was the first of many journeys made by the barge, for it continued to ply the Thames for over a century and was not finally taken out of service until 1849. An impressionistic suggestion of its presence at a royal water-borne function *circa* 1819 was made in a small oil painting by John Constable. The painting is in the Victoria & Albert Museum and so, for a time, was the barge, though it has now finally been berthed in the much more fitting surroundings of the National Maritime Museum at Greenwich. Here it rests, the undisputed peer of the other royal barges and shallops which accompany it, a witness to Kent's inventive genius and to the skill of the craftsmen who helped him to translate his ideas into reality.

In 1733 it was announced that Anne, the Princess Royal, was to marry the Prince of Orange. The wedding, postponed from November 1733 because of the Dutch Prince's indisposition, took place on 4 March 1734 at St James's Palace, in the chapel built in 1623–7 by Inigo Jones. Here Kent performed another service for the royal family, for he put up appropriate decorations 'in a very expensive manner, and in a very fine taste; that and the other preparations will cost the king £15,000.'[9]

This kind of festive decoration was not entirely new to Kent, for in 1727 he had provided in Westminster Hall a triumphal arch on the occasion of George II's coronation, and an engraving of it had been made.[10] Following this precedent he now published an engraving of the scene at the royal wedding (Jean Rigaud was the engraver, and Kent's preliminary drawing is in the British Museum). Perhaps he still had memories of a distant day back in 1714 when he had witnessed in Parma Cathedral the ceremony at which the Duke of Parma's daughter was 'sposato' to the King of Spain; two cardinals had officiated, and Kent had sketched some of the decorations in his notebook. Certainly he now decorated the chapel of St James's in a not dissimilar manner, making much use of drapery, with 'as much finery as velvets, gold and silver tissue, galloons, fringes, tassels, gilt lustres and sconces could give.'[11] His instinct for the theatre was thus given full rein, and was doubtless stimulated

[133]

by the fact that this was an evening ceremony (the procession to the chapel began to form up at 7 p.m.) and so was dramatically lit by thousands of candles. The grandeur of the scene is admirably captured in the engraving, work on which he may well have supervised with a feeling of satisfaction, content in the knowledge that he had at last succeeded in settling the score with his old foe William Hogarth.

For originally Hogarth had asked the Queen's permission, via a friend at court, to make a painting of the ceremony, and then to engrave it for public sale. At the time he was engaged upon a 'conversation piece' painting of the royal family, for which he had already made two preliminary studies (still extant), and permission to paint the wedding scene was readily granted. But he had reckoned without Kent, who over the intervening period of almost ten years had uncharacteristically neither forgotten nor forgiven the incident of the St Clement Danes altarpiece and who now, like the sinister nobleman in Browning's poem 'My Last Duchess', 'Gave commands/Then all smiles stopped together.' When Hogarth arrived at the chapel to make preliminary drawings, 'he was by Mr. Kent's interest ordered to desist', and on complaining was personally ejected by the Lord Chamberlain.[12] An appeal to the Queen merely produced the reply that although she had originally granted permission for Hogarth to paint the wedding she had not realized that in so doing she was trespassing on Kent's prerogative. Furthermore, all work on the royal group portrait was now brought to an abrupt end. Truly, as Vertue remarked, 'these are sad mortifications to an ingenious man. But it's the effect of caricatures [with] which he has heretofore toucht Mr. Kent and diverted the town, which now he is like to pay for, when he least thought on it.'[13]

52 Tail-piece from the *Odyssey*. Though Classical in conception, this is perhaps the starting-point for Kent's ideas for the royal barge. Nor should his experiences of the richly decorated Venetian state barges (such as the Doge's own *Bucentaur*) be forgotten

A few years later in 1739 Hogarth was forced to endure the pain of seeing Kent secure the appointment of Portrait Painter to the King, on the death of Charles Jervas. As usual Kent 'obtained a grant of that employment by interests of friends at court',[14] though it was generally accepted that portraiture was the weakest of his accomplishments. 'His portraits bore little resemblance to the persons that sat for them', remarks Horace Walpole, and elsewhere dismisses a painting by Kent of Burlington's daughters which he saw in the old house at Chiswick as 'a bad picture'.[15] Kent evidently found his own inability to capture a likeness very irksome; Vertue discloses that 'in many attempts in portrait painting and for the great ministers of state he could not succeed, which sometimes mortified him. . . . He attempted to paint portraits and succeeded not, especially Hon. Mr. Pelham his great patron – at last this he could not overcome.' It seems that Kent's deficiencies in this field were so notorious that despite his appointment the King 'declared he would never sit to him for his picture.' Shortly afterwards some wit (perhaps Lord Chesterfield) made up a scurrilous jingle that circulated in fashionable society and is found in various forms of which Vertue's is probably nearest the original:

> As, to Appelles, Ammon's son
> Would only deign to sit,
> So to thy pencil, Kent, alone
> Shall Brunswick's form submit.
>
> Equal your envied honours, save
> This difference still we see;
> One would no other painter have –
> None other would have thee![16]

Nevertheless Kent was not without commissions, though it is perhaps significant that many of these were apparently for portraits of George II (certainly not done from life) for despatch to embassies overseas, where the royal features were less well known. According to Vertue these commissions were secured for Kent by the Duke of Grafton. One such portrait of the King, signed and dated 1741, is still extant at Rokeby in Yorkshire. It is not a good likeness, and indeed Kent's failure to capture convincingly the features of most of his sitters may explain why few of his portraits seem to have survived – after a decent interval they were simply consigned to well-deserved oblivion. Disappointment on the part of the sitters may perhaps also explain the presence in his studio after his death of the portraits of Lady Bruce and Miss Denham, not to mention yet another of George II.

However, one important portrait still extant is that of Alexander Pope, now in the Blue Velvet Room at Chiswick. This is a roundel situated over the door leading into the Red Velvet Room; it is dated on the back 1735, and shows the poet wearing a red coat or gown with a brown fur collar and a red turban of the sort worn informally indoors by gentlemen at that time (Handel sports one rakishly in the famous Vauxhall statue by Roubiliac that is now in the Victoria & Albert Museum). Pope must have been fond of the coat, for he was painted in it several times by Jonathan Richardson, to whom he sat more often than to any other portraitist. A comparison between Kent's portrait and other likenesses of Pope suggests that it is reasonably faithful, though perhaps a trifle too gaunt and ascetic, even given Pope's constant poor health. On the other hand it is considerably more lively than either of Kent's other two attempts to portray his friend – the tail-piece to Homer's *Odyssey* (see p. 75) and a similar profile on the ceiling of the 'Belisarius Room' at Raynham (p. 102).

Consciousness of his own limited powers as a portrait painter coupled with a reluctance to let his old friend down may have been behind Kent's apparent hesitation in completing a portrait of Pope for their mutual friend Hugh Bethel. ('Mr. Kent enquires always of you', writes the poet to Bethel, who like Kent was a Yorkshireman.) It is clear from the correspondence that Kent had originally agreed to paint the portrait. But in February 1743/4 Pope is forced to ask Bethel, 'if Kent will still put off my picture, will you have a copy of Vanloo's?' Eventually it seems Kent was cajoled to get down to work. 'The last thing I did before I was confin'd was to sit the first time to Mr. Kent for you; it wants but one sitting more, and pray tell me where, or with whom it shall be left for you?' (19 March 1743/4).[17] Nothing further is known of this portrait, and it seems that Kent had delayed too long, for Pope was already seriously ill and just over two months later was dead.

In happier times and in characteristic vein Pope had taken advantage of his friend's new royal appointment to have a little dig at the latter's well-known foibles, in a letter to Lord Burlington (19 January 1739/40):

> If His Majesty's Principal Painter (for so I read in . . . the Gazetteer) would follow my example here for as many months (for so many at least it will take) to cleanse his pencil, and purify his palette, from all that greasy mixture and fat oil they have contracted, he would paint like a Raphael and look like an Angelo: whereas if he proceeds in his carnality and carnivoracity he must expect not to imitate Raphael in anything but his untimely end.[18]

An unusual portrait in which Kent seems to have risen somewhat above his normal level in this type of work is that of Burlington's younger daughter Charlotte on horseback (Plate 53). The likeness itself is fresh and appealing, and one hopes compensated for any previous failure Kent may have had in capturing the sisters on canvas. But the picture – which is at Chatsworth – poses problems. It is inscribed on the back, possibly in Burlington's own hand, 'The horse painted by Van Bloomen. The landskip by Horizonte. The figure and portrait of Lady Charlotte Boyle by Mr. Kent 1747.' Jan Frans van Bloemen, known as Orizonte, was an Antwerp-born artist who was indeed famed for

53 Portrait of Lady Charlotte Boyle, the figure by Kent but the horse and landscape ascribed to others. Perhaps Kent's most successful portrait

his landscapes (see p. 203) but is never known to have left Rome once he had settled there in 1681; he died in 1749. His brother Pieter van Bloemen, though noted as a painter of horses and known to have been in Rome *circa* 1688, was back in Antwerp by 1694 and died there in 1720. The precise origins of the portrait therefore remain obscure, although there is no reason to doubt Kent's authorship of the figure and features. Nevertheless it seems not to have been commissioned, for at the time of his death it was hanging in his dining room (? in Savile Row) and was bequeathed to Lady Charlotte in his will.

A number of opportunities for portraiture of a different kind came Kent's way, in the form of sculptured monuments. Since the majority of these (there are nine or ten in all) were created in the early 1730s, the selection of Kent as designer smacks more of a vogue than of any firm conviction as to his merits in this field, while the actual likenesses of the deceased were created by the skill of the sculptors concerned.[19] Nevertheless the monuments are a not inconsiderable feature of Kent's total output, and it would no doubt have gratified him to know that three of them are still amongst the most famous in the country, though it must be confessed that their fame is due more to the men they commemorate than to the skill of their designer. They are those to the Duke of Marlborough in the chapel at Blenheim Palace and to Shakespeare and Isaac Newton in Westminster Abbey.

The Marlborough monument was completed in 1733. On a marble pedestal a black marble sarcophagus is flanked by two allegorical figures representing Fame and History, whilst above them are grouped the figures of John and Sarah Churchill and their two sons (their four daughters are totally ignored). From beneath the sarcophagus there struggles the half-crushed figure of a dragon, representing Envy (doubtless Kent had noticed a similar creature on the tomb of Pope Gregory XIII in St Peter's at Rome). Across the front of the base pedestal is a marble relief representing the Duke at what was probably the proudest moment in his life – accepting the surrender of the French Marshal Tallard at Blenheim. In style strikingly and unashamedly Baroque despite the Duke's Classical costume and laurel-leaf crown, the monument was executed by Rysbrack for the sum of £2,200 at a time when he had (as Vertue puts it) 'great employments for quality and gentry' and could ask £35 for a single bust. He had come to England in 1720 at the age of 26. His rapid success, though attributable to his great talent, probably also owed something to discerning patronage, and once again Burlington's influence must almost certainly have been of crucial importance. The Marlborough tomb is without doubt one of his finest works, from the family group itself to the relief panel showing the surrender, for which a terracotta model exists in the Soane Museum. It is doubtful whether Kent had much to do with this detailed work other than giving it general approval as part of his overall scheme; such things could be confidently left to Rysbrack, who by 1732 – according to Vertue – had already made a bust of Kent, though whether completed in marble or only in terracotta we are not told. That there was genuine friendship between them is attested by the fact that Kent in his will left Rysbrack a mourning ring. They also appear together in Gawen Hamilton's group portrait *A Conversation of Virtuosis* (1735).

The Marlborough monument was not Rysbrack's first work in this genre for Kent, for the monument to Newton (d. 1727) was finished in April 1731, two years previously. The figure of the great scientist lies easily on top of the sarcophagus, his elbow resting on a pile of books, beside him two *putti* holding up a diagram of the solar system. Above is a huge globe marked by signs of the Zodiac and showing the path of the 1681 comet as predicted by Newton, the globe itself supporting a mourning figure representing Astronomy. The front of the sarcophagus bears a relief showing children playing with various objects symbolic of Newton's career and including a telescope, a prism and a furnace (he was at one time Master of the Mint). The monument is by no means as arrestingly dramatic as that to the Marlboroughs, but the general scheme has been carefully thought out, the head of Newton is bold and the features fine. Horace Walpole was later to condemn as 'an absurdity' the fact that 'the obelisk at the back is . . . loaded with a globe and human figure',[20] but today such criticism is seen as mere carping. Vertue rightly commends it as 'a noble and elegant work of . . . Rysbrack, much to his reputation', but is rather sour about the fact that Kent's name appears on it as well although all he did was to provide the design.[21] In the collections of the Plymouth City Museum and Art Gallery is a preliminary drawing for the Newton monument by Rysbrack himself; it has no connection with Kent's design and shows a boldly inventive talent which on this occasion Rysbrack was compelled to suppress, contenting himself solely with exercising his virtuosic technique. A question mark must hang over the full-length statues of Inigo Jones and Palladio which he completed for Lord Burlington some time before 1730, and which still stand in their original positions, one at each side of the main entrance stairway at Chiswick. Rysbrack's original authorship of these has seldom been questioned; nevertheless there exists (in the Victoria & Albert Museum) a drawing by Kent of the Jones figure which could have been either a pattern for it, or merely copied from it after its completion. (But see note on p. 249.)

In 1733 Rysbrack completed another of Kent's designs, intended to complement the Newton monument on the opposite side of the thirteenth-century choir screen into which both were set. This is a memorial to Lord Stanhope (d. 1720), a gallant soldier who amongst other exploits captured Minorca for the Crown; he too reclines in a similar posture to that of Newton, though against the background of a marble tent surmounted by a helmeted figure (Victory perhaps, or Fame). In accordance with the Classical outlook which helped to make Rysbrack's work so acceptable to the Palladians, both Newton and Stanhope are shown wearing Roman costume; so, for that matter, is Marlborough, although as has been noted above the general design of this monument is far more traditionally Baroque than perhaps either Kent or Rys-

54 The Newton and Stanhope monuments in Westminster Abbey, in their original setting before Blore's alteration of the choir-screen

brack would have cared to admit. 'Mr. Kent's payments for his works and drawings especially were high enough commonly', Vertue tells us,[22] and goes on to state that Kent received £50 each for the Newton and Stanhope monuments (designs for both are to be found in the Victoria & Albert Museum). Neither, regrettably, is seen to best advantage amidst the Gothic Revival fripperies with which the architect Edward Blore concealed the remnants of the medieval screen in 1833–4 (Plate 54).

Intriguing questions are raised by two drawings in the British Museum which show the front and side views of an equestrian statue on its plinth; these are inscribed 'The statue of Prince Eugene of Savoy formerly standing in Carlton House gardens, by Kent'. The drawings are almost certainly not by Kent, though they could be by Vardy. All trace of the statue seems to have vanished, and there is no indication either of the material or of the sculptor, but inevitably it brings to mind Rysbrack's great figure of William III at Bristol – said to be his only equestrian work.

Less than ten years after completing the Newton monument Rysbrack found himself the victim of 'the great and unproportioned exultation of that statue

[140]

of Shakespeare . . . done by Scheemakers . . . which has effectually established his credit and reputation, and at the same time obliterated in some degree that of Rysbrack's insomuch that he feels the effect in the decline of business.'[23] The reputation of Shakespeare as England's greatest dramatist had been gradually growing ever since the early eighteenth century, and several editors including Pope himself had tackled the text, incidentally subjecting it to indignities and bowdlerizations which would not be tolerated today. Bands of admirers, the equivalent of modern fan-clubs, formed to propagate the name and works of the Bard, including one especially formidable group of women calling themselves 'Shakespeare's Ladies'. It seems to have been these ladies who in 1738 promoted the idea of the monument, and also persuaded the manager of Drury Lane theatre to put on a benefit performance of *Julius Caesar*, the proceeds (in the event, some £200) going towards the project. But there was also an organizing committee with Pope and Burlington as members, and few can therefore have been surprised that Kent was selected as designer.

The choice of Scheemakers as sculptor, however, was perhaps less predictable. Peter Scheemakers, the son of a Flemish sculptor, had studied in Italy and was making his second visit to England where he was to remain until 1771, eventually retiring to Antwerp where he died in 1781. Apparently he laboured without outstanding success at first, producing a series of busts and monuments of high quality but without the necessary flair to catch the public imagination. The Shakespeare commission changed this, 'tossed this sculptor above on the summit of the wheel [of fortune], and so became the admiration of the public', as Vertue puts it, adding that the 'considerable employments of profit and honour' which Scheemakers subsequently enjoyed were also due to business acumen and a policy of undercutting Rysbrack's prices. 'As Mr. Rysbrack for a marble bust, model and carving his lowest price was 35 guineas, the other would and does do it for near ten guineas less.'[24]

Scheemakers was nevertheless a fine craftsman and the Shakespeare monument, completed in 1740, bears eloquent testimony to his skill. Though there is some evidence that the success went somewhat to his head ('This little fellow, since he has done [the] Shakespeare monument, thinks himself above all others', remarks Vertue severely), he would apparently disarm his critics by saying cheerfully, 'I am a little impudent fellow – no matter, I can't help it.'

The Shakespeare monument gave an important stimulus to the concept of the Poets' Corner, and remains one of the most striking memorials there. It is now so well known as to have become something of a sculptured cliché; this is unfortunate, for its quality merits closer attention. Within a framework composed of a Palladian door-frame complete with pediment and dentil moulding stands the figure of the Bard, elbow on a pile of books, one leg crossed over the other, cloak flowing, his right hand holding a page bearing Prospero's speech on 'The cloud-capp'd towers . . .' from the final moments of *The Tempest*. His features seem to be an idealized amalgam of the well-known engraving by Martin Droeshout and the bust over his grave in Stratford-on-Avon parish church, and are a good deal more attractively romantic than either of these (especially the bust, which has been described by a modern author as portraying 'a moon-faced ninny').[25] But perhaps the most interesting point, so obvious that it is usually missed, is that Shakespeare's costume conforms more or less to what he would actually have worn, instead of the Classical style usually applied to important statuary at this period.

At the base of the plinth against which the figure leans there appear in relief the heads of Henry V, Richard III and Queen Elizabeth I. These drove Horace Walpole – ever a stickler for the proprieties, as he saw them – into a frenzy. 'What an absurdity to place busts at the angles of a pedestal, and at the bottom of that pedestal!' he protested, and then went on to pose what is in fact a valid question: 'Though Queen Elizabeth's head might be intended to mark the era in which the poet flourished, why were Richard II [sic] and Henry V selected? ... What reason can be assigned for giving them the preference?'[26] There can be no certain answer to this; all that can be said is that Kent no doubt consulted with Pope on the literary aspects of the monument, and that no such niggling criticism had any effect on its general popularity, either then or now. In 1743 Scheemakers made a replica for Henry Herbert, ninth Earl of Pembroke and a member of the Burlington circle, 'in fine free stone with its little pedestal and ornaments' for the sum of £100 18s. 4½d.; this still stands in the front entrance hall of the family seat, Wilton House, a worthy reminder of the tradition that Shakespeare himself with his company gave the first performance of either *Twelfth Night* or *As You Like It* in the house early in January 1600/1.

The Shakespeare monument was not the first collaboration between Kent and Scheemakers, nor their first within the Abbey. In 1730 there was erected in the south aisle their memorial to General Monk, Duke of Albemarle (d. 1670). Here, against the background of a black obelisk, the armoured figure of the Duke standing at one side is balanced on the other by a seated female figure supporting herself on a medallion which bears a portrait of the Duke's son. It is a worthy but somewhat humdrum composition, the non-impact of which perhaps explains why the two artists concerned produced no further joint work until ten years later. Certainly the Monk monument has none of the style and originality that gives such life to the Shakespeare memorial.

A third sculptor with whom Kent was associated was Giovanni Battista Guelfi, whom Burlington seems to have brought back with him from Rome in 1715 and who also lodged in Burlington House. He, like Kent, profited from the confidence of his noble patron, who as well as making constant use of his services for almost twenty years 'much commended him to the nobility for an excellent sculptor [and] procured him many works' (as Vertue puts it).[27] Regrettably he turned out to be 'much opinionated, and as an Italian thought nobody could be equal to himself in this country.' His work fell out of favour and in 1734 he went back to Italy, settling finally in Bologna. 'It's thought that Lord Burlington parted with him very willingly' – the bloom had long since worn off. But it is probable that with their Italian background Guelfi and Kent got on well together,[28] and they are known to have collaborated on at least two church monuments – a large one to Thomas Watson Wentworth in York Minster (*circa* 1731) and another to Thomas and Katharine Stringer in the church at Kirkthorpe, Yorkshire (1731/2). The Wentworth monument has the husband (bewigged but otherwise confusingly clad in Roman toga and buskins) leaning against a plinth with his wife sitting dutifully at his feet; now situated in the north choir aisle, it has suffered slightly from losing the original pyramidal background as a result of being moved from another part of the Minster, but remains none the less a powerful and impressive piece of work. The Stringer monument is more restrained, presenting two separate busts of man and wife standing on a ledge over their inscription and backed by a marble slab surmounted by cherubs and coat-of-arms. The keynote here is simplicity, albeit of a kind touched with nobility.

Guelfi and Kent together also contributed jointly to a curious project commissioned by Queen Caroline. At her request Kent designed a Hermitage, *circa* 1731, for the grounds at Richmond, and this was ornamented inside with niches containing the busts of four famous thinkers – Newton, Locke, Samuel Clarke and William Wollaston; later, that of Boyle was added (1733) and later still that of Bacon. Guelfi was the sculptor originally selected, but although he probably completed two or three of the busts (certainly the one of Clarke is by him) it appears that the remainder were in fact executed by Rysbrack. At the time of writing all are on loan from the Royal Collections to Kensington Palace, where they adorn the Privy Chamber. It is a curious fact that Kent in his will bequeathed to Lady Isabella Finch 'four heads busto's Newton Clark Lock and Woolaston', and that for some reason this is repeated in the codicil as 'my four models of Newton, Lock, Woollaston and Doctor Clark'. These may have been Guelfi's terracotta studies for the finished busts; their presence in Kent's collection was another close link between himself and the creation of the Hermitage.

The exterior of the Hermitage was resolutely rustic, although behind the rusticity of the façade could be traced the formality of a Palladian front complete with pediment and central arched doorway. 'The stones of the whole edifice appear as if rudely laid together, and the venerable look of the whole is improved by the thickness of the solemn grove behind it, and the little turret on top with a bell to which you may ascend by a winding walk.'[29] The rough exterior contrasted strongly with the octagonal interior which remained strictly formal in its proportions, decorations and furniture, despite some attempt to decorate the domed ceiling – via whose central *oculus* light was admitted – with a frieze of imitation fronds (not sharp enough to pass as stalactites). A section of it illustrated in Vardy's *Some Designs of . . . William Kent* (plate 33)

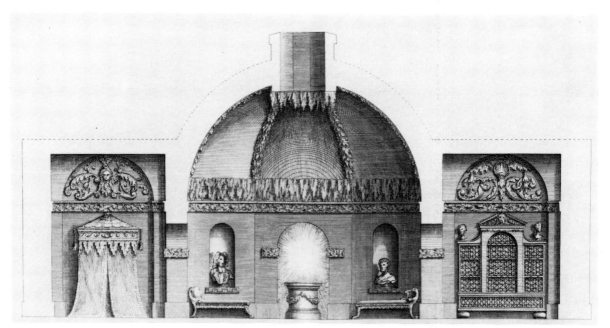

55 Interior of the Queen's Hermitage showing the tented entrance, a bookcase and busts (that
of Boyle replaced by a sunburst). Plate 33 in *Some Designs of . . . William Kent*

shows an apsidal end with niches containing two of the busts and a Classical
plinth; the furniture shown consists of two elegant couches and a thoroughly
Kentian bookcase, while the entrance is constructed to resemble a tent
(Plate 55). The plinth, though empty, seems to have behind it a source of light
like a sunburst, and is undoubtedly described in the following passage from
the *Gentleman's Magazine* for April 1733:

> The 4 bustos so often mention'd stand in niches at each quarter in the walls
> of the vaulted dome, but the bust of Mr. Boyle stands higher than these
> on a pedestal, in the inmost end, as it were, the most sacred recess of the
> place; behind his head a large gold sun, darting his wide spreading beams
> all about and towards the others, to whom his aspect is directed.

Why the bust of Boyle is not actually shown in the engraving is a mystery.

A rash of verses about the Hermitage and the busts broke out in the *Gentleman's Magazine* during 1732–3. Some, like the following, were rudely critical:

> Three holes there are, thro' which you see;
> Three seats to set your arse on;
> And idols four – of wizards three,
> And one unchristian parson.

(April 1733)

Criticism, however, was balanced if not outdone by blatant sycophancy:

> Flow swiftly, Thames, and flowing still proclaim
> This building's beauty, and the builder's fame;
> Tell Indian seas thy Naiads here have seen
> The sweetest grotto and the wisest Queen,
> Whose royal presence blest this humble seat;
> How small the mansion, and the guest how great!
>
> (December 1732)

The author of these lines was Stephen Duck, an agricultural labourer and largely self-taught lesser poet who through a fortunate introduction to the Queen was appointed custodian of the Hermitage and holder of the unusual office of Royal Thatcher; he later became Rector of Byfleet.

In a letter from Pope to Burlington, written probably in 1732, occurs the following curious passage: 'Pray lay your commands upon Kent, to send you the short Dialogue I writ in his behalf, between the General [? Dormer] and myself, shewing the cause why nobody takes notice of him when they speak of the Hermitage. He is modest, and afraid to give offence, so has kept it in his pocket, nor ever dared to show it to the General, by which means my wit is lost in obscurity.'[30] The document has disappeared (perhaps destroyed by Kent), so it is hard to tell whether it was some piece of raillery, or whether Kent's authorship of the Hermitage really was disputed or ignored.

Three or four years later Kent took these ideas several stages further by designing (also for the Queen at Richmond) an extravaganza called Merlin's Cave (completed in 1735). This stood on the site of the well-known Rhododendron Dell, one of the attractions of Kew Gardens today. A thatched rustic exterior looking curiously like a group of African native huts concealed a roof-lit chamber whose vaulted ceiling was supported on rough columns suggestive of trees. This too is illustrated by Vardy (plate 32) with a section which reveals the absence of furniture except for two bookcases whose Kentian outlines have been thinly disguised by what might be termed applied rusticity.[31] There were no busts, but the Cave contained six ill-assorted waxwork figures of Minerva, Elizabeth of York, Queen Elizabeth I and her Muse, and Merlin himself with an assistant. These were kept in a sort of three-bayed Gothic showcase in the apse of the Cave; its outline, though not its contents, may be seen in Vardy's engraving.[32] The waxworks were shown to visitors by Stephen Duck, who in the 1770s was to figure together with the Queen in a poem by William Mason. The poem attacks the landscaping of the Old Park at Richmond by 'Capability' Brown, who included in his scheme the destruction of the Cave:

56 Interior of Merlin's Cave, perhaps showing the Queen (right) with attendants. The wall-cases containing the waxworks can be seen in the background. Plate 32 in *Some Designs of . . . William Kent*

To Richmond come; for see, untutor'd Brown
Destroys these wonders which were once thy own.
Lo! from his melon-ground the peasant slave
Has rudely rush'd, and levell'd Merlin's Cave;
Knock'd down the waxen wizard, seiz'd his wand,
Transform'd to lawn what late was Fairy-land;
And marr'd with impious hand each sweet design
Of Stephen Duck and good Queen Caroline.[33]

The absurdity of the waxworks was not Kent's idea (see note 32). But it may well have set a trend, for just as hermitages, grottoes and rustic retreats of all kinds became popular, so it was not unusual for owners to install a waxen inhabitant, suitably dressed, to add verisimilitude. Occasionally even real 'hermits' were engaged, though most found the spartan régime to which they were committed too much for them and quietly decamped. Hermit posts were advertised, and contracts were normally for seven years, though few would-be professional hermits lasted that long; one who did, called Finch, probably only survived in the job because his cell (at Burley-on-the-Hill) boasted a thatched

[146]

roof and two fireplaces. Kent himself is said to have designed the thatched cell in the grounds of Badminton, although this is actually a small rustic cottage of stout construction.

The point about the Hermitage, Merlin's Cave, and all other similar follies that sprouted up in gardens and grounds from the 1730s onwards is that to a greater or lesser extent all were manifestations of the taste for Gothic, or imitation medievalism – and here again Kent was a pioneer. Eighteenth-century Gothic is often assumed to have begun with Horace Walpole at Strawberry Hill. This, however, was its second phase. Public awareness of the medieval heritage was in fact probably first stirred by Pope who despite his devotion to Classicism nevertheless also found himself deeply responsive to the emotive power of medieval buildings (especially ruined ones) and to the romantic appeal of landscape. His poem 'Eloisa to Abelard', published with his collected works as early as 1717, evokes a setting replete with grots, caverns, rills, groves, 'darksome pines' and caves. There can surely be few more powerful passages in romantic literature than the description in the same poem of 'Black Melancholy' who sits surrounded by

> A death-like silence and a dread repose:
> Her gloomy presence saddens all the scene,
> Shades ev'ry flow'r, and darkens ev'ry green,
> Deepens the murmur of the falling floods,
> And breathes a browner horror on the woods.

And in terms of painting perhaps only Caspar David Friedrich could have done justice to the following:

> In these lone walls (their days eternal bound),
> These moss-grown domes with spiry turrets crown'd,
> Where awful arches make a noon-day night,
> And the dim windows shed a solemn light.

The same artist is strongly recalled also in a strange and again essentially romantic notion to which Pope confessed in his later years:

> I have sometimes had an idea of planting an old Gothic cathedral in trees. Good large poplars with their white stems (cleared of boughs to a proper height) would serve very well for the columns, and might form the different aisles or peristiliums, by their different distances and heights. These would look very well near; and the dome rising all in a proper tuft in the middle, would look as well at a distance.[34]

Pope seems to have been one of the first English writers to use the adjective 'picturesque' in its modern sense; following his lead, people began to regard natural objects such as mountains and waterfalls with a new and rather awestruck respect, to see ancient ruins in a different and more appreciative light, and to invest medieval personages with a glamour they probably did not merit. Moreover he himself began the romantic enthusiasm for grottoes with his own remarkable grotto in his garden at Twickenham, begun about 1718 (see p. 202). But it was Kent who designed what is certainly one of the earliest above-ground Gothic follies in the country, at Shotover in Oxfordshire. This consists simply of a castellated façade pierced by three arches and with a tower at either end, and was probably designed in the 1720s.[35]

Kent's interest in Gothic remained with him throughout his career. No doubt initially stimulated by Pope, it may also have received encouragement from Queen Caroline. Her interest in medievalism is illustrated not only by such fanciful excesses as Merlin's Cave ('You *deserve* to be abused for such childish, silly stuff', retorted George II on being told that she was being criticized in the press for her extravagance),[36] but also by her commissioning Rysbrack to make busts of the Black Prince and Henry V. (Did she, one wonders, have anything to do with the selection of the busts at the foot of the Shakespeare monument?) So it may well have been at her behest that Kent painted three canvases (still in the Royal Collection) with themes from the life of Henry V – *The Battle of Agincourt, The Meeting of Henry V with the Queen of France*, and *The Marriage of Henry V*. (A small drawing of an archer, which is in the Victoria & Albert Museum collections, appears to be a study for the central group in the battle scene (Plate 57).) The royal household accounts show that Kent received £166 6s. 'for pictures' between May 1730 and March the following year, most probably for these works. They enjoy a unique significance in being perhaps the only canvases on medieval subjects to be painted in this country during the first half of the eighteenth century. (It would be fascinating to know whether the subjects evoked in Kent any memories, however dim, of a strange picture he saw and noted in his Tour diary of 1714 in the collection of one of the great Italian families, which depicted 'King Edward the Third a-making one of them a Knight of St. Giorgio, and [on] each side of the King of England [the] King of France and King of Scotland'. No Italian was admitted into the Order of the Garter by Edward III, so this painting must have been either allegorical or else pure fantasy.) Inevitably the historical details of costume, weapons, conduct of battle, etc., are for the most part wildly improbable and the characters shown are emphatically of Kent's own time, while in the battle scene the buildings overlooking the field of action recall not France but the Castel Sant' Angelo in Rome, a brooding and sinister landmark well known to Kent. However, accurate background research was not considered essential until the nineteenth century, and even today many a Hollywood epic has suffered from lack of it, evoking laughter in all the wrong places.

Nevertheless this cavalier disregard for reality could be considered a positive asset to the series of illustrations which Kent produced for the Thomas Birch edition of Spenser's *The Faerie Queene*. That this epic work, a triumph of Elizabethan imagery masquerading as a medieval fable, could attract readers

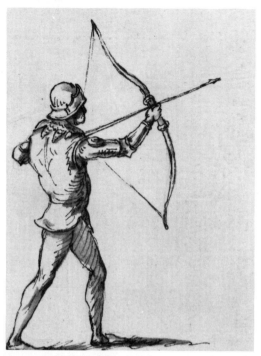

57 Drawing of an archer: probably a study for Kent's painting *The Battle of Agincourt*

in the austere Augustan age, is proof that an undertow of romanticism was already running strongly. Birch's edition did not appear until 1751, by which time Kent was dead (indeed it has been suggested – though not convincingly – that some of the final illustrations were completed by another artist); obviously, however, he must have been working on them for some time previously. A number of the original drawings have been preserved and are in the Victoria & Albert Museum (Plates 58–61). Kent's personal affection for the poem is evinced by the sheer number of illustrations he provided for it – no less than thirty-two, a total unsurpassed until Walter Crane produced his version (edited by T. J. Wise) in 1896. Here it must again be emphasized that, whatever Kent's origins, he was not uneducated, though perhaps to some extent self-taught. His literary interests are further attested by a lively drawing in the Chatsworth collections of a scene from Cervantes showing the exorcising of Don Quixote's library, and by another in the British Museum illustrating the opening passages of John Bunyan's *Pilgrim's Progress*, and perhaps intended as a frontispiece for it. Continuing Italian influence is proclaimed by three small illustrations (also in the British Museum) to Torquato Tasso's poem *Gerusalemme Liberata* (1574); these are very much in the style of the *Faerie Queene* drawings and suggest that at some time Kent was contemplating a similar published edition of Tasso. History too attracted his attention, not only the English variety indicated in his Henry V canvases, but French as well;

[149]

58 Design for book II, canto vi of Spenser's *The Faerie Queene*. Published with the caption 'Guyon Leaves the Palmer & Crosses the Idle lake with Phaedria'

59 Design for book V, canto ii of *The Faerie Queene*. Published with Kent's caption, 'Arthegal Fights the Sarazin Polente'

60 Design for book I, canto vii of *The Faerie Queene*. Published with the caption 'Prince Arthur Slays the Giant Orgoglio & Releases the Redcross Knight'

61 Design for book I, canto iv of *The Faerie Queene*. Kent's title to this drawing was simplified in publication to 'The House of Pride'

[151]

in a letter at Chatsworth of 16 November 1732 he tells Burlington 'I have just now with me a French bookseller, that brought me the French Antiquity beginning with William the Conqueror. . . .' It is highly probable that his attention was first directed to Spenser by Pope, who expressed his own admiration for *The Faerie Queene* in the following anecdote:

> After reading a canto of Spenser . . . to an old lady, between seventy and eighty years of age, she said that I had been showing her a gallery of pictures. I don't know how it is, but she said very right; there is something in Spenser that pleases one as strongly in one's old age, as it did in one's youth. I read *The Faerie Queene* when I was about twelve, with infinite delight; and I think it gave me as much, when I read it over about a year or two ago.[37]

Horace Walpole felt that the illustrations to *The Faerie Queene* showed up Kent in the worst possible light as an artist, calling them 'the most exercrable performance you ever beheld. . . . Whoever would search for his faults, will find an ample crop in a very favourite work of his, the . . . Fairy Queen.' He then goes on to castigate 'the wretchedness of drawing, the total ignorance of perspective, the want of variety, the disproportion of the buildings, and the awkwardness of the attitudes. . . . There are figures issuing from cottages not so high as their shoulders, castles in which the towers could not contain an infant, and knights who hold their spears as men do who are lifting a load sideways.'[38] Nor was Walpole the only critic of these pictures. 'It is said that Mr. Kent frequently declared he caught his taste in gardening from reading the picturesque descriptions of Spenser. However this may be, the designs which he made for the works of that poet are an incontestable proof that they had no effect upon his executive powers as a painter.' So wrote William Mason the poet,[39] and it must be admitted that as regards draughtsmanship and general technique the illustrations are often poor. Yet they are imaginative, and in some cases the very unreality of proportions and perspective may be thought to enhance the fantasy of the subject matter – though it is doubtful whether this effect was intentional on Kent's part.

The various characters in *The Faerie Queene* are dressed by Kent in a pseudo-medieval manner whose non-historical basis is here of no importance. In fact the costumes and backgrounds – especially the castles, which have about them the flat, cardboard cut-out look of stage scenery – impart to the whole allegorical fantasy a further dimension of pantomime, and once again we are reminded of Kent's continuing interest in the theatre. For the most part his ideas seem to have been entirely his own. However, in the illustration showing Prince Arthur slaying Giant Orgoglio (Book I, Canto vii) the ruined tower in the background has some interesting antecedents, for it may be compared with similar buildings drawn both by Inigo Jones and by Filippo Juvarra, the Italian architect and theatrical designer (see pp. 230, 233). Jones made two drawings, both showing a very similar castellated tower, for the masque *Britannia Triumphans* (1638). Juvarra's tower was the principal feature of the backcloth which he provided for scene VII of Alessandro Scarlatti's opera *Il Ciro*, performed at Rome in 1712. Kent may well have seen the opera, although he could also have seen or owned a copy of the printed libretto in which Juvarra's scenes were reproduced as engravings. But it is a moot point whether any of these designs actually prompted the idea for Giant Orgoglio's castle, which may yet be another piece of pure Kentian fantasy. And fantasy is very much the keynote of the illustration 'Britomart with her Nurse consulting Merlin' (Book III, Canto iii), in which Kent unleashed a veritable Pandora's Box of horrific Gothic monsters, drawn with obvious verve and enthusiasm.

It should be mentioned here that the majority of Kent's drawings are executed not in pencil but in pen-and-ink, often with the addition of monochrome washes. An elaborate study (in the British Museum) for a scheme of indoor decoration, consisting of a painting in an architectural setting, is a rarity indeed, for not only is it larger than most of Kent's surviving drawings, it is also enlivened by the liberal use of watercolour. One's suspicions are aroused by this uncharacteristic trait, and they are not allayed by the terse inscription 'by Kent' which appears in a corner of the drawing.

'As Kent's genius was not universal, he has succeeded as ill in Gothic.'[40] This dogmatic statement by Walpole could perhaps be condoned if it concerned the paintings and to a lesser extent the illustrations. But it does not; it is aimed primarily at architecture, the one field in which Kent's personal brand of Gothic is remarkably successful. Perhaps the folly at Shotover was the jumping-off point; at all events something prompted Henry Pelham to invite Kent *circa* 1729 to design and build a Gothic-style house for him, including in it genuine extant pre-Tudor buildings of 1475–80. This was Esher Place, Surrey, now vanished (except for the brick gatehouse) but after its completion in 1739 a house which evidently aroused a good deal of interest, until eclipsed by Walpole's own Strawberry Hill (Plate 63). Contemporary engravings (such as those in Badeslade and Rocque's supplementary fourth volume to *Vitruvius Britannicus*) show a west front clearly inspired by the main gateway of Hampton Court and an east front terminating in angular bays rising up through all three storeys; battlemented throughout, the whole concoction had (or so it appears in the prints) a disconcertingly cardboard look to it. The gatehouse consists basically of two angular, four-storey turrets joined by a central, three-storeyed section – a typical form of what had become, at the period *circa* 1475 when it was originally built, an important status symbol (another example is Sissinghurst Castle). To this Kent added a porch with an ogee-arched entrance, reconstituted battlements, and replacement arched and quatrefoil windows. In the entrance hall behind the porch he devised a circular staircase of marble to complement the original brick-built spiral staircase; the latter survives but Kent's has vanished, its place indicated only by the remains of some highly individual if structurally implausible fan vaulting on the ceiling. Vardy shows one of the chimney-pieces of Esher (plate 36), but this is basically Palladian and pays only the lightest lip-service to Gothic in the form of a lozenge-shaped frieze below the mantelshelf. For substantial tangible evidence of Kent in his Gothic mood we should go first to Hampton Court, where in 1732 he rebuilt part of the Clock Court including the vaulted gatehouse; this fits in very well with the original Tudor parts of the palace, though it is said that in fact Sir Robert Walpole persuaded Kent to follow existing precedent rather than to build in the Classical manner as he had at first intended. For this one feels grateful; yet Kent was obviously not insensitive to the historical appeal of the palace – how could he be, with his interest in medievalism? – and indeed he made a drawing of the hall which is now in the British Museum. It shows Henry VIII seated on a dais and receiving the French Ambassador; Kent's manuscript inscription reads 'Mommerancy [? Montmorency] Embassador from ye King [of] France to Henry ye 8th at Hampton Court.' This drawing formed the basis for a magnificent engraving which John Vardy published in 1749, acknowledging Kent as its source but reducing the role of the figures and placing much greater emphasis on the architecture, in particular the great hammer-beam roof.

In another of Kent's drawings, also in the British Museum, the main gateway and front façade of Hampton Court occupy the foreground of a landscape, somewhat telescoped since it also includes a view of Esher in the distance. The margins of this drawing contain short but interesting manuscript annotations which seem to show that Kent was attempting to write a poem on the subject of the confluence of the river Mole with the Thames, and that the drawing illustrates this (certainly the river – which also appears in the drawing – is filled with seahorses and tritons which look distinctly out of place in the pastoral setting).

Large, spacious medieval interiors such as the Hampton Court hall in fact evoked a sympathetic response in Kent (it was certainly no accident that the interior of Merlin's Cave was planned like a round Templar church with an apsidal end). Thus when called upon to provide screens for the interiors of Westminster Hall (1738/9) and Gloucester Cathedral (1742) he did so without hesitation in the Gothic style, even though his personal form of Gothic bore only superficial resemblance to the medieval styles on which it was superimposed. Neither screen exists now, but both are illustrated by Vardy (plates 48 and 49), and together they neatly encapsulate Kent's architectural Gothic manner. This is seen to have been very much his own creation, consisting of a limited vocabulary of favourite pseudo-medieval motifs (in which the ogee arch and the quatrefoil take pride of place) applied as a flimsy façade to solid, Classically based structures. The latter can be sensed, as it were, lurking just beneath the surface, and even breaking through it; the columns and pilasters, for instance, remain firmly Classical in conception and appearance, although being faceted instead of rounded (Plate 62).

62 Gothic screen for Westminster Hall. Interestingly paralleled by the setting for the 'House of Pride', this screen perfectly encapsulates Kent's Gothic manner in architecture, with ogee arches and quatrefoils predominating. Plate 48 in *Some Designs of . . . William Kent*

This is wedding-cake decoration – but of the best kind. The effect is cheerful and pleasing, not portentous, the execution taut and sharply defined. It is as effective on a small scale as on a large; this is exemplified by two designs in Vardy (plates 22 and 31), for a candlestick and for a silver standish respectively. (The latter, designed specifically for Merlin's Cave, has an owl – Gothic night-bird *par excellence* – as the central lid finial. Kent seems to have been interested in owls, and to have studied them fairly closely. They ornament another of the candlesticks in Vardy (plate 21), as well as the richer of the two library writing tables at Chatsworth. His illustration of Gay's fable 'The Two Owls and the Sparrow', no. XXXII, is competent and assured, and there are drawings at Chatsworth which, although probably not by him, suggest that the Burlington household may at one time have included a tame owl which could have been his model.) Vardy also shows the Gothic pulpit which Kent provided for York Minster (plate 51), and this is especially valuable since here we see a large item of traditional church furniture which is not Classically based and perhaps represents the nearest that Kent ever got to a pure Gothic style. Clearly the York pulpit had considerable charm, even delicacy.

[155]

63 Esher, rebuilt and Gothicized by Kent in the landscape setting which he devised for it

The assertion is sometimes made that Kent also constructed a screen for York. This is not borne out by the facts. What he did, in 1736, was to demolish a wooden screen of indeterminate medieval date which then stood behind the high altar and to move the altar back one bay so that it stood as it now does immediately in front of the stone screen. By 1736, in consultation with Burlington, he had also re-paved the Minster, replacing the gravestones with which the floor was then covered with a geometrical pattern in slabs of stone and blue marble; this paving was renewed in 1971–2. (Possibly his mind went back to 1715, when together with Thomas Coke he had visited Siena Cathedral and had scribbled down in his notebook that 'the pavement before the high altar is most wonderful for the inlay'd work of stone, brown, black and white.') The pulpit came in 1740, together with a new throne in the same style; three years later Kent also redesigned the pews (for ladies only) which stood in front of the pulpit. All this perished in the fire of 1829 which almost totally gutted the Minster Choir.[41]

Occasionally Kent was inspired to go beyond the self-imposed limits of his decorative medieval style and to produce something quite startling in Gothic-inspired originality. In the late 1730s his old friend General Dormer invited

[156]

him to make alterations and additions to the family home, Rousham in Oxford-shire. Wings were accordingly added in the Jacobean style of the original and the main façade lightly battlemented. Inside, the parlour remains as a fine and valuable example of Kent in Classical mood, notably the ceiling which is second only to the Presence Chamber at Kensington Palace in providing a definitive exposition of his Roman grotesque style. In total contrast, the dining room (then the library) has a Gothic ceiling of structural complexity unique in Kent's work, in which a honeycomb pattern of squares and hexagonal vaults clusters round a large central vault. This vaulting, though obviously medieval in inspiration, is composed in a thoroughly original way and carried out with a kind of *élan* totally foreign to genuine medieval architecture.

Kentian Gothic is a purely decorative style taking its inspiration from a dis-torted and generalized view of the medieval era. Moreover Kent could never have brought himself to abandon the balanced and symmetrical proportions of Classicism in favour of the asymmetry characteristic of true medieval build-ings, as James Wyatt was later to do at Lee Priory (1785) and Ashridge (1808). 'Icing-sugar Gothic', if one may so call Kent's brand of medievalism, preceded by some fifteen years Horace Walpole's first attempts to remodel Strawberry Hill (from 1744), and indeed set a trend of its own. Walpole himself completely failed to appreciate Kent's personal brand of Gothic; his comment on the Glou-cester choir screen was that 'Kent knew no more there than he did anywhere else how to enter into the true Gothic taste.'[42] Rousham, he found, 'has rein-stated Kent with me; he has nowhere shown so much taste'; yet even here, although he thought the library 'delightful', he felt that Kent had 'stuck as close as *he* could to Gothic', thus damning with noticeably faint praise.[43] No doubt he would have been deeply distressed to know that his own ideas on the subject, as exemplified at Strawberry Hill, would be dismissed as mere frivolity by the serious-minded theorists of the nineteenth-century Gothic Revival.

Kent's most important follower in Gothic was the architect and builder Batty Langley, who in 1742 published a comprehensive pattern book with an immensely long title, here for convenience shortened to *Gothic Architecture, Improved by Rules and Proportions*. The designs are Langley's own, not Kent's, but they closely reflect the Kentian spirit and confirm that Gothic was yet another area of architecture and decoration upon which Kent firmly left his mark.

CHAPTER SEVEN
BUILDING ON THE GRAND SCALE

By the mid-1730s Kent's position as the most fashionable and sought-after all-purpose artist of the day was unassailable. 'Mr. Kent at Court and amongst people of quality, call'd on for drafts &c. on all occasions', noted Vertue in 1734,[1] and this succinct word-picture is reinforced by Gawen Hamilton's 1735 group portrait of an artists' club in which appears the stout, dapper figure of the middle-aged Kent – erect, assured, and perhaps just a little bit pompous (Plate 64). His place in society now secure, it no longer mattered to him as much as it might have done earlier that in April 1733 Lord Burlington suddenly threw up all his official appointments and retired from Court. This precipitate action naturally aroused intense interest, and the gossip-mongers were kept busy trying to nose out the cause. 'The reason everybody gives that I converse with is, his not having the White Staff [i.e. the office of Lord Steward]', wrote the Hon. Charles Howard to his father Lord Carlisle, and continued, 'Let it be what it will, his doing it at this time, considering how much notice always was taken of him at Court, and he looked upon as being particularly well with the Ministry, has caused great speculation.'[2] Lord Hervey also asserts that Burlington resigned 'in great wrath' on being disappointed of the Stewardship.[3] Vertue, on the other hand, links Burlington's withdrawal from public life specifically with Kent, commenting that the former 'endeavoured and engaged in Mr. Kent's interest so far as to be opposed by the Court interest, which created some ill blood or resentments.'[4] In other words, the decision to resign was made in a fit of pique when some scheme involving Kent was, for once, actually thwarted by an anti-Kent lobby. Whatever the reason, Burlington was not the sort of man either to acknowledge defeat or to go back on his word, so he stuck to his decision; by December of 1733 Sir Thomas Robinson, in a letter to Lord Carlisle, reported that 'He has quite quitted London, sent for all his pictures from Burlington House, and is making very great and beautiful additions to Chiswick.'[5] Lady Burlington for a time stayed on at Court, mainly (it was whispered) because she could not bear to be parted from the Duke of Grafton.

[158]

64 *A Conversation of Virtuosis*, by Hamilton, 1735. Kent is on the far right (dividers in hand), admiring an antique bust, the beauties of which Rysbrack is explaining to Wootton. Appropriately, the figure of Kent is balanced at the opposite side of the canvas by that of Vertue

Perhaps Burlington's greatest consolation at this time was the knowledge that at least he would now be able to devote more time to cultural pursuits, and that he left the Court with his reputation as the supreme arbiter of Classical taste untarnished. That reputation had received a further boost in 1730 with the publication of *Fabbriche Antiche Disegnate da Andrea Palladio*, drawings of Roman baths by Palladio from Burlington's own collection; he seems to have found some of them in 1718, hidden in an obscure corner at the Villa Maser, and to have bought the rest from the Bishop of Verona. The drawings (engraved by Fourdrinier) are prefaced with a foreword by their owner in impeccable Italian. A second volume was apparently mooted; in 1734 Vertue speaks of visiting Chiswick, where he was flattered to be shown 'infinite numbers of designs of Palladio of which some has been engraved at his Lordship's expense to make a book. . . . He showed it me himself and promised me a copy of it when done, tho' he intends not to part with above 20 (a great honour and favour to come).'⁶ Regrettably the 'great honour' did not materialize, and neither did the book.

However, the publication of the original volume had already stimulated Pope to compose his famous lines on Burlington's artistic status. These are contained in the poem originally entitled 'Of Taste' (1731), later 'Of False Taste', and finally 'Of the Use of Riches' (the fourth of the *Moral Essays*). The poem is subtitled 'An Epistle to the Right Honourable Richard Earl of Burlington. Occasion'd by his publishing Palladio's Designs of the Baths, Arches, Theatres &c. of Ancient Rome'. Its central theme is that the true understanding of Classical taste, as exemplified in Burlington, is open to abuse by those who do not have his learning and sensitivity.

> In you, My Lord, Taste sanctifies Experience,
> For Splendor borrows all her Rays from Sense.
> You show us, Rome was glorious, not profuse,
> And pompous Buildings once were things of use.
> Just as they are, yet shall your noble Rules
> Fill half the Land with Imitating Fools,
> Who random Drawings from your Sheets shall take,
> And of one Beauty many Blunders make. . . .
> Yet thou proceed; be fallen Arts thy care,
> Erect new Wonders, and the Old repair,
> Jones and Palladio to themselves restore,
> And be whate'er Virtruvius was before.

This peroration is preceded by a lengthy description of 'Timon's Villa', an imaginary mansion on whose building no expense has been spared but which in the end is nothing but a vulgarly ostentatious pile, 'a labour'd Quarry above ground!' Daily life at the Villa is a mannered and meaningless ritual, and Timon himself an ignoramus with more money than sense who – for instance – values the books in his library not for their contents but for their expensive bindings.

Unfortunately but inevitably it was immediately assumed that Timon and his Villa were synonymous with the Duke of Chandos and Canons, and indeed the parallel was too close to be ignored. It seems incredible therefore that Pope protested – apparently in all sincerity – that no such comparisons were intended, and said as much in letters to both Chandos and Burlington (the letter to Burlington also being published as the foreword to the third edition of the poem). Chandos, who was an open-hearted and generous sort of man ('Thus gracious Chandos is belov'd at sight', Pope himself had written in the 'Epistle to Lord Cobham'), at once accepted Pope's protestations at their face value, but this cannot entirely have stilled the gossip. Matters were not helped by the publication of the satirical Hogarthian print, *Taste, or Burlington Gate*, in which the Duke is spattered with whitewash by Pope as the latter ascends a ladder towards the commanding figure of Kent atop the Burlington House gateway. As for Burlington – did he, one wonders, feel a twinge of uneasiness at finding his own reputation as the oracle of taste enhanced at the expense of a man whose only fault was that his zeal was unmatched by the extent of his learning?

Throughout this unedifying episode Kent, it seems, was a bystander. Indeed he may not even have been in England when Burlington's book, the cause of the trouble, appeared, for he is said (by Cunningham in his *Lives*, for example) to have paid a second visit to Italy in 1730 with the joint purpose of buying yet more works for art for Burlington and of cultivating his own knowledge of architecture.[7] If such a visit indeed took place it perhaps shows how both Kent and Burlington were gradually accepting the fact that the former's true abilities might lie in architecture rather than painting, in which case a further trip to Italy would be beneficial. (Yet Kent himself, despite his ever-increasing involvement in architectural matters, never lost sight of his original calling. When in the early 1740s – according to Vertue – he sent a drawing of himself to Paris to be engraved there by Ravenet, the inscription he supplied read: 'Gulielmus Kent Magnae Britanniae Regis Pictor et Architectus'.) As usual where Kent was concerned, Burlington later went to uncharacteristic extremes in defence of his protégé; on an occasion when Kent's competence as an artist was once again being called in question, the angry Earl 'declared that if Kent was not the first or best painter in England, he was certainly the best architect.'[8] The really surprising feature of this dogmatic statement is Burlington's oblique admission that Kent had not after all turned out to be the 'Raphael secundus' that had once been expected.

The first fruits of Kent's architectural work was Kew Palace. Although externally this was not, as we have seen, a particularly interesting building it was certainly competent, and its lack-lustre façades were amply compensated for by the splendours within. Kent's second main task as an architect on behalf of Prince Frederick was to superintend a number of necessary and far-reaching alterations at the Prince's newly purchased town residence, Carlton House. Had the purchase taken place some years earlier the fact that the Prince bought the house from the Dowager Countess of Burlington (who in turn had acquired it from her son) might have been thought to have affected the choice of architect. But by 1732, when the transaction took place, Kent was already well able to stand on his own feet, so that Lord Burlington's departure from Court in the following year had no effect upon his career. Indeed the very year of Burlington's retirement saw Kent at the zenith of his influence as an official of the Office of Works, concerned with the architectural planning and design of important public buildings.

The first of these was the Royal Mews at Charing Cross. There had been royal stables here since the seventeenth century, but by 1731 these had

65, 66 Exterior and interior of the Royal Mews. Probably the most impressively monumental
stabling ever built in Britain

become so ruinous that it was deemed proper to demolish them and to supply a new building, at a cost of just over £14,000. Kent's authorship of the final stage is not attested officially but by the legend 'Guilielmus Kent, Archit: et Pict: Invenit et Delint.' on an engraving of the plan, and – even more conclusively – by his own handwritten remark that, having been with the King and Queen to the Banqueting House at Whitehall where they inspected his restoration of the Rubens ceiling, 'from thence I waited on them to the Mews, to look upon that building of my design.'[9] And the design was undeniably impressive. The façade, 235 ft long, presented a sequence of twelve blind, round-headed arches with an attic storey above; the sequence was interrupted by three rusticated and arched gateways, the central one rising to a pediment above the roofline and the two outer ones surmounted by domed open cupolas (Plate 65). This sober yet magnificent frontage concealed behind it stabling for fifty-six horses with a wide central alleyway between the stalls and two staircases giving access to the upper floor. The interior itself had an almost cathedral-like effect, the central aisle being flanked on both sides by a series of giant pillars and archways, with each opening containing a horse's stall (Plate 66).

Inevitably Burlington's name was also associated with the Mews, and James Malton later went so far as to state that the building was constructed 'from the designs of the Earl of Burlington'.[10] No doubt, as usual, Kent consulted his patron over the designs, especially as this was his first piece of official architecture; however, the evidence quoted above as to Kent's ultimate responsibility would seem to be conclusive, and is not devalued either by the fact that the central gateway seems to have been based on the entrance to Burlington House, or that the ground floor façade of the Westminster School dormitory also presents a long sequence of arcades. In this connection it is interesting to reflect on the possible extent to which Inigo Jones's arcaded piazzas at Covent Garden may also have influenced Kent in his design.

The Great Mews, as it was called – and spelt variously Mewse, Meuse or even (by Kent himself) Muse – was completed in 1733, and although it seems originally to have been only one part of a larger scheme none of this was built. Behind Kent's stable block there were other areas, notably the Green Mews in which lived the coachmen, stablemen and grooms, but the entrances to these yards were unimpressive, not to say mean; Kent supplied a striking new design (now in the Soane Museum) for at least one of these entrances, suggesting a semicircular railed enclosure with entrance gates and flanked by two Palladian pavilions, each with a rusticated archway entrance surmounted by a cupola as on the main façade. This would vastly have improved the general appearance of the area, which for the most part was squalid and seedy, detracting not only from the nobility of the Great Mews but also from James Gibbs's fine church of St Martin-in-the-Fields which stood nearby. Business interests, however, prevailed – just as they had done in 1666 when Wren tried to rebuild the City of London on modern lines – and Mews and church stood surrounded by a huddle of utterly undistinguished buildings, like two great galleons stranded on the rocks, until some opening up of the site took place in the 1820s. For the Mews the end came in 1830, when it was demolished to make way for the National Gallery. By then it had long ceased to fulfil its original functions; the horses had been removed to Buckingham Palace in 1824, and the building had since housed in turn a menagerie, a museum and exhibition hall, and the Public Records Office. Demolition, though regrettable, was perhaps after all an honourable end.

As the Mews was nearing completion in 1733 Kent had already embarked upon his next official commission. The Treasury buildings, facing on to the north corner of Horse Guards Parade, were old and unstable; something new would have to be provided. Plans were submitted by the Office of Works at the beginning of August 1733 and permission to proceed was granted on 14 August. Once again Kent's authorship is attested from unofficial sources only, one of which – as in the case of the Mews – is an engraving. It shows the north façade of the Treasury and is inscribed 'As designed by W. Kent 1734'. The design is for a three-storey rusticated frontage with round-headed windows, two single-bay end projections and a three-bay central section with four Ionic columns and a pediment ornamenting the upper storey. Each window in the top two storeys has a balustrade before it.

The engraved design presents a façade of fifteen bays, but in the event only seven (which included the central pedimented section) were built; they are still standing. The front overlooking the Treasury garden, though based on the same design, is very much plainer – without balustrades or rustication. This suggests that future expansion, though probably considered unlikely, was not entirely ruled out. As to the source of the design, Inigo Jones's ideas for a new Palace of Whitehall and, to a lesser extent, those for the river frontage of Somerset House, may both be cited with some conviction. The influence of Jones on the architectural thought of Burlington, Kent and the other Palladians should never be forgotten. It was in 1738 that Burlington received from Sir Hans Sloane what was to be one of his most prized possessions – an ornamental gateway designed by Jones in 1621 for the Great House (or Beaufort House) at Chelsea. This consists of a round-headed rustic arch flanked by columns and surmounted by a pediment; it was set up with great solemnity in the grounds of Chiswick Villa where it still remains.

It was not, however, a gift. 'I assure you that you could not have conferr'd a greater obligation upon me, and since you are so good as to say that I may find a mason to value it, I will order Mr. Pickford to wait on any person you shall appoint, and whatever they or you shall think the door worth, I shall readily agree to.'[11] Writing thus to Sloane on 25 July 1738, Burlington clearly indicates that he expected to pay for the 'door', and though the price is not disclosed we may be sure that it was not thought too high for such a prize.

An anonymous four-line piece of doggerel verse in the Chatsworth collections, apparently in Pope's handwriting, celebrates the setting up of the gate in notably irreverent terms:

> This Architectonical
> Gate Inigo-Ionical
> Was late Sir Hans Slonical
> And now Burlingtonical.

Better known and less flippant are some lines which are usually found in collected editions of Pope's works under the title 'On Beaufort House Gate at Chiswick'. Nevertheless they are not by him, and it is significant that their first appearance is in fact in a letter of Kent's written on 25 September 1739 to the Countess of Huntingdon. The probability must be that Kent composed them himself; they differ slightly from the usual printed version, and run as follows:

> 'On An Old Gate Brought From Chelsea To Chiswick'
> Ho! Gate, how came ye here?
> I came from Chelsea the last year.
> Inigo Jones there put me together;
> When was I dropping by wind and weather,
> Sir Hans Sloane let me alone
> But Burlington brought me hither.[12]

Returning to Kent's responsibility for the Treasury designs, this is also confirmed by Sir Thomas Robinson, who in a letter to Lord Carlisle writes: 'The new Treasury is just finished; I have sent your Lordship the upright of it [i.e. the engraved façade], as in my opinion 'tis one of the most perfect designs in the Island; and 'tis some satisfaction to me, as a Yorkshireman (and as I was entrusted by Lord Malton in negotiating the agreement between him and Mr. Kent), to reflect that the architect of this beautiful building is from henceforward to conduct and finish his Lordship's; and as he is determined to spare no expense, a few years will make it a pile sufficient to tempt strangers to visit the north, though there was not a Castle Howard or a Studley Park in the country.'[13] This raises a problem in that the letter is dated 23 December 1734 and the Treasury can hardly have been completed by then; indeed it was not until January 1736 that the transport to the site of heavy materials including stone and wood had ceased sufficiently for restoration of the nearby parkland to be undertaken. In view of this it seems that Sir Thomas can only have been referring to the design as being 'finished', not to the building itself.

The letter also suggests that there was a contract of some sort between Kent and Lord Malton for the rebuilding of his Lordship's country seat, Wentworth Woodhouse in South Yorkshire. In fact the rebuilding (of an older house) had already begun, probably in 1733, for in an earlier letter (6 June 1734) to Lord

Carlisle Sir Thomas Robinson recounts that he found the garden front finished and that a start had been made on the main façade. He further declares that 'when finished 'twill be a stupendous fabric, infinitely superior to anything we have now in England. . . . The whole finishing will be entirely submitted to Lord Burlington, and I know of no subject's house in Europe [which] will have 7 such magnificent rooms so finely proportioned as these will be.'[14]

The architect actually employed at Wentworth Woodhouse was Henry Flitcroft (1697–1769), said to have been originally a craftsman who, whilst working at Burlington House, had the misfortune to break a leg, and was then instead employed by Lord Burlington as a draughtsman. He it was who prepared for the engraver the Inigo Jones designs published by Burlington and Kent in 1727, and he was given a post in the Office of Works from which he eventually followed Kent as Master Carpenter (1746) and Master Mason (1748), ending up as Comptroller (1758). As an architect Flitcroft can best be described as worthy but pedestrian; he made up for this by a devotion to his chief patron and the Palladian creed in general so complete as to earn from his contemporaries the nickname of 'Burlington Harry'. While Flitcroft may have found this flattering, Lord Burlington probably did not; it will not have escaped his critical notice that Flitcroft's London church of St Giles-in-the-Fields (1731–3) is too close an imitation of Gibbs's St Martin for comfort, nor that Wentworth Woodhouse, when completed, would turn out to be basically an enormously elongated façade (606 ft) with its central section all too clearly inspired by Campbell's Wanstead. But while it may therefore have been misgivings inspired by Burlington's criticisms of Flitcroft's design that prompted Lord Malton to make an approach to Kent, that approach came to nothing and Wentworth Woodhouse was built as planned.

From 1733 to 1739 Kent worked intermittently on an official project which also never came to fruition but which, had it been completed, would undoubtedly have been one of the most impressive British architectural achievements of the eighteenth century. This was nothing less than a proposal to build a new and fitting setting for both Houses of Parliament. The remnants of the old medieval Palace of Westminster were no longer thought to be a suitable home for Parliamentary debate, and the fact that our politicians were so poorly housed did nothing at all – it was thought – for our image in the rest of Europe. 'Tis the good fate of our nation in this particular, that there remain yet two of the noblest subjects for architecture; our Prince's palace and our House of Parliament', wrote Lord Shaftesbury, continuing: 'For I can't but fancy that when Whitehall is thought of, the neighbouring Lords and Commons will at the same time be plac'd in better chambers and apartments than at present, were it only for Majesty's sake, and as a magnificence becoming the person of the Prince who here appears in full solemnity.'[15] Informed artistic opinion looked to the Palladians to give a lead, conscious that both Campbell in *Vitruvius Britannicus* (vol. II, 1717) and the Burlington/Kent duo in *The Designs of Inigo Jones* had published Jones's plans for a monumental new Palace of Whitehall, and hoping perhaps that these could lead to something similar though on more public lines. John Talman, in a letter written from Rome on 31 May 1710 describing his drawings of interiors (see p. 5), had continued: 'I hope if I have the honour to see Whitehall built after the noble designs of Inigo Jones, these drawings (which keep 5 men employed) may be of some use.' Specifically of course, the *cognoscenti* looked to Burlington, and it may well be significant that in the epistle 'Of False Taste', Pope urges his patron to erect public works in the manner of Vitruvius, Palladio and Jones until such time as he shall receive a specific royal command – 'Till Kings call forth the ideas of thy mind/Proud to accomplish what such hands design'd . . .'.

As it happened, Burlington was probably no longer at Court when Kent's first plans for the new Parliament building were produced in 1733, following a resolution of the Commons (14 March 1732/3) in which it was proposed to request the King 'to give directions for the building of a more spacious and convenient edifice that may be made use of for the reception of Parliament.' Yet Burlington remained very much an *eminence grise*, and although no further action was taken on this particular set of plans (nor, indeed, on any of the subsequent ones) an interesting comment is made by James Ralph in his book *A Critical Review of the Publick Buildings . . . in and around London*, published in 1734: 'I should be glad to see this noble project put into execution . . . and if it falls into the noble hands to execute we have long been flattered to believe it would, there is no room to doubt but the grandeur of this appearance will answer the majestick purpose 'tis to be employ'd in.' (The book, perhaps not surprisingly, is dedicated to Burlington.)

There is certainly one very clear link between Burlington and Kent in the designs for a Parliament building, and that is the former's 1730 publication on Roman baths, *Fabbriche Antiche*. Kent's plans, in their grandeur, scale and spatial relationships are obviously strongly influenced by these huge complexes. A number of his plans with their accompanying sections and elevations have survived, bearing witness to the fact that Kent was no idle dilettante but on the contrary took his public duties very seriously.[16] ('I had been at Richmond this morning with the Board of Works to see all was in order', he wrote to Lady Burlington on 31 August 1745, showing that he became no less assiduous as he grew older.) After 1733 there were two more official bursts of enthusiasm about a new Parliament building, in 1735 and again in 1739; Kent provided a corpus of drawings on both occasions, as well as some produced during the interim years which indicate that discussion of the project never completely died down until after 1739.

The designs also show that from the outset Kent envisaged a rectangular building standing in much the same position as the present Houses of Parliament, with its two main fronts looking onto the river and Old Palace Yard respectively (Plates 67, 68). The rusticated ground floor was to be given over

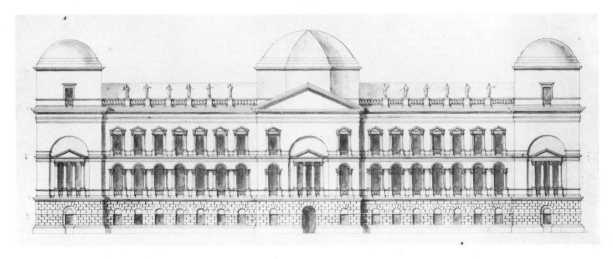

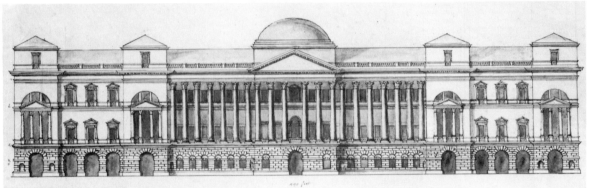

67, 68 Designs for the two main façades of the Parliament House, from the corpus of Kent's drawings for this immense project

to vestibules, offices, and staircases leading up to the *piano nobile*, on which would be (at opposite ends of the building) the main debating chambers for Lords and Commons with their subsidiary lobbies and offices. On this floor also accommodation was provided for the famous Cottonian Library, whilst an important feature was a basilican hall of monumental Classical proportions complete with a huge coffered barrel-vault ceiling. This hall is indicated externally by a central dome whose basic shape, with or without lunettes, remains unaltered throughout almost the entire sequence of designs. Kent also retained his vision of a great concave colonnade with central portico on the landward side contrasted on the river side with a flat façade also having a central pedimented portico. The influence of Jones is strongly felt in these designs, not only in such details as the long, unbroken lines of rectangular windows with predominantly triangular window-shades, but also in the surviving sketches for the interior. Kent's 1735 drawing for the House of Lords, for example, shows an impressive arcaded and galleried chamber whose orig-

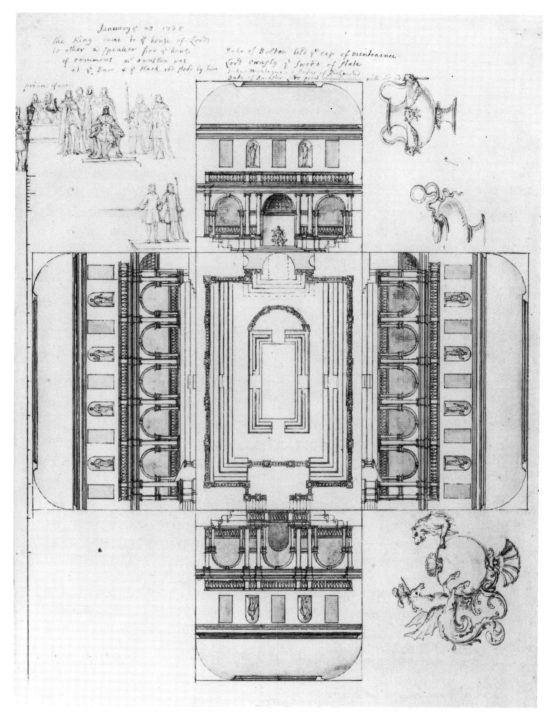

69 Interior design for the House of Lords. In the top left-hand corner Kent has sketched the
occasion of the King's visit to Parliament on 23 January 1735, and as is his custom has
used the same sheet for a few ideas on silverware

[170]

70 Wooden model for a proposed new palace at Richmond. The central dome is presumed to be missing, but the façade, with its double staircase recalling that of Chiswick, is still impressive

ins, conscious or unconscious, may well lie in certain of Jones's designs for the Palace of Whitehall (Plate 69).

Early in 1739 hopes were high that the project would come to fruition. The petition of 1732 was revived, the Office of Works re-submitted plans and estimates, and rumours began to circulate in the Press: 'We hear that a plan of Mr. Kent's and Mr. Ripley's for building a magnificent House of Lords and Commons has been laid before his Majesty and approv'd; it is said it will cost upwards of £200,000 and will be built in Cotton-Garden' (*Read's Weekly Journal*, 24 March 1739). Nothing happened. War with Spain that same year merged in 1741 into the War of the Austrian Succession; the national coffers were drained, and Walpole fell from power in 1742. The opportunity to build a new Palace of Westminster was lost, and would not return until almost a century later.[17]

Kent's Parliament designs also clearly influenced yet another official project which he embarked upon, probably in 1735. This was for a royal palace at Richmond, to replace Richmond Lodge in the grounds of which Merlin's Cave was then just approaching completion. On this occasion the main surviving design is not on paper but in the form of a pearwood model which is now in the Dutch House at Kew. The traveller and diarist Count Frederick von Kiel-

[171]

mansegge saw it at Richmond in a summerhouse called the Pavilion during 1761.[18] The model presents Kent's 'public manner' at an assured and professional level, but amongst the more interesting of its many architectural ingredients is the fact that almost certainly it too was intended to have a central dome (now missing). Here clearly was an idea, conceived originally for the Parliament building, which had caught Kent's imagination, and again he must have been disappointed that his design was not followed up. Nevertheless there were compensations, notably his succession in 1735 to the posts of Master Mason and Deputy Surveyor on the Board of Works, in place of Nicholas Dubois and Westby Gill respectively. One suspects that these titles meant a lot to him, and that he felt considerable pleasure, on opening a book such as Francis Drake's *Eboracum: or, the History and Antiquities of the City of York*, at finding himself announced in the list of subscribers as 'William Kent, Esq., Architect, Master Carpenter to His Majesty', even though by the time the book came out (1736) he had already been compelled to relinquish that post on promotion to Deputy Surveyor.

In the matter of Kent's two official appointments in 1735 Burlington probably played no part, having resigned his offices two years previously. It is much more likely that Kent owed his advancement, first, to Walpole – well satisfied with the recently completed Houghton – and, second, to the powerful Duke of Devonshire for whom in 1733 Kent, in the middle of his various official activities, had designed his first private mansion (if we ignore Kew Palace), Devonshire House in Piccadilly. This replaced a recently burnt-out seventeenth-century house, and consisted basically of a three-storey, eleven-bay block with the main entrance at first floor level approached by an external double staircase. There was no portico, and indeed the general impression conveyed by the elevation in *Vitruvius Britannicus* (vol. IV) is one of a plain severity only slightly less marked than at Kew. The fact that the house was hidden from public gaze behind a high wall must have helped still further to give it the appearance of a penitentiary. Nevertheless, as was so often the case with Palladian mansions, a stern exterior belied the riches within, and by all accounts Kent's interiors at Devonshire House were impressive enough. The actual plan was simple, the house being only two rooms deep at the level of the *piano nobile*. There was the usual grand entrance hall (the only apartment to rise through two storeys) but no main saloon as such, this being replaced by a series of drawing rooms and by a large library 40 ft long; all these rooms were interconnected and so formed an area for the continuous ceremonial parade of guests and visitors who came to admire the magnificent collection of pictures which adorned the walls. The house underwent drastic interior alterations in the later eighteenth century and again in the nineteenth, but a few remnants of Kent's work (mainly chimney-pieces and a ceiling or two) survived until the final demolition in 1924.

In nearby Dover Street the Duke's neighbour Sir William Stanhope had employed Kent to decorate and perhaps also to furnish his London home, Stanhope House, as Horace Walpole suggests in a letter to Sir Horace Mann describing a party held there: 'The house, which is most magnificently furnished, all the ornaments designed by Kent, and the whole *festino* put us more in mind of Florence, than anything we had seen here' (7 June 1748).[19] Sadly, all this too has vanished, apparently without trace.

The single great domestic project with which Kent's name is most frequently linked is the building of Holkham Hall, Norfolk. However, the scope and scale of his work here is considerably less extensive and, at the same time, more problematic, than was at one time generally recognized.

Holkham was the country seat of Kent's erstwhile travelling companion and patron in Italy, Thomas Coke. His Italian experiences behind him, Coke married some six weeks after returning from the Continent in May 1718 and at once began to live the hectic life of a young man-about-town in London. Nevertheless he also accepted the social responsibilities of his position by getting himself elected MP for Norfolk in 1722; this, coupled with his wealth and the fact that he had Sir Robert Walpole as a near neighbour in Norfolk, soon led to further advancement. In 1725 he was made a Knight of the Order of the Bath, in 1726 Serjeant-at-Arms in Ordinary (a post requiring personal attendance upon the Monarch), and in 1728 Baron Lovel of Minster Lovel in Oxfordshire. His considerable personal fortune was at various intervals augmented from such sources as the Dungeness lighthouse (he rented it from the Crown for an annual £6 13s. 4d., but against this was entitled to claim 1d. per ton from every vessel passing it), and the office of Postmaster General, a sinecure which brought in £1,000 per annum and also (so it was slyly hinted) gave him the opportunity to peruse society's private correspondence. When in 1733 Lord Burlington resigned his offices and left Court, his post of Captain of the Gentlemen Pensioners was assigned to Lovel. Finally, in 1744, the recently extinct Earldom of Leicester was revived and Lord Lovel became Viscount Coke of Holkham and Earl of Leicester. Although he is usually known today as Lord Leicester, it has to be remembered that he received the title only four years before the death of Kent who after 1728 consequently knew him mostly as Lord Lovel.

It was, however, while still on the Grand Tour as plain Mr Coke that he probably conceived the idea of building a great new mansion, as a fitting home for the paintings, sculptures and books which he was even then collecting in large quantities (see p. 31). This would be built at Holkham, and would replace the seventeenth-century family mansion there, Hill Hall. By 1721 work had already begun on the preparation of the area and by 1729 the heathland surrounding the old Hall had been completely enclosed, replanted with young trees and turned into a park whose focal point was a gigantic obelisk, 80 ft high. But the foundations for the new house were not dug until 1734. Why this delay? The simple answer is, lack of money. Thomas Coke spent his considerable fortune not only on collecting; he also drank, gambled, hunted, and speculated in some ill-fated South Sea schemes, as well as repairing, enlarging and refurnishing his London home (Thanet House, in Great Russell Street). The result was debts of more than £70,000 by the end of 1721. Eventually matters were more or less resolved and although the future Lord Leicester was never to be entirely free of financial worries (it took him years to pay off the loans which had to be raised in 1721 – indeed some of the debts were bequeathed to the great-nephew who succeeded him) he was able to continue amassing books and antiques, and also to commission new work, especially sculpture from living artists such as Rysbrack, Roubiliac and Scheemakers. He was likewise a great music-lover and was a supporter of Handel, though this sometimes earned him the criticism of the anti-Handel lobby, as appears in a letter he wrote to Burlington in October 1736: 'I am sorry to hear operas do so badly – you know as a virtuoso I encourage both, and have subscribed to Hendell [sic], for which I have been severely reprimanded by my bretheren.'[20] At the other end of the social scale he was consistently if covertly generous to those less fortunate than himself, disbursing money (as the family account books show) to a wide range of suppliants from persons 'of decay'd fortune' to prisoners.

Above all, the improvement in his financial situation enabled him to make a start at last on the project most dear to his heart – the building of Holkham Hall. We may take it that the project had long been discussed with Kent and Burlington, both jointly and individually, for all three must often have met since Kent's return to England in 1719. Moreover as the new park at Holkham developed Kent supplied designs for a number of the follies and other buildings which arose there, including the great obelisk itself. Nevertheless the earliest designs for Holkham Hall, which date from pre-1731, have no apparent connection with Kent; though drawn by Matthew Brettingham, Lord Leicester's clerk of works, there seems every reason to suppose that they were conceived by Leicester himself, whose knowledge of architectural theory was widely acknowledged to be second only to that of Burlington. In this connection it is interesting to recall that the young Thomas Coke was receiving instruction in architecture from Giacomo Mariari well before Burlington became specifically interested in it (see p. 25). Much later in life. Lord Leicester was to assume the architectural mantle of Burlington on the latter's death in 1753. In 1756 Robert Adam, whilst in Rome, was advised by the cultivated Sir William Stanhope that 'Lord Leicester is the Burlington of the times' whose approval was absolutely crucial to the success of every aspiring architect at home in England.[21] Nor should we forget that occasion on which, according to Kent, his Lordship informed an Italian nobleman, with supreme self-confidence, that Michelangelo knew nothing about architecture (see p. 80).

We should not therefore be in any way surprised to find that the origins of Holkham probably lay with Lord Leicester. The first extant elevations and plans, which are preserved in the British Museum, are drawn by Brettingham but annotated in a hand which could be either his own or Leicester's (their writing is deceptively similar); even at this early stage the house is shown as a square three-storey block with roof pavilions at the corners and a six-column portico – features retained in the final version. In the plan emphasis is placed on another continuing feature, an imposing colonnaded hall with a semi-circular double staircase leading up to the *piano nobile*. Echoes of both Wanstead and Houghton (not many miles distant) are strong, and indeed it seems that Colen Campbell was briefly employed by Leicester in 1724, although we do not know what ideas he produced.

Then at some time during the late 1720s a bold decision was taken to enlarge the area of the house by the addition of four subsidiary blocks or wings standing at each corner of the main block and connected to it by passageways. The attic storey of the main block (which would have made the ceilings of the state rooms unacceptably low) was correspondingly removed. The wings were severally designated for the chapel, kitchen, guests, and family, leaving the central block for the state rooms; a neat and significant division was thus made between public and private life by means of this plan, which Sir William Chambers in his *Treatise on Civil Architecture* was later to deem 'inimitably well contrived, both for state and conveniency' (p. 82). Indeed this whole question of convenience in a great house such as Holkham was so novel and surprising that others besides Chambers remarked upon it; for example, the travelling agricultural economist Arthur Young writes: 'let me come to what of all circumstances is in Holkham infinitely the most striking, and what renders it so particularly superior to all the great houses in the kingdom – *convenience*.'[22]

The idea of the wings was already common knowledge by 1731, for we find Lord Hervey writing in that year that despite the unattractive and bleak appearance of the site at Holkham, Lord Leicester 'comforts himself with a park in embryo, and a Burlington house with four pavilions on paper.'[23] Originally there had been only two, an idea inspired by Palladio's Villa Trissino at Meledo, but later this was abandoned in favour of another original Palladian model with four pavilions, the Villa Mocenigo on the Brenta. However, Palladio's elegant curved colonnades which at both these villas linked the wings to their parent block were discarded at Holkham in favour of straight, short corridors – a solution perhaps influenced by Burlington's method of linking the old house at Chiswick to the new Villa there. Although Burlington himself added similar wings to his brother-in-law's house, Tottenham Park, in the 1730s, it seems probable that the plans for Holkham preceded this.

In 1761 Matthew Brettingham published *The Plans and Elevations of the late Earl of Leicester's House at Holkham* which made very little reference to Kent and in which all the main engravings were signed only by himself. This upset some people including Horace Walpole, who commented: 'How the designs of that house, which I have seen an hundred times in Kent's original drawings, came to be published under another's name, and without the slightest mention of the real architect, is beyond comprehension.'[24] Matters were not much improved by the second edition published in 1773 with a text by Brettingham's son the younger Matthew which included such passages as the following: 'The care of proportioning the parts at large and the detail of each member of the building in particular, was committed by the Earl of Leicester to the superintendence of his own architect, the late Mr. Matthew Brettingham of Norwich ... who ... was allowed to equal, if not excel, all the professors of his time' (p. ix).

Seemingly the critics of the younger Brettingham chose either to ignore or to misinterpret some of his other comments, for example: 'The general ideas of the plans ... of Holkham Hall ... were first struck out [i.e. sketched] by the Earls of Leicester and Burlington, assisted by Mr. William Kent. ... [Lord Leicester] continued with uncommon diligence to improve and elucidate the first sketches of the plans and elevations concerted with the Earl of Burlington and Mr. Kent' (p.v). In thus defining Kent's position as a member of the design triumvirate rather than as the fountain-head Brettingham surely told no more than the truth. Walpole's comments seem to indicate the existence of an entire corpus of original Kent designs for Holkham, but in fact the majority of those which have survived are concerned with buildings and vistas for the park; only a few relate to the house itself, and they deal respectively with the north and south façades, the hall, and the library, though these are amplified by some of the plates in Brettingham's book which show ceiling and chimney-pieces and designs for other rooms as well. A great deal of time and energy has been spent by architectural historians, especially latterly, in proving to their own satisfaction that Holkham was Leicester's brainchild, in the overall evolution of which Kent and Burlington were participants rather than originators. This self-evident possibility hardly differs from what the younger Brettingham tells us, and does not alter the opinion – long held by many – that whatever its beginnings Holkham was the product of a constant exchange of views and a pooling of knowledge and ideas between the three principal participants.

Kent's drawings for the exterior of Holkham show only minor differences from the final result, except that he suggests rusticating the main block right up to the cornice. In the event rustication was used only at ground floor level, as had indeed been suggested as long ago as the pre-1731 drawings; the rest of the house appeared in its true colours of yellowish-coloured brick. The use of this material – most unusual in a period which preferred its buildings to be at least faced with stone – was not dictated either by chance or by financial considerations, but by a passage in Vitruvius which states that brick is the preferred material for the construction of villas. What was good enough for Vitruvius was more than good enough for Lord Leicester, especially so when it was found that bricks baked from a clay found on his own estate were both

Libraria di S. Giorgio Maggiore

71 The Library of S. Giorgio Maggiore, in an engraving by Vincenzo Coronelli, 1709 (a few
years before Kent saw it)

in colour and in texture so similar to genuine Roman bricks as to be indis-
tinguishable from them.

With the library and the hall we enter the realm of interior decoration, in
which Kent was of course thoroughly at home in every sense. It was typical
of Lord Leicester, with his great love of books, that the library should be the
principal apartment in the south-west or family wing of the house, with his
own rooms immediately adjacent so that he could slip in there at any hour
of the day or night. Here his old tutor, Domenico Ferrari, watched over a
fabulous collection of volumes and manuscripts that included the celebrated
Leicester Codex of Leonardo da Vinci, sold in 1980 to ensure the maintenance
of Holkham. The library is long and narrow, lined with pedimented bookcases
whose edges are ornamented with mouldings. Above the moulded coving of
the room the design of the ceiling essentially repeats that which Kent had seen
many years earlier in the Convent of S. Giorgio Maggiore at Venice (Plate 71).

On that visit he had been accompanied by Leicester himself, and we cannot ignore the possibility that once again the idea came from the patron, closely involved as he was with the building of his mansion in all its stages. On the other hand the ceiling at the Convent had obviously made a deep impression on Kent's mind when he saw it back in 1714 (see p. 26). The main differences at Holkham are that instead of the sequence of paintings as at S. Giorgio the flat area of the ceiling is heavily ribbed in the usual geometric manner, and there are no lunettes (Plate 72). The height of the room is also much lower than its Italian prototype. The entire colour scheme is white, with much gilding, though it should be recognized that the use of white as a foil to gilding was not an invariable Palladian practice. The alternatives, however, were generally less successful, as Arthur Young noticed when visiting Wanstead: 'I should remark that the gilding, being all on brown, is by no means set off with such lustre and brilliancy as that at Holkham.'[25]

In fact ribbed but otherwise plain ceilings, white paint and gilding are such consistent features of the decoration throughout Holkham that it sometimes seems as though they reflect a uniform pattern imposed by Kent. This is not the case. Indeed there is some evidence that Kent himself would have liked a different type of decoration, at least in some of the rooms. In the case of the library, for instance, his original design proposed that the lunettes and spandrels be painted with typical grotesques, nudes and shells, but this was never executed. Nor is there any trace of a ceiling painting which, as Kent told Burlington in a letter of 10 November 1738, he was about to do on cloth for Lord Leicester (though this could have been for Thanet House, not Holkham). Perhaps Leicester, with his chaste Classical tastes, decided that mural decoration would be out of place at Holkham; perhaps, too, he had no high regard for Kent as a painter. 'I don't wonder now', he writes to Burlington of a brother nobleman in 1736, 'that the noble Earl prefers Amiconi's to the Signor's scenes, but your Lordship perceives when I enter on this subject I don't know what I do, nor can I write, wherefore it is fit I should finish.'[26]

(Jacopo Amigoni, or Amiconi, to whom the Earl here refers, was born in Venice in 1675 and came to London in 1729 where he worked as a portraitist and decorative artist in the manner of Ricci. In the latter capacity he painted the ceiling of the newly built Covent Garden theatre in 1732 but may also have painted scenery, and it is possibly in this role that Lord Leicester here compares him with Kent. One suspects that Kent was fairly active as a scene-painter, although – given the ephemeral nature of all things theatrical – evidence of this is extremely scanty. Nevertheless he has been credited with designing the sets for Niccolo Porpora's semi-operatic cantata *Il Festa d'Imeneo*, performed on 4 May 1736 in honour of Prince Frederick's marriage, as well as those for Gay's *The Captives* in 1724 – see p. 70.

In fact almost all the ceilings of the state rooms, as well as their chimney-pieces, were based on designs taken from Inigo Jones; Kent never saw them,

72 Holkham: the library, with ceiling based on Kent's (and perhaps Lord Leicester's) memories
   of S. Giorgio Maggiore

and only the family wing of the house was completed during his lifetime. But
the younger Brettingham makes it clear that Kent was responsible for the
decoration of the family wing as a whole, not just for the library. 'The inside
of the Earl and Countess of Leicester's family wing, which contained their own
elegant apartment, was . . . finished from designs supplied by Mr. Kent, without
undergoing any material change.'[27] Some of the ceilings from these rooms
are illustrated by Brettingham, although the design for the library ceiling
(undoubtedly Kent's) is unattributed and a section through the library – Kent's
only large completed apartment at Holkham – is signed by the elder
Brettingham.

Apart from the library the family wing contained bedrooms, sitting rooms,
a dining room (called the Rustic Parlour), a bathroom and water closets (there
was even a form of central heating supplied by hot air) – all of them homely
and necessary apartments, but hardly magnificent ones. The family was
installed here by the end of 1741, though for some time afterwards they and

their guests continued to use the old original house, so close by as to be linked to the south-west wing by a covered wooden passageway called the 'arcade'. (Eventually Hill Hall was demolished.) Possibly, in view of his financial troubles, Leicester felt some relief, even surprise, that one wing had actually been completed and was habitable. It seems he did not believe in getting down to the actual details of interior decoration too soon, for in 1736, two years after building had started at Holkham, we find him writing the following to Burlington: 'I now begin to think of London [and] only wait till my pockets are full, which I hope will be next week. I shall wait on you with my portfeuill and make the Signor scold, for now we must think of the inside of the rooms.'[28] There was to be plenty of time for thought, for the main block containing the state rooms was not finally roofed over until 1749 (a year after Kent's death), and only one of the remaining three wings (that for the guests) was completed shortly before Lord Leicester himself died in 1759. Nevertheless Kent's own influence at Holkham outlived him, for the younger Brettingham attributes the designs of three ceilings and four chimney-pieces in the 'New Wing' (the guest wing) to him.

Kent did, however, develop the original idea for the hall. His drawings for this show not only the plan but sections which clarify the conception of the hall as an apartment entered at ground floor level and surrounded on three sides at the level of the *piano nobile* by colonnades; at the far end a double semicircular flight of stairs leads up to the *piano nobile* itself, the staircase-well rising about a colossal figure of Jupiter. The originality of this idea, in which access to the *piano nobile* is gained not by the usual grand exterior staircase but by an interior one, has often been stressed, and is made more emphatic by the fact that the exterior staircase to the portico on the garden front was never built. But, once again, Kent did not actually conceive the idea – undoubtedly it was Lord Leicester's, his general source for the plan probably being Roman temple architecture. ('The idea of the Great Hall was suggested by the Earl himself, from the judicious and learned Palladio's example of a basilica, or tribunal of justice, exhibited in his designs for Monsignor Barbaro's translation of Vitruvius.'[29]) The same source would account for the statue, while a prototype for the semicircular staircase already existed at Chatsworth, where Leicester could have seen it. (Horace Walpole too believed that Chatsworth was the inspiration, though he directly credits Kent with the Holkham stairs, calling the placing of the statue 'a noble idea'.) Yet even as we prepare to award the palm for the original idea of the hall to Lord Leicester, we are brought up sharply by the sudden recognition of its basic similarity to Kent's 1735 design for the interior of the House of Lords. That there is a connection seems certain, its exact nature less so. For example, do Kent's colonnaded galleries in the Lords derive from Holkham, or vice versa? The problem serves only to highlight the wider difficulty of coming to any firm conclusions about many of the details of Holkham's ultimate authorship.

In 1757, when the hall was already in building, Leicester – for reasons best known to himself – made dramatic alterations to the long-dead Kent's design. The interior wall on the north side, which would have carried the colonnade round three sides of the hall, was destroyed and the staircase converted into a single unbroken flight minus statue; niches and doors (some false) were introduced behind the colonnade, the stone balustrade became an iron railing, and a ribbed ceiling replaced Kent's flat one (was it for this he had provided the painting in 1738?), its plain coving now heavily coffered. The total effect of the hall is magnificent, but cold – not for nothing has it been compared to a huge, empty marble-lined bath. Somehow one feels that Kent would have been disappointed by it.

In the end Lord Leicester too was a disappointed man. Writing from Holkham in 1736 to Burlington he rounds off the letter with the usual expressions of goodwill, but concludes as follows: 'No compliments from me to Signor Cazzo Vestito who would not come to see me, tho' I had cherry brandy from France on purpose for him, which he shall pay for.'[30] This obvious reference to Kent may be mere friendly raillery. On the other hand it may be a veiled reproof and an indication that Kent – whose possible reluctance to visit his more distant commissions has already been noted (p. 63) – could hardly be persuaded to visit Holkham; indeed it seems doubtful that he ever willingly went there at all.

Leicester kept a bold face on things; a visitor to Holkham in 1757 received 'A very kind reception from the fat, laughing, joking peer of this house, whose taste in building is so elegant that it is far beyond conception or description.'[31] Increasingly, however, life became a charade. What with continual financial worries, bitter family strife, the death of his only son, and the slow progress of work on the house, there was little to laugh or joke about. By 1754 (when Kent and Burlington were both dead) even the house was ceasing to interest him. Probably the apartment which gave him most of what little pleasure he still felt, apart from the library, was the sculpture gallery. Situated in the main block and taking up the whole of the west front, this long and chastely Classical room 'bears a near analogy to that in the Earl of Burlington's elegant little villa at Chiswick.... The gallery of Chiswick ... is that of Holkham in miniature' (Brettingham). Painted almost entirely white throughout, except for a little gilding, it houses eleven statues and eight busts, several of antique origin and including the figure of Diana about which the embarrassing 'imbroglio' had taken place all those years ago in Italy. A number of the statues were bought in Italy on Lord Leicester's behalf by the younger Brettingham, who for a time occupied the place of agent which had once been filled by Kent.

In his half-finished mansion, surrounded by his pictures, books and statuary, Lord Leicester grew sad and old. In 1764, after Leicester's death, his widow put up over the entrance to the hall a typically resounding eighteenth-century declaration: 'This seat, on an open barren Estate/Was planned, planted, built, decorated/And inhabited the middle of the XVIIIth Century/By Thos Coke Earl of Leicester.' To Leicester himself it would have had a hollow ring. He had laboured long over Holkham, not only in providing designs of his own and constantly discussing alternative projects with his friends, but also to the extent of supervising almost every detail of the building process throughout the years. Now he found himself asking whether any of it had been worth the effort. Had he known them, he could have recalled the prophetic words of Sir Thomas Robinson who long ago in 1731, following a visit to the embryo Holkham, had communicated to Lord Carlisle his thoughts on the enormous task that the then Lord Lovel had set himself: 'His successors might reap an advantage, but life is too short for the first generation to receive much benefit, where there are so many disadvantages from Nature, and the whole to be compassed only by art, time, and expense.'[32] Moreover Leicester seems keenly to have felt the isolation of his position, both socially and geographically. 'It is a melancholy thing to stand alone in one's country', he wrote to the younger Brettingham, 'I look around, not a house to be seen but my own. I am Giant, of Giant Castle, and have ate up all my neighbours.'[33] In the end it all came down to practicalities, as he revealed when with uncharacteristic lack of generosity he complained of the elder Brettingham to the son: 'Your father has built a house more to look at than to live in, for all the chimnies smoke and cannot be cured.'[34] It is hard to imagine either Kent or Burlington allowing themselves to be greatly troubled by such mundane considerations, and is perhaps a measure of the depression into which their lonely old friend had sunk.

CHAPTER EIGHT
A NEW ELYSIUM

By the second half of the eighteenth century the view was already widely held that Kent's most significant artistic legacy was his imaginative development of the practice of landscape gardening. As with all his other pursuits except painting, he seems to have slipped into it almost by accident. It is difficult for us today, separated as we are from the 1720s and '30s by a time span that has since included the work of 'Capability' Brown, Humphry Repton, J. C. Loudon and William Robinson, to appreciate fully the contrast between the developed landscape garden and the Baroque garden that immediately preceded it, the more so since no complete original examples of the latter have survived in this country. We now look upon the landscape ideal as the accepted norm in garden planning and layout, but it was not always so; indeed it was not until the eighteenth century that the curve replaced the right-angle as the basis of design in this particular area of creative activity.

During the seventeenth century the formalities of the Italian Renaissance garden in this country had been tempered by two other external sources of influence, one French, the other Dutch. The French influence came from that great master of design, André Le Nôtre. First at Vaux-le-Vicomte, then at Versailles itself, Le Nôtre revealed his conception of the garden as a vast stage-setting, a backcloth for the daily performance of court ritual, its salient features capable of being appreciated as a single *coup de théâtre*. Amongst its main ingredients were wide alleys with mathematically planned intersections, great formal sheets of water enlivened by numerous fountain jets, and the ubiquitous parterres – raised beds whose swirling Baroque patterns were formed from box or other dwarf shrubs enclosing the contrasted colours of sand, soil, minerals, gravel, even brick and coal dust. (Flowers were seldom used for this purpose – they tended to be too untidy, and got out of hand too quickly.) Unlike Tudor knot gardens, which were self-sufficient, individual and often enclosed, each parterre formed one section of a grand design, on the same principle as the patterns in a carpet.

The influence of Le Nôtre gradually found its way here after the Restoration of Charles II in 1660, as indeed did so much else that was French in origin. Le Nôtre himself, though invited, never came to England; however, his pupil Daniel Marot was here from 1694 to 1698 in the service of William III and had a hand in the layout of the gardens at Hampton Court. Whilst Marot's birth and training probably predisposed him towards the French manner, he will have been well aware of certain Dutch characteristics which had been grafted on to that manner and which reached this country even before the accession of William and Mary in 1689. The flat nature of the Dutch landscape combined with the grid-like patterns imposed by its canals and dykes had forced Dutch gardeners to be more inward-looking than their French counterparts, and to sacrifice the grand manner in favour of a more intimate approach. Formal planning remained, but it was usually more sectional and on a smaller scale; at the same time, by way of compensation, it developed certain distinguishing features of its own, of which the most immediately obvious was a keen interest in topiary.

Topiary had enjoyed a certain popularity in England ever since Tudor times. Not everybody had approved of it– 'images cut out in juniper or other garden stuff: they be for children', growled Francis Bacon crossly.[1] Nevertheless it kept a certain place in the affections of gardeners, who after 1660 began to devote increasing attention to it. A further boost was given to its popularity with the arrival of the House of Orange in 1689, until by 1700 it seems that something very like a topiary mania was sweeping the country. Those who wish to see an extant example of this mania at its most extreme should visit Levens Hall, near Kendal, where the magnificent if bizarre topiary garden was laid out *circa* 1700 by a pupil of Le Nôtre named Beaumont. No other garden in Britain presents such a large assortment of shrubs and bushes cut into such a wide variety of curious shapes. But what are we to make of the following catalogue?:

> Adam and Eve in yew (Adam a little shattered by the fall of the Tree of Knowledge in the great storm, Eve and the Serpent very flourishing); the Tower of Babel, not yet finished; St. George in box, his arm scarce long enough, but will be in a condition to stick the Dragon by next April; a green Dragon of the same, with a tail of ground ivy for the present; . . . a lavender pig with sage growing in his belly; Noah's Ark in holly, standing on the Mount, the ribs a little damaged for want of water.

This joke at the expense of topiary enthusiasts was made in the publication *The Guardian* (no. 172, 29 September 1713), as part of a longer essay on gardening. The anonymous author presents his fictitious list as 'a catalogue of greens to be disposed of by an eminent town gardener. . . . He represents, that . . . the world stands much in need of a virtuoso gardener who has a turn to sculpture. . . . My correspondent is arrived to such perfection, that he cuts family pieces of men, women, or children. Any ladies that please may have their own effigies in myrtle, or their husbands in hornbeam.'

The author was in fact Alexander Pope, and behind the light, bantering tone of this deceptively gentle satire there lay a serious purpose. For Pope felt that artificiality in gardening had gone too far, and that the time had come to press for a more naturalistic approach. He makes clear reference to this in the earlier part of his *Guardian* article, stating that 'There is certainly some-thing in the amiable simplicity of unadorned Nature, that spreads over the mind a more noble sort of tranquillity, and a loftier sensation of pleasure, than can be raised from the nicer scenes of Art.' Yet he was not the first to have felt this way. In 1712 Joseph Addison in *The Spectator* (no. 414, 25 June) had already attacked topiary work as symbolic of the over-artificial in gardening:

> Our British gardeners . . . instead of humouring Nature, love to deviate from it as much as possible. Our trees rise in cones, globes and pyramids. We see the marks of the scissors upon every plant and bush. I do not know whether I am singular in my opinion, but for my own part I would rather look upon a tree in all its luxuriancy and diffusion of boughs and branches, than when it is thus cut and trimm'd into a mathematical figure; and cannot but fancy that an orchard in flower looks infinitely more delightful than all the little labyrinths of the most finished parterre.

Similar sentiments to those of Pope and Addison had also been expressed by Lord Shaftesbury, who in 1709 made the following strong plea on behalf of 'unadorned Nature':

> I shall no longer resist the passion growing in me for things of a natural kind, where neither art nor the conceit or caprice of Man has spoiled their genuine order by breaking in upon that primitive state. Even the rude rocks, the mossy caverns, the irregular unwrought grottos and broken falls of waters, with all the horrid graces of the wilderness itself, as representing Nature more, will be the more engaging, and appear with a magnificence beyond the formal mockery of princely gardens.[2]

However, Shaftesbury's interest in Nature was primarily moral – he com-mended it to the extent that it reflected the Divine creative will and the established order of the universe. Pope, on the other hand, seems partly to have developed his own theories on landscape and on a more relaxed attitude towards gardening through his readings of the Classical authors. In *The Guardian* he specifically commends to his readers Virgil's account of the garden of the elderly Cilician peasant, as translated by Dryden or Addison, and himself provides an instant translation of a passage in Homer describing the garden of King Alcinous. In fact most of the 34-line extract is taken up with a catalogue of the fruit trees and vines growing in the garden, details of its actual layout being confined to a few lines only:

> Close to the gates a spacious garden lies,
> From storms defended and inclement skies:
> Four acres was th' allotted space of ground,
> Fenc'd with a green enclosure all around. . . .

Sketchy details indeed, it might be thought, on which to found a whole theory of garden planning. The description of the Cilician veteran's plot is even less satisfactory, since Virgil deals almost entirely with the flowers and fruit trees growing there and does not discuss the plan at all. Yet there were other sources available to Pope which must have had as much if not more influence upon his thinking, although he does not mention them in *The Guardian*. The letters of the younger Pliny, for example, contain descriptions of his two country villas and their gardens – the Laurentian villa on the coast near Ostia, and the Tuscan villa in the foothills of the Apennine mountains. Although the actual details are not always clear, the general impression conveyed by these descriptions is that the gardens were predominantly formal; indeed, the despised topiary seems to have been a fashionable novelty at the Tuscan villa. On the other hand the Tuscan garden boasted a *ruris imitatio*, an area specifically suggesting rural country.[3]

Amongst English works that may have fired Pope's imagination we can include the 1685 essay 'Upon the Gardens of Epicurus', also entitled 'Of Gardening', by Sir William Temple. Though stating his own opinion that 'The best figure of a garden is either a square or an oblong', Temple allows that there may be other forms of gardening of which Europeans are entirely ignorant, such as those reputed to be adopted by the Chinese. 'Amongst us, the beauty of building and planting is placed chiefly in some certain proportions, symmetries, or uniformities; our walks and our trees ranged so as to answer one another, and at exact distances. The Chinese scorn this way of planting. . . . Their greatest reach of imagination is employed in contriving figures, where the beauty shall be great, and strike the eye, but without any order or disposition of parts that shall be commonly or easily observed' (pp. 185–6).

These effects, whatever they may have been, were man-made. On a higher plane Lord Shaftesbury's theme of the Divine order in Nature had already been sonorously explored by Milton in his description of the Garden of Eden, in which

> . . . the crisped brooks. . .
> Ran nectar, visiting each plant, and fed
> Flow'rs worthy of Paradise, which no nice art,
> In beds and curious knots, but Nature's boon
> Pour'd forth profuse on hill and dale and plain,
> Both where the morning sun first warmly smote
> The open field, and where the unpierced shade
> Imbrown'd the noontide bowers. Thus was this place
> A happy rural seat of various view. . . .[4]

It is significant that this passage is quoted in full by the gardener Stephen Switzer in his book *The Nobleman, Gentleman, and Gardener's Recreation*, published in 1715; Switzer's own comment on the passage is equally interesting:

> What a variety of natural thoughts is here found, as much beyond the trifling diminutive beauties of some of our modern gardens as the poem is superior to the meanest ballad! In those scenes 'tis hard to turn one's head any way without wonder and surprise, whilst in our modern gardens a few clipp'd plants and hedges is the utmost of our variety (p. 262).

Undoubtedly these were sentiments shared by Pope, who in addition to absorbing ideas from such sources as Pliny, Temple, Milton and Shaftesbury probably took especial notice of Addison's *Spectator* article of 1712. 'There is something more bold and masterly in the rough careless strokes of Nature, than in the nice touches and embellishments of art', writes Addison, and goes on to commend French and Italian gardens, 'where we see a large extent of ground covered over with an agreeable mixture of garden and forest, which represent everywhere an artificial rudeness, much more charming than that neatness and elegancy which we meet with in those of our own country. . . . Why may not a whole estate be thrown into a kind of garden by frequent plantations, that may turn as much to the profit, as to the pleasure of the owner?' He concludes that by judiciously mixing the natural with the artificial, 'a man might make a pretty landskip of his own possessions.'

Above all, the words of Alberti must have fired many a Palladian imagination as, in Leoni's translation, he discusses the ideal situation for building a house. Through the bounty of Nature, he writes, 'we very frequently meet with circumstances extremely noble and surprising, such as promontories, rocks, broken hills vastly high and sharp, grottoes, caverns, springs and the like; near which, if we would have our situation strike the beholders with surprise, we may build to our hearts' desire.'[5]

Soon after setting up house at Twickenham (often delightfully shortened at that time to Twit'nam) in 1719, Pope began to plan and design his own garden, a labour of love that was to occupy him for the rest of his life. ('My garden, like my life, seems to me every year to want correction and require alteration', he wrote to Ralph Allen in 1736.[6]) An unusual feature was that the house – insulated from the Thames only by a sloping lawn – stood on one side of the public road, the garden on the other, the two being connected by an underpass. Pope was to turn this apparent inconvenience to advantage, by converting the passageway into his celebrated grotto. A plan of the garden as he left it was published in 1745 by John Searle, Pope's gardener from about 1724 onwards. This shows that the garden's various features were cleverly arranged so as to convey a sense of size and space which in fact it did not possess, being actually quite small in area and basically rectangular. In the centre was a circular lawn, called the bowling green, which the visitor approached from the house through a grove of lime trees arranged in formal lines. Surrounding the lawn were plantations set between mainly irregular, meandering paths, a 'mount' or vantage point, a vineyard, an orangery, and a curious rococo Shell Temple. Views were punctuated or terminated by urns or statues, while at the very end of the garden Pope erected an obelisk in memory of his mother. In his letter to Lord Burlington of 28 November 1738 Kent mentions having seen a portrait by Jonathan Richardson of Pope 'in a mourning gown with a strange view of the garden to shew the obelisk as in memory to his mother's death', and adds frankly 'the allegory seem'd odd to me.'[7]

Horace Walpole gives an excellent word-picture of Pope's garden, noting its dramatic if small-scale impact upon the visitor: 'There was a little of affected modesty [in Pope,] when he said of all his works he was proud of his garden. And yet it was a singular effort of art and taste to impress so much variety and scenery on a spot of five acres. The passing through the gloom from the grotto to the opening day, the retiring and again assembling shades, the dusky groves, the larger lawn, and the solemnity of the termination at the cypresses that lead up to his mother's tomb, are managed with exquisite judgement.'[8] Kent himself made a lively drawing of the garden looking down through the Shell Temple and the grotto tunnel to the Thames beyond; despite a few typically fanciful touches such as a Baroque fountain, this is remarkably faithful to the facts as they are known to us. For good measure the drawing (now in the British Museum) also contains figures which are evidently those of Kent (complete with artist's palette) and Pope, as well as a large dog of Bounce dimensions.

Looked at simply as a plan, the features which most distinguish Pope's garden from the more formal type are the various serpentine paths which help to relax the rigidity imposed by the undeviating straight ones. Pope was not the first to practise such relaxation. For example, rudimentary meanders characterized the 'Wilderness' laid out at Ham House as early as the 1670s. They were favoured by Switzer and expressed by him (somewhat tentatively) in his published plans, as well as in written passages such as the following: 'Why should we esteem nothing but large regular walks, the only characteristics of a noble seat? But, for diversity, should not mix therewith serpentine meanders?'[9] How much of Switzer's actual work has survived is debatable, but he is known to have collaborated at St James's Park and at Blenheim with another famous gardener of the period, Charles Bridgeman, who also introduced subsidiary winding paths into his plans (e.g. at Blenheim and Stowe). Pope knew Bridgeman well, and in fact what little we ourselves know about Bridgeman as a man is culled mainly from Pope's correspondence. In a letter to Lord Oxford Pope describes Bridgeman as being 'of the virtuoso class as well as I (and in my notions, of the higher kind of class, since gardening is more antique and nearer God's own work than poetry)'.[10] Bridgeman, appointed Royal Gardener in 1728, joined with Pope in a number of garden projects including Marble Hill House and the Twickenham villa itself. Above all, both were concerned with Lord Burlington in the earlier stages of planning the gardens at Chiswick.

When Burlington returned from Italy in 1715 the Jacobean mansion at Chiswick was surrounded (as old prints show) by a garden of rigid formality. He set to work at once to remodel it, the first stage being completed by 1728. This is the date of the manuscript 'Voiage d'Angleterre, d'Holland et de Flandre' (see page 256, note 9). It contains a plan of the garden at Chiswick which, although not totally accurate, clearly shows the main avenue behind the building complex dividing eventually into three straight radiating walks, each terminating in a small building. (Several, if not all, of the garden buildings at Chiswick were designed by Burlington himself, beginning with the Casina of 1717.) Behind the villa itself the main area is shown laid out as a 'quincunx', a formal arrangement of small trees standing in grass, as in an orchard. To the left is shown a turf amphitheatre facing a small temple, before which is a round pond with an obelisk rising from its centre. This area remains unchanged to this day. It was in fact an outdoor orangery, and is so designated on the plan; the text of the manuscript, as well as contemporary prints, confirms that during the summer orange trees in tubs were set out in serried ranks along the several tiers of the theatre. The area beyond the point at which the main avenues diverge is shown as being filled in with plantations (marked simply 'bois') intersected by straight paths.

Contemporary views of the garden at this period confirm that it remained basically formal and was very far from being an example of 'unbounded Nature'. In fact the main inspiration behind it was Classical, tempered with recollections of gardens which Burlington had visited in Italy. Within its walks, as each carefully planned vista opened on to another, the visitor – it was hoped – would be gently nudged into a salutary recollection of antiquity. 'Every walk terminates with some little building, one with a Heathen Temple, for instance the Pantheon; another a little Villa, where my Lord often dines instead of his house, and which is capable of receiving a tolerable large family; another walk terminates with a Portico, in imitation of Covent Garden church.'[11] It is significant that in 1728, when work on this first phase of the garden was mainly complete, there appeared *The Villas of the Ancients* by Robert Castell, a protégé of Burlington (who financed the book's publication and to whom it is dedicated). In it Castell gives Pliny's accounts of his Laurentian and Tuscan villas in an English translation printed alongside the Latin originals, together with plans of the gardens and a commentary of his own. Castell distinguishes between three different styles which, he suggests, constituted the Tuscan garden in particular. In the first, 'Nature appears in her plainest and most simple dress; such as the first builders were contented with about their villas,

73 The grounds of Carlton House. Probably Kent's first influential contribution to landscape
    gardening

when the face of the ground itself happened to be naturally beautiful' (p. 117).
Another was the *ruris imitatio*, in which 'under the form of a beautiful country,
hills, rocks, cascades, rivulets, woods, buildings etc. were possibly thrown into
such an agreeable disorder, as to have pleased the eye from several views, like
so many beautiful landskips.' In between came 'the manner of the more regular
gardens', a style marked 'by the care used in regulating the turning and winding walks, and cutting the trees and hedges into various forms. . . . Through
its winding paths one as it were accidentally fell upon those pieces of a rougher
taste, that seem to have been made with a design to surprise those that arrived
at them through such a scene of regularities. . . .' It was in this half-way style,
declares Castell, that the main part of Pliny's Tuscan garden was based – and,
he could have added, that of Lord Burlington's villa as well; the element of
ruris imitatio was not introduced at Chiswick until later (and then only on
a restricted scale). Furthermore, while naturally growing trees and shrubs were
contrasted with severely angular clipped hedges at Chiswick, the extensive topiary apparently favoured by Pliny was rigorously excluded. Indeed Castell goes
out of his way to condemn the fashion with some vigour, maintaining that
'it cannot be supposed that Nature ever did or will produce trees in the form

74 Design for a small outdoor orangery or similar area. Perhaps the original source for the Chiswick Orangery

of beasts, or letters, or any resemblance of embroidery, which imitations rather belong to the statuary and workers with the needle than the architect; and tho' pleasing in those arts, appear monstrous in this' (pp. 117–18). It is surely not fanciful to hear in this the voice of Pope, any more than it is to suppose that Burlington's contribution to *The Villas of the Ancients* went a good deal further than mere finance.

It is at this point that Kent appears on the scene. As usual the exact circumstances of his becoming involved in garden design are shrouded in mystery; in addition the time sequence of the various projects remains vague, as does also – more often than not – the precise nature of Kent's contribution to them. However, it is safe to list his main gardening achievements as being at Chiswick, Carlton House, Esher, Euston, Claremont, Stowe and Rousham. If we except Holkham, for which he designed the obelisk (and probably the outline details of the park) in 1727, it is unlikely that he began this stage of his career much before 1730, although thereafter some of the schemes were to occupy him on and off for the rest of his life. It is also certain that he was involved to a greater or lesser degree in numerous smaller garden schemes though his actual participation in them is unrecorded – 'his genius leading him to . . .

ordering of gardens, visto's, views, prospects, groops of trees &c', as Vertue remarks, and continues (with perhaps some slight exaggeration), 'No noblemen's gardens were thought to be of taste, unless Mr. Kent had disposed or planted &c.'[12]

Kent's work for Prince Frederick at Carlton House also involved remodelling the garden (Plate 73). This was completed by 1734, with immediate and widespread effect, if Sir Thomas Robinson (writing on 23 December of that year to Lord Carlisle) is to be believed:

> There is a new taste in gardening just arisen, which has been practised with
> so great success at the Prince's garden in town, that a general alteration
> of some of the most considerable gardens in the kingdom is begun, after
> Mr. Kent's notion of gardening, viz. to lay them out, and work without
> either level or line. By this means I really think the 12 acres the Prince's
> garden consists of, is more diversified and of greater variety than anything
> of that compass I ever saw; and this method of gardening is the more
> agreeable, as when finished it has the appearance of beautiful nature, and
> without being told one would imagine art had no part in the finishing, and
> is, according to what one hears of the Chinese, entirely after their model
> for works of this nature, where they never plant straight lines or make
> regular design.[13]

This passage seems to indicate that Kent's own style in gardening was first successfully established at Carlton House rather than at Chiswick, where his earliest work was probably attempted. He may have been concerned in the design of the Chiswick theatre or Orangery (Plate 75), which as we have seen was completed by 1728; certainly there is a tradition that he spent the whole of a warm summer night there, rapt in happy contemplation of his handiwork, and equally certainly there is a drawing in the Chatsworth collections which could well be an early version of the Orangery design (Plate 74). More significant is his probable involvement in the design and creation of the *exedra*. This was an apsidal hedge of greenery (mainly yew) cut into niches; it terminated an oblong area of lawn laid down immediately behind the new Villa and lined with trees alternating with urns and statuary. The area was described *circa* 1760 by a visitor to Chiswick as follows:

> On descending from the back part of the house you enter a verdant lawn
> with clumps of evergreens, between which are two rows of large stone
> vases; at the ends next the house are two wolves in stone by the celebrated
> Scheemaker the statuary; at the farther end are two large lions, and the
> view is terminated by three fine antique statues, dug up at Adrian's garden
> at Rome, with stone seats between them, and behind [is] a close plantation
> of evergreens.[14]

The statues, from Tivoli, are said to represent Caesar, Pompey and Cicero; they still stand as described, and indeed as shown by Kent himself in a drawing

75 The Amphitheatre or Orangery at Chiswick, still largely unaltered today though bereft of its orange trees

now in the Devonshire collection (Plate 78). Also to be found are the lions ('The pedestals for the lions are ready to put up', wrote Kent to Burlington on 10 November 1738), the urns, a number of herms (sometimes ascribed to Guelfi), and the stone benches, these last now moved to the intersection of the three main avenues. Contemporary prints show that two stone sphinxes on pedestals, now situated at each side of the lawn about halfway down its length, were early adjuncts to the statuary, although exactly how early it is impossible to say. There was at the time, however, a superficial interest in Egyptian motifs which, whilst in no way approaching the Egyptian excesses of the Regency era, nevertheless prompted even Kent to create at Rousham the delightful Pyramid, a stone garden house with a pyramidal roof and a relief of an Egyptian head over the entrance (to say nothing of his use of the sphinx as a motif in furniture design – see p. 257, note 21).

It is certainly true that Kent's gift for landscaping is not much in evidence at Chiswick, being confined mainly to the creation of a 'wilderness' (centred on an obelisk from which radiated three straight walks) on the west side of the formal canal; this itself, shown as a severely regular L-shape in the 1728 manuscript plan, was later made deliberately irregular (see p. 201), and Kent may also have been responsible for introducing winding paths into the plan-

76 Kent's drawing of the obelisk and gateway at the eastern entrance to the Chiswick grounds. Both are still standing; set into the base of the obelisk is a Roman tombstone said to have been at one time in the Arundel collection. Man and dog together obey the call of Nature, unabashed by these solemn mementoes of Antiquity

77 Rejected design for the Chiswick *exedra*, probably based on a similar structure at the Villa
Mattei, Rome. The temple and obelisk of the Orangery can be seen behind the trees to the
left

tations at the end of the main garden. But he went no further. Possibly Lord
Burlington felt that there was a limit to the amount of *ruris imitatio* which
he could permit the newly enthusiastic Kent to introduce into the carefully
controlled Classicism of the Chiswick grounds. There exists (in the Devonshire
collection) a drawing by Kent of the *exedra* in which the semicircular hedge
is replaced by an architectural gallery of stone with a pyramid as its centrepiece
(Plate 77); it is significant that this idea was suppressed (surely by Burlington
himself), probably because it was not thought to be entirely in keeping with
Classical precedents – Castell's plan of the Tuscan garden shows, after all, a
somewhat larger prototype of the Chiswick *exedra*. Nevertheless Kent's idea
was not wasted, for it was to reappear later as the Temple of British Worthies
at Stowe.

Clearly Kent's first interest in garden planning was aroused by Burlington
and Pope, perhaps more especially the latter. He will have been conversant
with the progress of the Twickenham villa in all its aspects, and indeed at
one point was consulted about some structural alterations, notably to the
façade of the building. His ideas were submitted by Pope to Burlington, who
replied rather crushingly on 8 October 1732, 'I have considered your front,
and am of the opinion that my friend Kent has done all that can be, considering

78 Drawing by Kent of the *exedra* as executed, with the statues of Caesar, Pompey and Cicero. Through a gap in the trees on the right can be seen the Doric column, still standing though no longer topped, as it then was, by a copy of the Venus de Medici. Two cheerful dogs pursue a hare across the grass

the place', and then excused himself from writing any more as he was 'in the middle of company and cards'. Pope, however, knew his patron well enough not to take offence at this, and on 6 November sent an unsolicited follow-up report: 'I am very impatient to be building my portico, but Mr. Kent admonishes me to defer the brickwork and plastering till Spring, which I grieve to comply with.'[15] How far Kent was actually involved in the designing of the garden it is impossible to say. His letter to Burlington of 12 September 1738 contains the following intriguing passage: 'I forgot to tell you in my way to Esher on Sunday I call'd upon Mr. Pope, he's going upon new works in his garden that I design'd there. . .'. But by 1738 the basic planning of the garden was already well established. In *Some Designs of . . . William Kent* plate 25 shows 'Two vases with pedestals for Mr. Pope', and these are obviously large urns for garden use; the design proved popular and was often subsequently repeated (e.g. at Longford Castle). The Shell Temple was certainly sufficiently bizarre to have

79 Although this drawing suggests a corner of the *exedra* complete with stone lion and terms,
the location does not seem to be quite correct. Little prancing dogs are a sort of Kentian
trademark, and the negro page makes more than one appearance in this sequence of
Chiswick drawings

been dreamed up by Kent in one of his wilder moments, but was in being by 1725. (Ten years later it fell down, but was rebuilt.) All that can positively be said is that the total effect upon him of Pope's garden must have been considerable, Horace Walpole going so far as to say unequivocally that 'The design of the Prince of Wales's garden at Carlton House was evidently borrowed from the poet's at Twickenham.'[16]

What Pope and Burlington and their gardens did for Kent was to evoke in his mind certain associations with his sojourn in Italy which had so far been dormant, and thus to stimulate his fertile imagination in an entirely new direction. In the first place he was reminded of Italian scenery in general – of its grandeur, its contrasts, and that all-pervading sense of serenity and mystery which has been so evocatively captured on paper by the great eighteenth-century watercolour artist John Robert Cozens, or in literary passages such as the following:

> Farther up the . . . mountain, on the edge of a precipice high above the murmuring Anio, stream beloved of Horace and Virgil, Beato Lorenzo's cell clinging to the sun-baked rock, a place where I have seen swallows shelter in January; great woods of dark-leaved chestnut trees, and rising among them ruins, sometimes at dusk crowned by the sudden figure of a man, herdsman or brigand, that appears for an instant and vanishes without a sound.[17]

Kent might not have been able to express himself with the romantic insight and sensitivity displayed here by a nineteenth-century genius, the composer Hector Berlioz, but he would certainly have been in instant sympathy with Berlioz's intensely atmospheric word-vignette.

Second, he was further reminded of specific Italian gardens which he had visited. Two – those of the Palazzo del Tè at Mantua and of the Villa Medicea at Poggio a Caiano near Florence – are mentioned briefly in the manuscript journal of his tour with Thomas Coke, and although in each case he speaks only of the grottoes (he also says that Pratolino has 'a very fine situation') he cannot fail to have been impressed by these gardens as a whole. There were (and are) other famous gardens which he must also have known, especially those in Rome or its vicinity such as the Villa Medici, the Villa d'Este at Tivoli and the Villa Aldobrandini at Frascati. Contrasts of light and shade, the imminence of the surrounding untamed countryside, the use of water in the form of fountains and cascades, elevated situations overlooking valleys, imaginative planning based on architectural punctuation points, even specific items such as the *exedra* at the Villa Mattei in Rome – all these undoubtedly contributed in large measure to the formulation of Kent's mature garden style.

Much has been made in the past of the supposed connection between the Kentian landscape garden and the idealized Classical landscapes painted by Claude Lorrain, Salvator Rosa and Gaspard Poussin. It is misleading to suggest that Kent set out deliberately to re-create their vision of a timeless Elysium in terms of actual landscape. At the time of his death his studio did indeed contain some thirty landscapes, but only three were by Claude and these were all drawings, although there were also three paintings by Gaspard Poussin and one by Rosa. Several of the landscapes are described in the sale catalogue as 'small', and they included only one by Kent himself ('a small landscape with a water-fall'), plus another by Orizonte to which Kent had added figures. The four miniature landscapes painted on the ceiling of the Summer Parlour at Chiswick are almost certainly by Kent and are undeniably charming, but their appeal perhaps owes more to their size than to any conviction that they would have been especially compelling if conceived as normal canvases. Nothing in his letters suggests that Kent himself was particularly interested in landscape painting, he made no copies of landscapes and despatched relatively few home whilst in Italy (in the Massingberd correspondence Claude receives but a single mention). The misconception of Kent as basically a painter who set out deliberately to project preconceived subject matter on to the natural canvas of real landscape perhaps derives from a superficial reading of Walpole's essay 'On Modern Gardening', which contains such misleading phrases as 'He realized the compositions of the greatest masters in painting' (p. 138).

Much more to the point is the recognition that it was probably Pope who introduced Kent to the possibilities of looking at landscape with a painterly eye – a very different matter. Here indeed was another area in which Pope's considerable influence has tended to be overlooked. His remark, 'All gardening is landscape painting', seems little more than a facile generalization until it is later illuminated by further comment:

> The lights and shades in gardening are managed by disposing the thick
> grove work, the thin, and the openings, in a proper manner, of which the
> eye is generally the properest judge. Those clumps of trees [speaking of some
> in his own garden] are like groups in pictures – you may distance things
> by darkening them, and by narrowing the plantation more and more
> towards the end, in the same manner as they do in painting, and as 'tis
> executed in the little cypress walk to that obelisk.[18]

Here speaks Pope the painter *manqué*. He returns to the same theme in his epistle 'Of Taste', where in a famous eight-line passage he assigns to 'the Genius of the place' the power that

> Calls in the country, catches op'ning glades,
> Joins willing woods, and varies shades from shades;
> Now breaks, or now directs, th'intending lines,
> Paints as you plant, and as you work, designs.

Pope's early receptivity to the impact of landscape, ruins, and Nature generally is further shown, not only in poems such as 'Of Taste' and 'Eloisa to Abelard', but also in many of his letters to friends. Kent can hardly have remained immune, and while we need not dispute Walpole's assertion that 'The great principles on which he [Kent] worked were perspective, and light and shade', there is much to be said for the view that without the ideas of Pope and their practical if miniaturized expression in the Twickenham garden Kent might never have come fully alive to the possibilities of landscape.

Once his eyes were opened, however, he was able to work on a scale far larger than anything Pope had attempted (except as an adviser, e.g. to Lord Bathurst at Cirencester Park, to Lord Cobham at Stowe). In the essay 'On Modern Gardening' Walpole makes his famous summary of Kent's basic contribution to the landscape ideal; though often quoted it has lost none of its relevance:

> He leaped the fence, and saw that all Nature was a garden. He felt the delicious contrast of hill and valley changing imperceptibly into each other, tasted the beauty of the gentle swell, or concave scoop, and remarked how loose groves crowned an easy eminence with happy ornament, and while they called in the distant view between their graceful stems, removed and extended the perspective by delusive comparison. . . . The living landscape was chastened or polished, not transformed (pp. 138–9).

Kent's great achievement was to widen the horizons of the garden and thus to abolish the firm divisions between what was natural and what was artificial. In so doing he was greatly assisted by the adoption of the ha-ha or concealed ditch, by means of which fencing is avoided and the surrounding land absorbed into the general vista. The ha-ha was not Kent's invention; it first appears as an 'ah! ah!' in a French work of 1709 which was translated into English in 1712 by John James as *The Theory and Practice of Gardening*. Nor is there any humour involved; the ditch, James tells us, 'surprises the eye upon coming near it, and makes one cry Ah! Ah! from whence it takes its name.' Though Bridgeman is tentatively credited with the first recognizable use of the ha-ha, it was left to Kent to appreciate its full potentiality. In view of this it should perhaps (following Walpole's example) be renamed the 'Kent-fence'.

Kent's mature landscape style is thus seen to be an amalgam of the theories of Pope and Burlington, of his own recollections of Italian scenery both natural and artificial, and of a semi-subconscious assimilation of the Claudian manner in landscape painting. When to this heady mixture there were added generous portions of imagination, boldness and originality, the resulting concoction was irresistible. Yet he did not merely improve upon what he found; he introduced and developed stylistic 'trademarks' that both identified his own works and pointed the way forward for future developments. The essence of naturalism is irregularity; hence – as Walpole noted – 'His ruling principle was, that nature abhors a straight line', in deference to which he caused flat ground to undulate where necessary. In Kent's philosophy trees grew and flourished as Nature intended, unscathed by shears, saw or pruning knife, their roots and boles freed from unsightly and suffocating undergrowth; furthermore he is credited with the idea of introducing clumps of trees on the lawns surrounding houses, to relieve the monotony of unbroken expanses of grass. Walpole in 'On Modern Gardening' rather unkindly takes him to task over this for being too unadventurous: 'His clumps were puny, he aimed at immediate effect, and planted not for futurity. One sees no large woods sketched out by his direction' (p. 804). In the context of Kent's total achievement this is surely a minor fault, and in any case his surviving plantations have in fact matured to an extent obviously not foreseen by Walpole.

In compensation Walpole rightly rhapsodizes over Kent's treatment of water, pointing out that he discarded formal canals, cascades and cataracts in favour of naturalistic winding streams shaded by vegetation. The first, rather hesitant example of this is probably the 'river' at Chiswick, which started life as a formal L-shaped stretch of water perhaps designed by Bridgeman or Burlington himself; a series of kinks and bends was then introduced into it, creating a pleasing irregularity and so changing the formal into the informal with minimum difficulty and maximum effect.[19] (Thomas Whately called it 'the best serpentine river for its size I have seen'.[20]) The final stroke was the building in 1738 of a rustic cascade at the south end of the canal. This cascade, triple-arched and constructed of rough-hewn stones, was one of several which Kent designed, all of them undoubtedly based on similar garden features seen in Italy, such as the rustic fountain in the gardens of the Villa Aldobrandini. It replaced a much more severely Palladian structure which would not have been in keeping with the new freedom of the canal, and was constructed by the mason Joseph Pickford (see p. 95). Pope's friend, the benevolent and philanthropic Ralph Allen of Bath, was no doubt flattered to be told by Pope in a letter (*circa* 30 March 1743) that high praise 'has been given your rusticks, by the greatest judge Mr. Kent, who prefers them to all he ever saw artificial in the world', the reference being probably to a cascade or similar structure in the grounds of Allen's splendid new mansion Prior Park.[21] Drawings at Chatsworth show that there were ideas for a rustic cascade system at Chatsworth itself, probably supplementary to Thomas Archer's formal cascade-house and step system which are still extant there.

The cascade at Chiswick leads us to consideration of another, fundamental aspect of Kent's garden planning – the provision of architectural features of all kinds, not simply as objects in themselves or mere punctuation points (as at Chiswick) but as contributing in one way or another to the total effect of the landscape. Here Kent was not exactly a pioneer; there is for example good evidence both at Blenheim and at Castle Howard that Vanbrugh had an excellent eye for the dramatic placing of temples and so forth. But Vanbrugh's parklands, like his buildings, are conceived on an heroic scale, and do not allow for the pictorial immediacy of Kent's less austere vision.

The different types of Kent's garden buildings may be loosely placed in three main categories. In the first and least original come 'eyecatchers', deliberately placed to terminate a view or to create a focal point, such as the obelisks at Houghton and Chiswick. Some of these eyecatchers, however, may also come into the second category, which is that of follies and Gothic extravaganzas, such as the sham castle at Shotover (see p. 148). Kent's most ambitious exercise in garden Gothic was Merlin's Cave, but he also designed a number of smaller manifestations of this taste, such as the 'Cuttle Mill' at Rousham, a ramshackle building prettified by the addition of a façade, church-type windows and pinnacles, all in Kentian Gothic. Strangely, however, he does not seem to have shared the enthusiasm for grottoes then prevalent, of which the most famous example was Pope's at Twickenham. Pope fashioned his grotto from the underpass leading from his house to the garden; in a well-known letter to his friend Edward Blount (2 June 1725) he describes the view looking from the grotto into the garden, and how 'you look down thro' a sloping arcade of trees, and see the sails on the river passing suddenly and vanishing, as thro' a perspective glass.'[22] Like all good grottoes in that age of scientific curiosity it was set throughout with minerals, fossils, pebbles and suchlike as well as 'shells interspersed with pieces of looking-glass in angular forms; and in the ceiling is a star of the same material, at which when a lamp . . . is hung in the middle, a thousand pointed rays glitter, and are reflected over the place.'[23] Pope loved his grotto (it still survives), composed a sonnet 'On His Grotto at Twickenham' and appears sitting in it in two separate sketches by Kent, both in the Chatsworth collection. (The larger of these two drawings is sometimes ascribed to Lady Burlington, but the style is much more like that of Kent in his less formal mood, and the outsize butterflies or moths which are also a feature recall those on one of Kent's designs for a candlestick – see p. 238). Pope's grotto was a refuge for meditation: 'Thoughts, which at Hyde Park Corner I forgot/Meet and rejoin me, in the pensive grot', he wrote in Book II, Epistle II of his Horatian Imitations. Yet Kent, although he must have known it well, does not seem to have found inspiration in it; perhaps the whole ethos of grottoes was too gloomy for his taste. The few he created were unremarkable, and he seems to have forgotten how greatly he had admired the grotto at Poggio a Caiano in 1714, describing it in his journal as 'a very fine grotto adorn'd with shells and petrified stone with pretty waterworks and Galatea coming out of her grotto drawn by dolphins'.

On the other hand a whole range of architectural works conceived under the direct influence of Classicism, and forming the third class of Kent's garden buildings, is an essential part of his landscape style. For these temples and pavilions are not introduced haphazardly, nor simply for their pictorial value. They were intended to stimulate a nostalgic respect for Classicism and its virtues; as Alberti put it, in his proposals for the ideal site: 'Nor should there be wanting in the prospect remains of Antiquity, on which we cannot turn our eyes without considering the various revolutions of men and things.'[24] Furthermore, scholars such as Pope and Burlington knew that in Classical times the ancients habitually placed their temples and other sacred buildings in artificially 'natural' settings, *ruris imitationes* in fact; at Tivoli, for example, the Emperor Hadrian excavated an entire valley (now known as the Vale of Tempe) apparently as a naturalistic backcloth for a small temple of Venus. More importantly, there also survives at Tivoli the ancient so-called Temple of the Sibyl; standing high above the famous waterfalls, this venerable circular building in its wild and luxuriantly green setting epitomizes even today the distinctively Classical relationship between the natural and the spiritual. It clearly made a great impression on Kent, who obviously knew it well – so well, in fact, that he introduced a derivative of it into the background of his earliest published work, the 1720 frontispiece to Gay's *Poems on Several Occasions*. Later it was to reappear in a drawing for a suggested revamping of the great cascade at Chatsworth, and was probably also the model for the Temple of Ancient Virtue at Stowe (although here the additional influence of Hawksmoor's magnificent Mausoleum at Castle Howard must also be taken into account). It has been called 'the most frequently imitated ancient building in the landscape garden', having been repeated in some twenty or more locations throughout Britain.[25] But although Kent may have initiated this Sybilline fervour, or at least helped to promote it, his understanding of the Classical attitude towards sacred buildings and their accepted settings enabled him to create many other types of Classically inspired architectural felicities and to place them unerringly in his landscapes.[26] This, of course, is exactly what Claude does in his paintings, but it in no way invalidates the belief that Kent came to his landscape style independently of Claude, whose canvases to some extent paralleled but certainly did not directly inspire Kent's work.

A more potent influence is likely to have been the Flemish-born landscape artist Jan Frans van Bloemen, known as 'Orizonte' because of the importance which he attached to distance in his paintings. Little if any account seems so far to have been taken of his impact on Kent, who in all probability knew him in Rome, but it is worth noting that the sale catalogue of Kent's picture collection lists three landscapes by 'Horizonti', in addition to a fourth with figures added by Kent himself (see p. 199). Orizonte's landscapes, which show the general influence of Gaspard Poussin, are notable for the emphasis placed in very many of them on architectural features, to such an extent in some that it would be more correct to regard them as architectural studies with landscape backgrounds. It is easy to see how much this sort of thing would appeal to the architecturally minded Kent, rather than painted landscape pure and simple.

In 1730, at just about the time his thoughts were turning decisively in the direction of landscaping, Kent produced four engraved plates illustrating James Thomson's poem *The Seasons*. They represented idealized landscapes dominated

80 'Spring', from Thomson's *The Seasons*. The villa in its landscape setting echoes Kent's Italian experience, though in general terms rather than in detail

81 Detail from 'Summer', from *The Seasons*. This scene could easily pass for one of Kent's full-size canvases

by figures, some human, some divinely sky-borne in the manner of Kent's own ceiling paintings. A number of interesting points are raised by these illustrations: for example, the poem 'Winter' gave Kent the opportunity – seldom if ever grasped by artists of his time – of showing Nature in rough as opposed to smiling mood (Plate 82), while his rendering of the scene in 'Summer' in which Damon discovers Musidora and her companions bathing in the stream (Plate 81) is a personal recollection of the many Italian paintings he must have seen, not only on the theme of the Judgment of Paris (a comparison suggested by Thomson himself in the poem) but also on that of Diana and Actaeon. (Thomson refers to three girls; Kent, perhaps through a misreading of the text, provided four, but in later editions went to the opposite extreme and reduced them to one.) Both in content and composition the engravings are not without merit, though a laudable desire to convey visually as much as possible of the content of Thomson's poems results in serious overcrowding. Three of the landscapes also contain buildings, and whilst one of these is clearly if tentatively

82 'Winter', from *The Seasons*. A rare pictorial evocation, for its period, of Nature in violent mood

reminiscent of Chiswick, the other two certainly evoke echoes of Claude, especially the Tuscan farm buildings featured in the illustration of 'Winter'. But once again one sees this as an unconscious recollection, rather than a conscious re-statement.

It is interesting to note that, with two exceptions, the various landscape backgrounds in Kent's illustrations to Spenser's *The Faerie Queene* – on which he was working during his later years – not only have nothing in them of Claude or Orizonte but do not even reliably reflect Kent's own landscape style. The first exception is a plate showing a temple-like building with dome and portico (not unlike the Temple of Venus at Stowe), standing in a sloping, landscaped park that boasts a winding stream, a bridge, and some of the famous clumps (Plate 58). Most interesting of all, at the highest point of the garden may be seen an arcade that is certainly first cousin to the Rousham Praeneste (see p. 215). (The idea of Praeneste is also repeated as one of the ingredients in a large, extraordinarily jumbled and crowded drawing at Chatsworth not connected with *The Faerie Queene* or indeed anything else; this is a sort of architectural *capriccio* in which landscape is reduced to a rocky, tree-crowned promontory with a waterfall and a mountainous background complete with exploding volcano, Plate 83.) The second exception also recalls Rousham in suggesting a landscape of carefully controlled vistas created by plantations.[27]

These two illustrations apart, however, one is initially both baffled by Kent's reported comment that he got his ideas on gardening from reading Spenser (see p. 152), and sympathetic towards Horace Walpole's assessment of the landscape backgrounds in *The Faerie Queene* as 'hills tumbling down themselves, no variety of prospect, and three or four perpetual spruce firs'.[28] If any precedent for them is to be found it lies not in the work of Claude, still less in that of Orizonte, but in that of Domenichino, with which Kent was of course entirely familiar.

Further reflection may nevertheless show that while Kent's actual landscapes are in no sense a re-creation of Spenser's scene-painting (there are very few descriptions of landscape in *The Faerie Queene* and those which are to be found are of the sketchiest), the great Virgil-like epic with its Classical parallels illuminated in his mind's eye a particular kind of poetic landscape which was to find unique expression at Rousham. For this was, after all, the period during which the evocation of pictorial images of landscape through the medium of literature was a subject of ever-increasing interest, and when the power of evocative texts began to be specifically linked to the impact of both natural and artificially created landscape. Indeed it would not be an exaggeration to say that landscape gardening actually grew out of literature. This important additional ingredient must always be reckoned with when assessing the planning and design of the eighteenth-century landscape garden. Many an eye-catcher was placed, many a view created, with the intention of awakening a specific emotion in the beholder through the association of ideas; Kent himself

83 Pen-and-ink drawing of a fantastic landscape, in which some rather misplaced natural elements are combined with Claudian monuments and activities

clearly understood this practice, behind which the principal theorist, as ever, was undoubtedly Pope.

It is intriguing to speculate whether Kent's psychological makeup may not have contributed in some way to his success as a landscape designer. This connection is suggested by a passage in Thomas Whately's 'Essay on the Different Natural Situations of Gardens'. Whately discusses what he deems to be the four basic 'dispositions of grounds', the third being the relevant one here. 'A third disposition is that of grounds running by gentle falls and risings easily into each other. In situations of this kind are placed many of the English modern gardens; and particularly, those which Kent delighted in laying out. Such a situation, as it is generally attended with great verdure, cultivation and populousness, naturally creates in the mind that sentiment of chearfulness which society and action are apt to create' (p. 142). It is the 'sentiment of chearfulness' which is the key and which suggests that an equable and optimistic temperament such as Kent's is peculiarly well suited to the harmonious pursuit of landscape gardening.

The two garden schemes which typify Kent's work at its best were both carried out between the years 1731 and 1741, at Stowe and Rousham respect-

84 A beautifully atmospheric and lyrical drawing of an unidentified landscape by moonlight

ively. The garden at Stowe, Lord Cobham's Buckinghamshire seat, had been laid out by Vanbrugh and Bridgeman on formal axial lines bounded by military-style bastions (a device also fittingly used by Vanbrugh at Blenheim). These are clearly shown in a plan of the grounds published in 1739 by Bridgeman's widow, although by that time Kent's alterations were already taking place. Kent's association with Bridgeman probably began at Chiswick and at Pope's Villa, but will have been strengthened by official contact between the Board of Works and the royal gardens. Though Kent threw off many of the constraints still practised by Bridgeman, there is no reason to suppose that their personal relationship was anything but amicable. But it was perhaps fortunate that neither was still living in 1766 when the following trenchant if sweeping comment appeared: 'The best disposed pleasure grounds, parks &c. in the kingdom were designed by the late Mr. Kent, who . . . was the first who ventured to attack and cut up the Dutch minced-pies of Bridgeman, and others of the same sublime taste and genius.'[29] Kent needed the practical experience and abilities of Bridgeman and others to help him translate his ideas into reality. So far as is known he himself never made an actual plan of a garden; his landscapes exist only in the form of sketches which he presumably left to others to recast as measured drawings.

Kent's principal work at Stowe is concentrated in the area known as the Elysian Fields, a landscaped valley encompassed by trees and with a stream flowing through it. Three temples were built here to Kent's design – those of Ancient Virtue, Modern Virtue and British Worthies. The didactic choice is significant, and was certainly not Kent's own. It seems to have been based on one of Joseph Addison's essays in *The Tatler* describing a vision of a broad avenue which 'lay in a direct line, and was terminated by the Temple of Virtue. . . . The persons who travelled up this great path were such whose thoughts were bent upon doing eminent services to mankind, or promoting the good of their country.'[30] This particularly appealed to Lord Cobham and his circle as a means of demonstrating iconographically Cobham's disillusion with Walpole's ministry (which he repudiated in 1733). Pope, who frequently visited Stowe, probably also had a hand in the matter. Kent's Temple of Ancient Virtue (Plate 86) was probably – as already noted – a repetition of the Temple of the Sibyl, and originally contained statues of four famous Greeks – Homer, Socrates, Epaminondas and Lycurgus, representing the ultimate achievement in the fields of poetry, philosophy, military science and law. The Temple of Modern Virtue, on the other hand, was significantly presented as a picturesque ruin (it has now completely disappeared!).[31] More immediately arresting than either, however, is the Temple of British Worthies (Plate 85), which still symbolically faces the Temple of Ancient Virtue across the waters of the Styx (as the stream was fancifully called). The design for this curious feature, already rejected at Chiswick (see p. 195), was certainly taken from Italian sources of which a now vanished *exedra* in the grounds of the Villa Mattei in Rome seems the most likely; as to ornamenting it with niches containing busts of the famous, there was ancient and widespread precedent in Italy for such practice, of which Cobham, Pope and their friends would have been well aware. The sixteen busts at Stowe were executed by Rysbrack and Scheemakers, and at first sight the choice of subjects seems curiously arbitrary. The inclusion of Shakespeare, Inigo Jones, Newton, Pope himself – these are understandable. But what, one might well ask, have King Alfred, Queen Elizabeth I, William III, Francis Drake or John Hampden in common with them? And who was Sir John Barnard?

The point of it all was that these were people whom Cobham and his circle considered to embody the virtues which they found so lacking in the Walpole administration. (Sir John Barnard was a City of London MP who was one of Walpole's most formidable opponents in Parliament.) The Temple of British Worthies may therefore be seen as a cross between a moral exhortation and a political manifesto in stone. The Worthies gaze across the Styx towards the Temple of Ancient Virtue, into which they too may hope one day to be admitted. Though apparently so diverse, they divide up naturally into the two categories of creative thought on the one hand and action on the other. They also accord with the vision of Addison, whose great dream road 'was planted on

85 Stowe: the Temple of British Worthies. Kent's successful re-usage of his rejected design for the Chiswick *exedra*

each side with laurels, which were intermixed with marble trophies, carved pillars, and statues of lawgivers, heroes, statesmen, philosophers and poets.' But knowledge of the underlying symbolism is not necessary for an appreciation of Kent's skill in creating so unique an area, in which scenery and buildings blend together with truly Claudian felicity.

One further temple building by Kent at Stowe demands attention, if only because it illustrates the complexity of thought which so often lay behind apparently quite simple schemes. The Temple of Venus consists of an arcaded quadrant with a central pedimented portico, originally making a single chamber. The Temple appears as plate 46/47 in Ware's *Designs of Inigo Jones and Others*, and – as has been suggested on p. 207 – has a stylistic affinity with the building in *The Faerie Queene* illustration showing Guyon leaving the Palmer. There is, however, additional interest in the fact that the room behind the portico originally contained murals – rated by some as obscene – by the contemporary but shadowy Venetian artist Francesco Sleter, whose only important decorative work in England seems to have been the paintings on the ceiling of the Long Gallery at Mereworth Castle. These murals illustrated Spenser's story in Book III, Cantos ix and x, on the theme of Malbecco and his wife Hellenore who was driven by the behaviour of her miserly and jealous old husband to abandon herself to a group of eager satyrs. Kent himself had illustrated the episode, and probably suggested its appropriateness here to Lord Cobham, on the grounds that Venus (who is obliquely involved in the story) was not only goddess of love but also – together with the even less inhibited deity Priapus – the tutelary genius of the ancient Classical garden. Significantly, Sleter also painted a figure of her on the ceiling, but both this and the murals have now vanished. Why Kent did not paint them himself is not known, unless Lord Cobham had but a poor opinion of his artistic powers.

Kent's temples at Stowe seem to have been completed between 1731 and 1735; today they remain as the chief evidence of his work there, since the garden itself has undergone much alteration. He undoubtedly also made moves towards introducing a more natural informality into the garden, although the whole area of the Elysian Fields is now considerably more overgrown than he would have wished. Nevertheless his numerous other commitments, official or otherwise, will not have given him the opportunity to do more than pay a few infrequent visits and send plans, designs and written instructions. More and more, therefore, he and Lord Cobham came to rely on the services of Lancelot (later 'Capability') Brown, a young Northumbrian-born gardener whom Cobham brought to Stowe in 1740. While it was probably Kent's idea to turn the formal walk down to the lake into an expanse of grass lined with his favourite clumps of trees, and to make the octagon-shaped lake itself into an irregular form (which was done in 1744), the actual execution was left to Brown. Small wonder therefore that Brown's landscape style, for which he is justly famous, is the logical continuation of Kent's, though for the most part shorn of literary and Classical allusion.

Inevitably Brown imprinted his personal style on the various gardens with which he was concerned, and it is therefore fortunate that neither he nor any other celebrated gardener followed Kent at Rousham. This beautiful place remains largely as Kent intended, and is thus the finest extant example of his work in gardens. Walpole found it 'the most engaging of all Kent's works', and described it as being composed of 'the sweetest little groves, streams, glades, porticos, cascades and river imaginable; all the scenes are perfectly classic.'[32] As Walpole suggests, there is a sense of intimacy about Rousham which was missing from Kent's other schemes, so far as we can tell. Invited to Rousham by General Dormer in 1737, he worked simultaneously on house and garden until 1741, and in the garden seems once again to have followed in the footsteps of Bridgeman; indeed the garden as Kent found it was of the semi-formal transitional type associated with his predecessor, to whom sufficient credit is not always given for laying down the general directions in which Kent's subsequent development of the site took place.

86 Stowe: the Temple of Ancient Virtue. A re-creation in Kent's own terms of the Temple of
the Sibyl at Tivoli

Before the north face of the house stood terraces leading down to the river Cherwell; these were converted into a grassy slope (the original 'bowling green') with a sculptured group by Scheemakers, *A Lion attacking a Horse* (after an ancient Classical model at Tivoli) at its head. The view from the slope across the river was enlivened by the Gothicized Cuttle Mill, and the picture completed on the horizon by a tentatively Gothic screen of arches actually called the Eye-catcher; this, however, may not have been designed by Kent, and its effect today is totally negated by a screen of trees which has grown up on the skyline behind it. To the west, the river bends sharply and then bends again further on; in the angle formed at this bend Kent converted an overgrown valley containing a series of ponds into the Vale of Venus, a tree-shaded place with a central pool and two rustic cascades, where Walpole professed to see the influence of Pope's garden at Twickenham. The pool (two higher ones have now disappeared) is additionally fed by a captivating shallow steam that meanders along, northwards of the Vale, through a winding course of specially constructed masonry that embraces at its centre an octagonal pool and a small building: these two features together constitute the Cold Bath. More than any other extant feature of Kent's work in gardens, the little stream emphasizes his belief not only that 'Nature abhors a straight line' but also that Man's task was to guide her gently, not to force her into aberrations of regularity or go to the opposite extreme of allowing her complete freedom.

Still farther to the north of the Vale of Venus a new vista was opened up to include a view of the medieval Heyford bridge, just outside the grounds. However, in order to maintain the element of surprise, one of Kent's favourite areas of trees, strategically planted, ensures that the view is only obtainable from a spot at the end of a grass walk that runs above the Vale. This walk meets another, the Elm Walk, opening northwards from the foot of the Vale, and both converge at a statue of Antinous (or Apollo), which from elsewhere in the garden may be seen against the trees masking the more distant bridge. A further path skirts the river throughout the length of the garden; to the visitor following this path each area of the garden, instead of merging into the next, is revealed as a separate composition, as though one were walking through a picture gallery. This above all is the place where today one feels most strongly the connection between Kent's actual landscaping and the pictorial theories of Pope which lay behind it. The effect of Kent's landscaping at Rousham owes much to the fact of its having been carried out on a fairly steep slope, as the riverside walk emphasizes.

Rousham is mercifully free from the over-numerous buildings and statuary which at one time ornamented the grounds of Stowe (though many of these were not by Kent); it does, however, boast one feature unique amongst Kent's numerous examples of garden architecture. This is the seven-arched stone arcade called Praeneste (Plate 87). The design is foreshadowed by one of Palladio's as published by Burlington in his *Fabbriche Antiche*, but the name is

87 Rousham: Praeneste. This Classically inspired arcade is unique in British garden
architecture

the Latin equivalent of the modern Palestrina where stood the Roman Temple
of Fortune; part of the temple complex consisted of a series of arcades, which
may have suggested the connection to Kent. The Rousham Praeneste is sited
along the narrow neck of land uniting the older, original garden with Kent's
new improvements halfway up the slope; it thus acts both as a tangible link
between the two, and as a focal point for the design of the entire garden. From
the seats within it the visitor sees, as it were, a series of framed vignettes of
the river valley below and the countryside beyond. Another, though less vital,
focal point is the temple known by the unclassical and prosaic title of
Townesend's Building, after the Oxfordshire mason who constructed it; it
stands at the end of the upper grass walk, considerably diminished from Kent's
original conception, but acting as a convenient place for viewing the bridge
(Plate 89). It is pleasant to find also, at the outer corners of the bowling green,
two trellis-work summer houses (described as 'two green seats') that have
survived from Kent's day. (Another of the same design was provided for Kew
and is illustrated in Chambers's *Plans, Elevations . . . and Views of the Gardens
. . . at Kew*, plate 8.)

The making of the garden at Rousham was not a simple matter. It involved,
amongst other things, moving tons of earth, planting numerous 15 ft conifers,
re-aligning a road, widening the river and establishing a ha-ha. At one point
in the spring of 1738 over 140 men were at work. Yet, as usual, Kent himself
seldom appeared on the scene – probably not more than once or at most twice
a year – so that most of the work of supervision fell on the shoulders of General
Dormer's steward William White. In November 1738 we find White expressing

88 Detail from Plate 58 showing a Praeneste-like arcade in a setting not unlike Rousham, although the domed building recalls the Temple of Venus at Stowe

the hope, in a letter, that Kent can soon be cajoled into paying a visit: 'The time Mr. Kent will be most wanted . . . will be about the beginning of next February, could he then be prevailed upon to take a trip down.' In July 1741 the General himself writes to a relative that 'if Kent can be persuaded to come I will take it very kindly.'[33] Little time was left him for the enjoyment of his newly made garden, for he died in the following December and work on the garden ceased, although it seems by then to have been completed in all essentials. There is evidence that the General's inheritance of Rousham from his brother cost him dear in terms of health, and Kent graphically if confusedly sums up the situation in the following report to Burlington (10 November 1738):

> The General has been exceeding ill – I thought it impossible he could have got over it, but now Dr. Hoult thinks he'll do well – it's not to be imagin'd that an estate could make such an alteration in a man – if I thought anybody would leave me an estate that I could be such an animal, I could wish they would knock me on the head sooner than give [me] that estate.[34]

It has already been suggested that although Kent probably did not con-

89 Rousham: Townesend's Building, with the statue of Antinous (or Apollo)

sciously think of his landscapes in terms of actual paintings, he did make use of his artist's training in matters of contrasted light-and-shade and perspective. To these should be added colour. Inevitably this was mainly in tones of greens and browns, but it is interesting to note that Kent seems to have been the first to introduce evergreen conifers into his plantations, perhaps recognizing their potential as a foil to the seasonally changing tints of deciduous oak, elm and beech. (Conifers were also suitable substitutes for the sombre ilex and cypresses found in Classical gardens.) It is also significant that flowering trees and shrubs were planted at Rousham on Kent's instructions, for so far as is known these did not normally form part of his schemes. He may well have been encouraged in this by Philip Southcote, a landowner who bought an estate called Woburn Farm, near Chertsey, Surrey, in 1735 and set about turning it into a 'ferme ornée' (literally, prettified farm). Kent knew Southcote, who claimed also to have persuaded him to re-introduce flowers into his gardens. Certainly Southcote was an enthusiastic advocate of flowers, hitherto not favoured in large gardens; Whately considered that at Woburn the flower beds were 'rather too profusely strewed' and that, as for the plants themselves, 'a more moderate use of them would . . . have been better, and the variety more pleasing, had it been less licentious.'³⁵ There was no fear of Kent's indulging in such floral excesses. Regarding his technical approach to gardening, it is worth pondering whether his interest in, and limited work for the theatre may not have had almost as much influence on the composition of foreground and background, on the preparation of views and vistas that change and dissolve as the spectator moves around, as did his artist's training.³⁶ It is significant that in order to appreciate the full effect of these devices the visitor to Rousham, as to other landscape gardens, was expected to follow a carefully planned route in his perambulation of the grounds. Elysium did not yield up its treasures lightly.

Amongst Kent's other landscape commissions, Claremont, Esher and Euston were the most considerable. The first two were contiguous in Surrey and moreover were owned by brothers – Claremont by the Duke of Newcastle (who had purchased it from Vanbrugh, its architect and original owner, in 1714) and Esher by the Hon. Henry Pelham. Euston, seat of the Duke of Grafton, was in Suffolk. At each of these Kent followed his now established practice of turning older, formal gardens (the layout of the Claremont garden had been established by Vanbrugh and Bridgeman) into naturalistic parkland ornamented with temples and other architectural items. Existing sketches for all three show much use of the famous clumps, and Walpole remarks that 'A small lake edged by a winding bank with scattered trees that led to a seat at the head of the pond, was common to Claremont, Esher, and others of his designs.'³⁷ Of Esher, Walpole commented: 'Esher I have seen again twice and prefer it to all villas. . . . Kent is Kentissime there.'³⁸ The last phrase is often quoted as referring only to the grounds, but the context seems rather to indicate that Walpole is speaking either of the house, to which Kent had also made some alterations (see p. 153), or of the estate in general. More to the point is a sentence which he wrote in 1763, long after Kent's death, in a letter describing another visit to Esher: 'The day was delightful, the scene transporting, the trees, lawns, concaves, all in the perfection in which the ghost of Kent would joy to see them.'³⁹ Esher was well established by 1738, for it was in that year that Pope (in the second of the two Dialogues appended as the 'Epilogue to the Satires of Dr. John Donne') penned his famous reference to

. . . Esher's peaceful grove
(Where Kent and Nature vie for Pelham's love).

Euston on the other hand was probably the least problematic of all Kent's landscape commissions, Nature apparently already having done much of his

90 The grounds of Euston with a view of the Temple. Although the sheet is signed 'J. Vardy 1755' and the building itself may well have been drawn by him, the landscape appears to be by Kent despite the pencilled date. Indeed the foxhounds could hardly be by anyone else.

work for him; it was a place where (as Sir Thomas Robinson wrote to Lord Carlisle) 'the woods and lawns are disposed in so agreeable a manner, that a little art and expense will make it a most charming place.' Kent opened up the approaches to the house, applied his serpentining technique to the formal canal (this was done by 1731), and erected buildings including gatehouses and a magnificent temple (completed in 1746). This fine creation, intended as a banqueting house, consists of an octagonal domed chamber at *piano nobile* level, with supporting wings; with the exception of Worcester Lodge at Badminton (see pp. 224–6) it is the most successful and impressive of all Kent's extant garden buildings (Plate 90).

In 1743, while Kent was still living, Walpole visited Euston in company with Lord Leicester; in a letter of 20 June to Sir Horace Mann he describes it as 'one of the most admired seats in England – in my opinion, because Kent has a most absolute disposition of it. Kent is now so fashionable, that, like Addison's Liberty, he

> Can make bleak rocks and barren mountains smile –

I believe the Duke wishes he could make them green too.'[40]

Walpole took this occasion to make another unfavourable comparison between 'Mr. Kent's passion, clumps' and the grandeur of the old woods surrounding the estate, complaining that the planting of clumps consists merely of 'sticking a dozen trees here and there, till a lawn looks like the ten of spades. Clumps have their beauty', he concedes, 'but in a great extent of country, how trifling to scatter arbours, where you should spread forests!'

No doubt on the occasion of this visit Walpole and Lord Leicester discussed together the progress of the work at Holkham, both inside and outside the house. While we may look on Kent's 1727 design for the Holkham obelisk as one of his earliest contributions to outdoor planning – perhaps even the earliest – the record of his involvement at Holkham continues on into the 1740s; in 1743 a seat was built to his design for a viewpoint in the grounds known as the Mount, although his first designs for it had been submitted in 1733 or earlier. The overall planning and layout of the park, begun well before work started on the house, is shown by estate maps to have conformed remarkably closely to Kent's intentions.

Sad to say, not all Kent's customers were completely satisfied, and in particular he seems to have fallen foul of the Duke of Newcastle. Vertue relates the circumstances as follows:

> With all these good successes as Mr. Kent enjoyed, he had the misfortune to disoblige somehow or other the Duke of Newcastle, who had long employed [him] to conduct his works at Claremont to a vast expense and great improvements in buildings, gardens, vistos &c; at last, for all his trouble and labour for years, the Duke rewarded him only with one hundred pound bank bill and employed another man, and no ways would better reward him – which was no little mortification to Kent's mind, and might be the original cause of the mortification in his body of which he died.[41]

Whatever the exact nature of this 'misfortune', and whether or not Kent's brooding over it actually contributed to his death as Vertue suggests, it seems to have come at the end of his life and must have cast a shadow over his last months or weeks. Yet even then he must surely have been consoled by the reflection that, in association with thinkers such as Pope and Burlington, and practical men such as Bridgeman, he had carried forward what was virtually a revolution in the concept of gardening. He it was who had successfully interpreted Pope's advice to Burlington in the famous epistle 'Of Taste', to 'Consult the Genius of the place in all' (a phrase which Pope himself had borrowed from Shaftesbury's *The Moralists*). The inane formalities of Timon's garden, in which

> Grove nods at grove, each ally has a brother,
> And half the platform just reflects the other

[220]

were no longer acceptable. Pope had clearly voiced the guiding principles:

> To build, to plant, whatever you intend,
> To rear the column, or the arch to bend,
> To swell the terras, or to sink the grot,
> In all, let Nature never be forgot.

And on another occasion he had declared that the rules of gardening could be summed up as 'the contrasts, the management of surprises, and the conceal-ment of the bounds'.[42] Kent's gardens embodied those principles to an extent which even Pope and Burlington, in the earlier years, can hardly have envi-saged and were the visible expression of Pope's rhymed advice. They were also the outcome of a fusion of many varying influences, for in this case it is obviously facile to assign to any one form of influence an importance over the others – to claim, for example, that the influence of painting predominated over that of architectural symbolism, or vice versa, in Kent's mind. His stature in gardening is due above all else to his ability to act as a catalyst and he would, one feels, have appreciated the unwitting tribute to his genius paid by Count Kielmansegge when the latter, discoursing upon English gardens in general, was moved to write that 'you are sometimes in doubt whether you are looking at a garden or at an ordinary landscape.'[43]

Not everyone found Kent's landscaping completely convincing. An interest-ing passage occurs in a letter of 26 November 1756 from Robert Adam to his brother John, in which he expresses the hope that certain landscape draw-ings which he has been making will prove that he is competent to develop the art of landscaping 'to a greater length than Kent and his disciples have yet brought it, as I have a great ease in drawing and disposing of trees and buildings and ruins picturesquely, which Kent was not quite a master of, as all his trees are perpendicular and stiff and his ruins good for nothing.'[44] Adam expects that although his brother 'may conclude me very bold if not presumptious in asserting against so great a man', he will in the end agree. This assessment of Kent's artistic stature as being virtually unassailable is an interesting comment on his continuing influence on taste in general eight years after his death.

Kent clearly threw himself into his gardening activities with a characteristic zest which led to some foolish miscalculations, such as (if Walpole's story is to be believed) the planting of dead trees in the grounds of Kensington Palace, a gesture intended as an aid to absolute naturalism but which only evoked ridicule. Such errors, however, were few and in no way dimmed his enthusiasm. Reference has already been made to Whately's connection between gardening and a happy disposition (in addition to the passage quoted on p. 208 he twice more asserts that a richly verdant, undulating scene creates feelings of 'chearfulness'). It might be thought that in Kent's case his enthusiasm could have been tempered by the solemnities of Classical precedent, as at Chiswick, or by ponderous didactic symbolism, as at Stowe. Yet even Stowe has its lighter moments. Vertue lists the famous persons represented in the Temple of British Worthies; last of all, he notes: 'On the back side, Sigr. Fido, a dog'.[45]

There does not seem to have been an actual bust of Fido, but in an arched recess behind the Temple is still to be seen a tablet on which was cut a long inscription (now barely legible), describing Fido as 'an Italian of good extraction' and eulogizing his virtues in the familiar hyperbole of eighteenth-century epitaphs. 'He hunted not after Fame, yet acquired it. . . . Tho' he liv'd amongst the Great, he neither learnt nor flatter'd any Vice. He was no Bigot. . . . He was a perfect Philosopher, a faithful Friend, an agreeable Companion, a loving Husband. . . .' Such words could be found on hundreds if not thousands of contemporary monuments. In the case of this particular memorial, however, the twist came in the final words: 'Reader, this Stone is guiltless of Flattery, for he to whom it is inscrib'd was not a Man, but a Greyhound.'[46]

This was a joke which must greatly have appealed to Kent (though we should not treat the tribute as insincere – eighteenth-century gentry were just as attached to their dogs as are their modern descendants). At the same time he will have appreciated the implied satirical comparison between the natural virtues of Fido and the vices of Lord Cobham's place-seeking political opponents. Indeed it seems as though satire flourished in especially fertile soil at Stowe, for Kent himself paid direct homage to it in the form of a monument to the dramatist William Congreve (d. 1729). Situated on an island in the lake, the monument (dating from 1736) takes the form of a pyramid on top of which there squats the figure of a monkey looking into a mirror. Thus do Congreve's plays reflect the follies of humanity. This witty parallel, expressed in uncharacteristically Rococo terms, illuminates the solemn groves of Stowe like a shaft of sunlight on a cloudy day, and though perhaps owing its original inspiration more to Pope than to Kent, is as much a tribute to Kent's 'chearfulness' as to Congreve's memory.

CHAPTER NINE
THE FINAL FLOWERING

In 1742, after twenty-one years of power, Walpole fell finally from office, forced into resignation by popular enthusiasm for a war with Spain which it seemed he alone did not want. 'Ring your bells now, but you will soon be wringing your hands!' was his exasperated comment. With his departure from the political scene William Kent obviously lost a formidable ally, but Walpole's going was not the principal reason behind a falling-off in official Board of Works business which can be detected in Kent's last years. After all, Walpole's place as leader of the Whigs was taken by another of Kent's patrons, Thomas Pelham, Duke of Newcastle, for whom Kent remodelled the grounds at Claremont – the misunderstanding between the Duke and Kent seems not to have arisen until 1747 or 1748. Public business contracted mainly because government funds were diverted into prosecuting the war against France and Spain – the original quarrel (stirred up by the bizarre incident of 'Jenkins's ear') having burgeoned into the much more serious War of the Austrian Succession. In 1739 there had been the flurry of revived interest in the scheme for a new Parliament building, and Kent had hopefully reached for pen and paper and produced designs. But hostilities were already well under way; that same year saw Admiral Vernon's successful action at Porto Bello, a minor victory whose significance was enlarged out of all proportion by a jingoistic and bellicose public at home. Neither the climate of opinion nor the financial resources of the Treasury favoured an extensive programme of public works, and by the time conditions improved with the Peace of Amiens in 1748 it was almost too late: although Kent may have provided designs for the new Horse Guards block, he did not live to see them carried out.

It often seems initially as though private commissions during the last decade of his life were equally sparse, but this was not the case. In the first place a number of commissions which were begun during the 1730s, including Holkham and Rousham, continued on into the 1740s. In the second, those commissions which were newly placed during the 1740s, while no less important to Kent himself, have not received the same amount of public attention that has been paid to such places as Chiswick, Houghton and Holkham. Yet there is no doubt that they represent some of his finest work.

During the early 1740s Kent was summoned to Badminton by the third Duke of Beaufort (who died in 1745). As regards the house itself, built originally in the later seventeenth century, Kent is credited with adding on another storey and ornamenting the façade with a somewhat ungainly pediment flanked by two low cupolas; the rustic entrance porch, also ascribed to him, is unimaginative, copy-book stuff. On the other hand it was a bold stroke to extend the single-storey wings of the house and to terminate them with four identical pavilions, one at each corner of the main block. The pavilions are strong, four-square masses; each face presents a strongly rusticated arch, above which a segmental lunette is surmounted by a pediment (Plate 91). Comparisons with Vanbrugh are inevitable but not inappropriate, although the original inspiration could well have been James Gibbs's two fine creations known as the 'Boycott Pavilions' which stand on a rise in the grounds at Stowe. It is assumed that Kent also carried out alterations and improvements inside the house, but the only area which can be ascribed to him with confidence is the entrance hall which was redesigned with plaster frames and accompanying relief panels to complement a series of paintings on the theme of the Duke's sporting activities. Nevertheless the carved door-frames and ornamental half-columns are probably those of the original seventeenth century hall, while the plaster ceiling is not in Kent's manner at all and is almost certainly later. The paintings include four by the Duke's protégé Wootton, on the themes of hawking, racing and hunting, while over the fireplace there is a life-size canvas of a highly prized Arabian stallion. Such pictures emphasize the point that in Kent's day, and for many years afterwards, the hall of a large mansion was not merely a convenient access point to the rest of the house; it was also a waiting room for servants and tenants and, as such, was not considered a fitting place for the display of valuable paintings. Consequently either no pictures at all were hung there, or else those which were hung tended to be of a bucolic or sporting nature only.

Apart from the pavilions it cannot be said that Kent's presumed work on Badminton House itself is outstanding. It is, however, amply redeemed by the noble and inspiring Worcester Lodge that stands at the entrance of the park, some three miles distant from the house itself. Here there are no doubts; 'it is the design of Kent', firmly states Richard Pococke, Bishop of Ossory, a peripatetic cleric who visited Badminton in 1756.[1] Even if the Bishop had not said so, we could hardly doubt Kent's authorship, for the Lodge is an assured work of his maturity. It is in two stages – a rusticated base, two storeys high and pierced by the central archway, and an upper section of the same height with great central round-headed windows echoing the shape of the gateway beneath them; above each rises a pediment, and the whole is surmounted by a cupola, the angular base of which recalls Chiswick (Plate 92). The gatehouse

91 Badminton: one of the pavilions. As conceived by Kent, the arcades were open; the infilling
of three of the pavilions took place at a later date

is extended at each side by single-storey lodges topped with quirky pyramids.

The cupola of Worcester Lodge is not the only reminder of Chiswick. From each side, at the level of the upper section, there project balustraded galleries which repeat that of the Link Building designed by Lord Burlington to join his new Villa to the original Jacobean complex. Perhaps, indeed, there were further thoughts of the Link at the back of Kent's mind as he designed and prepared the upper storey of Worcester Lodge. For, like the Link, this is basically a single grand apartment designed for the occasional banquet – a room, in Dr Pococke's words, 'which commands a most glorious prospect. . . . Here the Duke often dines in the summer.'[2] And again like the Link, it is richly decorated throughout; Kent is at his best here, and the coved compartment ceiling is one of the finest things of its kind that he ever designed, in the complexity and profusion of its ornament (Plate 93). A final comparison with Chiswick

[225]

92 Worcester Lodge. Arguably the most impressive entrance to any private park in Britain, the Lodge evokes memories of Chiswick without descending to mere pastiche

suggests itself – the coving is deeply recessed behind the cornice, which thus receives the same kind of prominence as in the Blue Velvet Room at the Villa. The conclusion must be that at Worcester Lodge Kent was still influenced by his recollections of Burlington's miniature masterpiece.

Quite different antecedents seem to lie behind another late work, Wakefield Lodge. This was basically a hunting lodge on the Northamptonshire estate of Kent's patron the second Duke of Grafton, a keen huntsman both of fox and of deer. The existing unpretentious seventeenth-century house was too small for the Duke's purposes, so Kent was invited to provide something larger; this was probably in the mid-1740s, following his work at the Duke's Suffolk seat, Euston (the Duke's close links with the Burlington circle were an obvious factor in his consistent employment of Kent). Wakefield Lodge was probably not completed until after Kent's death, but it was ready by mid-1751, for on 22 July of that year Horace Walpole in a letter to George Montagu writes: 'I saw a pretty lodge just built by the Duke of Grafton in Whittleberry Forest; the design is Kent's, but – as was his manner – too heavy.'[3]

The original outlines of the house have since been spoiled by the addition of another storey, but it is still possible to see what Walpole meant and to

93 Interior of Worcester Lodge. A microcosm of Kent's decorative style at its richest

sympathize to some extent with his point of view; moreover prints and paintings exist which show the house before alteration. The main façade is slightly recessed between two end-blocks and is divided horizontally above the *piano nobile* by an emphatic cornice. The squat, single-storey portico, its flat roof surrounded by a balustrade, would raise suspicions of nineteenth-century origins did it not appear in contemporary illustrations, while the windows on the second storey of the façade take the most unusual form of semi-blind lunettes, the central one extending the entire width of the portico.[4] The effect of all this is to suggest an almost Vanbrughian sense of mass and weight, as though the building were being forced down into the earth. Perhaps only at Wakefield Lodge is it possible to understand, though not to sympathize with, Horace Walpole's barbed comment that 'Vanbrugh dealt in quarries, and Kent in lumber.'[5]

If in his later years Kent felt more in sympathy with the work of Vanbrugh, he nevertheless did not repudiate his earlier idols, amongst them Inigo Jones whose influence is also felt at Wakefield. The end-blocks are carried up into attic storeys, the gable ends of which recall the pavilions on the roof at Wilton, whilst inside, the galleried entrance hall (the only part of the main interior to escape alteration) repeats the cubic proportions beloved of the Palladians and based ultimately on those of the Queen's House at Greenwich. Another and even more specific reminder of Greenwich is a beautiful cantilevered staircase of stone with delicate iron balustrade; this adjoins a corner of the hall and was originally matched by another on the opposite side. The ceiling of the hall is the familiar Jonesian recipe of heavy beams forming a pattern of nine compartments with a central oval; as at Houghton, this oval frames the Garter motif as a compliment to the Duke, who had received the Order in 1721.

Recalling Kent's activities at Euston, it would be strange if the Duke had not invited him also to take a hand in landscaping at Wakefield, and although there are no specific references in the estate accounts linking Kent by name with the garden, there are nevertheless entries relating to the changing of contours, the planting of clumps, the provision of oaks, firs and beeches, and other details which all suggest his influence.

In the last decade of Kent's life some of his most striking architectural and decorative achievements were carried out not in the country but in London. We tend to associate the Palladians almost exclusively with country house building, but Sir John Summerson has shown that Burlington himself, Campbell, Leoni and Flitcroft all designed and built town houses in the vicinity of Burlington House.[6] The precise extent of Kent's work in this field is unknown, but (as his will shows) he owned a house in Savile Row which he may well have designed for himself; Summerson moreover associates him with the character of Savile Row in general and with the terminal building (demolished in 1937) at its northern end in particular. Also demolished (in 1900) was 16 St James's Place which account books show he built for Sir John Evelyn between 1740 and 1743.

For his patron the Hon. Henry Pelham, Kent provided a town house at 22 Arlington Street (formerly no. 17); this was begun in 1741 and was set well back from the street, overlooking Green Park. Although originally comparatively modest, it was extended in 1743 after Pelham bought the adjoining plot of land; in fact work on the house was still continuing after Kent's death and was completed in 1750 by Stephen Wright. By then, however, Kent had completed the most impressive room in the new part of the house – the Saloon or Great Room, distinguished by a fine ceiling whose decoration is of a type not previously associated with him. A deep coving rises to the flat rectangular ceiling proper which is somewhat densely patterned by the usual plaster ribs, but in addition the entire area is covered with small frames in different geometric shapes; these contain cameo-like mythological figures and emblems in *grisaille* on backgrounds of red and blue. The inspiration for this striking treatment is undoubtedly Italian, possible models being the Palazzo del Tè or the Villa Madama. Horace Walpole aptly described the room as being 'remarkable for magnificence',[7] and there are other indications that the house created quite a stir. Besides the Great Room it boasted an earlier Saloon with a fine plaster-ribbed ceiling and an impressive cantilevered staircase of three right-angled flights. Altogether it was a fitting home for the First Minister, an office to which Pelham succeeded in 1743 and which he held until his death in 1754. (It has recently been sympathetically restored by the Eagle Star Insurance Company which now owns it.) Nevertheless in some respects the house could not match another of Kent's creations – some would call it his finest – which in September 1742 began to arise on the opposite side of town. This was 44 Berkeley Square.

Kent's patron here was Lady Isabella Finch, a spinster daughter of the Earl of Winchelsea. Lady Isabella, who was First Lady of the Bed-Chamber to the Princess Amelia, had a social position to maintain even though she had no family; she therefore required – and got – a house whose comparatively small area was largely given over to rooms for parade and entertainment, with the private domestic apartments being reduced to an absolute minimum. She can hardly have realized, however, just what a unique masterpiece she would eventually acquire; indeed one is tempted to wonder whether she altogether appreciated it, for she is said to have been of a somewhat staid disposition, and there is nothing staid about the interior of 44 Berkeley Square.

The same cannot be said about the façade of the house, which gives no clue to the glories within; consequently these make an even greater impact upon the visitor (a ploy similarly used at Holkham). The façade is three storeys high and the width of three windows, those of the *piano nobile* having ornamental balustrades and triangular window-shades; in the centre of the bottom storey the unassuming front door shelters inside a round-headed arch whose strong rustication is echoed by equally pronounced quoins.

The front door admits us to a small and unremarkable entrance hall. Still the visitor receives no hint that he or she is about to experience one of the

[229]

most extraordinary *tours de force* ever achieved by a British architect. Nor indeed should this come until the visitor has ascended the lowest, single flight of the staircase to the half-landing and turned to complete his ascent by one or other of the curving reverse flights into which the stairs divide. Then the full revelation is made. Across the back of the landing above runs a screen of four Ionic columns supporting a concave cornice; behind the screen a single curving staircase leads up to the second floor landing which mirrors the outline of the screen below (Plate 94). Between the upper landing and the screen cornice there is a partition wall which is pierced by a lunette and two roundels containing busts. Above the whole ensemble is a barrel-vaulted ceiling ending in half-domes, one of which is glazed and so admits light.

A bald description such as this can give only the faintest idea of this amazing creation; it cannot do justice to the effect of gleaming white with the mouldings and other details picked out in gold, to the un-Kentian delicacy of the honeycomb ceiling patterns, to the graceful scrolled tracery of the ironwork balustrade (of a design also found at Holkham and at 22 Arlington Street). But perhaps it can at least stimulate interest in the seemingly inexhaustible fertility of Kent's imagination.

It is fascinating to speculate on possible sources for the staircase. Despite its magnificence it is necessarily conceived on a surprisingly small scale; a town house did not allow for expansive schemes such as the hall at Holkham, and the entire composition is compressed within the space of a rectangle with two apsidal ends – a familiar classical plan used, for example, for Lord Burlington's ground floor library at Chiswick and the Gallery above it, but one which is not immediately self-evident here. When the house was redecorated in the early 1960s a large mirror was placed on the half-landing, presumably to give a feeling of greater space, but this cannot be commended, for it totally destroys the element of surprise which Kent intended as an essential ingredient of the whole. At this point it is relevant to quote Horace Walpole's considered judgment: 'The staircase at Lady Isabella Finch's, in Berkeley Square, is as beautiful a piece of scenery and, considering the space, of art, as can be imagined.'[8] Surprise, scenery – these words lead us inevitably to assess this staircase in a theatrical context, and indeed 'theatrical' is the adjective most often used to describe it, with good reason. Certainly it has all the panache and invention of a clever stage set, designed to make the maximum effect within a confined space, and to announce itself to the spectator with the immediacy of a sudden revelation, as at the rising of the curtain. Kent, we know, enjoyed the theatre and had himself designed actual stage scenery. Is it possible, however, to be more specific? It is here that the name of the Italian architect and stage designer, Filippo Juvarra, comes intriguingly to mind.

Juvarra (or Juvara), born at Messina in 1676, came to Rome about 1700 and entered the studio of the architect Carlo Fontana, who himself had been a pupil of the great Bernini. Thus it was in the best tradition of the Italian

94 44 Berkeley Square: the Staircase. Here are an unfamiliar lightness and elegance which
were not lost on Kent's successors such as Robert Adam. The unfortunate modern mirror
is luckily somewhat masked by the flower arrangement

95 44 Berkeley Square: the main landing. This extraordinary and compelling composition
speaks for itself

Baroque that Juvarra received his training. At Rome he came to the notice of powerful patrons, notably the cardinals Buffo and Ottoboni, and made a reputation as a designer of stage sets in which his own architectural abilities were tellingly combined with Baroque illusionism. Later he was invited to enter the service of Victor Amadeus of Savoy, King of Sicily, whose court was based at Turin; here Juvarra built the three works for which he is best known – the Palazzo Madama, the Palazzo Stupinigi, and the great church of the Superga. In addition to being the royal architect he seems also to have doubled as an undercover agent for his master, just as Rubens had done a century earlier, and to have travelled to and fro through Europe in both capacities. He also served the monarchs of Portugal and of Spain, and was in Madrid when death overtook him suddenly in 1736.

It is entirely probable that Kent met Juvarra in Rome; the call to Turin did not come until 1714, and moreover Juvarra revisited Rome at least once before leaving for Portugal in February 1719. At the beginning of November 1720 he apparently left Lisbon by sea for London, where he spent about a month as the guest of the Portuguese ambassador before proceeding on to Italy via Paris. Again it seems reasonable to suppose that Juvarra took the opportunity of renewing his acquaintance with Kent, who in turn will have introduced him to Lord Burlington. The Chatsworth collections include a manuscript sketchbook by Juvarra with a dedication to Burlington; how it reached England is not known, but in this connection it is worth recalling the visit which Kent is supposed to have made to Italy in or about 1730, for the sketchbook is dated 1730 on the title-page while the drawings themselves are dated 1729. What more natural than for Juvarra to have asked Kent to carry the book home with him, as a present for Burlington – a man whose stature as an architect Juvarra acknowledged, and whose hospitality in London he remembered with gratitude.

Following his London visit Juvarra was back in Italy by early 1721. In that year there was built to his design, in the mainly seventeenth-century Palazzo Reale at Turin, a staircase of stunning originality. Within the confines of a high rectangular well a single flight rises to a half-landing where it divides into a double flight; this continues the ascent to the main landing, whence another single flight continues on up to the top landing. It is tempting to believe that somehow Kent knew of this 'scala delle forbici' (scissors staircase) as it is called; he could have seen the designs in London in 1720 as Juvarra passed through on the way back to Italy, or could even have seen it for himself in 1730. Both at the Palazzo Reale and at 44 Berkeley Square the spatial problem of constructing an impressive staircase in a confined space is triumphantly solved, while the element of surprise, of a gradual unfolding leading to a sudden stage *dénouement*, is an essential ingredient. There are also minor similarities such as the use of ironwork balustrades and the introduction of niches for statuary on the landings.

Equally, however, it has to be admitted that the building of dramatic stair-cases was something of a speciality amongst Italian Baroque architects, and Kent must have seen many examples during his Italian sojourn, especially whilst on his 1714 tour with Thomas Coke. One which particularly took his fancy then was at Bologna: 'At the Palace Marchese Ranucci a very fine stair-case', he writes in his journal, referring to the Palazzo Ruini-Ranuzzi (now the Palazzo di Giustizia). This staircase, designed by the Bolognese architect Giovanni Battista Piacentini, was very new when Kent saw it, having been completed in 1710.

In it Piacentini reverses the order of 44 Berkeley Square, in that two curving flights are succeeded at the half-landing by a single flight; they are also much wider, and the whole effect is far heavier. Nevertheless we cannot entirely ignore the effect of this and similar designs on Kent's thinking; what is certain is that when eventually he was presented with the opportunity of making his own highly personal variant of them, he did so with supreme skill and self-confidence, outdoing the Italian masters at their own game. Furthermore the purely decorative ingredients are in the Classical idiom. Paradoxically most of the Baroque decoration used to ornament Italian staircases seems curiously restrained as against the rich opulence of Kent's Palladian mouldings; nor do we find any such bold feature as his screen of columns – an idea perhaps developed from Inigo Jones's original practice of using such a screen to mask the true proportions of a room, as in the Corner Room at Wilton House.

No subsequent British architect has ever had the temerity to produce a close copy of the staircase at 44 Berkeley Square, but its influence can be detected in a number of different houses, amongst them Robert Adam's 20 Portman Square, London, and James Paine's Stockeld Park in Yorkshire. It is also notable that John Nash, faced at Attingham Hall, Shropshire, with the need to insert a staircase into a cramped space, solved the problem in exactly the same way, although here the double flight leads to no spectacular revelation but simply to a disappointing blind wall.

After the impact of the staircase at 44 Berkeley Square it might seem as though all else in this small jewel of a house must come as an anticlimax, but the splendid Saloon is hardly less impressive. It is entered through a door-way at the left of the main landing; towards this doorway the visitor is gently ushered, as it were, by the columnar screen whose curve is echoed in the scrolled balustrade. Once inside, the eye is immediately captured by the coved ceiling which is painted in the same manner with mythological subjects (the Loves of the Gods) on red and blue backgrounds as at 22 Arlington Street, to which it is a worthy rival (Plate 96). However, the gilt frames which surround the cameos are much more closely knit than at Arlington Street (where the effect might be described in part as 'exploded coffering') and the overall honeycomb treatment specifically recalls the *Sala dello Zodiaco* at the Palazzo del Tè.

There is no documentary evidence to show which of these two ceilings was

96 44 Berkeley Square: ceiling of the Saloon. This represents the final phase of Kent's ceiling
designs and is a most interesting departure from his earlier compositions, introducing the
concept of interlinked cameos

designed first. Nor do we know for certain that Kent actually painted either ceiling himself, but there seems no reason to doubt this. The walls of the Saloon have undergone change, and so has much else at 44 Berkeley Square; various alterations were carried out in both the eighteenth and nineteenth centuries, some of those in the former period being attributed to Henry Holland. The only room apart from the Saloon to have retained some of its original character is the former dining room which has a ceiling ornamented with a geometrical design in shallow plasterwork, two original doorways and an original chimney-piece. A generally sympathetic programme of restoration was carried out with skill and taste throughout the house when it was purchased in 1962 and converted into an exclusive club. The quiet opulence of the *décor* which now prevails is entirely in the spirit, if not the letter, of Kent's own work, which it admirably complements.

The staircase at 44 Berkeley Square, with its sense of movement and the dramatic, is the most overt expression of a perceptible tendency on Kent's part, during his latter years, to express his architectural ideas in a Baroque rather than a Classical idiom. For instance, the influence of Vanbrugh at Badminton and at Wakefield Lodge has already been noted, while the garden front of 22 Arlington Street is distinguished by three angled bay windows – not an approved Palladian feature. In the applied arts the fulsome, overblown shapes and decoration of his furniture are conceived almost entirely in the spirit of the Baroque. We should not, however, forget silverware. Kent's name is often associated with silver, but in fact several of his ideas for silver items were published by Vardy in *Some Designs of . . . William Kent*, and it would seem that these mostly date from the later 1730s and 1740s. Apart from a fine two-handled gold cup-and-cover designed for Colonel James Pelham and made for him by George Wickes in 1736 (it cost £300 and is still extant), and two or three pieces in a loosely Gothic idiom, including the standish for Merlin's Cave (see p. 155), the two most arresting designs are in a fantastical vein which in the case of the first can only be described as Baroque. This is for a multi-branched hanging chandelier 'for the King' (Plate 97) featuring sphinxes and acanthus leaves, at the top two cherubs supporting a crown over an heraldically inaccurate representation of the White Horse of Hanover, and terminating in a *cul-de-lampe* composed of scallop shells and acanthus. In looking at this design one is once again reminded of Juvarra, this time of his drawings for silverware, many of them preserved in the Museo Civico, Turin. It is of course not necessary for Kent to have seen any of them, for him to have produced a design such as that for the royal chandelier; nevertheless there are certain similarities in the treatment and decoration of the actual candleholders themselves (in particular the gadrooned edges), in a joint interest in sphinxes and scallop shells, and in the general approach.

The second of these two fantasies is described as a 'Surtoute' and is in fact an épergne or centrepiece (Plate 98). A shaped dish standing on scrolled legs

97 'Chandelier for the King': plate 23 in *Some Designs of . . . . William Kent*. Kent in lavishly
Baroque mood

rests upon a larger tray and supports a strange-looking pierced canopy, on
top of which there rests in turn a small covered tureen or dish; projections
from the main dish support a pair of octagonal casters. A piece based on this
unlikely model was actually made for Prince Frederick in 1745 by the
silversmith George Wickes, who nevertheless made several alterations to Kent's
original design. In the design there are none of the echoes of Juvarra noticed
in the chandelier; the general effect is altogether more light-hearted, and
indeed the form and treatment of the canopy suggests a feeling for the Rococo,
being faintly reminiscent in appearance of the Shell Temple (in the design of

98 'A Surtoute': plate 27 in *Some Designs of . . . William Kent*. A piece based on this
extravaganza was made for Prince Frederick in 1745

which Kent may have been concerned) in Pope's garden. This, however, is
a tentative excursion, paralleled only by such details as the robust butterflies
which surprisingly support the main stem of the Gothic candlestick design in
plate 22 of *Some Designs of . . . William Kent*, or by some of the illustrations
to Gay's *Fables*. For the most part it is the burgeoning opulence of the Baroque
which is the stylistic thread uniting Kent's silverware designs. None the less
it is worth bearing in mind that *Some Designs* was published at a time when
the outlines and decoration of English silver were already strongly reflecting
the influence of the international Rococo style, and it would be strange if even
such a traditionalist as Kent had not shown some awareness, however slight,
of this trend.

When all is said and done it is not with the Baroque and still less with the
Rococo styles that Kent is generally associated, but with the Classical as idio-
matically expressed by the Palladians. Thus it is fitting that the last building
to be completed under his immediate influence was a strong restatement of
Palladian beliefs. The military headquarters known as the Horse Guards, in

99 Tail-piece from the *Odyssey*. This fantastical ewer is a significant if exaggerated foretaste of the silverware items in *Some Designs of . . . William Kent*

London's Whitehall, consists on its west front of a central block with roof pavilions and a clock-tower with cupola, linked by recessed arms to a pedimented block at each side; a triple-arched passageway beneath the central block provides access to the accompanying parade ground and to Whitehall respectively. The façade is dominated by extensive rustication and by a range of characteristic windows within arched recesses; above all, the interplay between the various surfaces imparts a liveliness and a visual satisfaction which is too often taken for granted.

The Horse Guards replaced a seventeenth-century brick and timber building which had also consisted of a central block and two wings, together with a very similar central clock tower. Doubtless these features were retained to give a sense of historical continuity. Yet in most other respects there is little to distinguish the external design from those for a great Palladian country mansion such as Holkham. Indeed the Horse Guards is sometimes said to be based on a rejected idea for Holkham, and while this is probably untrue there is enough similarity between the two buildings to suggest that Holkham may at least have provided the inspiration.

The chief doubts, however, concern the extent of Kent's authorship. Architectural text books invariably state – quite correctly – that the Horse Guards was completed after Kent's death by John Vardy, in about 1760, and in addition Vardy is often specifically credited with the appearance of the east front. The ruinous condition of the seventeenth-century building was first brought to official notice in 1745, but it was not until 5 September 1749, almost eighteen months after the death of Kent, that the Board of Works submitted plans and elevations for the new building, and work did not begin on the site until the following April. Nevertheless a drawing in the Victoria & Albert Museum shows a design for the west façade not dissimilar from the completed work, and it is significant that although the sheet bears the name of Vardy the style of the drawing itself is rather that of Kent (Plate 100). It may well be, therefore, that there is more of Kent in the Horse Guards than has formerly been supposed.

In the field of architectural drawing it is important to make a distinction, as far as possible, between the techniques of Kent and Vardy, not only for the purpose of identifying individual sketches, as in the case of the Horse Guards design mentioned above, but also because on more than one occasion both of them seem to have collaborated in a single drawing. This is true, for example, of a design for a chimney-piece intended for the Treasury building. Here the drawing (also in the Victoria & Albert Museum) is presented on two conjoined sheets of paper; the upper sheet is signed 'For the Treasury WK 1737' and shows the overmantel (later completed almost as given), while the lower sheet is undoubtedly by Vardy who has contributed the fireplace.[9] Not all their joint efforts are so conveniently self-evident, however, and in dubious cases it is useful to remember that in general Kent's lines are altogether more lively and undisciplined than the meticulous, sober and draughtsman-like efforts of Vardy. This selfless disciple of Kent on the whole receives insufficient credit for the way in which he loyally promoted the best interests of his chief, under whom he served officially as Clerk in the Office of Works. An excellent draughtsman and a sound architect in his own right, Vardy drew and engraved for Kent regularly from about 1735 onwards, and after the latter's death completed not only the Horse Guards but also new accommodation for the Courts of Justice (demolished in 1850) which had been originally planned and designed by Kent as part of the grand scheme for the new Parliament complex.

Despite an enforced slowing down of activity on the public works front, Kent's last five or so years were probably as crowded as any that he had known. In addition to the larger commissions in both town and country – some new, some continuations of work begun earlier – there were many smaller ones in a variety of different fields. In 1746, for example, he returned to sculpture, in designing the Huntingdon monument for the church at Ashby-de-la-Zouch (see p. 258, note 24). During this period he also had the gratification of being admitted in 1743 to the select and exclusive Society of Virtuosi of St Luke, a club reserved for artists and connoisseurs, of which he was, according to

100 Design for the Horse Guards building. Although the sheet bears the name of Vardy, the drawing itself is much more in the manner of Kent

Vertue, an assiduous member. In 1744 his reputation was further enhanced by the publication, in flattering tandem, of *Some Designs of Mr. Inigo Jones and Mr. William Kent*, edited by Vardy. (Indeed his position and achievements were such that several modern writers have been understandably misled into styling him *Sir* William Kent.)

Yet clearly there were troubles and vexations too. Kent's detractors never ceased to snipe at him for one reason or another, and despite his robust humour there is no reason to suppose that he was insensitive to their barbs, as his attitude to Hogarth shows. 'I have been little in town', wrote Pope to Burlington, '[but] whenever I have, I have seen Kent, and endeavoured to comfort him, under all his calumniators and afflictions, with the representation that all great genius's have and do suffer the like' (19 December 1738).[10] There is no indication of what precise calumny was being fostered at Kent's expense on this occasion, but evidently he needed the solace offered by his friend.

The 1745 Rebellion created shock waves of panic throughout London society, and the Court and the nobility (though not the King) rushed frantically about trying to get their money and valuables out of the country. At the time of the earlier Rebellion in 1715 Kent had been a young man living in Rome: perhaps he remembered writing to the long-dead Massingberd, all those years ago, that 'They give out here the Pretender is a-going to be married to the King of Portugal's daughter and the Scotch [are] going to take the Pretender for their King, but I believe [it is] all Jesuit *nova*.' Now he looked on as history busily repeated itself, sending reports to the Burlingtons that reflect the confused, rumour-ridden atmosphere of the time. 'The situation of things and different accounts [are such that] one does not know what to write – I was bid to write to you by a friend of yours and mine that the affair in Scotland rather augments to the Pretender. . .' (12 September 1745). As the 'ribles' (his spelling) approached ever nearer he tried to turn his mind into other channels; a friend lent him Francesco Bianchi's *Del Palazzo de'Cesari* (Verona, 1738), and on 12 October following he told Burlington that 'as politics are not my genius, it divert[s] me much now at nights to look and read of these fine remains of A[n]tiquity.'[11]

It was a depressing period, and the strain told even upon his normally ebullient nature; at a dinner party with the Fairfax brothers, 'Nando and I was bravo'd down by Brian as two cowards that we at this time ought to have courage and resolution and not to be lamenting about the times; we have had foggy weather for this fortnight and never once see the sun, people are afraid of a distemper amongst the cattle about London, in short nothing talk'd about but what's dismal' (letter to Burlington, 12 November).[12] Yet even in such gloomy circumstances food, wine and good company still had their attractions, as is shown by another passage in the same letter: 'Now I am just come from dinner from my Lady Burlington [senior]; the two Nandos din'd there, a good doe pasty from the Duke [of] Somerset's park; we drank your healths and wish you all well here.' And the postscript shows that the faithful old servant may still be relied upon to carry out any commissions that may be laid upon him: 'The room you desir'd to have painted is done; if you want to have anything else done before you come that you may be comfortable at home in your own house, let me know – you know I'll do my best.'

Kent's old friend Alexander Pope died on 30 May 1744. The robust, good-humoured artist and the slight, waspish poet had complemented each other perfectly for over twenty years; now all that was left to Kent were his memories, not only of weighty discussions about artistic theories, but of many a rousing party and the endless schoolboy jokes about Pope's supposed gluttony. That Kent valued Pope's support and friendship we need not doubt, nor that he appreciated the extent of his friend's stature as a poet. Yet the vagaries of human nature never cease to surprise, and it comes as a shock to find that Pope left no memento of any kind to Kent in his will. One can only hope that Kent was forewarned of this inexplicable omission and that his regrets were not tinged with bitterness.

Burlington, of course, remained (he was to die in 1753). But the austere patrician and acknowledged arbiter of taste had by the 1740s opted out of all but family concerns. Though doubtless his advice was still readily available to those who sought it, such as Lord Leicester, he himself built no more, although he continued to make improvements at Chiswick, where he planted trees, erected sculptures, and even introduced a herd of Alderney cows. Though Burlington House was not neglected it was at Chiswick that his Lordship spent most of the time which could be spared from his Yorkshire estates, and Chiswick where he loved best to be. Amongst the visitors he entertained there during these latter years was George Vertue, who recalls the occasion as follows:

> The noble Maecaenas of Arts the Earl of Burlington, having employ'd me in some works, came to see me and invited me to come to Chiswick at his house – ordered a chariot purposely. Amongst his fine collections of

paintings [are also] sculptures, statues, busts, marbles, bronzes, all in a most excellent taste. View'd his gardens with his Lordship and Mr. Kent [and] his house, all over. . . . Amongst his books a printed quarto of Vitruvius in Italian, with notes in the margin by Inigo Jones – this I lookt over pretty carefully. He has also a MS. of King Charles First's pictures.[13]

It was formerly thought that the long and happy if unlikely association between Burlington and the Signor was marred by some kind of misunderstanding which arose towards the end of Kent's life. The Chatsworth archives contain a letter dated 5 January (altered from December) 1749, and written from Paris; at first sight it appears to be in Kent's handwriting, and begins with an apology for an unspecified misdemeanour:

My Lord: I shou'd be ashamed ever to remember that I left England without paying your Lordship my respects, and receiving your commands, but for the confidence I have in your goodness for my pardon. I know you are not ignorant of the cause which induced me to it, from a most unworthy proceeding; therefore I shall say no more of it. . . .

However, a closer inspection of this letter reveals a number of inconsistencies. The date places it several months after Kent's death, though this could be explained if the ill-written 9 were actually to be a 7, thus giving 1747. Although it concludes with the writer's protestation to be 'your Lordship's most faithful, obedient humble servant and old friend', it is not actually signed, and the handwriting, though superficially similar enough to Kent's to explain the attribution to him, differs from his in important calligraphic details. The style and punctuation are also superior to his. But the most serious objection to Kent's authorship is contained in the following passage:

But what has added to the general discontent [here] is the proceeding in the seizure of him they call P. Edward, who was taken at the Opera door as he got out of his coach, as possibly you must have heard, and ty'd hand and foot and carried to the dungeon at Vincenne. . . . This treatment is highly resented by all here, and most particularly by the fair sex, and the poets have exercis'd their vein upon it in strong satire.

This is a correct factual account of the arrest of Charles Edward Stuart, the Young Pretender, which took place on 10 December 1748 as a prelude to his official expulsion from France some days later. When the arrest was made Kent had already been in his grave for eight months; the Paris letter is therefore not by him, but by some other person closely connected with the Burlington family whose identity remains yet to be discovered. There is a sense of relief in finding that Kent did not after all end his life under a cloud, as had once been supposed.

Nevertheless a clue that all was not entirely well in Lord Burlington's household is given by Vertue. After recounting that Kent suffered from eye trouble and other unspecified sickness 'some three or four years' before 1748,[14] from which he appeared to recover (and certainly the references in his letters to successive if minor ailments increase noticeably after *circa* 1745), Vertue then states that 'his high feeding and life and much inaction brought on again (it's said) some disorders, which, with some appearance of secret differences in the Burlington family, inclin'd him to think of taking lodgings or apartments a little way out of town, which he had fitted up for to be there sometimes [as] a retirement.' What were these 'secret differences'? Was there some sort of family quarrel going on, of which Kent was an unwilling spectator? The most likely instigator of any such quarrel would seem to be the Countess, noted for a hasty temper which probably got worse after the death of her daughter. Perhaps even the presence of Kent himself was at last beginning to grate. It is easy enough to visualize a situation in which a highly strung and emotionally disturbed wife finds the continual presence and personality of her husband's oldest and closest friend an increasing irritation, while the husband himself remains seemingly insensitive both to her feelings and to what she sees as his friend's shortcomings. In such an atmosphere Kent could well have felt himself compelled to face up to the unthinkable and to consider quitting the shelter of Burlington House for good.

All this is mere speculation, and perhaps an apology is owed to the memory of Lady Burlington. But whatever the facts behind the mysterious quarrel, it is clear that Kent's last months were not happy. Added to domestic troubles was the Duke of Newcastle's refusal to grant him a proper recompense for his work at Claremont. Gamely he struggled on, ignoring as far as possible what Vertue calls the 'slow increase of his distemper', and concentrating on proposals for alterations at Hampton Court and St James's Palace, and on constructing new terraces at Holland House.[15] Then, quite suddenly, it all became too much for him. A dropsical inflammation flared up, and though nursed with the greatest care and attention at Burlington House throughout his final illness, which lasted about three weeks, nothing more could be done. He died on 12 April 1748, and after an impressive funeral which included nine mourning coaches, was laid to rest in his patron's family vault at Chiswick, a privilege for which he had sought leave in his will.

This will was drawn up in 1743, with a codicil added two days before Kent's death. The provisions it makes have been criticized in that, whilst distributing his collection of paintings and sculpture amongst his various friends, Kent made no distinction on behalf of his life-long patrons, the Burlingtons, other than leaving a pair of Sienese marble vases and a sculpture by Camillo Rusconi to the Earl and three paintings to the Countess. At the last, it seems, he had treated them only marginally better than Pope had apparently behaved towards him. Yet to accuse him of ingratitude is foolish. The Burlingtons wanted for nothing material, and Kent's real legacy to them was the memory of all the times spent so happily together, memory for which – as he well knew

– no tangible work of art could adequately substitute. Incidentally the codicil shows that, whatever the family disagreements may have been, these had not ultimately affected Kent's position, for not only does he slightly augment the original legacies to both Burlingtons, but he is described firmly and unequivocally as 'William Kent Esq. of Burlington House'.

The will also shows that in addition to his art collection and 'my house in Saville Street' Kent had a considerable sum of money to his credit. Surprisingly, however, there were relatives to be considered. His sister Esther, named after their mother, was to receive an annuity of £50 obtained from the rent of the Savile Row house, while her children William, Esther and Mary divided between them the residue of the estate after all other bequests. William was also named as executor, but sadly, as the codicil reveals, predeceased his uncle. The bulk of the money, however, significantly went to Elizabeth Butler (who received £600) and her two children, George and Elizabeth, each of whom received £300. It is not known for certain that George and Elizabeth Butler were actually Kent's children, but having regard to his generous treatment of them in the will this seems probable. They lost their mother tragically soon, for she died on 16 September 1748.

In his lifetime the genial and good-natured Kent made many friends. Such enmity as he aroused probably came more through envy and the method of his advancement than from actual dislike of his personality. Yet one man was not to be appeased even by his death. 'Neither England nor Italy ever produced a more contemptible dauber than the late Mr. Kent', commented Hogarth savagely.[16] In about 1754 he painted his four canvases on the subject of *An Election*, and these were engraved in 1757. The second of the four scenes in the series, entitled *Canvassing for Votes*, includes an inn sign-board on which amongst other details there is a representation of the Horse Guards building. Beneath the central arch there passes the royal state coach, followed by a troop of cavalry – but the arch is so low that the coachman has lost his head. With this rather cheap joke at Kent's expense Hogarth contrived to have the last laugh, though by 1754 it must have sounded distinctly hollow. And the office of Sergeant Painter, to which he was appointed in 1757, came nine years too late to cause Kent any annoyance.

At some point in his career William Kent designed a National Monument, temple-like in style and of indeterminate purpose (a drawing is in the Victoria & Albert Museum). There is no such national monument to Kent himself. Indeed none is needed, for here surely is another man to whom Christopher Wren's famous epitaph can be equally well applied – 'Si monumentum requiris, circumspice.' In the case of Kent our search must be wider and our horizons broader, for as these pages have shown the scale and scope of his achievements are not comprehended in a single place or an individual work of art. If this book acts as a satisfactory signpost or path-finder in the search, it will have served its purpose.

APPENDIX I
PORTRAITS OF KENT

The following is a list of the major portraits of Kent, although the whereabouts of several of them are unknown at present and some may no longer exist.

1   Head-and-shoulders by Luti, inscribed on the back 'Wi. Kent Rittrato Cavalier Benedetti Luti/Pinxt: in Roma 1718.' Perhaps identifiable with item no. 91 in the sale catalogue of Kent's effects: 'Cav. Luti. Mr. Kent, 3qrs, painted at Rome' (though admittedly a head is not the same as a three-quarter length). At Chatsworth.

2   Self-portrait with palette, completed by 1727. Over the staircase at Kensington Palace.

3   Probable self-portrait on a medallion in *Mercury and the Arts* on the ceiling of the Red Velvet Room at Chiswick.

4   Portrait by Dahl, described by Vertue as 'very like' (*WSAV* XXII, 1934, p. 24), completed by 1725. Lost.

5   Full-length by Aikman, completed by 1725. Placed in the hall at Wanstead (*WSAV* XXII, p. 24) and probably identical with the one seen there over the fireplace by Mrs Powys (*Diaries*, ed. E. J. Climenson, London, 1899, p. 205); probably also lot 365 in the 1822 sale at Wanstead ('A portrait of Kent the artist') which was sold to 'Carroll' for £24. 13s. 6d. Lost.

6   Head-and shoulders by Aikman, now known only through engravings as in e.g. various editions of Walpole's *Anecdotes*. The sitter wears a turban.

7   Three-quarter length signed by Dandridge, last recorded in 1910 at 31 Old Burlington Street, at that time the premises of a firm of interior decorators, Lenygon & Co. Probably *circa* 1730. The florid-faced Kent wears a turban, white shirt, coat with wide cuffs and frogged buttonholes. His left hand rests on a closed upright folio volume, his right gestures towards an unidentifiable architectural plan lying on the table before him. An indeterminate architectural background suggests a monument or obelisk. Illustrated in *Connoisseur*, vol. XXVIII, 1910, p. 211.

8   Also signed by Dandridge, similar to no. 7 above though smaller and without accessories. The coat is brown velvet, the frogs gold. Purchased by the National Portrait Gallery in 1909 from Shepherd Brothers of King Street, who also had no. 7 on their premises at the time. In neither case is the sitter actually identified as Kent, but there is no reason to doubt that it is he.

9   Three-quarter length at Nuneham, traditionally and not improbably said to be Kent. At one time attributed to Slaughter but re-attributed by the third Lord Harcourt to Kent himself. The sitter wears a wig, white shirt, coat with large buttoned cuffs, carries a palette and brushes in his left hand and a single brush in his right. Probably *circa* 1727. Illustrated in C. W. James, *Chief Justice Coke . . . at Holkham*, London, 1929, and in *Artwork*, vol. VII, 1931, p. 37.

10   Full-length in Gawen Hamilton's group portrait *A Conversation of Virtuosis*, 1735. Standing far right with Rysbrack, Wootton and Hamilton, in wig and frogged brown velvet coat (possibly the same one as in nos. 7 and 8 above), holding a pair of dividers. National Portrait Gallery.

11   Self-portrait sent to Paris to be engraved by Ravenet (*WSAV* XXII, p. 115). Inscribed 'Gulielmus Kent Magnae Britanniae Regis Pictor et Architectus.' Late 1742 or early 1743. Lost.

Kent is identified (either by name or in appearance) in several of the sketches which are preserved at Chatsworth, most if not all of these lightning portraits probably being from the observant pencil of Lady Burlington.

The Department of the Environment owns a half-length portrait of a man wearing black, with a white shirt and black turban; in one hand he holds a stylus, while the other – grasping a roll of paper – rests on the head of a Classical bust. The portrait is labelled as Kent, the artist Aikman, and is dated on the canvas 1704. At that time Aikman was still in Scotland (he did not come to London until 1723) and the unknown Kent had not yet left Yorkshire. Unless this major discrepancy can be explained – perhaps by a scientific examination which might show that the date is a corruption of 1724 – there seems little point in speculating further on the authenticity of the likeness.

Reference is sometimes made to Kent's appearance in an ill-preserved group portrait (at the Ashmolean Museum, Oxford) known as *An Assembly of Virtuosi* and inevitably attributed on occasion to Hamilton. But the table of identification which accompanies the picture dates only from the nineteenth century, and the shadowy figure named as Kent may not be him at all.

APPENDIX II
KENT'S DRAWINGS IN THE VICTORIA & ALBERT MUSEUM

The following are to be found in the Department of Prints & Drawings:

1 Designs for chimney-pieces: 208, 209
2 View of the Temple and grounds at Euston: 3309
3 Designs for the Horse Guards: 3317/8
4 Design for a chimney-piece at the Treasury: 3436.199
5 Designs for the Parliament House: 3518.1–18
6 A table for Houghton: 8156
7 Drawing of the statue of Inigo Jones at Chiswick: 8933.103
8 Design for a mural monument: 8933.121
9 Design for a statue of George II: 8933.231
10 Designs for the Stanhope monument: 8933.257/8
11 Design for a National Memorial building: 9141
12 Designs for *The Faerie Queene*: E.869–895.1928
13 A view at Tivoli: E.896.1928
14 An archer: E.897.1928
15 A fantasy (Time altering the hands of a church clock), and a sketch of a dog: E.898.1928
16 A sheet of figure studies: E.899.1928
17 A sketch of gladiators: E.900.1928
18 Design for a painted frieze: E.901.1928
19 Sketches of a building and a cook: E.903.1928
20 Design for the Newton monument: E.424.1946

Note
Since completion of the main text, another version of item 7 above has been added to the catalogue (8933.102). Except for the head, which is clearly that of Jones, it corresponds closely to the statue of Palladio at Chiswick. The supposition must now be that both statues are based on Kent's original ideas for a figure of Jones.

A SATIRICAL POEM

The following anonymous poem in the style of Pope (though certainly not by him) was sent in the form of a letter to the Countess of Burlington at Bath, and is dated 1736; it is now at Chatsworth.

Inscribed to Mr. Kent

Rare Architect, in whose exotick school
Our English connoisseurs may learn by rule
To spoil their Houses and to play the fool,
To all mankind (could we on paper live)
What charming Dwellings might thy Genius give,
And though when executed still we find
Thy plans have nothing to its use design'd,
Though to space, light, convenience you declare
Irreconcilable perpetual war,
With Halls where groping Moles should only feed,
And Librarys where Linx's eyes can't read,
With Doors to common purposes such foes
Some never open, others never close,
Windows inventing what the seer of old
Nor form'd to let in light nor keep out cold,
Chimneys in cupboards, of full means posses't
To fire the house, tho' not to warm the Guest,
Stairs which no mortal can go up or down,
And leaden Skulls each Emblem-dome to crown,
Though such in every shape in every part
We find thy unaccommodating art,
Yet who shall say thy works are not Divine
When all must own there is no House of thine
In which (amongst the many have been try'd)
The Devil *would* or mortal *can* reside.

Not[e] on Chiswick

Possess'd of one great Hall for state,
Without one room to sleep or eat,
How well you build let flatt'ry tell
And all mankind how ill you dwell.

NOTES

Abbreviations are used as follows:

CAP	*The Correspondence of Alexander Pope*, ed. G. Sherburn (Oxford, 1956)
CHW	*Correspondence of Horace Walpole*, ed. W. S. Lewis (New Haven, 1937–)
CL	*Country Life*
HKW	*The History of the King's Works*, ed. H. M. Colvin (London, 1976)
HMC	*Historical Manuscripts Commission Reports*
WSAV	*Walpole Society Annual Volume*

CHAPTER 1   *A Second Raphael*

1   'The family name, which he modernised to Kent, was originally Cant.' J. Thompson, *Historical Sketches of Bridlington* (Bridlington, 1821), p. 113n.

2   They were published by the Walpole Society in a series of volumes between 1930 and 1955. The principal references to Kent are in Notebook III, published as *WSAV* XXII, 1934, and the main account of his life is on pp. 139–41. This reference will not be invariably cited; all other references are cited below in the normal way.

3   *Anecdotes of Painting in England*, ed. R. Wornum (London, 1849), vol. III, p. 777.

4   C. Burney, *A General History of Music [etc.]*, 2nd edn (London, 1799), vol. IV, p. 640.

5   J. Addison, *Remarks on Several Parts of Italy &c* (London, 1705), p. 303.

6   Bodleian Library MS. Eng. Letters e.34. The same library also houses the letter to Samuel Gale, MS. Eng. Misc. C.114.

7   Letter to Burrell Massingberd (see note 9 below).

8   To the same, 24 November 1714.

9   It is now in the Lincolnshire Archive Office, as is also Massingberd's correspondence with his shipping agents Chetham, Winder & Co., and with Sir John Chester. Massingberd's own letters are in the form of drafts.

10   An excellent description of the ceremony will be found in P. J. Grosley, *New Observations on Italy and its Inhabitants*, trs. Thomas Nugent (London, 1769), vol. II, pp. 161–4.

11 R. Thoresby, *Ducatus Leodiensis*, 2nd edn (Leeds, 1816), pt III, p. 57.

12 This at least is the tradition, but it is not convincingly substantiated; on the other hand Kent, in his letter to Massingberd of 24 November 1714, refers specifically to Chiari, not Luti, as 'my master'.

13 The Wentworth correspondence is in the British Library, Add. MS. 22,229.

14 R. and J. Adam, *The Works in Architecture [etc.]* (London, 1778–1822), vol. I, p. 3 n. E.

15 Mariari is identified by J. Tanner in 'The Building of Chicheley Hall' (*Records of Buckinghamshire*, vol. XVII, 1961–5), who states that his letter survived in the Massingberd/Kent correspondence. When I consulted the correspondence in 1982 I did not find this letter.

16 There are *grisaille* panels of trophies in the entrance hall at Bretton Park which may be by Kent. The house was rebuilt for Sir William Wentworth between 1720 and 1728.

CHAPTER 2   *Travels in Italy*

1 Richard Lassels, *The Voyage of Italy* (London, 1670). All these extracts are taken from the unpaginated preface.

2 Holkham MS. 733; 734 is also relevant. A microfilm is deposited in the Bodleian Library.

3 C. W. James, *Chief Justice Coke, his Family and Descendants at Holkham* (London, 1929), p. 187.

4 Bodleian Library, MS. Rawlinson D.1162.

5 *WSAV* XXII, 1934, p. 138.

6 See J. Lees-Milne, *Earls of Creation* (London, 1962), p. 109.

7 James, op. cit., p. 191.

8 *CAP*, vol. III, p. 417. 'All that has nothing of the Ancient gust is call'd a barbarous or Gothique manner, which . . . has nothing in it that is noble.' C. A Du Fresnoy, *The Art of Painting*, trs. John Dryden, London, 1695, p. 93. At the same time, however, the Goths – as a loose ethnic group – were held to have some good qualities including rugged independence and great hardihood.

9 Lord Shaftesbury, 'Advice to an Author', *Characteristicks of Men, Manners, Opinions, Times*, 5th edn (Birmingham, 1773), vol. I, p. 338.

10 Ibid., p. 333.

11 Ibid., p. 338.

12 Chatsworth MS.

CHAPTER 3   *Swift Success*

1 *South Western Star*, 5 November 1892.

2 *The Architecture of Sir Roger Pratt . . . Printed . . . from his Note-Books*, ed. R. W. T. Gunther (Oxford, 1928), p. 78.

3 'The staircase is painted by Sebastiano Ricci in his best manner, the ceilings by Kent in his worst.' H. Walpole, *Journals of Visits to Country Seats*, *WSAV* XVI, 1928, p. 39.

4 Kent also worked at about the same time in the Duke's London mansion, Chandos House in St James's Square, completing the commission by 1724. There was later a strange suggestion that his ceiling painting for the main bedroom should be re-used in the Ducal mausoleum at Canons (see p. 53).

5 *Passages from the Diaries of Mrs. Philip Lybbe Powis . . . A.D. 1756 to 1808*, ed. E. J. Climenson (London, 1899), p. 205. In his painting *Assembly at Wanstead House* Hogarth's setting is the Great Hall, but the details are indistinct and it is not possible to make out anything of Kent's ceiling nor to tell whether the picture over the fireplace is indeed a portrait of him. Hogarth's painting is now in the John Howard McFadden Memorial Collection at the Philadelphia Museum of Art. The ceiling was not universally admired. On a visit to Wanstead in 1727 the Scottish baronet Sir John Clerk of Penicuick noted: 'The Saloon is a fine room well finished in stucco, the roof [sic] painted by Kent (a very indifferent piece of work) and the ornaments above gilded.' J. Fleming, *Robert Adam and his Circle* (London, 1978), p. 24.

6 *WSAV* XVIII, 1930, p. 100.

7 Ibid., XXII, 1934, p. 76.

8 Ibid., XVIII, p. 100. Seeking the latest decorative style for his new house Mavisbank in Midlothian, then being built for him by William Adam, Sir John Clerk consulted the painter William Aikman. In reply Aikman wrote from London on 15 July 1725 as follows: 'I observe your commission for a picture to your staircase; at present I know nobody here [who] could perform it to your mind, for Mr. Kent is so busy about the staircase and gallery at Kensington that he can find no time to undertake it. Sir James Thornhill is but a heavy draughtsman and extravagantly dear.' Fleming, op. cit., p. 39.

9 *WSAV* XVIII, p. 101.

10 T. Beckwith, 'Anecdotes of the Lives of . . . Painters [etc.]' (*circa* 1780), Victoria & Albert Museum Library MS. L.5020-1975.

11 *HMC*, Portland MSS., vol. VI, 1900, p. 150.

12 *HKW*, vol. V, p. 199.

13 The Privy Chamber is sometimes confusingly called the Queen's Drawing Room. In fact it seems that Queen Caroline re-designated the apartment as her Drawing Room. See C. Hussey, 'Kensington Palace: The State Rooms', pt III, *CL*, vol. LVI, 1924, p. 952.

14 *WSAV* XXII, p. 19.

15 This discovery was made in 1953. See *HKW*, p. 200.

16 In his *Journals of Visits* (see note 3 above) Walpole records having seen a portrait of Peter hanging in St James's Palace in 1758 (p. 17).

17 C. H. C. and M. I. Baker, *The Life and Circumstances of James Brydges, First Duke of Chandos* (Oxford, 1949), p. 415.

18 Lord Shaftesbury, 'Treatise VII, Viz. A Notion of the Historical Draught or Tablature of the Judgement of Hercules', *Characteristicks of Men, Manners, Opinions, Times*, 5th edn (Birmingham, 1773) vol. III, pp. 347–8.

19 *WSAV* XXII, p. 19.

20 Lord Hervey, *Memoirs of the Reign of George the Second*, ed. J. W. Croker (London, 1848), vol. I, p. 59.

21 Ibid., p. 426.

22 *Anecdotes of Painting in England*, ed. R. Wornum (London, 1849), vol. III, pp. 777–8.
23 Victoria & Albert Museum Library MS. L.518-1945.
24 *WSAV* XXII, p. 55.
25 Ibid., p. 138. Nevertheless Kent apparently provided a sofa and chairs for a small Chinese-style temple (later called the House of Confucius) which Goupy designed for Kew. See Sir William Chambers, *Plans, Elevations, Sections and Perspective Views of the Gardens and Buildings at Kew* (London, 1763), p. 4.
26 *WSAV* XXIV, 1936, p. 163. Almost certainly Trench is the 'Mr. French' to whom Lord Raby commended Sir William Wentworth for advice about buying pictures (see p. 29). Confusion over his name extends even to such modern authorities as Redgrave, Bénézit and Thieme-Becker, all of whom give descriptions of his life and work under both spellings without any connection or cross-reference between the two.
27 Ibid.
28 However, several people clearly entertained high hopes of him. William Aikman, in his discussion of a suitable artist for Sir John Clerk's staircase (see note 8 above), continues: 'In September next I expect my friend Mr. Trench from Italy where he has been these two years past, studying colouring under the famous Solimena. . . . We expect he will do something in a right manner when he returns. So soon as he comes I will speak to him about your roof piece and doubt not he will undertake it at a reasonable rate.' Nothing happened, and in the end the idea of a painted ceiling was abandoned in favour of plasterwork (Fleming, op. cit., pp. 39, 42). This incident also reinforces the point that Solimena was widely esteemed at the time, especially as a colourist. Kent himself owned four paintings by Solimena which are listed in the sale catalogue of his effects.
29 According to Hogarth himself, Vanderbank's Academy was set up 'in an old Presbyterian meeting-house . . . with the addition of a woman figure, to make it the more interesting to subscribers'. It lasted for a few years, but eventually the treasurer absconded with the funds, the landlord distrained on the furniture, and the venture collapsed (J. Ireland, supplement to *Hogarth Illustrated*, London, 1798, pp. 65–6). Kent's membership is attested by Vertue who gives a list of the original subscribers in *WSAV* XXX, 1955, p. 170.
30 It is illustrated in Sir T. Cox, 'William Kent as Painter', *Artwork*, vol. VII, 1931, p. 28.
31 *WSAV* XXII, p. 35.
32 It is impossible to take seriously Vertue's assertion that after returning to England Kent 'was obliged to satisfy his Yorkshire master for his time' (i.e. his indentures) except in terms of financial compensation – which doubtless would have been paid by Burlington.

CHAPTER 4   *The Signor and his Friends*

1 *CAP* vol. IV, pp. 162–3.
2 The bells were not actually part of the harpsichord mechanism but were in fact an early form of the modern orchestral Glockenspiel. Within the limits of the period Handel was one of the foremost orchestral innovators of his day.

3   Gay here spells Handel's name according to the original German pronunciation which fell out of use when the name became anglicized.

4   J. Spence, *Anecdotes . . . Collected from the Conversation of Mr. Pope* [etc.] (London, 1820), p. 214.

5   *CAP* vol. II, p. 181.

6   E. Croft-Murray, *Decorative Painting in England 1537–1837* (London, 1962–70), vol. II, p. 231.

7   *CAP* vol. II, pp. 415–16.

8   *Anecdotes of Painting in England*, ed. R. Wornum (London, 1849), vol. III, p. 779.

9   *CAP* vol. II, p. 181.

10 Ibid., vol. IV, p. 165.

11 Ibid., vol. III, pp. 516, 518.

12 Ibid., vol. IV, p. 163.

13 Ibid., p. 150. Hugh Bethel was a mutual friend whom Kent had originally met in Italy – 'Mr. Bethel has . . . bespoke one picture of every hand that is famous' (letter to Massingberd, 5 November 1712). Kent was later supposed to paint a portrait of him for Pope but never completed it (see p. 136). The Murrays were the future Lord and Lady Mansfield.

14 Umbrageous = suspicious, jealous, apt to take offence (*OED*).

15 Chatsworth MS.

16 *CAP* vol. IV, p. 163.

17 Ibid., vol. III, p. 517.

18 *CHW* vol. XVII, 1955, p. 438.

19 *CAP* vol. IV, p. 43.

20 Kent had an unlikely successor in the painter G. F. Watts, who in the 1850s was also called 'Signor' by Mrs Prinsep's literary/artistic circle at Little Holland House, Kensington.

21 Chatsworth MS. He was not alone in this. Writing to his wife on 5 July 1728, Lord Burlington remarks: 'I hope the venison came sweet – I shou'd have sent the buck but that the General [? Dormer] dined yesterday at Chiswick and has a rage for that diet.'

22 H. A. Tipping, 'Four Unpublished Letters of William Kent', *Architectural Review*, vol. LXIII, 1927, p. 182. 'Polly' was perhaps an Italian jack-of-all-trades craftsman.

23 *CAP* vol. IV, p. 163. Kent seems here to be quoting Lovel's own words, or at least an approximation: 'Like Michelangelo, where [in whose work] there is nothing of value.' In this context 'nove' makes no sense unless it is a mistake for 'dove'. Kent's Italian grammar and spelling are as careless as his English.

24 Ibid., p. 149.

25 The MS. is now in the Bodleian Library, Rawlinson D.540.

26 Vertu = a love of, or taste for, works of art or curios; a knowledge of, or interest in, the fine arts (*OED*).

27 *WSAV* XXII, 1934, p. 115.

28 The bulk of her letters to Burlington and Kent, and theirs to her, are at Chatsworth.

29 *CAP* vol. IV, pp. 323–4.

30 Ibid., pp. 139–41.

31 Ibid., pp. 196–7.
32 *HMC*, Hastings MSS., vol. III, 1934, p. 26.
33 *CAP* vol. IV, p. 329.
34 Spence, op. cit., p. 23.
35 *CAP* vol. I, p. 188.
36 Lord Hervey, *Memoirs of the Reign of George the Second*, ed. J. W. Croker (London, 1848), vol. II, p. 157.
37 Quoted in G. E. Cokayne, *The Complete Peerage of . . . the United Kingdom* (London, 1912), vol. II, p. 433, n.
38 To Lord Hartington, 27 September 1747. This letter and all other domestic correspondence quoted below it in this chapter are at Chatsworth.
39 *CHW* vol. XXXVII, 1974, p. 114.
40 Pleydell was persuaded by Lords Lovel and Burlington that Coleshill (burnt out in 1952) was designed by Inigo Jones, but the architect is now known to have been Roger Pratt.
41 *CAP* vol. III, p. 417.
42 Chatsworth MS.
43 P. H. Highfill, K. A. Burnim and E. A. Langhans, *A Biographical Dictionary of Actors, Actresses, Musicians . . . & Other Stage Personnel in London 1660–1800* (Carbondale, 1972), vol. II, pp. 450–1.

CHAPTER 5   *Decorations and Furniture*

1 That Kent, while still in Italy, was aware of contemporary architectural events in England is proved by his letter of 8 June 1718 to Massingberd in which he asks, as a favour to himself and Mariari, for 'a design of the church made in the Strand', i.e. St Mary-le-Strand built by James Gibbs between 1714 and 1717.
2 *Anecdotes of Painting in England*, ed. R. Wornum (London, 1849), vol. III, p. 778.
3 *HMC*, Hastings MSS., vol. III, 1934, p. 26.
4 H. A. Tipping, 'Four Unpublished Letters of William Kent', *Architectural Review*, vol. LXIII, 1927, p. 180.
5 Ibid., p. 182.
6 Ibid., p. 209; *CAP* vol. IV, p. 150.
7 Chatsworth MS.
8 *WSAV* XXII, 1934, p. 73.
9 An anonymous MS. of 1728 entitled 'Voiage d'Angleterre, d'Holland et de Flandre' speaks only of 'Une belle maison qui sera composée de deux corps de logis joints par une colonnade ou peristille' (Victoria & Albert Museum Library MS. L.1255-1912). There is no mention of the Link, which may indicate that at this date it had yet to be built.
10 *HMC*, Portland MSS. vol. VI, 1900, p. 160.
11 *HMC*, Castle Howard MSS., 1897, p. 85; A. Young, *A Six Weeks Tour through the Southern Counties of England and Wales* (London, 1768), p. 33. Two important drawings by Kent (one dated 1725) showing his proposed decorations for the north and south walls of the Saloon, together with the arrangement of pictures, were sold at Sotheby's on 7 July 1983.

12 W. Coxe, *Memoirs of the Life and Administration of Sir Robert Walpole, Earl of Orford* (London, 1800), vol. III, p. 351.

13 Quoted by R. Vivian in 'Houghton Hall, Norfolk', *CL* vol. XXII, 1907, p. 133, who attributes the lines to Pope. Pope, however, is not their author, and I have not been able to trace their source.

14 H. M. Colvin, *A Biographical Dictionary of British Architects 1660–1840* (London, 1978), p. 694. Hawksmoor in a letter to Lord Carlisle referred to Ripley as 'our useless Surveyor' (*WSAV* XIX, 1931, p. 145). Nevertheless in Kent's will Ripley received a bust of Michelangelo with its wooden pedestal, as well as a mourning ring.

15 M. Verney and P. Abercrombie, 'Letters of an Eighteenth-Century Architect', pt III, *Architectural Review*, vol. LX, 1926, p. 51.

16 Lord Hervey, *Memoirs of the Reign of George the Second*, ed. J. W. Croker (London, 1848), vol. I, p. 113.

17 *HMC*, Portland, p. 160.

18 Ibid.

19 *HMC*, Castle Howard, p. 86.

20 MS. 'Journal of a Jaunt into England 1759'; quoted by J. Fleming, 'In Search of Landscape Gardens', *CL* vol. CXXX, 1961, p. 200.

21 *HKW* p. 201; C. Hussey, 'Kensington Palace: The State Rooms', pt III, *CL*, vol. LVI, 1924, p. 952. This may refer to the re-designated Privy Chamber; see chapter 3 *supra*, n. 13. The appearance of the Privy Chamber, with Kent's side tables, is indicated by W. H. Pyne in *The History of the Royal Residences* (London, 1819), vol. II (plate entitled 'Queen Caroline's Drawing Room'). A Kentian sphinx side table appears in the same (plate entitled 'Old Dining Rooms').

22 A. Cunningham, *The Lives of the Most Eminent British Painters, Sculptors and Architects*, 2nd edn (London, 1830–3), vol. IV, pp. 303–4 (an upholsterer, by Cunningham's time, was a general purveyor of furniture and fittings). The Walpole reference is *Anecdotes*, vol. III, p. 778.

23 *HMC*, Portland, p. 161.

24 *Anecdotes*, vol. III, p. 778.

25 *Lord Hervey and his Friends 1726–38*, ed. Lord Ilchester (London, 1950), p. 27.

26 *HMC*, Hastings, p. 28.

27 *CHW* vol. XIX, 1955, p. 175. Perhaps the cradle had an affinity with a remarkable baby carriage ascribed to Kent and now at Chatsworth; made for the children of his patron the Duke of Devonshire, the body is in the shape of the ubiquitous shell and the traces formed like serpents. Traction was provided by a goat.

28 Victoria & Albert Museum, Dept of Prints & Drawings, 93.B.21, no. 417.

CHAPTER 6   *Royal Commissions and Gothick Gusto*

1 Richmond Lodge was an old building not unlike Kew House in appearance, with numerous but small rooms. It had been acquired in 1721 from the Earl of Arran by George II when Prince of Wales; his wife took an especial fancy to the Lodge and its grounds, eventually purchasing it for herself out of her own allowance.

2 Sir William Chambers, *Plans, Elevations, Sections and Perspective Views of the Gardens and Buildings at Kew* (London, 1763), p. 2.

3 A further name for it was the White House.

4 H. Walpole, *Journals of Visits to Country Seats*, WSAV XVI, 1928, p. 38.

5 Chambers, op. cit., p. 2.

6 The drawings are in the collection of the RIBA.

7 *Lord Hervey and his Friends 1726–38*, ed. Lord Ilchester (London, 1950), pp. 115–16, Hervey himself was originally supposed to be one of the entourage, but (as he confessed in a letter to a friend), 'pleaded chicken, headache, fear of sitting up etc., and got off.'

8 *Anecdotes of Painting in England*, ed. R. Wornum (London, 1849), vol. III, p. 779.

9 HMC, Castle Howard MSS., 1897, p. 125.

10 This arch, constructed of wood and plaster, stood against the north wall framing the entrance to the Hall. The archway itself was surmounted by a heavy pediment supporting a joint medallion portrait of the new monarch and his consort, together with figures of Fame, Neptune and Britannia, and was flanked by four gigantic female caryatids. It was portentous but can hardly have inspired joy. For an illustration, see *HKW*, pl. 67.

11 Lord Hervey, *Memoirs of the Reign of George the Second*, ed. J. W. Croker (London, 1848), vol. I, pp. 226–7.

12 *WSAV* XXII, 1934, p. 68.

13 Ibid.

14 Ibid., p. 140.

15 *Anecdotes*, vol. III, p. 777; *Journals of Visits*, p. 22.

16 *WSAV* XXII, p. 98.

17 *CAP* vol. IV, pp. 500, 509.

18 Ibid., pp. 220–1.

19 Kent's first monument commission, a memorial to John and Thomas Wainwright, is considerably earlier than the others (*circa* 1722) and bears no portrait; it is in Chester Cathedral, and its design (a wall plaque featuring two *putti* supporting an oval inscribed panel with surrounding garland) looks back to Italian sources.

20 *CHW* vol. XXXV, 1973, p. 151.

21 *WSAV* XXII, pp. 50–1.

22 Ibid., p. 141.

23 Ibid., pp. 115–16.

24 Nevertheless Rysbrack's professional association with Kent was not finally ended. The monument in the church at Ashby-de-la-Zouch which ostensibly commemorates the ninth Earl of Huntingdon has as its principal feature a relief bust of his widow the Countess on a large urn, which itself stands out in high relief against the supporting obelisk behind. The monument was commissioned by the Countess *circa* 1746, the design provided by Kent, the bust carved by Rysbrack, and the whole erected by Pickford *circa* 1750 after Kent's death.

25 C. Deelman, *The Great Shakespeare Jubilee* (London, 1964), p. 18.

26 *Anecdotes*, vol. III, p. 779.

27 *WSAV* XXII, p. 74.

28   'This Sig. Guelphi works under the direction of Mr. Kent at the house of Lord Burlington' (ibid., p. 51).

29   Anon. MS., 'Account of Royal Palaces . . . In and Around London' (*circa* 1755), Victoria & Albert Museum Library.

30   *CAP* vol. III, p. 329.

31   'Here is also a library consisting of a well chosen collection of the works of modern authors neatly bound in vellum' (anon. MS., see note 29 above). In a footnote to line 355 in book II, epistle I of his *Imitations of Horace* Pope defines Merlin's Cave as 'A building in the royal gardens of Richmond, where is a small but choice collection of books.'

32   The waxworks are also sometimes said to have been grouped round a table. But the figures in the engraving are clearly real people; a male courtier bends over a terrestrial globe, whilst a regal-looking lady sitting apart may be the Queen herself (Plate 56). Count Kielmansegge saw the waxworks in 'three niches in the wall', with Merlin in the centre (*Diary of a Journey to England in the Years 1761–1762*, London, 1902, p. 74). Their iconography has been closely examined by J. Colton, who also suggests that Merlin's Cave and its contents were profound if obscure symbols of the Queen's political beliefs ('Merlin's Cave and Queen Caroline: Garden Art as Political Propaganda', *Eighteenth-Century Studies*, vol. X, 1976, p. 1).

33   W. Mason, *Satirical Poems Published Anonymously*, ed. P. Toynbee (Oxford, 1926), p. 49.

34   J. Spence, *Anecdotes . . . Collected from the Conversation of Mr. Pope [etc.]* (London, 1820), p. 12.

35   B. Jones, *Follies and Grottoes*, 2nd edn (London, 1974), p. 51.

36   Hervey, *Memoirs*, vol. II, p. 50.

37   Spence, op. cit., pp. 296–7.

38   *Anecdotes*, vol. III, pp. 779–80.

39   See the notes to book I of his poem *The English Garden* (London, 1811).

40   *Anecdotes*, vol. III, p. 779.

41   In F. Drake, *Eboracum* (London, 1736), will be found a plate showing a plan of the pavement design.

42   *CHW* vol. XXXV, 1973, p. 154.

43   Ibid., vol. IX, 1941, p. 290.

CHAPTER 7   *Building on the Grand Scale*

1   *WSAV* XXII, 1934, p. 73.

2   *HMC*, Castle Howard MSS., 1897, p. 114.

3   Lord Hervey, *Memoirs of the Reign of George the Second*, ed. J. W. Croker (London, 1848), vol. I, pp. 226–7.

4   *WSAV* XXII, 1934, p. 139.

5   *HMC*, Castle Howard, p. 125.

6   *WSAV* XXII, p. 73.

7   On 17 June 1724 Benedetto Luti died in Rome. The *Biographie Universelle* states that 'Son cabinet d'estampes . . . fut acquis après sa mort par William Kent' and

further states that the collection amounted to over 14,000 items. If Kent did indeed acquire it, he may well have done so on this second trip to Italy, although the time lapse between 1724 and 1730 seems rather long.

   Kent is also said to have purchased a number of drawings by Fra Bartolommeo, then the property of the Italian collector Niccolo Gabburri. These included some important and rare landscapes which were sold at Sotheby's in London on 20 November 1957. Mariette in his *Abecedario* (vol. II, 1854, p. 275) states that Gabburri's collection was bought 'par un Anglais nommé Kent' after the former's death, but as this did not occur until 1742, and there is no firm evidence of Kent's having returned to Italy for a third visit, it is possible that the purchase was made during Gabburri's lifetime. Significantly, Vincenzo Marchese in his *Lives of the Most Eminent Painters . . . of the Order of S. Dominic* (trs. C. F. Meehan, vol. II, 1852, p. 130) merely says that the drawings 'passed into the hands of Niccolo Gabburri, and they were at last purchased by a Mr. Kant [sic] and removed to England.'

8   *WSAV* XXII, pp. 139–40.
9   Inscribed at the back of the 1714 tour journal.
10   J. Malton, *Picturesque Tour through the Cities of London and Westminster* (London, 1792), p. 33.
11   British Museum Sloane MS.4055, fol. 349.
12   *HMC*, Hastings MSS., vol. III, 1934, p. 28.
13   *HMC*, Castle Howard, p. 144.
14   Ibid., p. 137.
15   Lord Shaftesbury, 'A Letter Concerning Design', *Characteristicks of Men, Manners, Opinions, Times*, 5th edn (Birmingham, 1773), vol. III, p. 398.
16   The Parliament House designs are to be found in the collections of the RIBA, the Soane Museum and the Victoria & Albert Museum.
17   In the volume dealing with London and Westminster in the Buildings of England series (2nd edn, 1962), Pevsner states that in fact Kent's designs were used for the rebuilding in 1738/9 of the range running south of Westminster Hall (p. 476). Wittkower in his article 'Lord Burlington and William Kent' (*Archaeological Journal*, vol. CII, 1945, p. 151) has shown how closely Kent's designs for the Parliament House and Treasury relate to Burlington's own ideas.
18   Count F. von Kielmansegge, *Diary* (London, 1902), p. 74. It is also recorded as being in the same place in the anon. MS. 'Account of Royal Palaces', Victoria & Albert Museum Library.
19   *CHW* vol. XIX, p. 485. Kent's work on another town house, 10 Downing Street, is conjectural and would have been an official commission, perhaps at Walpole's behest. He is credited with the over-grand kitchen as well as the decoration of the Official Drawing Room.
20   H. A. Tipping, 'Four unpublished Letters of William Kent', *Architectural Review*, vol. LXIII, 1927, p. 210.
21   J. Fleming, *Robert Adam and his Circle* (London, 1978), p. 197.
22   A. Young, *A Six Weeks Tour* (London, 1768), p. 13.
23   *Lord Hervey and his Friends 1726–38*, ed. Lord Ilchester (London, 1950), p. 73.
24   *Anecdotes of Painting in England*, ed. R. Wornum (London, 1849), vol. III, pp. 780–1.

25 Young, op. cit., pp. 197–8.

26 Tipping, op. cit.

27 M. Brettingham *The Plans, Elevations and Sections of Holkham in Norfolk* (London, 1773), p.v.

28 Tipping, op. cit.

29 Brettingham, op. cit., p. vi.

30 Tipping, op. cit. Perhaps an acceptable translation of the crude tag would be 'Mr. Codpiece'.

31 The visitor was Admiral Boscawen of Hatchlands, Surrey, one of Robert Adam's first patrons in England. See C. W. James, *Chief Justice Coke . . . at Holkham* (London, 1929), p. 272.

32 *HMC*, Castle Howard, p. 86.

33 A.M.D.W. Stirling, *Coke of Norfolk and his Friends [etc]* (London, 1908), p. 62.

34 Ibid.

CHAPTER 8 *A New Elysium*

1 F. Bacon, *Of Gardens: An Essay* (London, edn of 1902), p. 15.

2 Lord Shaftesbury, 'The Moralists,' *Characteristics of Men, Manners, Opinions, Times*, 5th edn (Birmingham, 1773), vol. II, pp. 393–4.

3 Robert Castell's felicitous translation of *ruris imitatio* is 'A sudden imitation of the country' (*The Villas of the Ancients*, London, 1728).

4 *Paradise Lost*, book IV.

5 *The Architecture of Leon Battista Alberti in Ten Books* trs. G. Leoni (London, 1726), vol. II, bk VI, chap. iv, fol. 6.

6 *CAP* vol. IV, p. 40.

7 The portrait was recently rediscovered and is now in the Paul Mellon Collection at the Yale Center for British Art. See J. Riely, 'A Supplement to the Portraits of Alexander Pope', *Evidence of Literary Scholarship*, ed. R. Wellek and A. Ribeiro (Oxford, 1979), pp. 141–3.

8 H. Walpole, 'On Modern Gardening', in *Anecdotes of Painting in England*, ed R. Wornum (London, 1849), vol. III, pp. 803–4.

9 S. Switzer, *Ichnographia Rustica* (London, 1742), vol. III, p. 47. Kent's attitude was more forthright, causing Lord Leicester on one occasion to write of 'those unpicturesque, those cold and insipid strait walks [at Waghen Hall, Yorkshire] which make the Signor sick', although in fact Leicester's own grounds at Holkham were laid out on similarly formal lines (H. A. Tipping, 'Four Unpublished Letters of William Kent', *Architectural Review*, vol. LXIII, 1927, p. 210).

10 *CAP* vol. II, p. 264.

11 J. Macky, *A Journey through England [etc.]*, 4th edn (London, 1724), vol. I, p. 72. He prefaces these remarks on the Chiswick gardens by saying that 'The whole contrivance of 'em is the effect of his Lordship's own genius and fine taste.' The 'Covent Garden church' is of course St Paul's, designed by Inigo Jones and therefore of particular significance for Burlington.

12 *WSAV* XXII, 1934, p. 140.

13 *HMC*, Castle Howard MSS., 1897, pp. 143–4. The garden featured a cascade and a pavilion paved with marble, 'adorned with painting and sculpture and furnished with suitable magnificence, the chair of state alone costing £500' (W. H. Pyne, *The History of the Royal Residences*, London, 1819, vol. III, p. 2). This too sounds like Kent's work.

14 Anon., 'Account of Royal Palaces', Victoria & Albert Museum Library MS.

15 *CAP* vol. III, pp. 322–3, 329.

16 'On Modern Gardening', p. 803.

17 H. Berlioz, *Memoirs*, ed. D. Cairns (London, 1969), pp. 173–4.

18 J. Spence, *Anecdotes . . . Collected from the Conversation of Mr. Pope [etc.]* (London, 1820), pp. 144, 209–10.

19 R. Morris claims that 'Lord Bathurst was the first who deviated from straight lines, as applied to decorative pieces of water, by following the natural curves of a valley, when widening a brook' on his estate at Richings in Buckinghamshire (*Essays on Landscape Gardening*, London, 1825, pp. 2–3).

20 T. Whately, 'An Essay on the Different Natural Situations of Gardens', *Observations on Modern Gardening [etc]*. (London, 1801), p. 152.

21 *CAP* vol. IV, p. 450.

22 Ibid., vol. II, p. 296.

23 Perhaps Pope recalled a passage in Alberti: 'I was extremely pleased with an artificial grotto I have seen. . . . the walls were composed of various sorts of sea-shells, lying roughly together, some reversed, some with their mouths lying outwards, their colours being so artfully blended as to form a very beautiful variety' (*Ten Books of Architecture*, ed. cit., vol. II, bk IX, chap. IV, fol. 82).

24 Ibid., vol. II, bk VI, chap. IV, fol. 6.

25 C. Thacker, *The History of Gardens* (London, 1979), p. 186. A further manifestation appears in Ware's *Designs of Inigo Jones*, described simply as 'A Round Temple by W. Kent'.

26 Amongst the unidentified scenic designs for masques in the corpus of Inigo Jones's drawings at Chatsworth is an interesting one showing a circular Classical temple with pepperpot dome standing in a forest clearing. Apart from the dome, the temple is of the same Tivoli type, and invites speculation as to the extent to which this drawing may have influenced Kent in his landscaping.

27 The plates are: (i) 'Guyon Leaves the Palmer & Crosses the Idle Lake with Phedria', bk II, canto VI; (ii) 'Chrysogone's Two Infant Daughters Taken Away by Venus & Diana', bk III, canto VI.

28 *CHW* vol. IX, p. 116. In the *Anecdotes* (p. 780) he contradicts himself, to the extent of saying that in these same backgrounds 'the trees are seldom other than young beeches, to which Kent, as a planter, was accustomed.'

29 J. Gwynn, *London and Westminster Improved* (London, 1766), p. 62n.

30 Addison, in *The Tatler*, no. 123, 19/21 January 1709/10. It is interesting to note also that Thomson in the 'Summer' section of *The Seasons* (1730) gives a long list of Worthies including More, Raleigh, Sidney, Bacon, Boyle, Newton, Shakespeare and Milton (lines 571–630).

31 Cf. Addison, op. cit.: 'I found that the stones were laid together without mortar, and that the whole fabric stood upon so weak a foundation that it shook with every wind that blew. This was called the Temple of Vanity.'

32   'On Modern Gardening', p. 804; *CHW* vol. IX, p. 290.

33   The Rousham letters remain in the family archives; there is a microfilm in the Bodleian Library.

34   Tipping, op. cit., p. 182.

35   Whately, op. cit., pp. 99–100.

36   Again it is worth considering that Kent may have had in mind – consciously or not – some of Jones's designs for masques, especially those half-dozen or so drawings for backcloths and wings which represent 'vistos' across open country bounded by trees to a distant hill. A particularly romantic moonlit scene of this type was provided for the masque *Luminalia* (1638); for an illustration see S. Orgel and Sir R. Strong, *Inigo Jones, the Theatre of the Stuart Court* (London, 1973), vol. II, pp. 710–11.

37   'On Modern Gardening', p. 805.

38   *CHW* vol. IX, p. 71.

39   Ibid., vol. X, p. 72.

40   Ibid., vol. XVIII, pp. 254–5.

41   *WSAV* XXII, p. 141.

42   Spence, op. cit., p. 200.

43   Count F. von Kielmansegge, *Diary* (London, 1902), p. 56.

44   MS. at Blair Adam; see J. Fleming, *Robert Adam and his Circle* (London, 1978), p. 363.

45   *WSAV* XXII, p. 133.

46   The complete text of the epitaph is given in T. Martyn, *The English Connoisseur* (published anonymously, London, 1766), vol. II, pp. 111–12.

CHAPTER 9   *The Final Flowering*

1   *The Travels through England of Dr. Richard Pococke*, ed. J. J. Cartwright (London, 1888–9), vol. II, p. 32.

2   Ibid.

3   *CHW* vol. IX, p. 122.

4   The portico, despite its un-Kentian appearance, is very similar to the one which adorned the river front of Pope's villa at Twickenham, in which Kent also had a hand (see p. 196).

5   *CHW* vol. XXIV, 1967, p. 93.

6   J. Summerson, *Georgian London* (London, 1962).

7   *Anecdotes of Painting in England*, ed. R. Wornum (London, 1849), vol. III, p. 780.

8   Ibid.

9   See 'A Kent–Vardy Collaboration' by H. Barkley (*CL*, vol. CXXVIII, 1960, p. 791), to whom I am indebted for helpful information on this aspect of Kent's work.

10   *CAP* vol. IV, p. 154.

11   Chatsworth MS.

12   Ibid.

13   *WSAV* XXX, p. 141.

14 Ibid., XXII, p. 140. In fact in a previous passage (p. 115) Vertue specifically assigns the eye trouble (described as 'a strain or rather a paralytic in one eye', perhaps suggesting some kind of mild stroke) to February 1742/3.

15 'Mr. Fox . . . has made Holland House a very fine place; Kent's death has rather put a stop to much farther improvements.' *CHW* vol. XXX, p. 114.

16 J. Ireland, *Hogarth Illustrated* (supplement, London, 1798), p. 83.

SELECT BIBLIOGRAPHY

The following titles have been arranged under headings corresponding to the main areas of Kent's work. Several of them nevertheless apply to more than one such area, and a title not found under its expected heading may be found under another.

General and Biographical

ADDISON, J., *Remarks on Several Parts of Italy in the Years 1701, 1702, 1703*, London, 1705.

ANDREWS, J., *Letters to a Young Man on his Setting Out for France*, London, 1784.

ANON., *Remarks on the Grand Tour of France and Italy, Perform'd by a Person of Quality in . . . 1691*, 2nd edn, London, 1705.

ANON., 'Account of Royal Palaces and Other Notable Buildings . . . In and Around London', Victoria & Albert Museum Library MS., *c.* 1755.

BAKER, C. H. C and M. I., *The Life and Circumstances of James Brydges, First Duke of Chandos* [*etc.*], Oxford, 1949.

BECKWITH, T., 'Anecdotes of the Lives of . . . the Most Eminent Painters [etc.]', Victoria & Albert Museum Library MS.L.5020-1975, *c.* 1780.

BROWNELL, M. R., *Alexander Pope and the Arts of Georgian England*, Oxford, 1978.

COKE, T., Earl of Leicester, 'An Acct. of the Moneys . . . Recd. of Mr. Hobart upon Acct. of . . . Thomas Coke Esq. [etc.]', Holkham MS.733 (and 734), 1712–18.

COOPER, A. A., Earl of Shaftesbury, *Characteristicks of Men, Manners, Opinions, Times*, 5th edn, 3 vols, Birmingham, 1773.

COXE, Rev. W., *Memoirs of the Life and Administration of Sir Robert Walpole, Earl of Orford*, 3 vols, London, 1800.

CUNNINGHAM, A., *The Lives of the Most Eminent British Painters, Sculptors and Architects*, 2nd edn, 5 vols, London, 1830–3.

FLEMING, J., *Robert Adam and his Circle*, reprint, London, 1978.

FLOWER, Sir N., *George Frideric Handel: his Personality and his Times*, rev. edn, London, 1972.

GAY, J., *Trivia, or the Art of Walking the Streets of London*, London, *c.* 1715.

GAY, J., *Poems on Several Occasions*, 2 vols in 1, London, 1720.

GROSLEY, P. J., *New Observations on Italy and its Inhabitants*, 'Written in French by Two Swedish Gentlemen', trs. T. Nugent, 2 vols, London, 1769.

SELECT BIBLIOGRAPHY

HERVEY, J., Baron Hervey of Ickworth, *Memoirs of the Reign of George the Second*, ed. J. W. Croker, 2 vols, London, 1848.

Lord Hervey and his Friends 1726–38, ed. Lord Ilchester, London, 1950.

HIBBERT, C., *The Grand Tour*, London, 1969.

HIGHFILL, P. H., BURNIM, K. A. and LANGHANS, E. A. *A Biographical Dictionary of Actors, Actresses, Musicians . . . & Other Stage Personnel in London 1660–1800*, Carbondale, 1972–.

HISTORICAL MANUSCRIPTS COMMISSION *Reports [HMC]* (i) Hastings MSS., vol. III, 1934; (ii) Castle Howard MSS., 1897; (iii) Portland MSS., vol. VI, 1900.

HODSON, P., *William Kent: A Bibliography and Chronology*, American Association of Architectural Bibliographers, Publication no. 27, Charlottesville, 1924.

HONOUR, H., 'John Talman and William Kent in Italy', *Connoisseur*, vol. CXXXIV, 1954, p. 3.

IRELAND, J., *Hogarth Illustrated* (supplement), London, 1798.

JAMES, C. W., *Chief Justice Coke, his Family and Descendants at Holkham*, London, 1929.

JOHNSON, F., 'The Bicentenary of William Kent', *Transactions of the Georgian Society for East Yorkshire*, vol. II, ii, 1948, p. 24.

JOURDAIN, M., *The Work of William Kent*, London, 1948.

KENT, W., In MS.:
  (i) Correspondence with Burrell Massingberd: Lincolnshire County Archives.
  (ii) Correspondence with Lord Burlington *et al.*: Chatsworth and Althorp collections.
  (iii) Letter to Samuel Gale: Bodleian MS. Eng. Misc. C.114.
  (iv) Journal of 1714 tour in Italy: Bodleian MS. Rawlinson D.1162.

Sale catalogues:
  (i) 'Pictures, models, coins and drawings', 13, 14 February 1748/9. Bodleian Mus. Bibl. III 4° 17(25).
  (ii) 'Library', 13 February 1748/9 – . Bodleian Mus. Bibl. III 8° 20(2).
  An annotated MS. copy of (i), with omissions, is in Victoria & Albert Museum Library MS.L.867/8, *Sale Catalogues of the Principal Collections of Pictures . . . Sold by Auction . . . 1711–1759*, vol. II, [c. 1760].

LASSELS, R., *The Voyage of Italy, or A Compleat Journey through Italy*, London, 1670.

LEES-MILNE, J., *Earls of Creation; Five Great Patrons of Eighteenth-Century Art*, London, 1962.

LENNEP, W. van (ed.), *The London Stage 1660–1800*, 5 vols, Carbondale, 1965–8 (index 1979).

MARTYN, T., *The English Connoisseur*, 2 vols, London, 1766.

MISSON, F. M., *A New Voyage to Italy*, 5th edn, 2 vols, London, 1739.

NOTTINGHAM UNIVERSITY, *Apollo of the Arts: Lord Burlington and his Circle*, exhibition at the University Art Gallery, 1973.

PAULSON, R., *Hogarth's Graphic Works*, rev. edn, New Haven, 1970.

PEVSNER, Sir N., *Studies in Art, Architecture and Design*, 2 vols (vol. I: *From Mannerism to Romanticism*), London, 1968.

[266]

POPE, A., *The Works of Alexander Pope*, ed. Bishop W. Warburton, 9 vols, London, 1751.

The Correspondence of Alexander Pope [CAP], ed. G. Sherburn, 5 vols, Oxford, 1956.

POWYS, Mrs P. L., *Passages from the Diaries of Mrs. Philip Lybbe Powys . . . 1756 to 1808*, ed. E. J. Climenson, London, 1899.

ROSSINI, P., *Il Mercurio Errante: delle Grandezze di Roma* [etc.], Rome, 1741.

SPENCE, Rev. J., *Anecdotes, Observations and Characters of Books and Men, Collected from the Conversation of Mr. Pope* [etc.], ed. S. W. Singer, London, 1820.

STIRLING, A. M. D. W., *Coke of Norfolk and his Friends* [etc.], London, 1908.

TALMAN, J., MS. correspondence from Italy 1709–12: Bodleian MS.Eng. Letters e.34.

THOMPSON, J., *Historical Sketches of Bridlington*, Bridlington, 1821.

THORESBY, R., *Ducatus Leodiensis*, 2nd edn, Leeds, 1816.

TIPPING, H. A., 'Letters of William Kent to the Earl of Burlington', *Country Life* [CL], vol. LV, 1924, p. 741.

TIPPING, H. A., 'Four Unpublished Letters of William Kent', *Architectural Review*, vol. LXIII, 1927, pp. 180, 209.

TREASE, G., *The Grand Tour*, London, 1967.

VERTUE, G., *Notebooks*, 6 vols, *Walpole Society Annual Volume* [WSAV] XVIII, XX, XXII, XXIV, XXVI, XXX (index to vols I–V in XXIX), Oxford, London, 1930–55.

WALPOLE, H., Earl of Orford, *Anecdotes of Painting in England*, ed. R. Wornum, 3 vols (section on Kent, vol. III, chap. XXII), London, 1849.

WALPOLE, H., *The Letters of Horace Walpole*, ed. Mrs H. Toynbee, 16 vols, Oxford, 1903–5.

WALPOLE, H., *Journals of Visits to Country Seats*, WSAV XVI, Oxford, 1928.

WALPOLE, H., *Correspondence* [CHW], ed. W. S. Lewis, New Haven. 1937–.

WENTWORTH, Sir W., MS. correspondence with Thomas, Lord Raby, 1709–12. British Library BM. Add. MS.22, 229.

WHITLEY, W. T., *Artists and their Friends in England 1700–1799*, London, 1928.

WITTKOWER, R., *The Earl of Burlington and William Kent*, York Georgian Society, Occasional Paper V, York, 1948.

WITTKOWER, R., 'Lord Burlington and William Kent', *Archaeological Journal*, vol. CII, 1945, p. 151.

Architecture, Interiors, Furniture and Related Designs

ANON., 'Voiage d'Angleterre, d'Holland et de Flandre Fait en l'Annee 1728', Victoria & Albert Museum Library MS.L.1255-1912.

AYLMER, G. E. and CANT, R., *A History of York Minster*, Oxford, 1977.

BADESLADE, J. and ROCQUE, J., *Vitruvius Britannicus*, vol. 4, London, 1739.

BARKLEY, H., 'A Kent-Vardy Collaboration' [Chimney-piece in the Treasury], *CL* vol. CXXVIII, 1960, p. 791.

BEARD, G., 'William Kent and the Royal Barge', *Burlington Magazine*, vol. CXII, 1970, p. 488.

BEARD, G., 'William Kent and the Cabinet-Makers', *Burlington Magazine*, vol. CXVII, 1975, p. 867.

BINNEY, M., 'Wakefield Lodge, Northamptonshire', *CL* vol. CLIV, 1973, p. 298.
BINNEY, M., 'Chicheley Hall, Buckinghamshire', *CL* vol. CLVII, 1975, pp. 378, 434.
BOYLE, R., Earl of Burlington, *Fabbriche Antiche Disegnate da Andrea Palladio*, London, 1730.
BRETTINGHAM, M., the Elder, *The Plans and Elevations of the late Earl of Leicester's House at Holkham*, London, 1761. 2nd edn: *The Plans, Elevations and Sections of Holkham in Norfolk*, ed. M. Brettingham the Younger, London, 1773.
BRINCKMANN, A. E., *Die Baukunst des 17. und 18. Jahrhunderts*, 2 vols, Berlin/ Neubabelsberg, 1915–22.
CAMPBELL, C., *Vitruvius Britannicus; or, the British Architect [etc.]*, 3 vols, London, 1715–25.
CHAMBERS, Sir W., *Plans, Elevations, Sections and Perspective Views of the Gardens and Buildings at Kew*, London, 1763.
CHANCELLOR, E. B., *The History and Antiquities of Richmond . . . Ham &c.*, Richmond, 1894.
COCKE, T., 'Gothic at Gloucester', *CL* vol. CLXX, 1981, p. 2308.
COLVIN, H. M., *A Biographical Dictionary of British Architects 1660–1840*, new edn, London, 1978.
CORNFORTH, J., 'Devonshire House, London', *CL* vol. CLXVIII, 1980, p. 1750.
CUPPINI, G., *I Palazzi Senatorii a Bologna*, ed. G. Roversi, Bologna, 1974.
DOWNES, K., 'Chiswick Villa', *Architectural Review*, vol. CLXIV, 1978, p. 225.
DRAKE, F., *Eboracum: or, the History and Antiquities of the City of York [etc.]*, London, 1736, later edn, 1788.
GILBERT, C., 'James Moore the Younger and William Kent at Sherborne House', *Burlington Magazine*, vol. CXI, 1969, p. 148.
GIROUARD, M., '44 Berkeley Square, London', *CL* vol. CXXXII, 1962, p. 1648.
GWYNN, J., *London and Westminster Improved*, London, 1766.
HARRIS, J., 'A William Kent Discovery: Designs for Esher Place, Surrey', *CL* vol. CXXV, 1959, p. 1076.
HAYWARD, J., 'A Surtoute Designed by William Kent', *Connoisseur*, vol. CXLIII, 1959, p. 82.
HAYWARD, J., 'The Pelham Gold Cup', *Connoisseur*, vol. CLXXI, 1969, p. 162.
HISTORY OF THE KING'S WORKS [*HKW*], ed. H. M. Colvin, vol. V (1660–1782), London, 1976.
HUSSEY, C., 'Kensington Palace: The State Rooms', *CL* vol. LVI, 1924, pp. 884, 952.
HUSSEY, C., 'Raynham Hall, Norfolk', *CL* vol. LVIII, 1925, pp. 742, 782.
HUSSEY, C., 'Badminton, Gloucestershire' (pt III). *CL* vol. LXXXVI, 1939, p. 600.
JOURDAIN, M., 'Documented Furniture at Rousham', *CL* vol. CIV, 1948, p. 384.
KENT, W., *The Designs of Inigo Jones, Consisting of Plans and Elevations for Publick and Private Buildings*, 2 vols, London, 1727.
KIELMANSEGGE, Count F. von, *Diary of a Journey to England in the Years 1761–1762*, London, 1902.
KIMBALL, F., 'William Kent's Designs for the Houses of Parliament 1730–1740', *Journal of the RIBA*, vol. XXXIX, 1932, pp. 733, 801.
LAW, E., *Kensington Palace . . . an Historical Guide to the State Rooms, Pictures and Gardens*, London, 1899.

LEE, J., 'The Furniture of William Kent', *Apollo*, vol. LXV, 1957, p. 53.

LEES-MILNE, J., *English Country Houses: Baroque, 1685–1715*, London, 1970.

LINES, C., 'Raynham Hall, Norfolk', *Connoisseur Year Book*, London, 1955, p. 13.

MALTON, J., the Younger, *A Picturesque Tour through the Cities of London and Westminster*, London, 1792.

MUSGRAVE, C., 'A London Palazzo: 44 Berkeley Square', *Connoisseur*, vol. CLVI, 1964, p. 75.

NORTON, P., *State Barges*, London (National Maritime Museum), 1972.

OMAN, C. C., 'Silver Designs by William Kent', *Apollo*, vol. XCV, 1972, p. 22.

OSWALD, A., 'Ditchley, Oxfordshire' (pt II), *CL* vol. LXXV, 1934, p. 622.

OSWALD, A., 'Bretton Park, Yorkshire', *CL* vol. LXXXIII, 1938, p. 530.

PEVSNER, Sir N., *The Buildings of England* (series). Harmondsworth, 1951–.

POCOCKE, R., Bishop of Ossory, *The Travels through England of Dr. Richard Pococke*, ed. J. J. Cartwright, 2 vols, London (Camden Society Publications), 1888–9.

PYNE, W. H., *The History of the Royal Residences*, 3 vols, London, 1819.

RALPH, J., *A Critical Review of the Publick Buildings . . . and Ornaments in and around London*, 2nd edn, London, 1736.

RICHARDSON, Sir A. E., 'The Royal Barge: Notes on the Original Drawings [etc.]', *Journal of the RIBA*, vol. XXXVIII, 1931, p. 172.

SCHMIDT, L., *Thomas Coke, 1st Earl of Leicester: An Eighteenth-Century Amateur Architect* [exhibition catalogue], Holkham [1980].

SCHMIDT, L., 'Holkham Hall, Norfolk', *CL* vol. CLXVII, 1980, pp. 214, 298, 359.

SITWELL, S., *British Architects and Craftsmen*, rev. edn, London, 1960.

STRATTON, A., 'The King's Mews at Charing Cross', *Architectural Review*, vol. XXXIX, 1916, p. 119.

SUMMERSON, Sir J., *Georgian London*, rev. edn, London, 1962.

SUMMERSON, Sir J., *Architecture in Britain 1530 to 1830*, 5th rev. edn, Harmondsworth (Pelican History of Art), 1970.

SURVEY OF LONDON, vol. XIV. *The Parish of St. Margaret, Westminster*, pt III (Neighbourhood of Whitehall, vol. II) London, 1931.

SURVEY OF LONDON, vol. XVI. *Charing Cross. The Parish of St. Martin-in-the-Fields*, pt I, London, 1935.

TANNER, J., 'The Building of Chicheley Hall', *Records of Buckinghamshire*, vol. XVII, 1961–5.

TELLUCCINI, A., 'La Scala "Delle Forbici" di Filippo Juvara nel Palazzo Reale di Torino', *Bollettino d'Art del Ministero della Pubblica Instruzione*, 2nd series, vol. V, 1925/6, p. 206.

TIPPING, H. A., 'Houghton Hall, Norfolk', *CL* vol. XLIX, 1921, pp. 14, 40, 64, 98.

VARDY, J., *Some Designs of Mr. Inigo Jones and Mr. William Kent*, London, 1744.

VIVIAN, R., 'Houghton Hall, Norfolk', *CL* vol. XXII, 1907, pp. 126, 162.

WALPOLE, H., Earl of Orford, *Aedes Walpolianae* [etc.], 2nd edn, London, 1752.

WARE, I., *Designs of Inigo Jones and Others*, London, n.d., 2nd edn 1743; 3rd edn 1756.

WARE, I., *The Plans, Elevations and Sections . . . of Holkham in Norfolk* [etc.], London, 1735.

WITTKOWER, R., 'Un Libro di Schizzi di Filippo Juvarra a Chatsworth', *Bollettino Società Piemontese d'Archaeologia e di Arti*, n.s. vol. III, 1949, p. 94.

YOUNG, A., *A Six Weeks Tour through the Southern Counties of England and Wales*, London, 1768.

Painting, Illustration and Sculpture

ASHMOLEAN MUSEUM, *Catalogue of Paintings*, Oxford, 1961.
BRADLEY, L., 'Eighteenth-Century Paintings and Illustrations of Spenser's "Faerie Queen": a Study in Taste,' *Marsyas*, vol. XX, 1980, p. 31.
COHEN, R., *The Art of Discrimination: Thomson's 'The Seasons' and the Language of Criticism*, Berkeley, 1964.
COX, Sir T., 'William Kent as Painter', *Artwork*, vol. VII, 1931, p. 28.
CROFT-MURRAY, E., *Decorative Painting in England 1537–1837*, 2 vols, London, 1962–70.
CROFT-MURRAY, E., 'William Kent in Rome', *English Miscellany*, vol. I, 1950, p. 221.
CROFT-MURRAY, E., 'Decorative Paintings for Lord Burlington and the Royal Academy', *Apollo*, vol. LXXXIX, 1969, p. 11.
DEELMAN, C., *The Great Shakespeare Jubilee*, London, 1964.
EDWARDS, R., 'Conversation Pieces in Search of a Painter', *Apollo*, vol. LXVI, 1957, p. 90.
EICHHOLZ, J. P., 'William Kent's Career as a Literary Illustrator', *Bulletin of the New York Public Library*, vol. LXX, 1966, p. 620.
FITZGERALD, D., 'The Mural from 44 Grosvenor Square', *Victoria and Albert Museum Yearbook*, I, London 1969, p. 145.
GAY, J., *Fables*, vol. I. London, 1927.
GUNNIS, R., *Dictionary of British Sculptors 1660–1851*, rev. edn, London, [1968].
KERSLAKE, J., *Early Georgian Portraits*, London (National Portrait Gallery), 1977.
MIDDELDORF, U., 'William Kent's Roman Prize in 1713', *Burlington Magazine*, vol. XCIX, 1957, p. 125.
MILLAR, Sir O., *The Tudor, Stuart and Early Georgian Pictures in the Collection of Her Majesty the Queen*, London, 1963.
MISSIRINI, M., *Memorie per Servire alla Storia della Romana Accademia di S. Luca*, Rome, 1823.
ORBAAN, J. F. and HOOGEWERFF, G. I., *Beschieden in Italië omtrent Nederlandsche Kunstenaars en Geleerden*, 3 vols (vol. II: Archieven van Bijzondere Instellingen). 's-Gravenhage, 1911–17.
PHYSICK, J., *Designs for English Sculpture 1680–1860*, London (Victoria & Albert Museum), 1969.
QUENNELL, P., *Romantic England: Writing and Painting 1717–1851*, London, 1970.
RICHARDSON, J., *The Works of Jonathan Richardson*, new edn, London, 1792.
SPENSER, E., *The Faerie Queene*, 3 vols, London, 1751.
THOMSON, J., *The Seasons*, London, 1730.
THORNHILL, Sir J., MS. copy of memorandum appealing for payment of salary as Royal History Painter, Victoria & Albert Museum Library MS.L.518–1945, *c.* 1730.
TROTTMANN, H., 'Die Zeichnungen Cosmas Damien Asams für den Concorso Clementino der Accademia di San Luca von 1713', *Pantheon*, vol. XXXVIII, ii, 1980, p. 158.
WEBB, M. I., *Michael Rysbrack, Sculptor*, London, 1954.

WESTMINSTER ABBEY, *The History of the Abbey Church of St. Peter's, Westminster* [etc], 2 vols, London, 1812.

WIMSATT, W. K., *The Portraits of Alexander Pope*, New Haven/London, 1965. Supplement by J. Riely, in *Evidence in Literary Scholarship*, ed. R. Wellek and A. Ribeiro, Oxford, 1979.

Landscape Gardening

ALBERTI, L. B., *The Architecture of Leon Battista Alberti in Ten Books*, trs. G. Leoni, 3 vols, London, 1726.

ANON., *Stow [sic]: A Description of the Gardens [etc]*, Buckingham, 1756.

BATEY, M. 'The Way to View Rousham, by Kent's Gardener [John Macclary]', *Garden History*, vol. XI, ii, 1983, p. 125.

CARRÉ, J., 'Lord Burlington's Garden at Chiswick', *Garden History*, vol. I, iii, 1973, p. 23.

CASTELL, R., *The Villas of the Ancients*, London, 1728.

CLARK, H. F., 'Lord Burlington's Bijou . . . at Chiswick', *Architectural Review*, vol. XCV, 1944, p. 125.

CLARKE, G. 'The Gardens of Stowe', *Apollo*, vol. XCVII, 1973, p. 558.

CLARKE, G., 'Grecian Taste and Gothic Virtue', *Apollo*, vol. XCVII, 1973. p. 566.

CLARKE, G., 'William Kent: Heresy in Stowe's Elysium', *Furor Hortensis: Essays on the History of the English Landscape Garden*, Edinburgh, 1974.

COLTON, J., 'Merlin's Cave and Queen Caroline: Garden Art as Political Propaganda', *Eighteenth-Century Studies*, vol. X, 1976, p. 1.

FLEMING, J., 'In Search of Landscape Gardens' (pt III), *CL* vol. CXXX, 1961, p. 200.

FLEMING, J., 'William Kent at Rousham: an 18th Century Elysium', *Connoisseur*, vol. CLIII, 1963, p. 158.

FLEMING, L. and GORE, A., *The English Garden*, London, 1979.

HADFIELD, M., *A History of British Gardening*, rev. edn, London, 1969.

HUNT, J. F., 'Gardening, Poetry and Pope', *Art Quarterly of the Detroit Institute of Arts*, Spring 1974.

HUNT, P. (ed.), *The Shell Gardens Book*, London, 1964.

HUSSEY, C., *English Gardens and Landscapes, 1700–1750*, London, 1967.

HUSSEY, C., 'A Georgian Arcady: William Kent's Gardens at Rousham, Oxfordshire', *CL* vol. XCIX, 1946, pp. 1084, 1130.

JONES, B., *Follies and Grottoes*, 2nd edn, London, 1974.

LANGLEY, B., *New Principles of Gardening*, London, 1728.

MACK, M., *The Garden and the City*, London, 1969.

MASSON, G., *Italian Gardens*, London, 1961.

OSWALD, A., 'Euston Hall, Suffolk' (pt III), *CL* vol. CXXI, 1957, p. 148.

PRICE, U., *An Essay on the Picturesque [etc.]*, new edn, London, 1796.

PUGH, S., 'Nature as a Garden: A Conceptual Tour of Rousham', *Studio International*, vol. CLXXXVI, 1973, p. 121.

SERLE, J., *A Plan of Mr. Pope's Garden . . . with a Plan . . . of the Grotto*, London, 1745.

SWITZER, S., *The Nobleman, Gentleman and Gardener's Recreation [etc.]*, London, 1715. 2nd edn *Ichnographia Rustica: or, the Nobleman, Gentleman and Gardener's Recreation [etc]*, 3 vols, London, 1742.

TEMPLE, Sir W., 'Upon the Gardens of Epicurus: or, Of Gardening, in the Year 1685', *Works*, vol. I, London, 1720.

THACKER, C., *The History of Gardens*, London, 1979.

WALPOLE, H., Earl of Orford, 'On Modern Gardening', *Anecdotes of Painting in England*, ed. R Wornum, London, 1849, vol. III, chap. XXIII.

WATKIN, D., *The English Vision: the Picturesque in Architecture, Landscape and Garden Design*, London, 1982.

WHATELY, T., *Observations on Modern Gardening [etc.]*, new edn, London, 1801.

WHISTLER, L., 'The Authorship of the Stowe Temples', *CL* vol. CVIII, 1950, p. 1002.

WHISTLER, L., GIBBON, M. and CLARKE, G., *Stowe: a Guide to the Gardens*, rev. edn, Buckingham, 1968.

WILLIS, P., *Charles Bridgeman and the English Landscape Garden*, London, 1977.

WOODBRIDGE, K., 'William Kent as Landscape Gardener: a Re-appraisal', *Apollo*, vol. C, 1974, p. 126.

WOODBRIDGE, K., 'William Kent's Gardening: the Rousham Letters', *Apollo*, vol. C, 1974, p. 282.

WOODBRIDGE, K., 'Iconographic Variations: Classical and Gothic Themes in the English Landscape Garden in the 18th century,' *Lotus International*, vol. XXX, 1981, p. 10.

INDEX